Second Edition

Competence

in interpersonal

CONFLICT

William R. Cupach
Illinois State University

Daniel J. Canary
Arizona State University

Brian H. Spitzberg
San Diego State University

WAVELAND

PRESS, INC.

Long Grove, Illinois

For information about this book, contact:
Waveland Press, Inc.
4180 IL Route 83, Suite 101
Long Grove, IL 60047-9580
(847) 634-0081
info@waveland.com
www.waveland.com

10-digit ISBN 1-57766-649-6
13-digit ISBN 978-1-57766-649-3

Printed in the United States of America

7   6   5   4

CONTENTS

Preface   ix

1   The Importance of Conflict in Interpersonal Relationships   1

Why Study Conflict?   3
   Reason 1: To Fine-Tune Your Expertise   3
   Reason 2: To Learn That Conflict Is Common   4
   Reason 3: To Understand That People Develop
     Individually Through Conflict   5
   Reason 4: To Diminish Aggression   5
   Reason 5: To Maintain or Improve Your Physical Health   6
   Reason 6: To Achieve Satisfying Relationships   7

Defining Interpersonal Conflict   7
   Approach 1: Interpersonal Conflict as Pervasive   8
   Approach 2: Interpersonal Conflict as Explicit Disagreement   8
   Approach 3: Interpersonal Conflict as a Hostile Episode   8
   Approach 4: Interpersonal Conflict as
     Disagreement in Particular Episodes   9

Features of Interpersonal Conflict   10
   Levels of Conflict   10
   Types of Actual versus Perceived Conflict   11

Summary   16
Discussion Questions   17

2   A Competence-Based Approach to Interpersonal Conflict   19

Criteria Guiding Perceptions of Competence   22
   Effectiveness   23
   Appropriateness   27
   The Relationship between Effectiveness and Appropriateness   28
   Implications of Judging Competence   29

Factors That Facilitate Competence   29
  Motivation   30
  Knowledge   31
  Skills   32
An Explanatory Model of Interpersonal Conflict   33
  Distal Context   33
  Proximal Context   35
  Conflict Interaction   35
  Proximal Outcomes   36
  Distal Outcomes   36
Summary   38
Discussion Questions   38

3   **Conflict Messages**   **41**
The Topical Content of Conflict Interactions   42
Conflict Tactics, Strategies, and Styles   46
  Conflict Tactics   46
  Dimensions of Conflict Communication   47
  Conflict Strategies   50
  Communicating Conflict Orientations Nonverbally   52
  Conflict Styles   55
Patterns of Conflict Interaction   57
  Reciprocity   57
  Complementarity   60
  Topical Continuity   60
Reacting to Negative Conflict Patterns   61
Summary   62
Discussion Questions   63

4   **Background Influences on Interpersonal Conflict**   **65**
Distal Individual Factors Affecting Conflict Interaction   66
  Attachment Styles   67
  Argumentativeness   69
  Taking Conflict Personally   70
  Locus of Control   71
  Sex Differences in Managing Conflict   73
Distal Relational Factors Affecting Conflict Interaction   76
  Relational Development   76
  Relational Types: Different Blueprints
    for Close Relationships   80
  Characteristics of Developed Relationships   82
Summary   85
Discussion Questions   86

5 Proximal Influences:
Spontaneous Reactions to Conflict   **89**

Anger and Anger-Like Responses 91
   Causes of Anger 91
   Types of Anger 93
   Emotions Associated with Anger 95

Initial Reactions to the Conflict Situation 97
   Physiological Reactions 98
   Temporary Response Modes 100
   Scripts 100

Higher-Ordered Thoughts 102
   Attributions about Causes of Conflict 103
   Expectations for Achieving Goals 108

The Dyad as a System That Affects Each Person's Behavior 112
   System Properties 112
   System Dysfunctions 114

Summary 116
Discussion Questions 117

6 Conflict Outcomes   **119**

Proximal Consequences 120
   Attributions 120
   Emotions 122
   Judgments of Competence 123
   Communication Satisfaction 126
   Face Threat and Restoration 127
   Physical Health 129
   The Cumulative Nature of Proximal Consequences 130

Distal Consequences 130
   Relationship (Dis)Satisfaction and (In)Stability 130
   Effects of the Demand-Withdraw Pattern 133
   Positive Consequences Involve More Than
      Simply Avoiding Negative Behaviors 134
   Conflict Combines with Positivity to Predict Divorce 135

Summary 135
Discussion Questions 136

7 Intercultural Conflict Competence   **139**
   by Stella Ting-Toomey

Intercultural Conflict Competence:
   Criteria and Components 141
   IC Conflict Competence Criteria:
      Appropriateness and Effectiveness 141
   IC Conflict Competence Components:
      Knowledge, Mindfulness, and Skills 142

Intercultural Conflict: Antecedent Factors   143
   Culture-Based Value Dimensional Patterns   144
   Understanding the Complexity of Cultural Values Grid   146
   Individual Personality Tendency Patterns   150

Intercultural Conflict Communication: Process Factors   151
   Cross-Cultural National Conflict Communication Styles   152
   Cross-Ethnic Conflict Communication Styles   154

Developing Intercultural Conflict Competence:
   Process and Outcome   158
   IC Code-Switching: Communication Adaptability   158
   Mindful Transformation   159

Summary   161
Discussion Questions   162

8 Competence in Organizational Conflicts   163
   by Wendy H. Papa, Michael J. Papa, and Rick A. Buerkel

Organizational Conflict Viewed from
   a Competence-Based Approach   166

Organizational Conflict and the
   Explanatory Model of Interpersonal Conflict   167
   Distal Context   167
   Proximal Context   168
   Conflict Interaction   169
   Proximal Outcomes   169
   Distal Outcomes   169

Phases of Conflict   170
   Differentiation   170
   Mutual Problem Description   171
   Integration   172

Applying the Phase Model to Organizational Conflict   175
   Interpersonal Conflicts in Organizational Settings   175
   Bargaining and Negotiation   178
   Intergroup Conflict   179
   Interorganizational Conflict   182

Summary   189
Discussion Questions   190

9 Family Conflict   191
   by Tamara D. Afifi, Desiree Aldeis, and Andrea Joseph

Constructive versus Destructive Family Conflict   193

The Impact of Interparental Conflict on Children   195
   The Effects of Divorce and Conflict on Child Adjustment   195
   The Case of Triangulation   196
   Blended Family Problems   197

Parent to Child Conflict   198
Adolescence and Family Conflict   199
Misunderstanding as a Source of Family Conflict   199
The Role of Parenting Style in Family Conflicts   201
The Effect of Children's Conflict/Aggression
on Other Family Members   202
Transition to Parenthood   203
Sibling Conflict Effects on Parents   204
Examining Family Conflict in Families as a Whole   205
Conclusion: Competent Conflict
Management in Families   207
Discussion Questions   *209*

10   Intimate Violence   211
by Brian H. Spitzberg
Myths and Maxims of Aggression and
Violence in Intimate Relationships   214
Myth 1: Violence Is Obvious   214
Myth 2: Violence Is Gendered   221
Myth 3: Female Violence Is Motivated by Self-Defense   226
Myth 4: Intimate Violence Is Unilateral   228
Myth 5: Intimate Violence Is Chronic   229
Myth 6: Intimate Violence by Males Is about Power   229
Myth 7: Intimate Violence Is Harmful and Traumatizing   232
Myth 8: Physical Violence Is More Harmful and
Traumatizing Than Communicative Aggression   233
Myth 9: Intimate Violence Is an Incompetent Approach
to Conflict Management   235
An Interactional Model of Intimate Aggression   237
Intimate Violence Evolves from Intimate Conflicts   237
Intimate Conflicts Are about Transgressions   238
Transgressions Evoke Negative Emotions   240
Negative Emotions Escalate Conflict Severity   240
The Course of Conflict Depends on
the Interactants' Competence   241
Communicative Aggression Increases the
Risk of Intimate Partner Violence   246
Refining the Interactional Model   247
Competent Violence?   251
Summary   251
Discussion Questions   *251*

11 Mediating Conflict 253
by Claudia L. Hale and Amy Thieme

What Is Mediation? 256
   Mediation and Other Forms of Dispute Resolution 256
   Principles of Mediation 257
   The Goals of Mediation 258

How Are Mediations Conducted? 260
   How Are Mediations Initiated? 261
   Stage 1: Introductions 262
   Stage 2: Telling the Story 265
   Stage 3: Identifying the Issues 270
   Stage 4: Generating Options 271
   Stage 5: Writing the Agreement 275

What Skills and Knowledge Contribute
  to Mediator Competence? 276

What Skills and Knowledge Contribute
  to Disputant Competence? 279

Summary 280

Discussion Questions 281 ■ *Notes 281*

12 Looking Forward to Future Conflicts 283

The Inevitability of Conflict 284

The Value of Competence in
  Managing Interpersonal Conflict 285

Guidelines for Managing Interpersonal Conflict 288
   The Question Is Not If, but How 288
   Avoid Reciprocating Negative Affect 289
   Respond Proactively to Your Own Anger 289
   Do Not Inadvertently Reinforce Aggressive Behaviors 290
   Discern Each Person's Goals in a Conflict 290
   Save Face 292
   Recognize the Systems You Create 295

Summary 295

Discussion Questions 296

References 297
Index 339

PREFACE

Conflict between people is a natural feature of the human condition. When people interact and form relationships, conflicts inevitably emerge. Conflict presents us with both opportunities and challenges, in all types of interpersonal relationships. We experience conflict with friends and neighbors, spouses and best friends, parents and children, roommates and coworkers. How we manage our interpersonal conflicts powerfully affects our relationships, perhaps more so than any other kind of interaction behavior.

Conflict has both negative and positive consequences. Conflict can expose our greatest weaknesses, destroy our most valued relationships, and impart tremendous personal anxiety or fear. People often recall this negative side of conflict. Just as likely, however, conflict can help us solve problems productively, express strong beliefs and feelings, solidify important relationships, and function as an engine of change in any social system.

To understand interpersonal conflict, we need to recognize the ways in which communication conveys problems between people. Communication provides the means by which we recognize and express conflicts. In addition, communication most often distinguishes productive conflict from destructive conflict. People who manage their conflicts using appropriate and effective communication behaviors dramatically increase their chances of experiencing the productive aspects of conflict. Thus, we adopt an approach to managing conflict that values communication competence.

Throughout this book we focus on interpersonal conflicts. We concern ourselves principally with disagreements between individuals in a variety of personal and social relationships. There are two types of conflict this book does *not* address. First, we do not concentrate on "intrapsychic," or internal, conflicts—that is, conflicts experienced by a single individual. Thus, we do not take up issues such as cognitive decision making, personal problems, or methods of dissonance reduction. We examine the psychological features of conflict only to the extent of how they relate to conflicts between people. Second, this book does not address aspects of social conflict such as social movements, international disputes, or political diplomacy. Our focus remains on interpersonal conflict and how to manage it in an appropriate and effective manner.

This second edition of *Competence in Interpersonal Conflict* is long overdue. We have retained the original conceptual and organizing framework that guided the first edition. Feedback from readers reinforced our belief in the utility of the competence model for promoting successful conflict management. Within that framework, in this edition we have substantially expanded and updated our coverage of specific topics in an effort to reflect the growing base of scholarly knowledge. (The number of sources cited in this edition is nearly double the number of the first edition!) Dr. Brian Spitzberg joined us (Bill and Dan) as coauthor, and his efforts and expertise were essential to accomplishing the update. The experts contributing chapters on the contexts of conflict (i.e., intercultural conflict, organizational conflict, interpersonal violence, and mediation) also thoroughly revised their original reviews. This edition also features an important new contributed chapter on the context of family conflicts.

The first two chapters of the book lay a conceptual foundation for understanding interpersonal conflict. Our opening chapter gives several reasons for studying conflict. We also present different ways of defining conflict and illustrate the various types and levels of conflict. As you will discover, conflict is a pervasive and important aspect of who we are and what our relationships become.

Chapter 2 presents a conceptual framework to organize ideas about interpersonal conflict and its management. We discuss communication competence and why it is central to conflict management. We also present a model of conflict that clarifies the antecedents and consequences of conflict from a competence focal point.

In chapter 3 we describe the nature of conflict messages—the central feature of any conflict interaction. We survey the landscape of conflict topics and investigate the many possible message behaviors during conflict interactions. We describe these behaviors in terms of communication tactics, strategies, styles, and patterns of interaction, as well as the conceptual dimensions that characterize and distinguish among types of conflict behaviors. In chapter 3 you will learn much about the communicative methods of enacting and managing conflict.

Chapters 4 and 5 outline what we refer to as "distal" and "proximal" influences on conflict interaction. Distal influences concern ways in which different types of people tend to approach and manage conflict. We cite several key individual and relational background factors that give shape and meaning to specific disagreements. Proximal influences have to do with how people respond more or less spontaneously to conflicts. Anger and other kinds of negative stimuli can bring about reactions that people do not understand. We explore how people's instant interpretations of events can lead to different sorts of conflict communication. Finally, we examine how the partner's behavior provides an immediate source of feedback regarding one's own conflict messages.

Chapter 6 summarizes both short-term and long-term consequences associated with conflict interactions. These include blatant immediate outcomes such as thoughts and feelings. We also consider more subtle processes in which the effects of individual episodes of conflict accumulate either to solidify or undermine an interpersonal relationship.

Chapters 7 through 11 explore conflict in five unique settings. These chapters are contributed by well-respected scholars who are thoroughly familiar with their respective contexts.

In chapter 7, Dr. Stella Ting-Toomey discusses the challenges of managing conflict when the parties are from different cultures. Professor Ting-Toomey illustrates cultural and ethnic differences in conflict styles, and she demonstrates how the principles of communication competence apply to episodes of intercultural conflict. In particular, she emphasizes the importance of code-switching and mindful transformation processes in accomplishing intercultural conflict competence.

Dr. Wendy Papa and Dr. Michael Papa, along with Rick Buerkel, discuss organizational conflicts in chapter 8. They depict the phases of conflict in organization settings. Then they illustrate how conflicting parties can display competence in the various arenas of organizational conflict, including interpersonal conflict in organizations, bargaining and negotiation, intergroup conflict, and interorganizational conflict.

In chapter 9, Dr. Tamara Afifi, in collaboration with Desiree Aldeis and Andrea Joseph, review research about conflict within the family context. In particular, they elucidate the effects of interparental conflict on children, the processes in parent to child conflict, and the effects of children's conflict on other family members. They offer specific guidelines for competently managing the various forms of family conflict.

Dr. Brian Spitzberg tackles the subject of violence in intimate relationships in chapter 10. He debunks several myths about intimate violence and presents an interactional model of intimate aggression that integrates the relevant literature in a thought-provoking way.

In chapter 11, Dr. Claudia Hale and Dr. Amy Thieme elaborate the process of mediation, in which an objective third party assists individuals who experience difficulty constructively managing a conflict on their own. The authors draw on their professional experiences to apply the principles of communication competence to conflict disputants and mediators.

Chapter 12 looks ahead to future conflicts you will experience. We argue that adopting an ethical stance in managing your conflicts is both desirable and practical. We offer some general guidelines to assist you in constructively grappling with your own conflicts in the future.

In sum, *Competence in Interpersonal Conflict* focuses on how you can increase your competence at managing interpersonal conflicts in a variety of settings. We do not presume that you are lacking in competency; we only hope to enhance your present level of motivation, knowledge, and practical communicative skills at managing interpersonal conflicts.

We wish to express our heartfelt gratitude to Neil and Carol Rowe of Waveland Press for their inexhaustible professionalism and graciousness. This project would never have come to fruition if not for Neil's gentle prodding. When we dragged our feet, Neil was always both patient and encouraging. We appreciate the careful attention given to this edition by the members of Waveland's editorial and production staff, particularly Diane Evans. We also thank Jennifer Marmo, who updated and created new material for the Instructor's Manual to accompany this edition. This valuable addition should greatly facilitate the instructional value of the text. Finally, we feel especially fortunate to feature the outstanding efforts of our contributing authors: Tamara Afifi, Desiree Aldeis, Rick Buerkel, Claudia Hale, Andrea Joseph, Michael Papa, Wendy Papa, Amy Thieme, and Stella Ting-Toomey. Their expertise greatly augments the value of this book.

William R. Cupach
Illinois State University

Daniel J. Canary
Arizona State University

Brian H. Spitzberg
San Diego State University

chapter 1

THE IMPORTANCE OF CONFLICT IN INTERPERSONAL RELATIONSHIPS

CHAPTER OUTLINE

Why Study Conflict?
    Reason 1: To Fine-Tune Your Expertise
    Reason 2: To Learn That Conflict Is Common
    Reason 3: To Understand That People Develop Individually Through
      Conflict
    Reason 4: To Diminish Aggression
    Reason 5: To Maintain or Improve Your Physical Health
    Reason 6: To Achieve Satisfying Relationships
Defining Interpersonal Conflict
    Approach 1: Interpersonal Conflict as Pervasive
    Approach 2: Interpersonal Conflict as Explicit Disagreement
    Approach 3: Interpersonal Conflict as a Hostile Episode
    Approach 4: Interpersonal Conflict as Disagreement in Particular
      Episodes
Features of Interpersonal Conflict
    Levels of Conflict
    Types of Actual versus Perceived Conflict
Summary
Discussion Questions

You already know much about interpersonal conflict. You have been "trained" for thousands of hours about conflict strategies and tactics, and you have experienced many disagreements with relatives, friends, lovers, and others. These conflicts have ranged in importance, from small disagreements (such as which college football team is the best) to critical disputes that may have determined the future of a job or an important relationship.

Your conflict management training began very early. By 18 months of age, toddlers become more verbally expressive during conflict with parents (beyond saying "no"); by 36 months of age, children utilize different decision rules when responding to conflict (for example, rules when to defend yourself, rules how to obtain rewards, and rules indicating when it is alright to condemn others) (Dunn & Slomkowski, 1992). In addition, at about 18 months of age, children learn that alternative types of reasons are appropriate and effective in different situations (Dunn & Slomkowski, 1992). For example, you learn that claiming "other children do it" does not satisfy your parents' desire for a reason why you put a dead bug in your younger sister's oatmeal or why you broke the iPod you were forbidden to touch.

As you proceeded through adolescence, you engaged in a different sort of conflict. Specifically, you expanded your rights to take control over "personal" issues, such as your style of clothes, how to wear to your hair, and how late you should sleep in on Saturdays (Smetana, 1988, 1989). But most parents do not understand the importance of establishing rights over one's personal life. So the two of you (or three or more of you) argued and experienced tension like you have seldom felt since adolescence. People often do not understand that adolescents need to establish control over their own lives so they can leave home and begin their own families (Robin & Foster, 1989). Your own children do or will strive for personal control, just as you did.

After you became an adult, you may have placed more emphasis on romance, your conflicts thus reflecting the issues that partners must face, especially issues of interdependence (Braiker & Kelley, 1979). As you become involved in intimate relationships, how you negotiate daily activities becomes an essential part of your relationships. Not surprisingly, and simply because you are not used to doing things with someone else, conflicts emerge. Your conflicts seem to involve mundane and seemingly unimportant issues, such as who drives the car, what type of groceries you purchase, how you spend your leisure time, and who watches the children while the other person folds the laundry. In addition, however, your conflicts can reflect more important relational issues, such as how you express yourself and show affection (including sex), how you get along with in-laws, and how money is spent.

Over time you have realized that interpersonal conflict is complex. It often involves more than just a simple disagreement that can be repaired by one person apologizing and promising not to behave badly again. According to Selman (1980), people come to understand that interpersonal conflict involves a system of two people who have their own goals and perceptions of the issues at stake. You also realize that people are often inconsistent in their goals, beliefs, and behaviors. Perhaps most important, from an interpersonal perspective, you have developed some preferred responses for handing your disagreements. Since you already have learned a lot about conflict, then you might wonder why you should study it more formally.

Why Study Conflict?

Although some scholars assume that people know nothing about conflict, we do not. We believe you are well on your way to being an expert on interpersonal conflict, although you are probably not acquainted with the language that scientists and other scholars use to explain conflict processes. So why should you study conflict? We can think of at least six reasons.

REASON 1: TO FINE-TUNE YOUR EXPERTISE

One reason is that you can fine-tune your ability at managing conflict situations, and the information contained in this book is written for that purpose—to make you more competent in your interpersonal conflicts. *Competence* in communicating refers to your ability to achieve your goals while you fulfill relational and situational expectations (Spitzberg & Cupach,

1984). Achieving your own goals concerns your *effectiveness*; fulfilling other people's expectations concerns *appropriateness*. In a sense, competence refers to your ability to "get ahead" while simultaneously "getting along" with others. Interpersonal conflict involves two people who strive to achieve goals that may appear incompatible.

People may sacrifice being appropriate in order to achieve their own goals; or they may be so concerned about offending someone that they do not pursue what they want. So interpersonal conflict often presents you with a quandary about how to behave in an interpersonally competent manner. This book provides you with principles based on research to help you increase your competence at managing interpersonal conflict.

REASON 2: TO LEARN THAT CONFLICT IS COMMON

Supposedly the only certainties in life are death and taxes. In our opinion, these are not the only certainties—it is a virtual certainty that you have experienced and will continue to experience interpersonal conflict. Indeed, as Hocker and Wilmot (1995) have noted, conflict is a natural and inevitable everyday feature of everyone's interpersonal life. Findings from studies investigating different types of relationships support the view that conflict is pervasive (Argyle & Furnham, 1983).

Interpersonal conflict begins early and often with a parent. Dunn and Munn (1987) observed interactions between mothers and toddlers in age groups of 18, 24, and 36 months. During each hour of observation, these interactions involved about 7–8 conflicts (that is, exchanges of disagreement), about half of which were extended disagreements and the other half short spurts of disagreement. Even if we count only the extended disagreements as "real" conflicts, parents and toddlers averaged three to four conflicts per hour. Although parent-toddler conflicts tend to be frequent, they are brief and unresolved (Eisenberg, 1992). Typically they do not lead to escalation of negative feelings; and when negative emotions are involved in parent-toddler conflicts, they tend to occur at the beginning of the episode and then subside (Eisenberg, 1992).

Conflicts are routine for adolescents. In a study involving self-reports of their previous day, high school students reported an average of *seven* conflicts a day involving different types of relationships (Laursen, 1993). These students also reported a large *range* in the number of conflicts (0–39) that were experienced the previous day.

Adults report their romantic involvements entail quite a bit of conflict. One study of college dating couples found an average of 2.3 conflicts per week (Lloyd, 1987). The amount of conflict depends partially on the couple's level of satisfaction and stability. One study found that unhappy married couples experienced an average of one conflict a day, but more satisfied and stable couples experienced one conflict only every five days (Vincent, Weiss, & Birchler, 1975).

Although conflict is common, it does not have to be destructive. Conflict can also be constructive (Deutsch, 1973). The competent management of interpersonal conflict can lead to stronger relationships, alternative ways of seeing a tough problem, and durable solutions. In this light, the frequency of conflict is probably less important than *how* people communicate during conflict (Straus, 1979).

REASON 3: TO UNDERSTAND THAT PEOPLE DEVELOP INDIVIDUALLY THROUGH CONFLICT

Research in developmental psychology indicates that learning how to manage interpersonal conflict is necessary for personal growth. As Shantz (1987) said, "Conflict is a central concept in virtually every major theory of human development" (p. 283). Research reveals that conflict is embedded within much of parent-child interaction. The child wants to expand her social world, and the parent "educates" the child about the limits of her social world. Through interpersonal conflict we learn early how to detect another person's thoughts and feelings, how to clarify the other's intentions for his or her actions, how to understand the social rules that indicate appropriate behavior, and how to use strategies to obtain personal goals (Dunn & Slomkowski, 1992).

It is important to understand that people's differences in thinking, behaving, and appearance often lead to interpersonal conflict. Conflict arises because of incompatibility between people (Deutsch, 1973). To have a conflict-free environment, you must be able to read minds and aspire to fulfill the other person's wants. Thus, a conflict-free environment is impossible, since no one is an accurate mind reader and we all vary in our wants. Such inevitable differences lead to conflict.

Unfortunately, people typically do not seriously study the interpersonal skills that help them to reconcile incompatible thoughts and behaviors between themselves and others. Here, communication in conflict plays a fundamental role in our personal and social development. If we learn how to manage conflicts competently, we can increase the likelihood of obtaining goals that are valuable to us without alienating people who are important to us, which relates to the next reason for studying interpersonal conflict.

REASON 4: TO DIMINISH AGGRESSION

Although most people manage their conflicts in ways that allow them to sustain their personal relationships, many do not learn how to manage conflict. For the latter, interpersonal conflict can be a very negative, and tumultuous, event. According to one review, 15–25% of parents complained about conflicts with their adolescents, and over 20% of adolescents reported "tumultuous" growth marked by "many serious" disagreements with their parents (Montemayor, 1986, p. 18). These figures suggest that 20–25% of families with adolescent children experience disruptions that have emotional and psychological implications.

An extensive review by Marshall (1994) reported that about 20% of people in romantic involvements had experienced some form of physical violence in those relationships within the previous year. (Verbal and physical abuse are discussed in greater detail in chapter 10.) As will become apparent throughout this book, the competent management of conflict helps people to resolve issues in such a manner whereas they see a reliance on verbal or physical abuse as unnecessary and ineffective. In other words, clear education on interpersonal conflict can provide you with insights so you have strategic, as well as personal, reasons to decide against abusive tactics.

REASON 5: TO MAINTAIN OR IMPROVE YOUR PHYSICAL HEALTH

Learning how to manage conflict in a competent manner can reduce risks to your psychological and physical health. Substituting abusive behaviors with more productive ones should provide you with a safer social environment. Research also shows that the way in which people manage conflicts may directly affect their psychological and physical health. Cooperative and reasoned conflicts appear to be much healthier than conflicts laced with negativity.

The following study provides an example. Kiecolt-Glaser and colleagues (1993) recruited happy couples in their first year of marriage to participate in a study conducted at a university medical center. The couples arrived early in the morning and had their blood pressure checked. They then participated in a discussion of conflictual issues, and blood samples were taken at times during the discussion using an unobtrusive method (that is, participants were catheterized and did not know when their blood was being sampled). The couples stayed overnight in the hospital and had their blood sampled again the next morning before they left (about 20 hours after the conflict discussion). The study found that negative conflict behaviors (such as criticizing a partner, denying responsibility for one's part of the conflict, or putting down a partner) adversely affected blood pressure during the talk, and they negatively impacted the immune system 20 hours later.

These results are clear evidence that negative conflict messages damage one's physical health, not only immediately, but for at least about a day. These findings are even more impressive when we realize that the conflictual conversations took place in a secure environment, that the couples reported high marital satisfaction, and that the individuals appeared to be well adjusted with no history of drug use or mental problems (such as depression). Despite all these positive influences, at times the participants engaged in negative behaviors that resulted in damage to their health. Imagine the toll that naturally occurring, negative conflict behaviors take on people who are not in highly satisfying relationships, who may be already depressed or anxious about some event, and who may use drugs either socially or as a means of escape.

Another study examining how physiological responses connect to conflict was undertaken by Levenson, Carstensen, and Gottman (1994). On the basis of their results and other research, the authors reasoned that men are more aware than women of their own negative physical arousal during conflict. However, women experience more negative and persistent physiological outcomes than men in conflict. Levenson and colleagues concluded, "If sustained autonomic arousal is accepted as playing a role in the etiology of disease, then the health of women would be expected to suffer most in the most unhappy marriages, which are the marriages most likely to have intractable problems and repeated bouts of high-level conflict" (p. 66). In short, the health problems that result from mismanaged conflict can be severe.

REASON 6: TO ACHIEVE SATISFYING RELATIONSHIPS

A vast amount of research reveals that how you manage your conflicts powerfully affects your close, personal relationships. No other type of communication tests the character of one's relationship more than the interaction of interpersonal conflict (Canary & Cupach, 1988). Many researchers have discovered that particular patterns of interaction separate satisfied from dissatisfied couples (see chapter 3). For example, Ting-Toomey (1983) found that one pattern among dissatisfied couples is a series of interactions in which one person complains and the other person defends him- or herself. Ting-Toomey found that dissatisfied couples often engaged in a long series of these complain-defend interactions: 10 exchanges of such messages were not uncommon! She also found that satisfied couples did not engage in such patterns. Instead, satisfied couples engaged in more confirming sequences of conflict interaction.

In this book, we review other patterns, both constructive and destructive, to show how interpersonal conflict affects relationships. The work of many researchers attests to one simple principle: *How people manage interpersonal conflicts dramatically affects the quality of their close, personal relationships.*

Defining Interpersonal Conflict

Scholars, like all other people, vary in their conceptions of conflict (see Putnam, 2006). These differences are due partly to the complexity of conflict issues, and partly to the fact that scholars have different research purposes. For example, some are interested in how conflict functions in the development of young children; others are interested in explaining marital problems. Each approach to defining conflict imparts something important about the topic; each approach stresses different ideas about how conflict is expressed or experienced. For this reason, we briefly examine the different approaches to defining conflict.

Definitions of interpersonal conflict vary on two features—*behavior* and *episode* (Canary, Cupach, & Messman, 1995). First, some definitions of conflict specify particular kinds of behaviors that qualify as conflict, but other definitions do not limit conflict to specific behaviors. Second, some definitions describe conflict as a certain kind of interaction event, a distinct set of circumstances that produce conflict; other definitions of conflict do not describe the context surrounding disagreements. These characteristics lead to four definitional approaches, each of which indicates properties of interpersonal conflict.

APPROACH 1: INTERPERSONAL CONFLICT AS PERVASIVE

This first approach to defining interpersonal conflict indicates no behavioral or episodic features of conflict. In other words, *conflict is pervasive*; it can be manifested in all behaviors and regardless of situational factors. According to this definition, people can convey disagreements with each other using a plethora of behaviors. In addition, this definition does not limit conflict to a particular kind of interaction. For example, Sprey (1971) claimed that "the family process *per se* is conceived of as a continuous confrontation between participants with conflicting—though not necessarily opposing—interests in their shared fate" (p. 722).

This definition reminds us that conflict can emerge almost anytime, anywhere. As Sillars and Weisberg (1987) argued, interpersonal conflict contains a "surprise element." These scholars noted how conflict accompanies most of our activities. Conflicts cannot be separated from the experience of everyday living; they potentially occur in every interaction we have.

APPROACH 2: INTERPERSONAL CONFLICT AS EXPLICIT DISAGREEMENT

According to this definition, interpersonal conflict occurs in behavior but is not limited to a particular kind of situation. For example, Vuchinich (1990) defined verbal conflict as a "distinctive speech activity. . . . In verbal conflict, participants oppose the utterances, actions, or selves of one another in successive turns at talk. Linguistic, paralinguistic, or kinesic devices can be used to express opposition directly or indirectly" (p. 118). Approach 2 says that interpersonal conflict occurs whenever people disagree with each other in some behavioral way, regardless of their emotional responses. This definition focuses our attention on the interaction of people.

Relying on this definition, scholars have examined many different behaviors that are said to constitute conflict. Some scholars refer to conflict behaviors as cooperative versus competitive strategies, whereas others define conflict as confirming versus disconfirming behaviors. In addition, some researchers view conflicts simply as behavioral oppositions; others believe that some type of "significant disagreement" should accompany these behavioral oppositions. The point is that conflict emerges in a variety of messages (see chapter 3).

APPROACH 3: INTERPERSONAL CONFLICT AS A HOSTILE EPISODE

A third category of definitions acknowledges that conflict entails perceptual parameters. Research shows that people can easily identify conflict episodes. *Episodes* are situations that have a recognizable beginning and end, which can vary widely in the minds of different people (Pearce, 1976). But people often use their definitions of the situation to locate the beginning and ending of an interpersonal conflict.

People often identify conflict episodes by referring to their own feelings—anger, hostility, depression, or some emotion that causes them to recognize a situation as conflict (Guerrero & La Valley, 2006). For example, the frustration we feel when another person prevents or delays us from achieving our goals is an experience that indicates conflict. Although interaction behaviors are not specified, they may be implied.

This approach reminds us that interpersonal conflicts are actually experienced in our perceptions of events. Of course, the prototype of this definition is when people disagree simply due to a misunderstanding. Accordingly, this definition centers on the individual's experience more than on the conflict messages. We all know that people can have alternative experiences of the same event. In addition, some people are more sensitive than others to negative feelings and thus might experience a conflict longer or more intensely, and they may read more hostility into a conversation than was intended. Regardless of the intensity of feeling, people can experience interpersonal conflicts over time, extending the conflict episode for weeks, months, or even years. When a particular conflict issue within a relationship recurs in multiple interactions over time it results in what Roloff and Johnson (2002) refer to as *serial arguing*.

APPROACH 4: INTERPERSONAL CONFLICT AS DISAGREEMENT IN PARTICULAR EPISODES

This final definition specifies that interpersonal conflict must entail a behavioral form of disagreement. In addition, the conflict behaviors occur within identifiable situations that are commonly understood as conflict episodes. This definition provides a central focus for the study of conflict at the interpersonal level. For example, Hocker and Wilmot (1995) offer the following popular definition of interpersonal conflict within this approach: "*an expressed struggle between at least two interdependent parties who perceive incompatible goals, scarce resources, and interference from the other party in achieving their goals*" (emphasis in original, p. 21).

This definition specifies conflict in terms of behavior (expressed struggle) and episode (perception of incompatible goals, scarce resources, and interference). Hocker and Wilmot's definition implies that people use particular behaviors when faced with incompatibility. In addition, this approach emphasizes conflict as something that is *communicated*; you must express your disagreement with someone to have an *interpersonal* conflict. Finally, this definition focuses on the division of scarce resources in close relationships that are marked by interdependence. Table 1-1 summarizes the four approaches to defining interpersonal conflict.

We have our own preference regarding an approach to defining conflict, but because we want to include various points of view, and for the sake of discussion, we refrain from offering our opinion. Instead, we would like you to determine for yourself which approach seems most insightful. You can refer to your own experience with interpersonal conflict, discuss the four definitional approaches with class members, and/or talk about these ideas with your instructor (who also probably has a preference on the topic of how to define conflict). The idea we wish to impart to you is that conflict is multifaceted, and much territory has been covered in the research literature about conflict.

Table 1-1   Definitions (and Examples) of Four Prototypical Definitions of Interpersonal Conflict

Definition 1: Interpersonal conflict concerns any incompatibility between people that can be manifested in any behaviors in any situation (for example, your successful older brother always finds a way to let everyone else know just how successful he is, which makes you crazy and spoils family reunions).

Definition 2: Interpersonal conflict refers to behaviors that explicitly show a disagreement between two people (for example, two consecutive oppositions).

Definition 3: Interpersonal conflict refers to situations that involve feelings of hostility between people (you resent someone who broke up with you several years ago).

Definition 4: Interpersonal conflict refers to behaviors that explicitly show a disagreement between two people involved in situations marked by feelings of hostility (you confront your nephew about his stealing money from your wallet).

Source: Adapted from Canary, Cupach, and Messman (1995).

Features of Interpersonal Conflict

As we have seen, scholars vary in what they mean by the term *conflict*. What is common across most definitions of conflict is that it originates in perceived incompatibility between interdependent parties (Putnam, 2006). The nature of these incompatibilities is revealed by considering the various levels and types of conflict that occur.

LEVELS OF CONFLICT

Braiker and Kelley (1979) argued that conflict exists at different levels of interdependence. Individuals share an interdependent relationship with each other to the extent that they can affect each other's outcomes. Interdependence requires individuals to coordinate their actions in order to achieve their goals (Putnam, 2006). According to Braiker and Kelley (1979), different issues of interdependence reveal the following three different levels of conflict.

Level 1 conflict refers to problems regarding *specific behaviors*. These conflicts can pertain to disputes over such things as which TV program to watch, how long to cook vegetables, and if you should mail a package overnight or by regular mail. In addition, any time one person regards the concrete actions of another as annoying ("Please quit interrupting me when I am talking."), imposing ("Don't show up at my house without calling first!"), or offensive ("You have a lot of nerve criticizing me!") there is opportunity for conflict.

Level 2 conflict concerns coordination of relational *norms and roles*. At this level, you and your partner might disagree about what is expected from you in the relationship. Level 2 conflicts include disagreements such as whether one should share toys when asked, who should cook and clean, and whether the woman should take the man's last name when they marry. In other words, level 2 conflicts entail disagreements about *relational rules*. These rules govern important relational issues such as trust, respect, commitment, and power. When relational rules are violated, a relational transgression occurs (Metts & Cupach, 2007). Infidelity, deception, and betraying a confidence are typically regarded as serious relational transgressions. Conflicts at level 2 tend to be more serious and more difficult to resolve than conflicts at level 1.

Level 3 conflict regards *personal characteristics and attitudes*. These conflicts concern problems you might have with your partner's personality or beliefs. Examples of problems that might fuel conflict at this level include the disposition of an immature older sibling, the extreme jealousy of a romantic partner, and religious differences. Level 3 conflicts focus on someone's personality— the person's motives, qualities, faults, and (sometimes) strengths.

These three levels of conflict are often mixed during actual interaction. For example, you may disagree with your friend and believe that she agreed to call you if she was going to arrive late (a specific behavior). You may also view her failure to call as part of a larger problem of not showing consideration as a friend (a relational rule). In addition, such instances of her treating you with a lack of consideration have decreased your liking of this person and your desire to spend any further time with her (a personal issue).

TYPES OF ACTUAL VERSUS PERCEIVED CONFLICT

In addition to having different levels, interpersonal conflict varies to the extent it concerns actual differences or perceived differences. Conflicts can arise from real incompatibilities or incompatibilities that are largely imagined (Deutsch, 1973). *Both* actual and perceived conflict represent legitimate bases for disagreement. No one's perceptions are 100% accurate, and perceptions differ in the extent to which they are anchored in reality.

An illustration can show how people might have different bases for conflict. Although many people think they can recall exactly who said what in a conversation, the research indicates otherwise. Stafford and Daly (1984) found that their participants could only recall about 9% of what they said the previous hour. Even when it comes to important issues, people only recall about 35% of what they talked about the previous hour (Sillars, Weisberg, Burggraf, & Zietlow, 1990). As you might have hypothesized, these low figures for conversational recall drop even lower over time. Given this research, it is ironic that many conflicts concern who said what to whom, why what the person said was merely in response to the other person's statement, and so forth. People sometimes state that they wish for a video recording to prove how accurate they are ("If only I had a video recording of this, you would see how right I am!"). However, it is likely that *neither* person will recall the conversation very accurately, and a video recording of their talk would show that inaccuracy.

Deutsch (1973) showed how interpersonal conflict differs depending on actual and/or perceived bases for disagreement, and whether the perceptions accurately portray the objective bases for conflict. Five types of conflict are possible.

Parallel conflict (what Deutsch, 1973, called "veridical" conflict) is a conflict that has an objective basis and is accurately perceived by both parties. For example, if Margo and Peter both agree that their conflict arises from the fact that Margo does not want to commit to their relationship, whereas Peter does, then they have a verifiable basis for conflict and their perceptions parallel that basis.

Displaced conflict is an instance in which someone might have an objective reason for conflict and perceives that a conflict exists but has perceptions of the conflict issue that are off target. Extending the previous example, Peter (who is uncertain of his relational future) may begin to withhold a full range of affection from Margo (from not sleeping with her to sulking). Margo may become upset at Peter and confront him about sulking all the time. As long as they focus on the issue of sulking, the real conflict (about commitment) is displaced.

Another form of conflict in which the objective basis for conflict is inaccurately perceived is *misattributed conflict* (Deutsch, 1973). In this case, however, the inaccuracy concerns *who* is in conflict. If Peter blames Margo's ex-lover for their problems, Peter may never confront Margo. Instead, Peter may build a sincere hatred for the ex-boyfriend and pity Margo for her inability to make a commitment.

Latent conflict refers to conflict "that should be occurring but is not" (Deutsch, 1973, p. 14). Although an objective basis exists for conflict, neither person perceives it. Such is often the case when couples have real differences in values but pretend such differences do not matter. They continue to plan for the wedding and do not allow any serious talk about issues that might cause them to scrutinize exactly what they are getting into (as illustrated in the sentence, "Oh, I know we're different, but that will change after we're married"). On the other hand, an important finding has been that perceived agreement between people—and not actual agreement—is positively associated with relational satisfaction (e.g., Segrin, Hanzal, & Domschke, 2009; Sillars et al., 1990). Sometimes ignorance is bliss (but other times it leads to trouble).

In *false conflict*, people disagree but have no objective basis for their disagreement. False conflicts are the result of misunderstanding. If I perceive that you dislike my best friend, but in fact you very much like my best friend, the conflict arising from my perception of you is a false one. A clear example of false conflict arises when a jealous lover imagines intrigue and guile that do not exist. Jealous lovers may contribute to the conflict by using "detective" strategies, such as monitoring the partner by calling at unexpected hours, looking through the person's telephone bills and drawers, and other covert activities (Guerrero, Andersen, Jorgensen, Spitzberg, & Eloy, 1995). Although such jealousies are often based more on imagination than reality, the jealous person, who might even recognize the lack of factual data, may feel too insecure to admit his or her perceptual error.

In short, interpersonal conflicts differ in the extent to which they reflect real or perceived problems. Sometimes the perceptions of both parties match reality;

in other instances conflict concerns the wrong issue. Seeing the issue accurately does not guarantee that the conflict will be reduced. In fact, sometimes knowing precisely where objective differences exist can exacerbate conflict.

These various types of conflict also occur at different levels, from those about behavior, to those about relational rules, to those about personal evaluations. Table 1-2 illustrates the different levels of each type of conflict. The fact that conflict exists in different types and on different levels implies that we can expect interpersonal conflict to emerge in many different issues. The level of interpersonal conflict is tied to how the issue if framed. Some issues are seen as isolated events; others are seen as reflecting larger relational problems.

Table 1-2   Levels of Different Types of Conflict

Type of Conflict	Example
Level 1: Specific Behavior	
Parallel	At a party, your friend has consumed several drinks and wants to drive home. But you do not want your friend to drive after drinking so much alcohol.
Displaced	You don't like that your housemate talks nonstop. To drown out the talking, you turn on a football game. Your housemate doesn't like sports, so the two of you argue about what to watch on TV.
Misattributed	You discover the smell of cigarette smoke in your house, which you hate. You think your daughter's boyfriend has been smoking, and you warn him to not smoke in your house. In actuality, your daughter was the person smoking.
Latent	You don't carry condoms because you think that is tacky. Your partner doesn't either, though you think he should. Several times now you have been frustrated because both of you want to make love, but you know you should practice "safe sex." Still, it's too embarrassing to discuss.
False	Two friends are in a heated debate about health care reform. They see their points as contradictory, but in actuality they both are advocating the same point of view but with different and even complementary evidence.
Level 2: Relational Rules	
Parallel	You have a job offer that requires you to move across the country. Your family doesn't want you to leave and they plead with you to stay home. You really don't want to leave home but this job is too good to pass up.
Displaced	Your parents have been having a lot of conflicts, which you can't stand. So you run away for the weekend in hopes of distracting their attention from their own problems.

(continued)

Type of Conflict	Example
Misattributed	You are very upset with your mother for breaking up the family by asking your father to move out. Your father indicates how sad he is to go, but your mother won't discuss the issue with you or your sister. Years later, you discover your father had abused your mother.
Latent	You and your partner have been dating for about six weeks and you are falling in love. You do not want to date others and assume your partner feels the same way. But s/he had just concluded an emotionally draining relationship and cannot fathom making another commitment right now and has plans to see other people when convenient.
False	You are not happy with a friend who did not invite you to her wedding. She is not happy with the fact that you did not attend her wedding. In actuality, the invitation was sent to your previous address, but was not forwarded to you.
Level 3: Personality	
Parallel	An acquaintance advocates white supremacy. You are offended by this, and he is offended by your "liberal attitude."
Displaced	You find out that an instructor has been dating a former student of his. You don't think this is ethical, because you feel that there is a power imbalance in the teacher-student relationship that unprincipled male teachers can exploit. So you look for occasions to disagree with this "sleazy" teacher during lecture.
Misattributed	You heard a rumor about you that suggested you can't be trusted. In public, you confront the person you are sure began the rumor, someone you know to be a gossip and a liar. The person you confront easily dismisses your accusation, and points out that you don't know what you're talking about. You never find out who initiated the rumor, though you often get embarrassed at recalling the event.
Latent	Your brother routinely uses drugs. The problem is that he cannot care for his two young daughters (ages 2 and 4) when he is high. In fact, he likes to get high and take his daughters to the park to play. You hope he grows out of this phase.
False	You cannot understand why your roommate is so lazy. He sleeps until 10:00 AM, complains about all the work that he never does, and likes to take naps in the middle of the day. In addition, he doesn't care that his courses are suffering this term. The two of you argue about it all the time, and he gets so depressed that he drops out of school. Later you discover that he has *chronic fatigue syndrome* and is under a doctor's care.

Box 1-1 Working for the Minimum Wage Case Study

Michael and David had different reasons for working part-time as janitors. Mike was a graduate student who needed tuition money. Dave had a family with four children and no permanent job, so he hoped this part-time job would turn into something better. They worked for a large company, Zambam Inc., which won large contracts. But Zambam paid their employees as little as possible, which meant that Mike and Dave waxed floors and scrubbed toilets for minimum wage. Zambam also stretched its profits by underestimating how long particular jobs would take, thereby forcing employees to work fast and hard.

Zambam won a $10,000-a-month contract for a pharmaceutical firm (Sticka Pharmaceutical). After the initial cleaning, they put Mike and Dave on the account and allowed only four hours a night for them to clean the two office buildings and factory. Mike would go before Dave and empty trash cans, clean ash trays, and wipe off desks and railings. Dave watched out for the ever-menacing dust—he would dust, clean all the air vents, and vacuum. They both cleaned the bathrooms in record time. Despite this system, they would miss one or two trash cans or an air vent.

Within a few days, Sticka started to complain that air vents and trash cans were not cleaned, which was critical to that business. Zambam reminded Mike and Dave about their obligations to do a good job. So, Mike and Dave worked faster—and longer—than they were paid to. But that was not enough to do a thorough cleaning of the buildings. Sticka complained again to Zambam. Zambam warned Mike and Dave that they could lose their jobs.

Mike and Dave each felt the pressure. So they changed their routine to maximize their efficiency, and their new routine required split-second timing and coordination. Also, to keep their jobs, they put in twice the amount of work without pay.

Mike knew he was working as hard as anyone could, and he was fast. Dave was not as fast because he was concerned that they would miss that all-important air vent or that executive ash tray. Dave really needed the money more than Mike. Mike began to complain that Dave was taking too long—and they weren't getting paid that much to work there all night. Dave would wipe the sweat from his eyes and remind Mike about missing certain ash trays. They resented each other, despite the fact that they were friends.

One night, Dave spotted a full trash can Mike had missed. He blew up, "What is wrong with you? Can't you see it doesn't matter how fast you go if you don't clean everything!"

Mike said, "Look, don't you give me that! I could get this place clean in plenty of time if I didn't have to drag you along all night!"

Dave replied, "Look, dummy, I have to clean things you miss, and that's what's slowing us down here! Now get it together or we'll lose this account."

Mike shot back, "Don't call *me* stupid! At least I don't consider this a *career* opportunity."

Dave was so mad, all he could say was, "Watch yourself."

(continued)

A week later they were called into Zambam's main office and told they had lost the account. They were fired and handed their pay (minus their uniform fee) for the past two weeks—$160.59.

Perhaps the real loss was the friendship. Mike and Dave lost contact with each other after a few months. Years later each of them would shake his head at how hard they worked for so little.

Discussion Questions

1. What is the *level* of conflict between Mike and Dave (i.e., behavioral, relational, personal)? What *type* of conflict is this?

2. Was the conflict between Mike and Dave partly the company's fault for not providing enough resources for the account? Did Mike and Dave manage the conflict in a productive way?

3. How would you deal with this issue, if you were either Mike or Dave?

Summary

You already have had much training in interpersonal conflict management. You have probably developed some very clear ideas about conflict and how you can effectively manage it. The purpose of this book is to help you refine your expertise by increasing your understanding of interpersonal conflict and how it can be competently managed.

Early in this chapter, we provided six reasons why it is important to learn more about interpersonal conflict: to fine-tune your expertise; to realize that conflict happens quite frequently; to see how conflict links to your development as a person; to diminish aggression; to maintain or improve your physical health; and to sustain positive relationships. We hope that each of these reasons provides you with enough incentive to learn more about the topic.

We offered four definitional approaches that researchers have used to study interpersonal conflict. Examining these alternative approaches helps us realize that conflict involves a multitude of factors, and each definitional approach stresses some of those factors more than others. You must decide for yourself which approach is most informative.

In discussing the various levels and types of conflict, we noted that conflict issues range from those concerning behavioral differences to more serious disagreements about relational rules and personal characteristics. The various types of conflicts occur at different levels. Some conflicts are no more than minor disagreements that barely last a minute. Conflicts that concern fundamental issues about a relationship or about each other as people can last years.

Interpersonal conflict may appear to be unnatural and unfriendly. No one we know wakes up in the morning and asks, "Who can I get into a conflict with today!?" Most people prefer their lives and loves to continue in a smooth fashion. But neither life nor love is like that. Because we interact with others, conflict occurs. Some researchers see conflict as part of every conversation; others see it isolated to particular events within particular conversations. Regardless of the definition adopted, conflict represents a prominent and critically important experience in everyone's lives.

DISCUSSION QUESTIONS

1. Recall the last time you had a significant conflict with someone close to you. What was the cause of the conflict? At what level, or combination of levels, was the conflict—behavioral, relational, personal? Has the conflict been resolved?

2. The beginning of this chapter provides six reasons why people should study interpersonal conflict management. Which of these reasons represents the most convincing case, in your opinion? Can you think of other reasons that are not discussed here? Can you think of reasons why people should *not* study interpersonal conflict?

3. Please reread each of the definitions in table 1-1. Which definition is the most insightful to you? Why?

4. Argyle and Henderson (1984) discuss different "rules of friendship." Several rules in particular were found to distinguish the quality of friendship. That is, if these rules were held, then the friendship was a good one. For example, consider the following rules:

   a. Standing up for the other friend (to defend him or her) in his or her absence;

   b. Sharing news of success with the friend;

   c. Showing emotional support for the friend;

   d. Volunteering to help the friend in time of need; and

   e. Striving to make the friend happy.

   Discuss a conflict that stemmed from one or both persons not following one or more of these rules. Also discuss other rules of friendship that are important to you. How do these rules differ from those in romantic relationships, such as dating seriously and marriage?

chapter 2

A COMPETENCE-BASED APPROACH TO INTERPERSONAL CONFLICT

CHAPTER OUTLINE

Criteria Guiding Perceptions of Competence
    Effectiveness
    Appropriateness
    The Relationship between Effectiveness and Appropriateness
    Implications of Judging Competence
Factors That Facilitate Competence
    Motivation
    Knowledge
    Skills
An Explanatory Model of Interpersonal Conflict
    Distal Context
    Proximal Context
    Conflict Interaction
    Proximal Outcomes
    Distal Outcomes
Summary
Discussion Questions

Our approach to understanding interpersonal conflict is based on a model of communication competence (Spitzberg, Canary, & Cupach, 1994; Spitzberg & Cupach, 1984). A model that features communication competence is particularly helpful for understanding conflict management. You will recall from chapter 1, competence is a judgment regarding the effectiveness and appropriateness of communication. Conflicts represent "problematic" communication situations that challenge our communication abilities. Getting what we want and simultaneously meeting others' preferences can be quite difficult. Tension between the dual criteria of effectiveness and appropriateness is heightened in conflict situations, and often becomes the focus of disagreement.

Research has shown the importance of competence judgments in interpersonal conflict (Canary & Cupach, 1988; Canary & Spitzberg, 1989). As we will show later, conflict behavior affects the relationship between conflict parties. The manner in which two friends manage disagreements, for example, influences their friendship. How a husband and wife deal with their inevitable conflicts affects their satisfaction with their marriage. In short, the perceived competence of conflict communication strongly influences whether conflict behavior will produce positive or negative outcomes for the individuals, their relationship, and the larger social or organizational systems in which they participate. In technical terms, we say that *perceived competence mediates the link between conflict behavior and relationship outcomes*. In other words, conflict behavior affects judgments of competence, which in turn, affect relational outcomes. One way of thinking about this mediating role is whether or not any given conflict behaviors will have a negative or positive impact on the participants will depend on the extent to which those behaviors are viewed as competent or incompetent. When conflict behaviors are viewed as competent, even if the behaviors are aggressive or avoidant, then the likelihood of positive outcomes is increased. In contrast, when conflict behaviors are viewed as incompetent, even when they are cooperative or accommodating, they are likely to result in negative outcomes.

Figure 2-1 depicts a hypothetical example of the role of competence judgments. Ron is a salesman and Kathy is his supervisor. When Ron and Kathy have conflict, they implicitly judge each other's behavior. Ron assesses the competence of Kathy's conflict behavior. The more positive his judgments are, the more likely he will feel good about maintaining their relationship. Those positive feelings about the relationship in turn are likely to promote more positive interactions with Kathy, which promote her own positive behaviors. Similarly, Kathy's judgment of Ron's behavior filters the effects of Ron's behavior on Kathy's judgment of their interactions. If Ron and Kathy both see each other as managing conflict competently, it will enhance their ongoing working relationship.

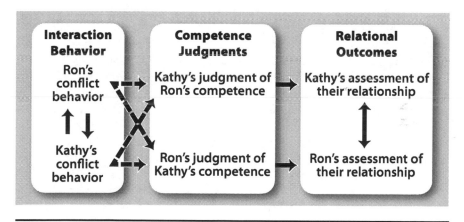

Figure 2-1   The mediating role of competence judgments in conflict situations.

The perception of another person's competence is partly influenced by one's own behavior. Individuals are behaviorally interdependent when they communicate. Thus, they not only influence each other's perceptions through their behavior; they also influence each other's behavior during conflict interactions (e.g., Sillars, 1980a). If Kathy is particularly aggressive in her conflict behavior it may lead to Ron's own aggressiveness. Thus, Kathy's own behavior indirectly affects her judgment of Ron's behavior because she influenced

Ron's behavior. This common tendency to mirror a conversational partner's behavior is called *reciprocity.*

Another reason for adopting the competence model is that it recognizes the complexity of conflict processes. Lists of prespecified skills or behaviors are unlikely to guarantee success in managing conflict. It will become apparent, we hope, that communication behaviors do not possess intrinsic meaning or have automatic effects on people. There is little value in preparing a cookbook of recipes for conflict success. The effects of conflict interaction directly depend both on how the participants *interpret and perform* conflict behaviors.

Judgments of competence are made in terms of a communication context. Contexts can be understood on several levels (Argyle, Furnham, & Graham, 1981). Strictly speaking, interactants' behaviors *constitute* the context—that is, regardless of where you are or what you intended to do, if you and another person are engaged in conflict, then it becomes a "conflict" encounter and context. How that conflict ensues, however, is affected by a number of contextual factors. One type of context that often affects conflicts is *culture*, or the enduring patterns of beliefs, attitudes, values, and behaviors that are capable of being passed on from generation to generation. The mutual influences of culture and conflict are examined in greater detail in chapter 7. A second type of context that significantly affects conflict is the *relationship*. You are likely to engage in conflict differently with your parents than you do with your romantic partner, and differently with your friend than you would with a boss. A third type of context is *environment*, or the physical place, media, and configuration of the conflict encounter. For example, (a) people tend to be more aggressive when temperatures are near 100°F than in cooler contexts, (b) people are more easily aggravated in crowded settings than in uncrowded settings, and (c) *flaming*, or engaging in exaggerated insults or swearing, is easier online than when face to face. A final form of context is *function*, which represents the purpose of the interaction. Conflict in a job interview is likely to occur differently than in a job layoff encounter. Conflict during a first date is likely to occur differently than in a relationship breakup situation. Each of these levels of context will tend to involve expectations for their rules and actions, and furthermore, the negotiation of these expectations, rules, and behaviors will often be at the center of the conflict itself. It follows, therefore, that judgments of communication competence (i.e., appropriateness and effectiveness) will depend significantly on the nature of the context and how it is negotiated. We elaborate on the standards employed for judging the competence of communication in the following section.

Criteria Guiding Perceptions of Competence

The quality of communication can be evaluated in many different ways. When we think of "good" communication, we think of such standards as: Is it clear? Is it supportive? Is it eloquent? Different standards are more or less relevant in different communication contexts. However, two standards are relatively universal. The criteria of *effectiveness* and *appropriateness* are general and apply to most instances of interpersonal communication (Spitzberg, 2000; Spitzberg & Cupach, 1984), including those involving interpersonal conflict. As explained in chapter 1, communication competence is a function of fulfilling *both* of these criteria. Here we consider how these two criteria are applied.

EFFECTIVENESS

Perhaps the most obvious benchmark for assessing communication is whether or not it is effective in accomplishing relatively preferred outcomes for the communicators. The most typical way of thinking about effectiveness is the extent to which communicators achieve their goals. This view, however, requires an important qualification. From time to time, interactants may face a true "lose-lose" situation, in which any decision or action is bound to result in an unwanted or undesirable outcome. In such a case it is still possible to be effective; a communicator is effective in a lose-lose situation by selecting the approach that minimizes the losses relative to other approaches. Facing a divorce, for example, may involve an inherently undesirable set of choices, but there are choices that are better than others at minimizing the damage to the individuals involved.

In most communication encounters, interactants go into the situation with some type or types of goals (Canary, Cunningham, & Cody, 1988). Even in unfamiliar situations, most communicators will apply goals from past situations that are somewhat similar to the current situation. For example, you may not have been to a political rally before, but you have seen, read, or heard about such meetings, and may have been to meetings of groups with political agendas, so you are able to generalize your expectations from those groups to your attendance at a political rally.

Goals represent the outcomes that people desire or prefer to achieve. To discern the extent to which communication is effective, it is necessary to know what goals motivate communication. While various classifications of goals have been offered by researchers, there are three general types of goals that are present in all interpersonal situations: instrumental goals, self-presentation goals, and relational goals (Canary & Cody, 1994; Clark & Delia, 1979). All three of these types of goals are present in any conflict situation, though the relative importance of each type varies.

If goals are the outcomes people seek in their conflicts, then it follows that in order to understand and behave more competently in conflict encounters, it becomes essential to develop a better understanding of the nature of goals. Goals are not necessarily static, stable intentions to behave in a certain way. Instead, goals are complex and evolving. Specifically, 10 characteristics can be identified about the nature of goals and the roles they play in everyday behavior (see table 2-1).

First, some situations permit only one or a few goals, whereas other situations permit many potential goals. In a courtroom dispute over the guilt or

Table 2-1   The Nature of Interaction Goals

1. Situations possess multiple goals and vary in the number of goals associated with them.
2. Goals are hierarchical; subordinate/proximal goals must be achieved in order to achieve superordinate/distal goals.
3. Goals vary in importance; some goals will be "sacrificed" in the pursuit of others.
4. Goals vary in complexity regarding the inputs and processes needed to achieve them.
5. Goals can entail both approach (you want to approach) and avoidance (you want to avoid) motivations.
6. Goals vary in mutual compatibility and exclusivity.
7. Goals vary in purity of valence; benefits entail some costs, and vice versa.
8. Goals vary in locus of motivation; some are internally generated, others are externally generated.
9. Goals are systemic and processual; they change through and during interaction.
10. Goals can be individual (identity), interpersonal (relational), and/or instrumental (tangible).

innocence of a defendant, most of the parties will have a relatively restricted number of goals. In contrast, in the early stages of a dating relationship, there are multiple potential goals for the direction of each participant's behavior.

Second, goals are hierarchical. Our higher-order goals help organize lower-order goals. So, for example, your desire to obtain a college degree requires the coordination of many more specific goals (e.g., registration, advising, daily schedules and activities, interactions with classmates and professors, etc.). Individuals impose hierarchical order on their interaction goals. At any given time, the most important goal has the strongest influence on our behavior, whereas the "secondary" goals qualify the manner in which the primary goal is sought (Dillard, 1990). If my primary goal is to get you to take a cooking class with me, my behavior is motivated to overcome your resistance. The manner in which I try to influence you and my degree of persistence, however, will be tempered by my perceived risks to our relationship if I push you too hard. My relational goal constrains my actions directed at accomplishing the primary goal.

Third, goals vary in their importance. Some goals (e.g., obtaining a college degree) are likely to be far more important than others (e.g., deciding on where to eat today). Some goals may be foregone in the interest of pursuing the more important goals (e.g., ending a dating relationship in high school due to the need to move away to a college in a different region of the country). Fourth, some goals are relatively simple to achieve, requiring only a few action steps (e.g., ordering a pizza delivery). Other goals (e.g., getting a college degree) involve many interdependent steps to be completed. Fifth, goals sometimes represent something you want to pursue, and sometimes they represent something you want to avoid. For example, you may want to pursue a party this weekend, but you want to avoid having a conflict with your parents about coming home this weekend.

Sixth, goals vary in the extent to which they are compatible or incompatible. For example, working full time may be incompatible with completing a college degree in a four-year time span. Seventh, some goals are almost entirely positive (e.g., sharing a fun time with friends) or negative (e.g., seeking revenge against another), whereas other goals have both positive and negative aspects to them (e.g., moving to an undesirable geographic location in order to start a better job than the one you presently have). Eighth, some goals emerge from "who you are," whereas others are more situational or opportunistic. For example, your desire to get a college degree may represent something that evolved from a variety of your personal experiences, background, and contemplation. In contrast, a friend calling you up to offer you a ticket to the game this weekend provides an opportunity for realizing a goal that might not have been prominent before.

Ninth, goals can be very fluid and evolutionary. You may go to a working lunch with a classmate or colleague, but develop a friendship or dating relationship during the process of the conversation. We normally think of goals as prospective. That is, we are cognizant of them prior to interaction, and we make plans and rehearse strategies for achieving them. However, this is not always the case. In fact, much of the time we are probably only dimly aware of our goals. They exist, but we pursue them automatically and relatively thoughtlessly. Moreover, goals may formulate and emerge during and after a conflict interaction. Hocker and Wilmot (1991) call these "transactive" goals. The fluid and changing course of interactions, as well as the ongoing mutual influence communicators have on one another, stimulate the emergence of transactive goals. Melissa may disagree with Shayna about when to launch a new employee relations project in their work division. Melissa may learn information from Hope during their conflict that alters her original position. Melissa may even decide, as a result of the new information, to advocate scrapping the original idea. Shayna may develop a goal to accommodate Melissa because Shayna realizes during the interaction that she is going to need Melissa's support later on for an unrelated project. Shayna and Melissa may even develop the goal to get to know each other better socially because they seem to think alike and share some values. The occurrence of transactional goals is consistent with the idea that competent communicators, above all else, must be adaptable to the dynamic circumstances of interactions.

A final distinction about goals is that they can represent different desired ends. Given the complex ways in which goals operate in interaction contexts, it is not surprising that goals also vary in the particular type of end-state toward which they are directed. There are different types of goals for different types of desired outcomes. One important approach to distinguishing goal types conceptualizes three basic goal intentions: instrumental, relational, and self-presentation (Clark & Delia, 1979).

Instrumental goals are concerned with resources we wish to acquire. Specifically, instrumental goals include gaining compliance from another, changing another's attitude or beliefs, obtaining assistance or support, and so forth (Cody, Canary, & Smith, 1994). These types of goals are distinguished by referring to relatively specific tangible outcomes. Often the primary source of interpersonal conflict is found in the competing instrumental goals of two people. David wants Mary to go away with him for the weekend, but Mary wants to stay home to finish a project for work. Mom wants little Jerry to come home to eat supper, but Jerry wants to stay out and play with his friends. An employee wants a raise whereas the manager wants higher employee productivity.

Relational goals represent the relationship status we wish to achieve or maintain with another person. Because interpersonal conflict is between two people, the relationship between them is always relevant to their mutual conflict. If Steve and Rachel are coworkers, the way they manage conflict with each other will be constrained by the desire to continue a smooth working relationship. And if Steve and Rachel are interested in pursuing a dating relationship, they may withhold disagreements about their attitudes to protect the fledgling relationship. Relational goals are often subsidiary, serving to constrain how instrumental goals are pursued (Dillard, Segrin, & Harden, 1989). When two individuals disagree about how to *define* their relationship, however, then incompatible relational goals can emerge as the primary conflict issue. For example, Zeke and Paula want to date each other; Zeke wants an exclusive relationship but Paula does not want to commit to Zeke. In this case, *relational* conflict seems inevitable.

Self-presentation goals pertain to the personal image or persona we wish to present when interacting with others. We always seek to leave a certain impression on those with whom we communicate (Schlenker, 1980). The identity we present and want others to accept during particular episodes of interaction is called *face* (Goffman, 1967). Most people want to be seen as intelligent and capable. Often, we wish to be perceived as likeable and friendly. During conflict, there are numerous impressions we may want to sustain: attractive, trustworthy, credible, powerful, sincere, fair, tough, and so forth. Successfully accomplishing our self-presentation goals can facilitate the accomplishment of instrumental goals. For example, if I think you are fair, I will be more likely to cooperate with you during conflict. There are exceptional circumstances, however, in which we seek to be seen as incompetent, such as when a person might bluff ignorance in a card game in order to "sucker" other players into losing their money.

Sometimes conflict stems from the fact that our face is "threatened" by the actions of others (Cupach & Metts, 1984). In other words, we perceive someone as interfering with our self-presentation goals. Whenever we are discredited our face is threatened. If we are ridiculed or criticized publicly, for example, our face is discredited (Cupach & Carson, 2002). Others can also unintentionally threaten our face by committing a faux pas or behaving fool-ishly (Miller, 1996). For example, if Ted brings his friend Tim to a party, and Tim gets drunk and makes a fool out of himself, then Ted feels guilt by asso-ciation. Whenever we feel that our face is threatened, our self-presentation goals are being thwarted. This can result in conflict with the person we per-ceive as responsible for creating our face loss.

Self-presentation goals sometimes interfere with instrumental goals, thereby complicating the management of conflict. For example, you may want help with your homework, but you don't want your roommate to think you are stupid. Or, you want to disagree with my opinion, but you don't want to seem arrogant. Or, you want to correct an errant employee, but you also want to be liked. There even may be times when we have an instrumental goal of avoiding more work than we want to perform, so we create the unde-sirable self-presentation impression that we are unreliable and lazy, so that we are not called upon to do a particular unpleasant job.

APPROPRIATENESS

There are normally multiple paths to achieving any particular goal; a concept known as *equifinality*. Most of the time we are dependent on other people in order to reach our goals. Thus, pursuing personal goals must take into account the following: (1) our goals may conflict with the goals of others and (2) how we pursue our goals produces consequences for others, regard-less of any real incompatibility. Thus, interpersonal competence demands that effective communication is also appropriate. In other words, pursuing personal goals must take account of the expectations of others. Of the multi-ple possible paths toward the achievement of a given goal, competence will depend on selecting the particular path(s) that are most appropriate to the other parties in the context.

Communication *rules* constitute one basis for judging the appropriateness of communication. According to Shimanoff (1980), rules "are followable pre-scriptions that indicate what behavior is obligated, preferred, or prohibited in certain contexts" (p. 57). Although individuals are in the best position to identify their own goals and the extent to which they are fulfilled, other peo-ple's judgments must be considered when evaluating what rules are relevant and whether they are followed.

Social rules are implicit in all social interaction. Although we do not think much about social rules, we certainly recognize them, especially when they are violated. In our society, we know that we are expected to treat others with politeness and civility (Brown & Levinson, 1987). Questions are sup-posed to be met with answers. Interrupting a conversational partner is gener-ally to be avoided (Grice, 1975; McCann & Higgins, 1984). When rules are violated, conflict may occur. For example, rules such as "do not criticize me" or "try not to say things to embarrass me" (Kline & Stafford, 2004), if vio-lated, could clearly lead to conflict. Conflict discussion may center on whether or not a rule was actually broken; whether or not the rule is "legitimate"; whether there is a relevant exception to the rule; whether there are other, more important rules; and the like (Newell & Stutman, 1988).

As interpersonal relationships develop more history and intimacy, partners increasingly rely on their own interpersonal rules. Partners tacitly establish their own mutual guidelines for behavior in their relationship. When conflict occurs in public, both social and interpersonal rules are in force. When conflicts occur in private settings, the interpersonal rules take precedence. Of course, individuals sometimes intentionally violate a known rule in order to escalate an emerging conflict. For instance, if you know your children do not want you to date others (although the divorce is final), you may deliberately begin looking for someone to date. Other times rules are unintentionally violated in the heat of interpersonal battle (for example, throwing a glass of water at someone without considering the consequences of that action).

Some rules pertain specifically to conflict communication. These rules govern what behaviors people believe should or should not be enacted during conflict. For instance, a couple may adopt a rule of never going to sleep angry, or not arguing in public. Honeycutt, Woods, and Fontenot (1993) examined differences among married and engaged couples with respect to endorsement of communicative rules for managing conflict (see Jones & Gallois, 1989). They found four different categories of rules governing conflict communication: *positive understanding* (e.g., one should be able to say "I'm sorry," one should listen to another), *rationality* (e.g., don't get angry, don't raise your voice), *conciseness* (e.g., one should get to the point quickly, one should be consistent), and *consideration* (e.g., don't make the other person feel guilty, don't mimic or be sarcastic). Violation of rules such as these, when they are accepted by relational partners, can create a unique type of conflict—conflict about rules about conflict.

Other rules may not be explicitly about conflict, but so closely associated with managing cooperative interaction that their ongoing negotiation seems bound to lead to conflicts. For example, Afifi (2003) identified a variety of tensions in stepfamily contexts, such as managing privacy boundaries, inappropriate disclosures, using family members as messengers or mediators, entrapping children in loyalty-disloyalty binds, and dilemmas of whether or not to reveal or conceal certain disclosures or information. In these contexts, it may not be entirely clear what the "rule" is, but people feel caught between what often seem to be contradictory rules.

THE RELATIONSHIP BETWEEN
EFFECTIVENESS AND APPROPRIATENESS

To put it bluntly, effectiveness represents getting your way, and appropriateness reflects getting along with others. It may seem like these are incompatible criteria, but often they are actually complementary. Getting what you want is often facilitated by getting along with others (Spitzberg & Cupach, 2002). Goals can be efficiently achieved because they are pursued within the limits of behavior defined by rules.

Of course, one can be personally effective while being inappropriate (e.g., cheating to win at poker; getting a partner's compliance by using threats and coercion). Aggressively getting goals met at the expense of others is personally effective, but interpersonally incompetent. By the same token, following rules and meeting the expectations of others shows that one is willing to collaborate, but is not sufficient to have one's own goals met.

IMPLICATIONS OF JUDGING COMPETENCE

Competence is not an absolute; it is not merely present or absent. Each person is relatively more or less competent in a given interaction. If a person achieves some of her goals, but not all of them, we would say that she was somewhat effective. If a communicator violates a minor rule, then behavior might be judged as momentarily improper. If an important rule is frequently and flagrantly ignored, then that person may be judged as severely inappropriate. Performing prohibited behaviors is likely to draw heavier sanctions than failing to perform preferred behaviors (Shimanoff, 1980). It is important to emphasize, therefore, that *competence is an evaluative judgment or impression of communication behavior* (Spitzberg, 2000; Spitzberg & Cupach, 1984, 2002). Competence is not defined by a particular type of motivation, knowledge, or skill. Instead, competence is an impression of a person's interaction appropriateness and effectiveness. This impression, in turn, is unlikely to be arbitrary—most of the time, it will be predictable by that interactant's motivation, knowledge, skills, and certain aspects of the context in which the interaction is being evaluated.

Factors That Facilitate Competence

Although there are occasional exceptions, most of the time we want to manage conflict competently. Nothing guarantees competence. There is no ideal personality type that is always competent. Nor can we specify certain behaviors that will always result in simultaneously meeting personal goals while accommodating the expectations of others. Conflict situations in particular are highly challenging to competent performance. Remember the nature of conflict—an expressed struggle in which another party is perceived as interfering with your ability to accomplish your goals. In such a context, you are likely to perceive the other party's interference as inappropriate, and the other party is perceived as preventing your own effectiveness. In this sense, conflict encounters are by definition challenging to competent communication (Spitzberg et al., 1994). There are three ingredients, however, that maximize your chances of being competent in any episode of conflict. They are motivation, knowledge, and skill (Spitzberg, 2000; Spitzberg & Cupach, 1984). Developing all three of these components will help you be consistently competent in your management of conflict.

Consider for a moment what it takes to be a competent stage or movie actor. From the perspective of competence developed here, it is ultimately the decision of the audience that determines the competence of the actor and his or her acting performance. This is not merely a matter of popularity—some actors are wildly popular or significant at the box office, but few of their audience members would evaluate them as particularly competent in their acting abilities. It is reasonable, however, to assume that certain characteristics of these actors increase the likelihood that they will be viewed as competent by their audiences. Specifically, the more motivated, knowledgeable, and skilled an actor is, the more likely it is that this actor will be perceived by audiences as competent. Likewise, actors lacking motivation, knowledge, or skills are at a distinct disadvantage at achieving any long-lasting sense of competence with their audiences.

MOTIVATION

As suggested by the previous discussion of goals, people enter conflict contexts with certain goals, and may emerge with different goals. These goals provide one important indicator of your motivation in any given context. Going into conflict situations with no notion of what your goals are, or being afraid of pursuing your goals, clearly places you at a disadvantage. Conflicts often present both approach (i.e., what you want to achieve) and avoidance (i.e., what you want to avoid) goals. Furthermore, it may be the conflict itself you wish to avoid. In order to manage a conflict competently, however, at some level it is important to be motivated by the need to be both appropriate and effective.

Despite the importance of competence, we sometimes *choose* to be incompetent. Have you ever felt strongly that your personal goals were very important? More important than being appropriate? You may have chosen to impose your point of view, knowing you abandoned tact and politeness. You may have felt pushed into being aggressive when the circumstances were strictly competitive. In this case, you were motivated to win the conflict; you were not motivated to be competent. Or at least, the other person interfered with your opportunity to be competent. There are also occasions where we choose the path of least resistance. For various reasons, we allow others to have their way at our expense. We choose, sometimes, to be personally ineffective—"to lose the battle in order to win the war." We simply decide that some goals under some circumstances are not worth pursuing (e.g., when a partner is in an especially bad mood and snaps at you without provocation). Again, sometimes we make the choice to be incompetent.

Motivation can be stifled, even when we want to succeed. Fear of failure is probably one of the strongest psychological barriers to realizing motivation. If we believe we cannot be successful in a certain situation, we are said to lack *self-efficacy*. Diminished self-efficacy in conflict stems from two types of beliefs: (1) thinking that we are incapable of performing behaviors that will produce the outcomes we desire and (2) thinking that if we perform the behaviors that are relevant, the behaviors won't produce the desired consequences anyway. The example in box 2-1 illustrates the frustration and communication incom-

---

Box 2-1   Low Self-Efficacy Undermines Motivation

Jennifer desperately wanted to confront her roommate Karen. Karen was always borrowing Jennifer's clothes without asking. This annoyed Jennifer, but she was reluctant to confront Karen. Jennifer grew up in a household where people avoided conflict and she simply was not accustomed to assertively standing up for her rights. She was afraid she would look foolish trying to confront Karen because she wasn't sure *how* to confront her. Jennifer didn't think she could persuasively formulate what she should say. Moreover, Karen was very outgoing, articulate, and somewhat controlling. She was also very good at making excuses. Jennifer felt that even if she confronted Karen, it would be wasted effort since her confrontation would surely be too timid and Karen would probably continue to wear Jennifer's clothes without seeking permission anyway. In the end, Jennifer said nothing, and when she complained to her friends about the problem, her friends would reply that they never would let Jennifer get away with it. Of course, her parents advised Jennifer to turn the other cheek and hope that next year she could afford her own apartment. In short, Jennifer had an important goal (of getting Karen to stop wearing her clothes without asking), but her lack of self-efficacy in the situation prevented her from having sufficient motivation to pursue the goal.

---

petence that can occur when a lack of self-efficacy undermines our motivation (Caprara, Regalia, Scabini, Barbaranelli, & Bandura, 2004).

KNOWLEDGE

Some actors would love to win an Academy Award, but wanting is not good enough—actors also need to be knowledgeable about their craft. Similarly, interactants seeking to perform competently in conflict encounters will be benefited by having knowledge of the situation and conflict processes. There are many types of useful information in a conflict encounter. Obviously, knowledge of one's own goals is important, as is awareness of the relevant social and relational rules in the context. We must also know what behaviors are most likely to result in goal achievement, and what the unintended consequences are for various behaviors. In addition, knowledge of conflict situations in general, and awareness of our social environment in particular, allow us to discern when we are "in" a conflict situation. Being socially "intelligent" means having a sense of what motivates people, understanding what various verbal and nonverbal behaviors "mean," and being able to predict fairly well what behaviors produce what consequences with what probabilities, under what circumstances (Hazleton & Cupach, 1986).

Knowledge is learned, and experience is the best teacher. Observing and participating in productive and destructive conflicts is where we learn. Paying attention to all of the consequences of our actions during conflict interactions helps us internalize typical conflict situations and perform appropriate and effective responses. Reading in this book about the antecedents, processes, and effects associated with conflicts should also equip you with some knowledge to help you manage your own conflicts.

SKILLS

Even actors who are motivated and knowledgeable in their craft sometimes simply lack the range and depth of acting skills necessary to achieve greatness in their profession. You can probably think of actors who are motivated to achieve greatness, and who study and practice their craft extensively, but simply lack the raw talent to perform as well as other actors. Similarly, if you like to play poker, and you meet with your friends regularly to do so, chances are you are motivated to win and know how to play the game. Nevertheless, you may not be as skilled in actually playing the game as some of your friends. For example, you know that it is both appropriate and effective to bluff your opponents during betting. Even though you know what behaviors to perform in order to bluff, you can't seem to pull it off effectively. Your friends always see right through your attempts to bluff, so you rarely win at poker. Clearly, some people are better than others in translating knowledge and motivation into skilled action.

Skills are reflected in the performance of communication behaviors. They are the *enactment* of knowledge and motivation. Without skill, we cannot be consistently competent. Skills are the moves you make during conflict, and in many ways, they are the only thing your fellow interactants have to know you by. They cannot know what your motivations are, or how knowledgeable you are, but they see you behave, and will base their judgments of you in large part on your behaviors.

Perhaps the most important interpersonal skill is *adaptability* (Spitzberg & Chagnon, 2009; Spitzberg & Cupach, 1989). This skill is general, yet complex. It involves tailoring communication behavior to the people and the situation at hand. Every conflict situation presents a unique bundle of constraints and opportunities. Adaptable communicators avoid overly stylized and rigid communication patterns. They do not manage conflict in the same way all of the time. Instead, they demonstrate behavioral flexibility. This requires having a diverse pool of communication strategies and tactics to draw from (see chapter 3), and being able to perform the right behaviors at the right time in the right context.

Most of the skills that are relevant to competent interpersonal communication in general apply to conflict situations as well. Skills are developed through practice. The more we use a skill, especially in contexts in which we can receive expert constructive feedback, the more we tend to improve it. A partial list of common behavioral skills is presented in box 2-2. Our goal is not to depict all of the possible interpersonal communication skills here. Instead, we simply want to refer to commonly cited behaviors that are positively associated with interpersonal competence.

Box 2-2   A Partial List of Interpersonal Communication Skills

Interaction Management
- coordinating the smooth flow of interaction
- introducing and closing appropriate topics
- turn-taking with minimal disruptive interruptions

Composure
- displaying relaxation, assertiveness, and confidence during interaction
- appearing in control of one's actions
- actions appear to have purpose

Other Orientation
- demonstrating attention to, interest in, and concern for the other person(s) in an encounter
- expressing empathy and supportiveness to co-communicators

Expressiveness
- showing dynamism, variability, and animation during conversation
- using appropriate gestures, vocalics, humor, etc.

Discussion Questions
1. Can you explain how proficiency in each of these skills might increase your chances of being competent during interpersonal conflict?
2. Not all of these skills are equally important. Which do you think are *most* important? Why? Which of these are you best at? Which of these do you need to improve on the most?

An Explanatory Model of Interpersonal Conflict

Figure 2-2 (on the following page) offers a model of the key components involved in interpersonal conflict. This model forecasts the features we will examine more closely in subsequent chapters. If you come to understand these components and how they interrelate, you will acquire the type of knowledge that can help you competently manage your own episodes of interpersonal conflict.

DISTAL CONTEXT

The model begins with what is called the *distal context* for conflict. Distal refers to the fact that these factors are somewhat removed from any specific conflict interaction. Such factors are "background" characteristics that exist prior to the initiation of any conflict episode. Distal context is "carried into" interaction by communicators. Conflict parties are generally influenced in subtle and indirect ways, yet very important ways, by distal context.

One important distal context factor is culture. As Professor Ting-Toomey demonstrates in chapter 7, when conflict parties are from different cultures, certain challenges emerge. Different cultures may emphasize the importance

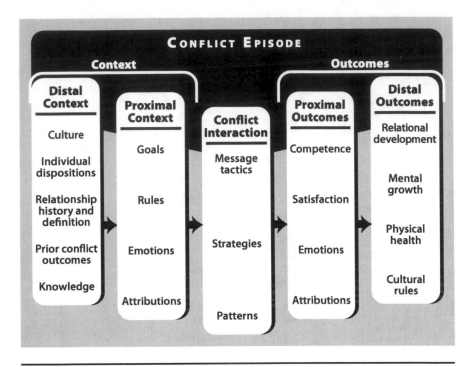

Figure 2-2   A model of interpersonal conflict.

of different rules, or place value on different goals. More importantly, perhaps, there are cultural differences in how people tend to manage conflict,
and in what they see as competence.

Individual dispositions also affect the course of conflict. In various loca-
tions throughout the book we will discuss how personality traits and sex differences influence conflict management practices. For example, individuals
with an argumentative personality trait may show more competitiveness during conflict. Individuals who are shy may tend to avoid conflict more often.
Do you think that men and women tend to manage conflicts differently? Do
we judge the same conflict behaviors exhibited by men and women to be
equally competent? Or do we expect that what is competent for men differs
from what is competent for women? Later, we will review the evidence on
this issue.

The relationship environment in which conflict occurs is also part of the
distal context. If you are happy in a current relationship, for example, you are
less inclined to blame your partner for conflict and you are more willing to
give your partner the benefit of the doubt (Bradbury & Fincham, 1990). If
you are satisfied and committed to a relationship, you generally want to keep
the relationship and this is reflected in the way you manage conflict. In other
words, your generally positive sentiments about the relationship have a halo

effect on conflict in the relationship. On the other hand, if your relational climate is negative, you will be more likely to entertain negative perceptions about your partner during conflict, and you will be more inclined to show negative behaviors.

Prior successes and failures in managing conflict, as well as knowledge, also predispose conflict behavior. For example, if Jane knows that Scott, who is otherwise a reasonable person, gets irrational and abusive when he is drunk, then Jane will avoid confronting Scott when he is drunk. If Bill knows that Larry is particularly sensitive about a certain topic of conflict, then Bill will take this into account when bringing up the topic with Larry.

PROXIMAL CONTEXT

Proximal context pertains to the perceptual environment that is immediately attached to a specific conflict episode. We have already indicated that goals and rules are important to assessing the competence of conflict behavior. In any given conflict episode, each person formulates and prioritizes goals. Perceptions of the rules that are relevant in a specific episode will constrain how the goals are pursued.

In addition, *emotions* and *attributions* set the tone of a conflict episode and can alter the path of conflict interaction. Emotions pertain to experienced arousal and the labeling of that arousal. We will consider emotions that are frequently associated with conflict, such as anger, contempt, guilt, and so on. If you *feel* angry during a conflict, for example, you are more likely to be defensive and conflict is more likely to escalate.

Attributions refer to people's explanations of behavior in terms of causality and responsibility. For example, behavior may be attributed to contextual circumstances ("She must be under a lot of stress") or to personality ("He's a jerk"). As we will consider later, these interpretations have considerable influence on the course of conflict interaction (Sillars, 1980a). Similarly, whether you blame the other person or take some or all of the blame yourself will affect your basic approach to managing a conflict.

CONFLICT INTERACTION

Conflict interaction constitutes the focal *process* of a conflict episode. Conflicts are recognized, expressed, and managed through communication. In the following chapters, we will describe various types and patterns of communicative behavior, both verbal and nonverbal. Communication behavior during a conflict is influenced indirectly by the distal context, and more directly by the proximal context. It is worth noting here, that proximal context not only precedes conflict communication, but also evolves with it. You will recall, for example, that goals can be emergent during a conflict. Similarly, emotions and attributions can be formulated during a conflict episode and can dynamically change. Thus, communication during a conflict episode both affects and is influenced by the occurring and ongoing emotions and attributions.

PROXIMAL OUTCOMES

Each episode of conflict has immediate consequences—some of which are intended, and some of which are inadvertent. These are called *proximal outcomes* in the explanatory model. Proximal outcomes evolve during a conflict episode and immediately after an episode of conflict interaction has ended. For example, productivity can be assessed following conflict. This includes a determination of what goals were accomplished and what progress was made in addressing the conflict issues.

As we indicated already, judgments of communication competence are made during and after conflict, and they are very important in influencing relational outcomes. These cognitive judgments are accompanied by feelings associated with the conflict interaction. When we perceive that conflict is handled competently, we tend to feel satisfied with the communication. If we achieve our goals, and if our partner has behaved appropriately, we experience communication satisfaction to some degree. Communication satisfaction can be considered the affective side of competence judgments. Satisfaction and perceptions of competence go hand in hand. Each tends to foster the other.

DISTAL OUTCOMES

Whereas proximal outcomes are immediate to the conflict episode, distal outcomes are somewhat removed and delayed. Various latent effects from conflict can emerge over time, such as personal growth and the development of cultural rules. An important distal outcome of conflict we mentioned earlier is the long-term growth and development (or deterioration) of the interpersonal relationship. Conflict interactions gradually influence such relationship characteristics as trust, intimacy, and relational satisfaction. The more important and the more intense the conflict episode, the greater the effects on the relationship. As we illustrated previously, these relational effects are determined, in part, by the interpretations placed on conflict behavior. In other words, the proximal outcomes mediate how communication behaviors affect eventual relational consequences.

Both proximal and distal outcomes from a current conflict become part of the distal context for the next conflict between the same parties. If, for instance, Ed trusts Jack less because of the way Jack has handled conflict in the past, then Ed's attributions are likely to be more suspicious and his communication more cautious the next time Ed and Jack engage in conflict. Thus, the model in figure 2-2 recognizes the fact that the current course of a conflict (and therefore its eventual consequences) is influenced by the outcomes of past conflict.

The case presented in box 2-3 brings forth many of the concepts discussed in this chapter. In reading the case, it is possible to draw out a number of concepts that are only in the background of the situation. For example, although we tend to take it for granted that everyone in the U.S. culture has a cell phone, there are still cultural differences in the availability of cell phone use, adoption, and coverage. It is important to consider what is *not* obvious as well as what *is* obvious in any analysis of a conflict situation.

Box 2-3 Phone Calls at 1:00 AM

Judy had just earned her MA degree when she met Derrick. They both were admissions counselors for colleges—she at a university in the Rockies and he at an eastern college—and they happened to meet at a conference in Miami, Florida. Although the rest of the country was cold that December weekend, Judy and Derrick drank fruit cocktails and swam in the warm ocean.

Judy believed she had met the perfect man. He was handsome, intelligent, witty, and (most of all) appeared sincere. Derrick was immediately drawn to Judy for many of the same reasons. They planned for a reunion in six weeks.

After they returned to their respective universities, Judy and Derrick talked on the phone for hours, and they e-mailed each other at least three times a day. Their desire to see each other was intense, but they couldn't afford a jet-set commuter relationship. They had to settle for visits every month or two, and phone calls, instant messages, or Facebook exchanges every day.

One problem they had to "negotiate" was *when* they would talk to each other. Derrick did not want to talk after 11:00 PM eastern time—or 9:00 PM mountain time—which was when Judy missed Derrick the most, especially on weekends. After 11:00 PM, Derrick would go to sleep. The few times that Judy did call after 11:00 PM, Derrick showed his displeasure.

At first, Judy did not feel justified in calling late at night. But after a few visits, and after they agreed they would date only each other, Judy wanted to be able to reach Derrick when she needed to. After all, she thought, what good are relationships if you can't even have a "phone date" on Saturday night. So she began calling after 11:00 PM EST. After a few nights, Derrick would not even answer the phone when he saw it was her number ringing on his phone; he simply let his voice mail record any message she left. This upset Judy and made her worry even more. She pleaded with him to be more accessible or to answer when she called.

So Derrick agreed that he would try to answer her when she called, and she agreed she would not call unless she really needed to. But Judy did not last long. She began calling routinely after 11:00 PM again, which angered Derrick. He saw the entire situation as the result of an insecure woman who had no business being in a long-distance relationship.

One night, after a lengthy conversation with Judy only an hour before, Judy called and Derrick answered her call, shouting in irritation, "What the hell do you *want* from me?"

Judy answered meekly, "I just want to connect with you before I go to sleep."

Derrick couldn't believe it: "Look, this is it—I can't take this anymore. You don't listen to reason and I can't meet your childish needs. Don't bother calling me ever again!" And then he hung up.

Of course, this sent Judy over the edge. She dialed his number several more times that night, always getting his voice mail message. All she wanted to do was assure him that she would "be good" from now on and not call at all hours. She desperately wanted to talk with him, but he would not answer. So she left a long message pleading to understand her, to give her another chance.

(continued)

Discussion Questions

1. What were Judy's goals in this conflict? What were Derrick's goals? Think about both their higher-order goals and their lower-order goals in the situation and in the relationship. What is the conflict really about?

2. How did Derrick's emotions and attributions about Judy influence his behavior? How did Judy's emotions and attributions about Derrick influence her behavior?

3. Other than prior conflict outcomes, what elements of the distal context do you surmise had an effect in this conflict?

4. Was Derrick competent? Was Judy? Explain.

Summary

In this chapter we introduced you to some of the key concepts that are important for understanding interpersonal conflict. We suggested that judgments of communication competence are central to conflict processes. Communicators assess competence with respect to the dual criteria of effectiveness and appropriateness. They are grounded in individuals' goals and shared rules. The tension between being effective and being appropriate is particularly acute in interpersonal conflict, and indeed, sometimes it is the primary source of conflict.

We identified three personal characteristics that, when combined, enhance your chances of being seen as competent in any given episode of conflict. They are knowledge, motivation, and skill. Perhaps the most important skill of all is the ability to adapt behavior to contextual circumstances.

Finally, we presented an explanatory model of interpersonal conflict. This model contains five classes of variables involved in understanding conflict processes and outcomes. These are distal context, proximal context, conflict interaction, proximal outcomes, and distal outcomes. These variables, and their important interrelationships, will be explored in greater detail in the chapters that follow.

DISCUSSION QUESTIONS

1. In this chapter we presented the hypothetical example of Ron and Kathy, a salesman and his supervisor. Suppose Ron and Kathy have a work-related conflict, e.g., they disagree about the performance appraisal that Ron received from Kathy. If Ron and Kathy are also living together, how do you suppose their close personal relationship might affect the way they communicate during a work conflict? How might their personal relationship affect the competence judgments they make about each other? In what ways can the work-related con-

flict affect their personal relationship outside of work? Is it possible for people like Ron and Kathy to keep conflict at work and conflict at home completely separate?

2. The fact that we have multiple goals operating simultaneously during conflict complicates things. Do our own self-presentation goals ever run contrary to our instrumental goals? How so? Do our relational goals ever conflict with our instrumental or self-presentation goals? How do these conflicting goals affect the conflict we have with another person?

3. What rules about managing conflict do you strongly endorse? Why do you endorse these rules? Where did they come from?

4. When we manage conflict with others, usually we have the self-presentation goal of wanting to appear fair, firm, credible, intelligent, etc. Imagine conflict situations where it might be desirable to give the impression that you are: (a) weak, helpless, hurt; (b) hostile, intimidating, angry; (c) indifferent; (d) naive, unaware.

chapter 3

CONFLICT MESSAGES

CHAPTER OUTLINE

The Topical Content of Conflict Interactions
Conflict Tactics, Strategies, and Styles
   Conflict Tactics
   Dimensions of Conflict Communication
   Conflict Strategies
   Communicating Conflict Orientations Nonverbally
   Conflict Styles
Patterns of Conflict Interaction
   Reciprocity
   Complementarity
   Topical Continuity
Reacting to Negative Conflict Patterns
Summary
Discussion Questions

Communication is central to all interpersonal conflicts. Interaction with others both generates conflict and provides the means to manage conflicts. Interaction between people creates the opportunity for conflict between them. That is, partners infer that they are in conflict by observing each other's symbolic behavior. Likewise, our intention to express anxiety, frustration, desire, resentment, anger, and so forth with the other person is made known through communication. When we confront conflict issues, they become explicit in the exchange of messages. Conversely, we can attempt to avoid disagreement by maneuvering around sensitive issues by carefully controlling what we do and don't say and do.

The communication of conflict can be based on an infinite number of topics, and can take on many different forms. It can be a calm and rational discussion; a subtle, nagging, unspoken tension; or an explosive, rancorous, knock-down drag-out fight. In addition, as we discuss later, conflicts involve *patterns* of communication in which people might reciprocate or otherwise perpetuate a sequence of messages for a time.

In this chapter we consider the concrete manner in which people communicate during their interpersonal conflicts. The sections that follow describe the communicative behaviors of conflict interactions.

The Topical Content of Conflict Interactions

One way to think about the content of conflict interactions is to consider the issues that provide the focus of disagreement. When you experience conflict with others, what is it about? Are conflict messages to be taken at face value, or do they reflect a deeper emotional need?

We first addressed this aspect of conflict in chapter 1. Recall that different levels of conflict represent different issues of disagreement. The three levels we discussed were conflicts about specific behaviors, conflicts regarding relational rules, and conflicts relating to personality (Braiker & Kelley, 1979). In addition, we can have metaconflict—that is, conflict about how we manage conflict. When you accuse me of fighting unfairly because I pout and withdraw from constructively talking through our disagreements, you are identifying a disagreement about the manner in which we resolve disagreements. If I complain that we can't resolve our differences as long as you keep yelling and cursing at me, I'm complaining about your way of handling our conflict. Such messages about messages, or statements that refer to the communication content or approaches to the conflict, are forms of metacommunication that become a manner of engaging in further conflict.

Specific topics of conflict are limitless. Almost any behavior we engage in, for example, can be seen by another as annoying, deficient, or belligerent to some degree. But the most common conflicts relate to the type of relationship shared by communicators. The most frequent conflicts of marital partners, for example, concern disagreements about sex, money, communication (or lack thereof), household chores, raising children, in-laws, jealousy, annoying habits, how to spend leisure time, and so forth (Gottman, 1979; Mead, Vatcher, Wync, & Roberts, 1990). Ex-spouses who continue to interact disagree about such things as differing expectations about child custody, visitation rights and rules, child support, lingering resentment toward the partner for the failed marriage, and interference by one partner in the other partner's life (Hobart, 1991).

Of course, not all conflict occurs within marital (or otherwise "romantic") involvements (e.g., Joshi, 2008). For example, box 3-1 discusses the most commonly mentioned topics of conflict among platonic friends—friends who sustain a friendship without sexual activities. As another illustration, a study of adolescents and parents found the 10 most common conflict topics to be characteristic of such contexts: fighting with siblings, doing homework, getting up in the morning, cleaning up a bedroom, putting clothes away, what the teen eats, helping out around the house, talking back to a parent, time for going to bed, turning off lights, bothering siblings, and cleanliness. As intuitive as such results may be, it is important to recognize what the least common topics were: drugs, getting in trouble in school, smoking, sex, who the teen's friends should be, clothing choices, and going on dates. The less common topics may be disproportionately more intense or significant in the course of the relationship, but less frequent in their occurrence. Indeed, the most intense topics of conflict included talking back to parents, fighting with siblings, and lying (Riesch et al., 2000). Another study found almost 70% of familial nagging conflicts consisted of chores or getting a child to do something or to stop doing something (Boxer, 2002). Although household chores may not seem particularly relational in their implication, given that all messages involve both content and relationship implications, when a parent or roommate complains about a chore not being done, the content level topic may be the chore, but at the relational level it is the lack of attributed respect of one person's expectations of the other that is at issue. Such perceived disrespect is a distinctly relational concern.

Box 3-1   Friendly Fire: Conflict Issues among Friends

Researchers interested in identifying sources of conflict in friendship asked more than 500 college students to describe their most recent conflict with a close, platonic friend. The investigators analyzed the descriptions and identified the most common general sources of disagreement.

The most common issue dealt with *violating a friendship rule*. Examples included the failure of a friend to fulfill a friendship obligation and improper interference with the autonomy of a friend's behavior. Obligations reflected common rules of friendship, such as keeping promises, repaying debts, being fair and equitable, being considerate and respectful, being supportive, being loyal, and respecting privacy.

The second most common source of friendship conflict was about *sharing activities*. For example, one friend reported: "We were watching TV. I wanted to watch the Eagles game, and she didn't, so we started arguing but eventually I won, so I watched the game."

The third most common source of conflict for friends pertained to disagreement about *sharing space and possessions*. These conflicts largely involved borrowing personal items and negotiating cohabitation. One example was disagreement between roommates about whose turn it was to do the dishes.

Other typical topics of conflict included *disagreements about ideas* (for example, debating about politics), *rival relationships* (for example, two girlfriends spending less time together because one of them acquired a boyfriend), *annoying behaviors* (for example, one friend complaining that the other procrastinates too much), *disapproval of relationship choices* (for example, one person not liking a friend's friend), *relationship intimacy* (for example, one friend desiring more of a sexual/romantic relationship than a friendship), and *communication breakdowns* (for example, one misinterprets a friend's joking comment as serious).

The authors compared the frequency of conflict topics for same-sex friends versus cross-sex friends. Same-sex friends reported more conflicts regarding *disapproval of relationship choices* and *sharing space and possessions* compared to cross-sex friends, whereas cross-sex friends reported more conflicts about *relationship intimacy, friendship rule violations, communication problems*, and *annoying behaviors* compared to same-sex friends.

The authors also explored sex differences in reported conflicts *within* same-sex and cross-sex friendships. In same-sex friendship, females were more likely than males to report conflicts about *sharing space and possessions*, whereas males were more likely than females to report conflicts about *sharing activities*. No significant differences between males and females were observed within cross-sex friendships.

Source: Samter and Cupach (1998).

Research suggests that satisfaction in relationships is associated with the frequency with which relational partners experience conflict in particular content areas. Kurdek (1994) asked partners from more than 200 gay, lesbian, and heterosexual couples to indicate how frequently they argued about each of 20 issues. On the basis of an analysis that discerned the way in which different conflict issues clustered together, Kurdek derived six general areas of conflict. These areas included:

1. Power (for example, over-criticism, lack of equality)
2. Social issues (for example, politics, personal values)
3. Personal flaws (for example, drinking/smoking, driving style)
4. Distrust (for example, previous lovers, lying)
5. Intimacy (for example, sex, lack of affection)
6. Personal distance (for example, job or school commitments, frequent physical absence)

Kurdek found that partners' relational satisfaction (measured at the same time as the reports of frequent conflict) was negatively associated with the frequency of arguing in areas of power and intimacy specifically. When Kurdek followed up one year later by measuring satisfaction in these couples again, he found that the reported frequency of arguing about power issues was associated with a decrease in relational satisfaction over the one-year period. These findings make intuitive sense, given the strong relational implications that attend issues of power and intimacy.

Conflict issues are important because they trigger disagreements and structure conflict interactions. It stands to reason that you need to understand what a disagreement is about if you are to manage it competently. But the topical features of conflict tell only part of the story—revealing the surface of disagreement. For example, Sanford (2003) found that couple conflict behaviors did not differ significantly between easier and more difficult topics. More *difficult* topics, however, tended to produce more negative communication behavior and less relationship satisfaction, regardless of a specific topic. In addition, the couple's level of relational satisfaction mediated the relationship between topic difficulty and communication behavior. That is, the degree to which topic difficulty influenced the negativity of conflict behavior depended on the degree to which the couple was generally satisfied or dissatisfied with their relationship to begin with. Thus, the topic of a conflict is important primarily to the extent that it is a more difficult or less difficult issue in the context of the relationship. The difficulty of resolving conflict on a topic, in turn, is therefore likely to depend on other factors in the relationship, including an understanding of the *forms* and *structures* by which the conflicts are enacted. To understand the nature and course of disagreement more fully, you must dig beneath the surface and explore how conflicts are enacted through communication. We consider this important subject in the following section.

Conflict Tactics, Strategies, and Styles

CONFLICT TACTICS

Interpersonal conflicts are exhibited in interactions between people, which are made up of specific individual actions enacted by each conflict participant. The most commonly studied, fundamental unit of communicative behavior in conflict is an individual's specific action at a specific moment in the interaction. These specific moves or actions are referred to as communication *tactics*, of which there is great diversity. Conflict tactics, for example, might involve a careful formulation of an argument to support our point of view, a request for information from our partner, a hint about what we want, an attempt to divert the topic to avoid confrontation, a joke to relieve tension, and so on. At any time people can select from a wide variety of tactics.

The diversity of potential behaviors makes it difficult to catalogue efficiently all the tactics that can be observed during conflict. Still, several researchers have carefully organized tactics (for example, Gottman, 1994; Overall, Fletcher, Simpson, & Sibley, 2009; Scott, 2008; Simon, Kobielski, & Martin, 2008; Ting-Toomey, 1983; Weiss & Summers, 1983). One such scheme, developed by Alan Sillars (see Sillars & Wilmot, 1994), is presented in box 3-2.

Box 3-2   Sillars' Classification of Conflict Tactics

Denial and Equivocation
- *Direct denial:* Statements that deny a conflict is present.
- *Implicit denial:* Statements that imply denial by providing a rationale for a denial statement, although the denial is not explicit.
- *Evasive remarks:* Failure to acknowledge or deny the presence of a conflict following a statement or inquiry about the conflict by the partner.

Topic Management
- *Topic shifts:* Statements that terminate discussion of a conflict issue before all parties have expressed an opinion or before the discussion has reached a sense of completion.
- *Topic avoidance:* Statements that explicitly terminate discussion of a conflict issue before it has been fully discussed.

Noncommittal Remarks
- *Noncommittal statements:* Statements that neither affirm nor deny the presence of conflict and that are not evasive remarks or topic shifts.
- *Noncommittal questions:* Unfocused questions that rephrase questions given by the researcher and include conflict-irrelevant information.
- *Abstract remarks:* Abstract principles, generalizations, or hypothetical statements.
- *Procedural remarks:* Procedural statements that supplant discussion of conflict.

Irreverent Remarks
- *Friendly joking:* Joking or laughter that is not at the expense of the other person.

Analytic Remarks
- *Descriptive statements:* Nonevaluative statements about observable events related to conflict.
- *Disclosure statements:* Nonevaluative statements about events related to conflict that the partner cannot observe, such as thoughts, feelings, and intentions.
- *Qualifying statements:* Statements that explicitly qualify the nature and extent of the conflict.
- *Solicitation of disclosure:* Nonhostile questions about events related to conflict that cannot be observed.
- *Solicitation of criticism:* Nonhostile questions soliciting criticism of self.

Confrontational Remarks
- *Personal criticism:* Remarks that directly criticize the personal characteristics or behaviors of the partner.
- *Rejection:* Statements in response to the partner's previous statements that imply personal antagonism toward the partner, as well as disagreement.
- *Hostile imperatives:* Requests, demands, arguments, threats, or other prescriptive statements that implicitly blame the partner and seek change in the partner's behavior.
- *Hostile joking:* Joking, teasing, or sarcasm at the expense of the partner.
- *Hostile questions:* Directive or leading questions that fault the partner.
- *Presumptive remarks:* Statements that attribute thoughts, feelings, and so on to the partner that the partner does not acknowledge.
- *Denial of responsibility:* Statements that minimize or deny personal responsibility for the conflict.

Conciliatory Remarks
- *Supportive remarks:* Statements that refer to understanding, acceptance, support, and so on for the partner and shared interests.
- *Concessions:* Statements that express a willingness to change, show flexibility, make concessions, or consider mutually acceptable solutions to conflicts.
- *Acceptance of responsibility:* Statements that attribute responsibility for the conflict to self or to both parties.

Source: Adapted from Sillars (1986). Used by permission.

DIMENSIONS OF CONFLICT COMMUNICATION

Categories of conflict tactics, such as those proposed by Sillars (see box 3-2), attempt to group behaviors that are functionally similar. Each behavior by each person, represented by a thought unit or a speaking turn, represents a tactic that can be observed, classified, counted, and analyzed. Most conflict interactions contain dozens, even hundreds, of conflict tactics strung together. To make sense of the numerous behaviors exhibited during conflict, it is useful to examine features that distinguish the types of conflict tactics from one another.

Thinking about dimensions of human behavior requires a move to an abstract theoretical level, but it is a level that has direct connections to the behavior of everyday mundane reality. For example, in physics it is commonly understood that there are four dimensions of reality—forward-backward (depth), upward-downward (vertical), right-left (horizontal), and past-present-future (time). Any human action can be plotted or mapped along such dimensions. But these dimensions describe purely objective physical features. Social scientists think in more interpretive terms, characterizing the more subjective meanings of human behavior. So, for example, although a person's physical features may be relatively objective, we evaluate people along underlying dimensions of meaning, such as attractiveness (unattractive-attractive), status (low status-high status), and so forth. One of the most important ways of understanding conflict behavior is in terms of the major common underlying dimensions by which we interpret such behavior, and the ways in which such behaviors function to influence the outcomes of conflict behavior. There have been many different approaches to identifying the underlying dimensions of conflict (Heyman, 2001), a couple of which are elaborated here.

Van de Vliert and Euwema (1994) identify two dimensions that are useful for distinguishing among conflict tactics: disagreeableness and activeness. *Disagreeableness* pertains to how unpleasant and straining, rather than pleasant and relaxed, the conflict behavior is perceived to be. *Activeness* regards the extent to which conflict behavior is responsive and direct, rather than passive and indirect. Any particular tactic during a conflict can be judged as more or less disagreeable and more or less active.

Referring to the conflict tactics presented in box 3-2, confrontational remarks (for example, hostile questions and personal criticism) would be perceived by most people as more disagreeable than conciliatory remarks (for example, concessions and supportive statements). Analytical remarks would probably fall somewhere in between confrontational and conciliatory remarks in terms of disagreeableness. With regard to activeness, confrontational and analytic remarks are relatively more direct and confrontational than are topic management and noncommittal remarks (Sillars & Wilmot, 1994).

More recently, a configuration of conflict dimensions has been increasingly recognized for its ability to differentiate important outcomes of interpersonal conflicts. This approach identifies two primary dimensions along which conflict tactics vary: directness and valence. *Directness* refers to the extent to which conflict behavior addresses the core issues under contention in a conflict. Saying, "I think we should visit my parents for Thanksgiving this year, since we visited your parents the last two Thanksgivings" represents a relatively direct comment, in which the core issue of family trips is under contention. There are obvious implicit relational implications (e.g., fairness, respect for each partner's familial obligations), but even these are relatively obvious in the conflict. In contrast, saying, "It seems like a long time since we've seen my parents" is far less direct in specifying the precise nature of the conflict. *Valence*, from the same root word that "value" and "evaluation" are derived, refers to the emotional and relational tone of a tactic, varying along a positive to negative continuum. Saying, "Honey, why don't we visit your parents this Thanksgiving—I'll bet they would appreciate that" implies a fairly positive attitude both toward the partner and toward the partner's familial connections. In contrast, saying, "It's really unfair of you to expect me to see your parents this Thanksgiving considering how much they dislike me" implies a negative evaluation of both the partner and the partner's family.

If these two dimensions are crossed, they create a typology of conflict tactics (see figure 3-1). Research indicates that the most common conflict tactics can be empirically distinguished along these dimensions (Overall et al., 2009). Figure 3-1 shows how tactics (including some from Sillars' [1986] typology) could be mapped along these dimensions. Indeed, in a longitudinal study of couples, the value of this typology was revealed by a rather peculiar finding. Couples were videotaped engaging in a discussion of difficult issues in their relationship and their conflict behavior was coded according to these dimensions and a set of tactics common to several existing coding systems. Over the span of the subsequent year these couples were asked the extent to which the relationship was satisfying and if the partner had made positive changes in regard to these difficult issues. It turned out that all negatively valenced and all direct tactics tended to be associated with less success (i.e., partner change) in the short term. Indirect positive tactics were associated with greater success in the short term. After a year, however, the only tactics seen during the initial observations that predicted positive change in partners were direct tactics, *both* positive and negative, although the positive direct strategies produced

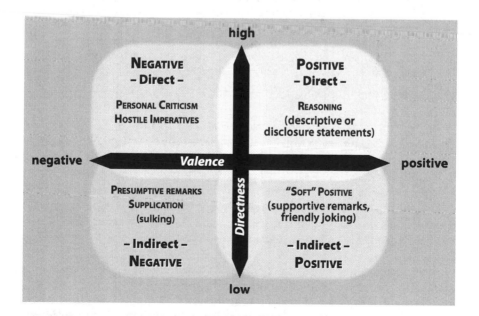

Figure 3-1   Dimensions underlying conflict tactics.

greater change than the negative direct strategies. It appears that although being direct with a partner about a conflict can be uncomfortable and ineffective in the short term, it can be effective in the longer term.

In chapter 6 we will discuss the idea that some conflict tactics are associated with constructive personal and relational outcomes, while other tactics are correlated with destructive outcomes. Remember, however, that the timing, frequency, sequencing, and patterning of tactics are much more powerful and meaningful than is the mere presence or absence of any single tactic.

CONFLICT STRATEGIES

Another useful way for studying conflict communication is to examine how an individual combines tactics into a coherent game plan during a conflict episode. Such a game plan, or group of conflict tactics, is called a *strategy*. A conflict strategy presents the general approach that tactics specifically institute; that is, tactics are the communicative messages that represent how people are oriented toward each other. For example, you may decide that you have had enough of your roommate piling her books and papers on the dining room table, so you confront her, but in a nice way. Your general strategy is to be agreeable and active. But when it comes to instituting the strategy, imagine that you engage in the following tactics (identified in italics):

> Do you have a second to talk *(request)?* I promise this will only take a second *(polite clarification of imposition)*. It seems to me that the dining room table has been full for the past week, mostly with lots of papers and books that happen to be yours *(descriptive statement)*. I realize you have been busy with two jobs and school and all *(supportive remark)*. And I know that there are habits of mine that are annoying *(acceptance of responsibility)*. I wonder if you could put your papers and books in the study, because I get frustrated when I can't eat in the dining room and I don't feel like I can move your things around *(disclosure statement)*.

This example includes six tactics that actualize the general strategy of cooperation.

Conflict strategies efficiently describe your orientation to a conflict based on and instituted by tactics you employ. Researchers have shown consistently that conflict tactics can be organized into three general strategies: *integration* (working *with* other people), *distribution* (working *against* other people), and *avoidance* (working *away from* other people). Although the labels used by different researchers vary, these three strategic approaches to conflict have been observed in numerous studies (for example, Canary & Cupach, 1988; Putnam & Wilson, 1982; Ross & DeWine, 1988; Sillars, Coletti, Parry, & Rogers, 1982).

The integrative conflict strategy reflects a cooperative confrontation: it is direct and positive or neutral in tone. That is, the integrative strategy provides a generally agreeable and active approach to conflict. It follows from a desire to solve problems and to seek mutually acceptable solutions. Key to this strategy are tactics such as these:

1. Seeking and disclosing information
2. Making supportive comments and listening in a supportive manner
3. Mutually defining the problem
4. Seeking areas of commonality and agreement
5. Negotiating fair solutions

The integrative approach to conflict seeks to identify shared goals and promote the interests of both parties. The assumption is that there are creative solutions in which each person can be satisfied with the outcome. Some authors argue that compromise, in which conflict parties "split the difference," is not integrative because both parties give up something to obtain what they desire (Filley, 1975). However, compromise can be considered integrative when goals are truly incompatible and collaboration fails to yield a mutually acceptable solution. Compromise also ensures equity when there is insufficient time to explore more creative alternatives.

The distributive conflict strategy is another active approach to conflict, but compared to the integrative strategy, it is at the opposite end of the agreeableness continuum. Distributive behavior is usually competitive, stemming from an attitude that one can gain or win only at the expense of another person. In belligerent forms of distribution, people don't care enough even to consider how a particular message might affect the other person. Regardless of its intensity, distributive conflict focuses on the individual rather than on the partner's or mutual needs. The distributive strategy includes tactics such as the following:

1. Threats, demands, and prescriptions
2. Coercion, hostility, and intimidation
3. Personal criticisms, put-downs, and ridicule
4. Defensiveness and hit-and-run tactics
5. Sarcasm and contempt

The avoidance conflict strategy is low in the activeness dimension, in contrast to integrative and distributive strategies. In fact, the objective in using avoidance might be to keep tensions buried. Still, avoidance can be either cooperative or competitive (Fitzpatrick, Fallis, & Vance, 1982). That is, avoidance can be relatively agreeable or disagreeable, depending on the context and the manner in which it is performed. Some tactics of avoidance include (Canary et al., 1995):

1. Withholding a complaint when confrontation is deemed to be too costly
2. Making irrelevant remarks to divert interaction from conflict to a non-threatening topic
3. Acquiescing to the requests or demands of another
4. Verbally denying that there is a conflict
5. Withdrawing from the interaction (for example, leaving the room)

6. Not voicing complaints for fear of retaliation (the "chilling effect") (Cloven & Roloff, 1993)

Any listing of strategies may imply a rather static compilation or repertoire. It is important to note, however, that there are many different lists and taxonomies of tactics and strategies (e.g., Heyman, 2001; Overall et al., 2009). No list is likely to be exhaustive, and any given interactant behavior may occasionally straddle multiple categories. Furthermore, it is important to emphasize that interactants are not limited to any one strategic approach. For example, studies find that about one-third to one-half of kids in middle childhood and young teens employ more than one strategy in conflicts they recall or imagine (Joshi, 2008; Scott, 2008). Identification of strategies is simply a convenient way of simplifying the vast and diverse territory of tactics into a more comprehensible map of behavior.

COMMUNICATING CONFLICT ORIENTATIONS NONVERBALLY

Competence at managing conflict requires the appropriate and effective use of not only verbal strategies and tactics, but also nonverbal communication. How we communicate nonverbally can radically affect our relationships with others (Gottman, 1979). As with verbal strategies, nonverbal behaviors used during conflict reveal people's orientations toward each other in terms of their positive versus negative affect as well as their level of involvement (Sillars et al., 1982).

Communicating Positive versus Negative Affect. Nonverbal behaviors convey a sense of our evaluation of the conflict and the partner. Interaction partners are often quite sensitive to nonverbal cues during conflict. As you might imagine, positive and negative affect can be expressed through several nonverbal messages. Here we highlight some of the more important ones.

First, as you might expect, people tend to respond negatively to a partner's negative evaluations of them. People rarely like to be treated with spite or malice. According to Gottman (1994), such messages convey disgust and contempt. People convey *disgust* by making a face to indicate their illness at the partner or the partner's behavior (as if to say, "You make me sick!"). The two most common nonverbal indicators of disgust are wrinkling the nose (as if you smell something) and raising the upper lip (that is, wrinkling the nose at the same time as showing one's teeth) (Gottman, 1994). *Contempt* is conveyed by rolling the eyes (as if to say, "What an idiot!") and by using the dimpler muscle (that is, moving one side of your mouth laterally, as if to say, "I doubt that").

Anger refers to the negative feelings we have from being frustrated by someone who has committed an objectionable action (Clore, Ortony, Dienes, & Fujita, 1993; see chapter 5). Through their nonverbal behaviors, people communicate anger both intentionally and unintentionally. People can show their anger intentionally by raising their voices, drawing closer to the partner in an intimidating manner, and clenching their fists. People can also show anger without intending to—with a flushed face, clenched teeth, and (more among women than men) tears (Cupach & Canary, 1995; Russell & Fehr, 1994). In addition, some people feel overwhelmed by their own anger and thus retreat from it and try to suppress it. Anger is a natural response to one's environment, and the appropriate expression of anger (for example, increased involvement) can lead to positive outcomes (see chapter 6). That is, if one can communicate one's frustration without showing malice, anger can work to the benefit of both parties (Gottman & Krokoff, 1989). For example, increased volume and rate of speaking indicate involvement and intensity, but these nonverbal behaviors do not have to be used in a threatening manner.

Sillars and colleagues (1982) examined the extent to which integrative, distributive, and avoidance conflict strategies corresponded with various nonverbal behaviors. Some of the more relevant findings include the following:

1. Speech productivity (the length of time spent talking, number of words used, and so on) was positively correlated with integrative behaviors but negatively associated with avoidance.

2. Adaptors (fixing one's hair, fidgeting, and so on) were positively linked to avoidance but negatively associated with integrative behaviors.

3. Eye glances (looking quickly at the partner and then elsewhere) were positively associated with avoidance but negatively linked to integrative behaviors. Conversely, eye gazes (focusing on the partner) were positively associated with integrative behaviors and negatively associated with avoidance and distributive behaviors.

4. Speech rate (the speed at which one speaks) was correlated much more positively to distributive behaviors than to integrative behaviors.

5. Response time was negatively correlated with integrative behaviors, indicating that people with a cooperative orientation do not hesitate to exchange messages with each other.

These findings suggest that people convey an integrative approach nonverbally by focusing on the partner, speaking for longer periods of time, and not engaging in adaptors. Avoidance was linked to a lack of productivity and eye gaze, but was indicated in adaptors. Distributive tactics were associated with a higher speech rate but less productivity, indicating that some negative responses involve one-line "zingers" that are used in a "hit-and-run" fashion (Sillars et al., 1982).

Communicating Involvement. Nonverbal messages indicate emotional involvement in conflict. Newton and Burgoon (1990) examined how people's nonverbal communication corresponds to their verbal messages during conflict interaction. These researchers examined how each of 17 nonverbal behaviors correlated with verbal strategies and reported three major findings:

1. More active, intense, and involving nonverbal behaviors were linked to the distributive tactics of invalidating the other person, accusing the other person, and asserting oneself. Such nonverbal behaviors

included using animated gestures, shaking one's head, speaking in a loud or sharp voice, speaking quickly, and being fluent.

2. Content validation verbal tactics (or focusing on the content more than on the person) were associated with less active nonverbal behaviors. That is, content validation was accompanied by the nonverbal behaviors of being calm and relaxed, speaking in a mellow and slow voice, and using a lower and deeper pitch (versus the higher pitch one uses when excited).

3. Supporting the partner was associated with active nonverbal messages that indicated a genuine concern for the partner's experience. Such nonverbal behaviors included facing the other person directly, being facially expressive and animated, and showing one's involvement both physically and vocally (through use of back channels, for example).

Examining nonverbal responses as a reflection of positivity versus negativity and of involvement can lead to some interesting analyses. Newton and Burgoon (1990), for example, found that showing cooperation and involvement was positively associated with assessments of being satisfied with the conflict and with the relationship. Some nonverbal behaviors exhibited during conflict reveal incompetence. For example, *whining* represents a negative but involved nonverbal response to conflict. As Gottman (1994) summarized, "Whining is heard as a high-pitched, fluid fluctuation of the voice, generally with one syllable stressed toward the end of the sentence. It reflects dissatisfaction in a very childish way. It often is characterized by a 'thin edge' to the voice and an irritating nasal quality" (p. 27). Similarly, the tactic of *stonewalling,* or refusing to discuss the issue, is clearly communicated nonverbally. Stonewalling is conveyed by negative and uninvolved nonverbal behaviors such as inattentiveness or blank staring, crossed arms, and flat intonation when one does respond ("If you say so").

Nonverbal messages operate in almost all communication contexts (Burgoon, Buller, & Woodall, 1989), and they reflect important dimensions other than affect and involvement. For example, Ostrov and Collins (2007) used unwanted and intrusive touch and resource control (e.g., taking a toy away from a peer) as indexes of social dominance. These researchers conducted a relatively unique study where teachers observed children in social interactions in second and third grade, assessing the children's internalizing (e.g., crying, tantrums) and externalizing (e.g., impulsivity, aggression, low popularity). Then these assessments were related to the same individuals as teens and young adults. They found that for men both internalizing and externalizing behavior as a child predicted unwanted intrusive touch in adult romantic relationships, and internalizing problems as a child predicted their resource control in their adult relationships. For women, internalizing and externalizing problems as a child predicted unwanted intrusive touch and externalizing problems as a child predicted resource control in their adult romantic relationships. It appears that templates are set in childhood that significantly affect our adult nonverbal behavior in conflicts.

Box 3-3   Negative Affect Says "Interpret This the Opposite Way!"

Statements said with negative affect can mean the opposite of what they literally say (Gottman, 1979). For example, agreement said with negative affect typically indicates disagreement; a compliment said with negative affect can reveal ridicule; and mind reading—that is, indicating what you believe is on your partner's mind—with negative affect is often personal criticism.

Consider the following dialogue between a mother (Debby) and her teenage daughter (Megan). First imagine that positive or neutral nonverbals are used with each italicized word. Then imagine that the italicized words are expressed with negative emotion.

Debby: Megan, I'm going to the store. Do you need anything?

Megan: Yes, I *need* some new ballet slippers.

Debby: But I didn't *plan* to go to the dance studio—I said I was going to the *store.*

Megan: I *know,* but I thought you could *drive* by the dance studio on your way back.

Debby: *Oh sure,* I can do that. *Do you need anything else?*

Megan: If you're *sure* it wouldn't be too much trouble—I could *use* some nylons.

Debby: Megan, you *always* seem to be needing nylons. *How many pair have you bought in the past week alone?*

Megan: A couple, I guess. Well, *can you get them for me or not?*

Debby: *If you promise* to do something for me.

Megan: *What is it?*

Debby: Clean the dishes. *You did such a good job last time that I would appreciate your doing them again tonight!*

Megan: Yeah, *OK,* no problem! *I have plenty of time before dance class tonight!*

In conflict interaction specifically, nonverbal behaviors combine with verbal communication strategies to reflect a person's orientation toward the conflict and the other party. As a rule, nonverbal messages that reflect involved and positive, or cooperative, orientations appear more competent than nonverbal messages that reveal an uninvolved and negative, or competitive, orientation.

CONFLICT STYLES

Have you ever known someone who consistently seems to try to avoid conflict? Or do you know someone who always seems to try to strike a compromise and bargain for a fair middle ground? A general tendency to perform certain behaviors repeatedly in different situations is referred to as a person's communicative *style* (Conrad, 1991; Sternberg & Dobson, 1987; Sternberg & Soriano, 1984).

Conflict styles reflect people's proclivity for using similar conflict tactics or strategies in different contexts, with different people, or across different times. For example, you may have a characteristic style for how you handle conflict with coworkers and you may show a similar and consistent style of handling conflict with your roommate. Our conflict styles represent our habitual inclinations for handling disagreements; we use them without much thought.

A more cognitive view of conflict styles is based on the idea that your method for handling conflict reflects two dimensions: (1) the extent to which you wish to satisfy your own goals and (2) the extent to which you are willing to satisfy the other person's goals (Blake & Mouton, 1964, 1970; Kilmann & Thomas, 1977; Rahim, 1983; Simon et al., 2008). Crossing these two dimensions results in five different conflict styles, as depicted in figure 3-2. Several researchers have relied on this approach to define conflict styles, although the labels for the styles differ from one author to another. The terms used here are drawn from Rahim (1983), who has constructed a self-report instrument to measure people's conflict style in the workplace. His measure has been successfully used in more informal contexts as well (Hammock, Richardson, Pilkington, & Utley, 1990; Utley, Richardson, & Pilkington, 1989). The five styles are as follows:

1. *Integrating* (which is similar to the integration strategy discussed earlier) shows a high concern for both your own goals and the other person's goals. This style includes problem-solving communication, a desire to collaborate, and attempts at open exchange of relevant information.

2. *Avoiding* reflects a low level of concern with both your own goals and the other person's goals. Conflict avoiders tend to withhold complaints, avert open discussion of conflictual issues, and withdraw from interactions involving conflict. Since avoidance is a passive approach to disagreements, it can be cooperative insofar as it permits the other person to get what they want. Avoidance can be competitive when it frustrates the other person's attempt to achieve their goals.

3. *Dominating* is similar to the distributive strategy we identified previously. This style shows a high level of concern for one's own goals and a low level of concern for the other's goals and reflects competitive and power-oriented thoughts.

4. *Obliging* reflects a low level of concern for your own goals and a high level of concern for the other's goals. This style involves minimizing conflict by accommodating the needs of the other person and giving in to their wishes.

5. *Compromising* shows moderate and roughly equal concern for your own goals and the other person's goals. This style involves attempts to negotiate, to give and take, and to seek a middle ground.

These styles are related to the conflict strategies we discussed previously. Integrating and compromising styles are similar to the integrative strategy, although pushing for premature compromise could be considered a distributive strategy. Avoiding and obliging styles are similar to the avoidance strategy, and the dominating style resembles the distributive strategy. The difference is simply that a conflict strategy represents a general approach within a particular episode of conflict, whereas a conflict style depicts a person's tendencies and preferences for handling all conflict.

Although we all have preferable ways of managing our disagreements, we

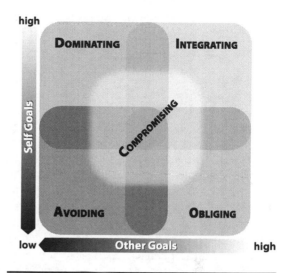

Figure 3-2 Styles of managing interpersonal conflict.

do not always behave accordingly. A supervisor, for example, may usually show an integrating style when managing conflict with subordinates. When faced with a specific instance of a noncompliant or belligerent subordinate, however, the supervisor may shift to a more coercive, distributive strategy (Conrad, 1991).

Patterns of Conflict Interaction

Patterns of conflict behavior between partners offer insight above and beyond summary descriptions of each individual's behavior. Although examining the tactics of each individual is informative, observing patterns is useful for understanding the relationship between conflict participants. Parties to conflict influence one another's behavior, and this influence can be seen in conflict patterns (Messman & Canary, 1998).

RECIPROCITY

One of the most common conflict patterns is *reciprocity*. In a reciprocal pattern, one person's behavior mirrors the behavior exhibited by the other person; that is, a particular tactic by one person begets a similar tactic by the other person. If someone teases you, you tease back. You give someone a compliment, and it is met with a compliment that matches yours. Your insulting remark draws an insult from the insulted person. One partner's complaint results in the other partner's countercomplaint, as in this example:

Wife: Why must you make so much noise while I'm trying to talk on the phone?!

Husband: Well, if you didn't call someone every time I am just about ready to put dinner on the table, maybe I would be more considerate!

Reciprocal patterns of behavior are quite common in everyday interaction. They are heightened during episodes of conflict (Alberts, 1988; Pike & Sillars, 1985; Ting-Toomey, 1983). Table 3-1 presents some of the common reciprocal patterns that have been detected by researchers.

As table 3-1 shows, reciprocated behaviors can be either positive or negative. For example, research suggests that in children's conflicts, positive conflict behaviors tend to be reciprocated (Joshi, 2008). Conflicts escalate in intensity as chains of reciprocated negative behaviors build (Alberts & Driscoll, 1992; Ting-Toomey, 1983) and negative feelings intensify. The participants feel more and more threatened and consequently respond with greater and greater defensiveness. The accumulating negative feelings are further inflamed by a tit-for-tat pattern in which each negative act stimulates a more negative response, which in turn increases the negativity of the response to the response, resulting in an ever-intensifying escalatory spiral. In short, reciprocation incites reciprocation.

Table 3-1   Common Reciprocation Sequences

Pattern	Example
Negative Reciprocation Patterns	
Complaint-countercomplaint	A: Do you mind not smacking your food so loudly? B: Do you mind not being such a grouch all the time?
Proposal-counterproposal	A: Let's go to my family's house for the holidays this year. B: Let's go to Florida and send everybody a card instead.
Disagreement-disagreement	A: I think Obama has done a great job, given the Republican opposition he's faced in Congress. B: No way! He's been an ineffective leader! A: Yeah way! He did more in his first year than Bush did in eight. B: No way! A: Yeah way! B: No.
Defensiveness-defensiveness (indifference)	A: I don't care what you think—this is my decision. B: I really don't care either.

Attack-counterattack (showing contempt)	A: You make me sick the way you kiss up to your sister like that. You look downright measly! B: Yeah, well that's some talk coming from the biggest kiss-ass of all time!
Metacommunication-metacommunication (said with negative feelings)	A: How can I talk when you won't listen? B: How can I listen when you won't talk?

Positive Reciprocation Patterns

Validation (argument exchanges)	A: I think that we should not save any more money until the credit cards are paid off. It makes little sense to save at 10% when we owe at 15%. B: I agree with your point in general. I just want to have some more money in the bank for emergency situations.
Validation (contracting)	A: Let's go to my family's house for the holidays this year. B: OK, I can do that, if you agree that we can go to Florida next year.
Convergence (joint arguments)	A: I think Obama has done a great job, given the Republican opposition he's faced in Congress. B: The Republicans certainly have a different agenda from Obama's. A: He accomplished more in his first year than Bush did in two terms. B: He certainly has worked hard.
Supportiveness-supportiveness	A: I want to have this baby, though I respect your wishes in the matter too. B: I appreciate that, and you should know that I respect what you want, whatever that is.
Cajoling	A: Ah, come on—admit it! You were flirting with her! B: I'll admit I was flirting if you admit you were flirting with her too! (Both laugh.)
Metacommunication-metacommunication (said with positive feelings)	A: I can't talk with you while you play that instrument. B: I know, it's hard to talk when someone seems distracted.

Source: Adapted from Alberts (1988); Alexander (1973); Canary, Weger, and Stafford (1991); Fitzpatrick (1988b); Gottman (1982); Ting-Toomey (1983).

COMPLEMENTARITY

Complementarity is the degree to which one person's communicative response relies on the partner's. Unlike reciprocity, however, complementarity reflects a pattern in which one response connects to a logically opposite type of response. For example, a confrontational remark followed by a conciliatory comment is a complementary pattern. One of the most common complementary patterns in conflict interactions is the *demand-withdraw* sequence (sometimes called the pursuit-retreat pattern). It goes something like this:

Wife: You haven't spoken two words since you got home. What's wrong?

Husband: Nothin'.

Wife: C'mon. I can read you like a book. I know when you're miffed about something. What is it?

Husband: I told you, nothing.

Wife: Are you mad that I invited the Parkers over for dinner without checking with you first? You told me the other day that we should try to do something with them this week.

Husband: No. I *told* you, nothing is *wrong!* (He starts to read the newspaper.)

As this above example illustrates, in the demand-withdrawal pattern, one person confronts a conflict issue while the other person avoids it. This pattern has been found in children's conflicts (Joshi, 2008) and studied extensively in romantic, marital, and family relationships (Caughlin & Scott, 2010).

Just as with negative reciprocal disagreements, extensive demand-withdraw patterns escalate the intensity of conflict and typically result in an unpleasant stalemate. Other common negative complementary patterns include *attack-defend* (one person's attack is met with self-defensive statements), *mind reading-disagreement* (one person's interpretation of the other's mood or motive is met with disagreement), and *control-obedience* (one person's unreasonable demands are met with immediate acquiescence).

TOPICAL CONTINUITY

Sillars and Wilmot (1994) contend that *topical continuity*—that is, the number of different issues raised during a conflict episode—constitutes an important feature of the structure of conflict interactions. Conflicts are sometimes simple in their topical structure; a single, specific issue of disagreement clearly dominates discussion. Often, however, conflicts expand to include multiple topics, and the issues of disagreement become complex and interrelated.

The discussion of substantive issues often reveals more general relational issues, which themselves become part of the conflict. If Taylor forgets to pick up her friend Lauren from work, as promised, the ensuing conflict discussion may overtly concern Taylor's "irresponsible" behavior. Beneath the surface, however, Lauren may be concerned about what Taylor's behavior means in terms of their friendship. Does it demonstrate a lack of respect for Lauren? Is it a sign that Taylor does not value the friendship? Does Taylor's behavior imply that the relationship is not fair and equitable?

As conflicts become more serious, they tend to involve more and more issues. For example, with greater levels of intensity and the corresponding defensiveness, people tend to introduce more complaints and reciprocations of them. Accordingly, people can become distracted by the introduction of a large number of issues, and they tend to drift from topic to topic, not resolving much of anything.

Intense and repeated conflict, however, often involves fundamental relational issues, even if they are not explicitly part of the conflict discussion. Hence, though some people might discuss many topics when the conflict escalates, other people might fixate on particular problems that are believed to be the "one" or "main" issue left unresolved (Sillars & Wilmot, 1994). For example, one might see all conflicts stemming from a transgression that occurred long ago, or from a lack of consideration, or from a lack of true affection. We discuss how conflict parties frame their particular conflict issues more in chapter 5, when we discuss proximal effects on conflict behavior. The point here is that conflict tactics vary, and both jumping from topic to topic *and* reverting back to one topic do not appear to be competent ways of managing conflict.

Reacting to Negative Conflict Patterns

Accommodation can nullify negative escalating conflict. Rusbult and her colleagues (1991) define accommodation as "an individual's willingness, when a partner has engaged in a potentially destructive behavior, to (a) inhibit tendencies to react destructively in turn and (b) instead engage in constructive actions" (p. 53). Recall that destructive actions are negative behaviors that undermine interpersonal relationships; constructive behaviors promote and maintain interpersonal relationships. Thus, accommodation helps break a chain of reciprocated negative behaviors. As we will discuss in chapter 6, the willingness and ability to avoid or at least to counteract negative reciprocity is important in producing positive personal and relational outcomes.

Related to the idea of accommodation is the concept of *message variety* (Sillars & Wilmot, 1994). Patterns of conflict behavior show relatively more or less diversity in the structure of communication behaviors. Lockstep, highly reciprocal, and highly predictable patterns of interaction tend to be constraining. As conflicts escalate in intensity, patterns tend to become more rigid, repetitive, and predictable.

Rigidity can perpetuate unproductive sequences of talk that fail to manage disagreement. On the other hand, flexibility in communication patterns affords the opportunity to counteract escalation and to compensate for accumulated negative actions and feelings. Research shows that satisfied married couples engage in negative acts, similar to their dissatisfied counterparts. However, satisfied couples (versus dissatisfied couples) stop negative cycles of interaction once they begin, allowing for constructive management of differences (Burman, Margolin, & John, 1993; Gottman, 1994). We will elaborate on this and other factors associated with different conflict tactics and patterns in chapter 4.

These are just a few of the patterns of conflict, but there are many more. You may find it interesting to identify and name patterns you observe or experience. For example, Boxer (2002) examined natural texts of familial conflict and formulated a behavioral definition of a form of conflict most people can identify in their relationships: *nagging*. According to Boxer, nagging "incorporates several sequential acts: the first move is a request. When the request is repeated it becomes a reminder. When a reminder is repeated it becomes nagging" (p. 51). Furthermore, this entire sequence can be repeated.

Summary

Interpersonal conflicts are recognized, experienced, expressed, and ultimately managed through communication. Thus, understanding conflict messages becomes essential for understanding the processes and outcomes of conflict.

Conflict messages pertain more or less to sources of disagreement between people. Perhaps the most common source of disagreement is incompatible behavior. Unfair demands, rebuffs, insults, criticisms, and offensive or annoying behaviors are inevitable in human interaction, and they frequently instigate conflict (Peterson, 1983; Witteman, 1992). Just as common are disagreements about how shared relationships are to be defined. These conflicts revolve around such issues as who has more power, what level of intimacy is appropriate for the relationship, and what the privileges and obligations of each partner in a relationship are.

Conflict interactions are made up of many conflict tactics, the most fundamental unit of behavior. A conflict tactic is one message behavior by one person at one moment in time. Conflict tactics can be characterized and differentiated from one another in a number of ways. For example, tactics can be identified according to (1) how relatively disagreeable the behavior is judged to be and (2) how relatively active or passive the behavior is. Alternatively, tactics can be judged to be (1) more direct or indirect and (2) more positive or negative in emotional and relational tone.

During an episode of conflict, tactics can be combined to represent one of three strategic orientations: integrative, distributive, or avoidant. General predispositions to behave in certain ways across episodes of conflict are represented by conflict styles.

Patterns of conflict interaction depict the mutual influence exerted by conflict participants. Reciprocity and complementarity patterns are the most common types observed. Extended chains of reciprocated negative behaviors and complementary patterns of demand-withdrawal typically are associated with conflict escalation. As we'll see in chapter 6, they are also associated in a negative manner with relational satisfaction.

DISCUSSION QUESTIONS

1. Describe an instance in which you intentionally used the strategy of conflict avoidance. What did you do to avoid conflict? Why did you use the avoidance strategy? Do you think you were successful? Why or why not? Do you think the other person knew you were avoiding conflict? In general, when is the strategy of conflict avoidance desirable? What are the drawbacks of this strategy? When do you think you should avoid using an avoidance strategy?

2. If someone uses the avoidance strategy on you, how can you effectively confront them? How do you know for sure that they are avoiding you? What decision rules do you use in your own relationships to determine whether or not to confront someone directly with an issue likely to elicit conflict? Do these rules change from relationship to relationship, and context to context, or do they reflect part of your conflict style?

3. You might have gathered that using an integrative strategy should always be preferred over a distributive strategy. Can you think of instances in which a distributive strategy would be preferred over an integrative one?

4. Do you have a predominant conflict style? What is it? Why do you suppose you have that particular style? What do you think is good about that style? What are its drawbacks?

5. What style of conflict exhibited by other people gives you the most difficulty (that is, is most frustrating or annoying for you)? Why?

6. Examine table 3-1. Can you think of other reciprocated patterns of negative or positive conflict behaviors?

7. Research indicates that women often confront men, and that men withdraw in the face of women who are confronting them. The exception to this rule occurs when the issue under discussion is the man's concern (that is, something the man wants the woman to change). How do you explain these findings? Do these run contrary to your understanding that men are supposed to be more assertive? If so, why?

chapter 4

BACKGROUND INFLUENCES ON INTERPERSONAL CONFLICT

CHAPTER OUTLINE

Distal Individual Factors Affecting Conflict Interaction
    Attachment Styles
    Argumentativeness
    Taking Conflict Personally
    Locus of Control
    Sex Differences in Managing Conflict
Distal Relational Factors Affecting Conflict Interaction
    Relational Development
    Relational Types: Different Blueprints for Close Relationships
    Characteristics of Developed Relationships
Summary
Discussion Questions

Students are often asked to discuss how they would behave in hypothetical interactions. Almost always, an astute student will note that how he or she might behave "depends on the situation." Of course, this student is right—we never behave the same way in all situations, and we adjust our responses to meet the behavioral requirements of situations. In the next two chapters, we specifically present situational factors that affect how people respond in various conflict interactions.

You will recall from chapter 2 that "distal" antecedents refer to factors that contextualize conflict. Such distal factors refer to the background setting of the interaction episode, and many such factors exist in conflict. In this chapter, we discuss issues dealing with individual and relational distal factors. (Later in the book, family, intercultural, and organizational issues are discussed by scholars who are expert on those particular contexts.) *Individual* factors regard salient predispositions that people have toward managing conflict, including differences due to sex and gender. *Relational* factors concern such issues as the character of the relationship (e.g., level of satisfaction and trust), relational development, and types of relationships and their accompanying expectations. Our selection of the particular factors we discuss is, as before, guided by the research literature on the topic.

Distal Individual Factors Affecting Conflict Interaction

Some people seem to look for interpersonal trouble, or they don't go far out of their way to avoid it. Other people avoid conflict at all costs. In this section, we explore five salient individual difference factors that affect conflict interaction: attachment styles, argumentativeness, taking conflict personally, locus of control, and sex/gender differences.

ATTACHMENT STYLES

Attachment theorists and researchers have focused on how very young children form attachments with their parents and/or caregivers, and how variations in attachments affect behavior. According to Bowlby (1969), Ainsworth, Blehar, Waters, and Wall (1978), and Hazan and Shaver (1987), three attachment styles develop in early infancy: *secure, anxious/ambivalent,* and *avoidant.* The secure child is confident in the caregiver's nurturance and love, and s/he feels little distress when the caregiver leaves him or her alone. The anxious/ambivalent child is unsure about the parent's loving support and becomes quite distressed when the caregiver does not show love. The avoidant child feels more self-reliant but still wants the caregiver's attention. Simpson, Rholes, and Phillips (1996) summarized these attachment "styles" accordingly:

> Children who have *secure* relationships use their caregivers as a base of comfort and security to regulate and ameliorate distress when they are upset. Children involved in *avoidant* relationships do not seek support from their caregivers. Instead, they control and dissipate negative affect on their own often in a highly self-reliant manner. Children with *anxious/ambivalent* relationships make inconsistent and conflicted attempts to glean emotional support from their caregivers, actions that reflect their underlying uncertainty about the caregiver's availability and supportiveness. (p. 899)

Importantly, our early attachment styles can affect how we relate to people later in life. According to Simpson, Collings, Tran, and Haydon (2007), early attachment styles affect how children later play with others and perform in school; and these styles continue to affect us through adolescence and adulthood. Simpson and colleagues provide compelling data to show that the development of adult attachment begins at infancy and sets the stage for how people form attachments through childhood, adolescence, and then adulthood. Likewise, Hayashi and Strickland (1998) found that the most important predictor of feeling secure in an adult romantic relationship concerns whether the person grew up with at least one parent who was accepting, loving, and fostered independence. Approximately 60% of college students self-report being "secure," 25% are "avoidant," and about 15% are "anxious/ambivalent." Still, some modifications in attachment styles occur between infancy and adulthood simply because our sources for attachment and experiences of close relationships change (Simpson et al., 2007).

Research on adults shows variation due to attachment styles. *Secures* tend to be at ease with closeness, trust, and depending on other people, and can acknowledge distress and seek support (Ognibene & Collins, 1998). Secures view themselves more favorably than do other attachment types, and they tend to see family members and friends as being reliable and trustworthy (Feeney & Noller, 1990). The *anxious/ambivalent* person wants closeness but also fears being abandoned (Collins & Read, 1990). Anxious individuals experience more emotional highs and lows in their relationships, engage in more jealousy, and become more obsessively preoccupied with their partners, when compared to other attachment types. They also tend to seek deep commitment in relationships (Feeney & Noller, 1990). The *avoidant* adult conceals feelings of insecurity. That person fears intimacy, hides his or her distress, and chooses not to depend on other people. Avoidant people often do not trust others, and they prefer self-reliance and emotional distance (Feeney & Noller, 1990). Because avoidant people place less emphasis on relational closeness, it is not surprising that avoidant men display less warmth and support to their partners, even when their partner is discussing a topic important to them (Simpson et al., 1996).

Critically, attachment styles coincide with how we cope with conflict. Conflict makes attachment styles salient because conflicts imply a disconnect that separates close relationship partners. In brief, secures are more likely to use integrating and compromising conflict strategies in their relationships compared to avoidant and anxious/ambivalent individuals (Pistole, 1989). Moreover, secure individuals do not become as emotionally distraught during conflict interactions and recover physiologically more readily than do nonsecure individuals (Powers, Pietromonaco, Gunlicks, & Sayer, 2006). The reason secures are not distressed during conflict is that they believe their partner fundamentally cares for them and that they can work through their distresses successfully. Interestingly, people who are not secure but have a secure partner also respond less negatively to conflict interactions than do people who have nonsecure partners. In a similar manner, Bippus and Rollin (2003) found that friends of secure people view them using more integrative behaviors than do nonsecures.

Anxious/ambivalent individuals are less secure about their attachments in close relationships. Although they have a positive assessment of their partner, they are less sure about their own desirability. And this combination plays out in both negative and avoidant conflict behaviors. For instance, Simpson et al. (1996) found that anxious/ambivalent types responded in less positive ways toward their partner, especially when discussing an important conflict issue. Ambivalent women, in particular, engaged in negative conflict behavior and displayed high stress and anxiety when compared to secure women. However, Pistole (1989) found that anxious/ambivalents were more accommodating to their partners. It is possible that anxious/ambivalent people who want affirmation and affection use signs of anger and other negative behavior to demand attention but also give in to their partner if they believe they are receiving enough attention and affection.

Avoidant individuals attempt to mask any feelings of insecurity. Because they want to appear self-reliant, avoidant people disengage themselves from conflict interaction. For example, Simpson et al. (1996) found that highly avoidant individuals minimize their involvement in conflict interactions, experience less anger and stress during conflict than do anxious/ambivalent people, and they engage in communication that was judged by raters to be of poor quality.

The literature reviewed here indicates that attachment styles can have profound effects on how people manage conflicts in their important relationships. However, this literature also reflects an individual difference presumption. More precisely, it would appear critical that the dyad contain at least one person whose attachment style is secure. The logic underlying this assertion is based on the research reviewed above showing that, in comparison to other attachment styles, secure individuals report more stable and satisfying involvements. Moreover, Creasey (2002) reported that one person's attachment style can "moderate the effects of his/her partner's attachment representations" (p. 366). Likewise, Canary, Erickson, Tafoya, and Bachman (2002) found that marriages that contained at least one secure individual were more satisfying, and they involved more constructive conflict behaviors when compared to marriages where neither partner was secure. In short, conflict behaviors enacted in personal relationships are a function of *both parties'* attachment styles.

Finally, we should mention that scholars have developed a two-dimensional model of attachment, which has been used in several studies as well (Bartholomew & Horowitz, 1991). Bartholomew and Horowitz's dimensions are (1) positive versus negative view of self and (2) positive versus negative view of others. These dimensions cross to create a four category system of attachment styles (e.g., see Guerrero & Burgoon, 1996). Our intent here is not to debate whether the three or four categories are more informative; rather, we want to indicate that one's attachment styles learned during infancy and molded during childhood and adulthood present an important distal factor that can affect your conflict behaviors.

ARGUMENTATIVENESS

Infante and Rancer (1982) defined argumentativeness as "a generally stable trait which predisposes the individual in communication situations to advocate positions on controversial issues and to attack verbally the positions which other people take on these issues" (p. 72). Two important features of this definition should be noted.

First, argumentativeness refers to a predisposition to behave, not actual behavior. Accordingly, some people are more inclined than others to engage in verbal debate on controversial issues. Second, argumentativeness does not refer to attacks on the person's character. In fact, according to Infante and Wigley (1986), attacks on a person's character and sense of self-worth describe *aggressive* communication.

Research by Infante and colleagues (e.g., Infante, Trebing, Shepard, & Seeds, 1984; Infante & Wigley, 1986) suggests that highly argumentative people are seen as very competent in managing conflict situations, simply because they focus on the ideas under dispute and not the flaws of the other person. In fact, this research provides evidence for a "skill deficiency model" of aggression (e.g., Infante, Chandler, & Rudd, 1989). More precisely, Infante and colleagues showed that people who do not have the skill to engage others in analysis of ideas are more likely to resort to personal harm than do those who possess a proclivity for arguing ideas.

For example, Infante et al. (1984) had students who varied in their argumentativeness rate the extent to which they would use four different aggressive messages on a roommate who was thought to be either accommodating or obstinate (i.e., would give in to a reasonable request or not). As predicted, highly argumentative people did not indicate that aggressive messages were acceptable in either condition, although moderate and low argumentatives did indicate increased preference in aggressive behaviors when the roommate was seen as obstinate. Apparently, the highly argumentative person's focus on ideas preempts a desire to resort to personal attacks.

On the other hand, highly aggressive individuals would readily use attacks on the person. For example, one study found that highly aggressive people are distinguished by the following: using verbal aggression to appear "tough," engaging in rational discussions that degenerate into fights, wanting to be mean to the partner (for whatever reason), and holding disdain for the partner (Infante, Riddle, Horvath, & Tumlin, 1992). Infante et al. (1992) found that highly aggressive people were more likely than low aggressive people to attack the competence of the partner, attack the partner's personal background, attack the partner's physical appearance, tease the partner, ridicule the partner, swear at the partner, and nonverbally degrade the partner.

Why might people engage in aggressive behaviors and not argument? Infante and Wigley (1986) offer four reasons that explain the use of aggression:

1. *Frustration*: you see your goal as being deliberately blocked by the other person;

2. *Social learning*: you model the behavior of those who raised you or those who you admire;

3. *Psychopathology*: you might attack someone who represents in some way an unresolved pain or fear; and

4. *Skill deficiency*: you lack the ability to communicate in an appropriate and effective manner.

Infante and colleagues have shown that the predisposition to argue about ideas is negatively associated with the use of aggressive behavior (e.g., competence attacks, ridicule) (for a review, see Infante & Rancer, 1996). Our goal throughout this book is to indicate the productive ways to manage conflict, such that conflict can be managed without attacking the other person maliciously.

TAKING CONFLICT PERSONALLY

Taking conflict personally (TCP) refers to the tendency of an individual to associate interpersonal conflicts with a negative emotional climate. Specifically, Hample and Dallinger (1995) describe the person who takes conflict personally as feeling "threatened, anxious, damaged, devalued, insulted" (p. 306). "Face becomes an issue which overwhelms the substantive grounds of conflict. Self-defense is the first priority, and this leads to impulses to fight or flight, for competition or withdrawal" (p. 306). Taking conflict personally leads to feeling pressured, to seeing conflict as competitive in nature and having a winner and loser, and to becoming defensive in attitude and behavior.

Hample and Dallinger developed an instrument to measure TCP. Their work shows six specific aspects of TCP: (1) directly personalizing conflict, feeling hurt by it; (2) feeling persecuted; (3) experiencing a high degree of stress; (4) not believing that conflict can produce positive relational outcomes; (5) believing that conflict can lead to unfavorable relational outcomes; and (6) disliking conflict interaction.

Research by Hample and Dallinger (1995) found that the dimensions of TCP are associated with approaching or avoiding conflict in expected ways. Those reporting high scores on direct personalization of conflict, stress, and perceiving negative relational effects, also reported that they tended to avoid arguments. Those who reported that conflict produces positive relational consequences and who liked conflict, tended to approach arguments with others. It may occur to you that the TCP measure and argumentativeness (discussed above) are similar concepts. Indeed, they may be two sides of the same coin. Argumentativeness represents your intention to behaviorally approach or avoid argumentative situations, whereas TCP reflects your emotional reaction to engaging in an argument.

LOCUS OF CONTROL

"Locus of control" refers to expectations for ourselves to achieve certain outcomes (Lefcourt, 1982). For example, whether or not you do well in a class can be seen as the result of your own ability (e.g., you have the intelligence it takes) and effort (e.g., your grade depends on how much you study), or the result of chance (e.g., correct guessing on exams) and whether or not the teacher rewards you (e.g., the teacher is fair, is a soft grader).

An *internal* locus of control refers to your believing that your outcomes—both successes and failures—result from your own ability and effort. Accordingly, you see the "A" on the test and think, "Yes, I earned that one!" We refer to such people as "internals." An *external* locus of control refers to the belief that your outcomes are due to chance, fate, or powerful others. Relying on an external orientation, you might see the "A" on the test and think, "Whew—I was flat-out lucky (or it was an easy test)." Such people are known as "externals." Of course, there are people who vary in their control orientations—for example, when they see their success due to internal factors ("I earned that A") and they see their failures arising from external factors ("That test wasn't fair"). Such people are called "defensive externals."

As scholars have noted, people vary in their locus of control orientations depending on the domain of behavior (e.g., Brenders, 1987; Lefcourt, 1982). That is, you might have an internal locus of control for making friends, for your own health, and for solving problems. But you could at the same time have an external locus of control concerning political decisions (e.g., who is elected president), economics (e.g., balancing the budget), and your own personal achievements (e.g., getting excellent grades).

Research has shown that locus of control specific to the domain of interpersonal relations affects how people manage conflict and solve their relational problems in general. For example, Miller and colleagues (1986) found that having an internal locus of control regarding marriage problems correlated positively with productive and positive discussion of problems. Those with an internal locus of control appear to try harder to succeed, using the problem-solving tools at their disposal. On the other hand, those with an external control orientation appear to give up easily and withdraw from the conversation or rely on forceful tactics to coerce the partner into complying (Goodstadt & Hjelle, 1973).

Directly relevant here, Canary, Cunningham, and Cody (1988) found that people have different locus of control orientations regarding conflict itself, as measured by the conflict locus of control (CLOC) scale. Consistent with previous research, we found that internal CLOCs relied more on integrative, cooperative messages, whereas external CLOCs reported using more distributive, competitive, and avoidant messages (see chapter 3). More recently, Caughlin and Vangelisti (2000) reported similar results using the CLOC scale. Table 4-1 presents some sample items from the CLOC scale.

Table 4-1   Example Conflict Locus of Control (CLOC) Items

Internality

Effort	I can work out almost any interpersonal problem if I try hard enough. (S)
	I have found that if I do not put forth much effort, I cannot resolve conflicts with others. (F)
Ability	I have good communication skills that help me resolve my interpersonal problems successfully. (S)
	If a conflict turns out badly, it's because the people having the disagreement lack the ability to work things out. (F)

Externality

Chance	If I am lucky, then my conflicts turn out to my benefit. (S)
	How poorly my interpersonal problems are resolved is often due to chance. (F)
Powerlessness	If conflicts are resolved to my benefit, it's because other people are willing to resolve them that way. (S)
	If my thoughts are not consistent with the other person's, then I fail to get what I want. (F)

Note: S = success item; F = failure item.
     Internality = effort + ability; Externality = chance + powerlessness.
Source: Adapted from Canary, Cunningham, and Cody (1988), p. 434.

In table 4-1, we show that CLOC refers to both internal and external orientations. Items representing both success and failure at obtaining favorable outcomes from conflict are presented as examples. As you examine table 4-1, ask yourself whether you agree more with the internality items or the externality items. Our hope is that you balance any external control orientations with an internal control orientation, so that you can make a positive difference in the way you manage conflict. People who believe that they can control the outcomes of their conflicts tend to work harder to produce productive outcomes.

SEX DIFFERENCES IN MANAGING CONFLICT

Much has been written about sex and gender differences in communication behavior (for a representative anthology, see Dindia & Canary, 2006). Sex and gender reflect the primary labels we use to understand people and their social interactions. As Cross and Markus (1993) pointed out, "People are socialized to consider gender a primary piece of information about a person, and gender knowledge significantly influences most subsequent interactions and thoughts about the person" (p. 56). In this book, we refer to *sex* as the biological differences between men and women (and boys and girls), and we refer to *gender* as the social-psychological-cultural meanings attached to one's sex (although we know that variations on these definitions exist). If one's sex and gender affect interaction, then in what ways might they affect conflict behavior? The answer to this question is more interesting than one might imagine at first glance.

First, consider that people develop schema for interacting with men and women. That is, people develop blueprints about appropriate and effective behaviors in different settings (Pavitt & Haight, 1985) Such blueprints depend on expectations tied to people's roles. For example, you have different blueprints for how a "teacher" should behave, how a "friend" should behave, how "a spouse" should behave. We also have blueprints for how "men" and "women" should behave. If we lack any other information about a person, then we must rely on the information at our disposal. Most often, we immediately notice the person's sex/gender, and we rely on the expectations we have for sex roles (Eagly, 1987).

Much of the time, people's sex role expectations are based in stereotypes of men and women. The stereotypical man is seen as task-oriented, activity-oriented, assertive, and emotionally strong; the stereotypical woman is kind, relationally sensitive, and emotionally expressive (Deaux & Lewis, 1984). Eagly (1987) labels these two sets of stereotypical expectations as reflecting the view that men by and large are "instrumental," whereas women are "communal." If people do in fact behave according to these stereotypes, then we would expect men to behave in very assertive and dominating ways during conflict and we would expect women to be passive and cooperative (Bradley, 1980).

In fact, in most studies that assess conflict styles (see chapter 3), we see a reflection of men as assertive and even aggressive and women as passive and cooperative (e.g., Berryman-Fink & Brunner, 1987; for a review, see Gayle,

Preiss, & Allen, 1994). Literally, on the face of it, it appears quite reasonable to act in ways that reinforce sex role stereotypes when there is no other information available (Geis, 1993). This helps to explain why we can be especially surprised when a woman acts in a hostile manner by rushing headlong into us, or when a large man apologizes with a tone of respect for bumping into us. As one might expect, when people negatively violate our expectations for behavior based on sex role stereotypes we might be offended at their lack of appropriateness (Bradley, 1980). But do such expectations occur when other information is available—as in close relationships?

We explored the idea that sex stereotypes are consistently found in the conflict and anger research literature regarding close relationships (Cupach & Canary, 1995). We were a bit surprised at what the research indicates.

1. First, most of the research on sex differences in close relationships finds more *similarities* than differences when it comes to self-reported *and* observed conflict behavior. For example, relying on self-reported conflict, Kelley and associates (1978) found that men and women engaged in more similar behaviors than dissimilar behaviors. Relying on observational methods, Margolin and Wampold (1981) found that husbands and wives acted in a similar manner in about 75% of the types of behavior analyzed.

2. Of the differences that are discussed, it appears that men and women act in ways *opposite* of what one would expect given stereotypes. More specifically, women (not men) are more assertive and at times aggressive. Men (not women) are more withdrawn and passive. Both sexes are equally likely to use cooperative behavior during conflict. For example, in the Margolin and Wampold (1981) study, husbands relied more on withdrawal (by not paying attention to the spouse) and avoidance (by offering excuses), but wives were more assertive in their use of complaints and criticisms of their husbands.

   Following their review of several studies on the topic, Schaap, Buunk, and Kerkstra (1988) concluded: "All in all we think that self-report and observational research supports the following statements. Women tend to be more emotional and show more negative affect, while men are inclined to be more rational and withdrawn" (p. 236). These authors also qualified these generalizations in terms of other background factors, such as relational satisfaction. Regardless, these data indicate that women, relative to men, appear to be more assertive in conflict situations that are familiar to them (Falbo & Peplau, 1980; Putnam & Wilson, 1982).

3. There is a tendency for women to pursue the conflict topic and for men to withdraw (see also Caughlin & Vangelisti, 2000). But that tendency depends on the amount of equity in the relationship. It appears that the person who wants the relationship to change will confront the partner, but the person who does not want the relationship to change

will withdraw, regardless of one's sex. As Heavey, Layne, and Christensen (1993) pointed out, "it is reasonable to assume that the person who wants the change will express more negative affect simply in the process of elaborating their dissatisfaction" (p. 26).

Box 4-1 Doing (Unexpected) Gender in Conflict

Tammy was a slight woman raised in the deep South. The reason we mention that is because of the lilting tone that would linger on her vowels a moment longer than those who are accustomed to hearing Yankee talk. She was everything a southern lady should be and more.

Tom was a medium-build sailor. He had joined the Merchant Marines when he was 21 and had sailed around the world five times. He was not shy. During one of his stops in Savannah, Tom met Tammy and they began to date.

At first, everything went smoothly. Tammy was sometimes offended by Tom's crude manner. But she convinced him that she was worth changing.

After several weeks, Tom begin to feel anxious whenever he and Tammy would disagree. He tried to change his manners, but they were never as polished as hers were.

Tammy: Tom, please stop fidgeting.

Tom: Sorry. Pass the pepper.

Tammy: Had you listened more carefully to your mother, you should have said, "*Please* pass the pepper." What am I to do with you? (She passes the pepper.)

Tom: Sorry.

Tammy: What would you like to do after supper?

Tom: I don't care—whatever you want to do.

Tammy: Tom, since when do I look like a concierge at the Sheraton?

Tom: What?

Tammy: You know—"concierge"—do I look like an English teacher too?

Tom: Sorry.

Tammy: Soooo?

Tom: What?

Tammy: Sooo, what are we doing after supper?

(Tom stops eating and looks down.)

Tammy: Listen, Tom, I want you to wear the proverbial pants, but you must take control.

(Tom continues to look down. After a full minute, he decides to speak.)

Tom: Do you want any dessert?

Do you find the above dialogue to be offensive? Why? How does the above dialogue compare with real life interactions you have experienced or witnessed between men and women?

4. Women and men tend to report similar reactions to issues. For example, both women and men bristle at questions about their integrity. No one likes their self-worth questioned, especially when it comes to such issues as one's competence in a work role or role as a partner, lover, relative, or friend (Campbell & Muncer, 1987). As Frost and Averill (1982) concluded in their summary of the literature, "As far as the everyday experience of anger is concerned, men and women are far more similar than dissimilar" (p. 297).

5. Women and men respond behaviorally to anger in similar ways, with one exception: Women tend to use tears more as a response to anger (Frost & Averill, 1982). Men sometimes (mistakenly) think tears are a sign of weakness and capitulation. However, men should realize that tears sometimes should be taken as a sign of anger.

6. Any sex differences that have been found are largely wiped out by more immediate influences on conflict behavior. Such influences include the issue under discussion (e.g., who seeks change), the partner's immediately preceding behavior (e.g., whether the partner was nasty or nice), and other proximal influences. We will look more specifically into proximal influences in the next chapter.

In order to summarize the extensive research on sex differences in conflict, we propose the following principle, which we term the *principle of ignorance*: *Lacking any information besides the person's biological sex, people tend to behave in conventional, stereotypical ways with regard to managing conflict.* However, once we get to know someone better—and it may not take long—we change our blueprints for interaction, which leads to the *principle of familiarity*: *In familiar situations, women and men behave opposite of what we might expect when assuming the principle of ignorance.*

Distal Relational Factors Affecting Conflict Interaction

Of course, interpersonal conflict requires *two* people, not just one. Accordingly, we should examine the development and nature of the relationship that emerges between two people (in addition to the individual differences we have been discussing so far). The remainder of this chapter focuses on relational factors that have a distal effect on conflict interaction.

RELATIONAL DEVELOPMENT

The first relational factor that has an important distal effect on conflict concerns where the relationship has been. Two alternative senses of "relational development" can be witnessed in the research. One sense concerns how the relationship has increased in intimacy (i.e., knowing the partner in a personal manner). A second sense regards how relationships change over the life span.

Box 4-2 Fatal Attractions

Have you ever been "turned off" by some feature of your partner that was initially attractive to you? Was her arrogance once seen as self-worth? Was his annoying, snarfuling laughter once seen as cute? If so, then you are not alone, according to a study published by Diane Felmlee (1995), a sociologist at University of California, Davis.

"Fatal attractions," according to Felmlee, refer to those social qualities that draw us to someone, but over time become rather repulsive. According to this research, about 30% of the respondents reported that some initial attractions turned fatal (i.e., disliked later). Dr. Felmlee suggests three reasons why these fatal attractions occur:

1. We are attracted to features in other people that we do not possess. But over time, the lack of similarity takes its toll. For example, you might find someone "interesting," because she reads so much literature. Later, however, you tire of spending all your time in the library.

2. We are attracted to features that really stand out, which may mean that the person has a particular feature in extreme. For example, you might like someone who "takes a stand" and is "honest all the time" about his feelings. But after a while you find this blunt honesty to be boring and dogmatic.

3. We are attracted to features that may not be conducive to a long-term association. For example, you might be attracted to someone because she is really "sociable" and "knows how to party." After a few months you find her to be flirtatious and untrustworthy.

What are some fatal attractions? Felmlee (pp. 302–303) found that college students reported the following as especially deadly:

1. *Fun.* Yes, that's right, being perceived as "fun" had some drawbacks. For example, one respondent noted how she was attracted to a man because she could have fun with him—over time, however, she saw his fun-loving nature as immaturity. Another example was a woman attracted to a man's humor, only now she finds him silly.

2. *Caring.* One person cited the partner's deep interest in her as an initial attraction, only to be turned off by his deep possessive nature later.

3. *Competent* (masculine stereotype). This means that a person is seen as effective and able to achieve instrumental goals. For example, one man was attracted to a woman's intelligence and confidence, later to be turned off by her "ego."

4. *Physical.* One man listed as many as 10 physical features that drew him to his partner, then objected that their relationship was based primarily on physical characteristics. Maybe beauty *is* only skin deep.

5. *Excitement.* It appears that being perceived as exciting causes some problems later as well. Some people's initial attraction to excitement transformed into perceptions of the partner being irresponsible or too different.

(continued)

6. *Easygoing.* Although this quality only comprised about 5% of fatal attractions, they are worth noting. Here, for example, you might have liked someone because he is not "anal" about time. Now, however, he is never on time for a date.

7. *Different.* Again, this quality only comprised about 5% of fatal attractions. But, according to Felmlee, being different over the long haul really bothered more people than not. So, going out with someone to "expand your horizons" may not work out.

Of course, you may have experienced other kinds of "fatal attractions." Why do fatal attractions occur, based on your experience or observation of others? Are fatal attractions avoidable or must we get to know someone before they become clear?

Trajectories for Intimacy. As Braiker and Kelley (1979) noted, increases in intimacy mean increases in conflict. The reason is that closer involvements entail more interdependence, and increased interdependence requires more coordination to do things, more knowledge of the other, and more opportunities for conflict to emerge. However, "intimacy" means many things (Perlman & Fehr, 1987), and research on critical events indicates that people have more than one type of intimate relationship. (As you may have guessed, most of the research on this involves romantic relationships.)

Huston, Surra, Fitzgerald, and Cate (1981) reported two studies that examined in retrospect how romantic relationships increase in intimacy, from the acquaintance stage to marriage. In both studies, these authors found three types of relationships. *Accelerated* couples become very committed to each other quite quickly, which is their defining feature. Within three months, on the average, these couples were more than 75% sure they wanted to marry. *Prolonged* couples, on the other hand, refrained from commitment. Prolonged couples were less sure about each other (i.e., 75% commitment to marriage takes about 18 months to two years). An important defining feature of the prolonged couple is that they engage in more conflict than other types of couples. It is possible that their lack of commitment leads to conflict or may result from the conflict. Finally, *intermediate* couples, as the name implies, reach a high commitment stage in a period between the accelerated and prolonged types. These couples are 75% sure of marriage between six to nine months. Interestingly, the intermediate types had the smoothest progression to commitment; that is, they had the lowest score on an index of turbulence (the ratio of decreases in commitment divided by the total number of significant commitment-changing events). Interestingly, intermediate and prolonged types reported a higher degree of love than did accelerated couples.

No doubt there are variations on each of these couple types, and you have probably experienced different relationships that varied in their intensity and intimacy. This research implies that there is not "one correct way" to develop a relationship and its corresponding conflict. Some relationships are smooth-running and partners reach consensus early, whereas others involve roller-coaster rides that entail more conflict. These alternative developmental patterns thus provide a background context for how conflict is managed.

Social Penetration.   Altman and Taylor (1973) posited social penetration theory to explain how people come to know each other over time. Altman and Taylor liken increases in intimacy to peeling away different sections and layers of an onion to arrive at the core. These authors presented four stages whereby people theoretically get to know each other more intimately. In brief, the stages are as follows:

1. An initial *orientation* stage: communication is largely based on social convention;

2. *Exploratory affect exchange*: increased intimacy on a number of topics begins;

3. *Affective exchange*: increased intimacy at greater levels, as well as number of topics, occurs; and

4. *Stable exchange*: communication is free and spontaneous, and penetration of the partner's personality core occurs.

According to Altman and Taylor, as a relationship progresses through these stages, communication between partners involves a greater number of topics, more unique symbols only the other person knows, greater efficiency in communication, more spontaneous occurrences of working together, more openness, and more evaluation.

In other words, people in close relationships gradually obtain much information about each other. They see each other on numerous occasions and in several types of situations. These observations provide information about the person that is used to assess the seriousness of the conflict, the intensity of the partner's responses, and a gauge of what is appropriate and effective communication. According to social penetration theory, then, as relationships develop partners have more information to "use" during conflict, experience more areas for evaluating each other, and possess a wider variety of conflict tactics that they can use with each other (see Fitzpatrick & Winke, 1979). Theiss and Solomon (2006) found that moderately intimate partners experience more arguments, become more direct about their conflict issues, and are less likely than less intimate partners to avoid conflicts. Also, perceived irritations from the partner positively correlated with being direct. Still, of all the factors Theiss and Solomon examined, intimacy appeared to predict being direct with one's partner. Such findings can extend to other relationships as well. Siblings and roommates, for example, who must share space often fight over who has rights to use the bathroom, who can watch the TV, or who should clean up a particular mess.

Relational Development Over the Life Span.   Just as people change over their lifetimes, so does their communication behavior (Nussbaum, 1989). It is no wonder, then, to discover that people's manner of managing conflict is affected by life span issues. Sillars and Wilmot (1989) provide a careful review of how life span changes affect conflict interaction. Some of the intriguing points they raise include the following.

Many younger couples interact in a way that reflects an "adaptation to the rapid pulse of family life in the early stages" (Sillars & Wilmot, 1989, p. 230). Young couples must learn how to live with each other, how to respond to declines in relational satisfaction, and how to negotiate parental roles (if they have children). Perhaps in synch with these many rapid changes, young couples engage in dynamic conflict behaviors that are confronting, analytical, and sometimes funny (Sillars & Wilmot, 1989).

As people slide through middle age, they turn to other issues. According to Sillars and Wilmot (1989), "Whereas young couples struggle to achieve a comfortable balance between individual autonomy and interdependence, midlife couples are more likely to have found equilibrium, with interdependence occurring in many ways that the couple cannot articulate" (p. 237). People's conflict behavior tends to reflect this sense of midlife arrival (assuming no separation is occurring): conflict tends to be more carefully and analytically articulated (Sillars & Wilmot, 1989).

Sillars and Wilmot (1989) showed that during later years, people report higher levels of relational satisfaction and interdependence. However, older couples' interactions are by and large constrained, especially in comparison to younger couples' interaction. During conflict, this sense of high interdependence and accommodation appears in the form of reduced confrontation and analyses of relational issues. Instead, many older couples are quite passive in their conflict interactions, although some older couples present case studies of "conflict habituated" types—always bickering.

RELATIONAL TYPES: DIFFERENT BLUEPRINTS FOR CLOSE RELATIONSHIPS

Recall that romantic relationships develop in alternative ways (i.e., accelerated, prolonged, and intermediate types). Likewise, there is no single model for established relationships. According to Fitzpatrick (1988a), there are several different types of marriages, and each type has its own preferred mode of managing conflict.

Fitzpatrick (1988a) identified three "pure" marital types, based on years of research. These types include *traditionals*, *separates*, and *independents*. Traditionals are marked by their adherence to "traditional" values (e.g., the woman taking the husband's last name, the man performing the breadwinning role, the woman cleaning the house). Separates (as their name implies) prefer to live in the same house but in different rooms. In other words, they are detached from each other emotionally and informationally. Independents seek partners who would help them achieve their own personal goals, and they do not adhere to traditional values. As Fitzpatrick and others have shown, the type of model for marriage one has dramatically affects the kinds of conflict that emerge.

Traditionals have conflicts, but they are reserved for important issues and entail cooperative sequences (Fitzpatrick, 1988b). Their cooperation may be due to their mutual adoption of traditional roles. For example, there should be no disagreement about who will cook and who will clean, because it is assumed that the woman will do that. Research on division of labor (e.g., Berk, 1985) verifies that traditional expectations about household performance often remain intact even if the woman works a full-time job. Separates avoid conflict, simply because they do not want to share ideas or feelings. One study found that separates would sometimes *actively* constrain their partners' behavior (Witteman & Fitzpatrick, 1986). However, the research largely suggests that separates would prefer to avoid conflict altogether and never enter a discussion about it. Independents, who get miffed if the partner somehow deters them from their goals, prefer to engage the partner than refrain from conflict (Fitzpatrick, 1988a). Fitzpatrick (1988b) summarized one set of findings in the following manner:

> The Traditionals attempt to confront their conflicts with one another and do so with less negativity than do the other couples. Independents do not respond well to a spouse's attempt to avoid discussing serious difficulties and confront them when they attempt to withdraw. At the act level, Separates show contentious behavior toward the spouse but appear to withdraw immediately from the discussion if the spouse contests their statements. (p. 250)

Box 4-3   Same Neighborhood, Different Worlds

Mark and Cleo were raised next door to each other, though you could swear they came from different countries. Like his parents, Mark was very traditional. He believed that women were the "fairer" sex who should be taken care of, and they in turn should provide a warm and nurturing home. Cleo, on the other hand, was raised in a home where the mother and father worked full-time jobs. Cleo learned that with careful planning and hard work she could make her mark on the world.

Simply because they ran into each other quite often, Mark and Cleo became engaged. Mark had visions of how he would come home to Cleo and a hot meal. Cleo had visions of how Mark would share equally in all the tasks they faced. They both realized they had differences but hoped they would pass in time. Of course, they didn't.

After the honeymoon, Mark was quite displeased that Cleo remained at her job at the counseling center. It wasn't a good job, and besides, she was ignoring her "real" duties at home and didn't keep regular hours. Cleo, on the other hand, was totally nonplussed at Mark, mainly for one reason: he never helped around the house. If anyone was going to have a hot meal, she would have to cook it. (Mark's involvement in cooking resided entirely in barbecuing hamburgers.) The dishes would stack up for days. Mark would watch ESPN and wonder when Cleo would come home. At times they had it out, and their conflicts went something like this:

(continued)

Cleo:	(from the kitchen) I can't get at anything in here!
Mark:	(from the TV room) Why *is* the kitchen such a mess?
Cleo:	Search me! When was the last time you did the dishes?
Mark:	Me? Why should I do the dishes? I work long hours at work.
Cleo:	Oh yeah? And *I* don't work? You really don't value my job, do you?
Mark:	What? Of course I do! But how long are you going to stay there? I thought we were going to start a family.
Cleo:	Well, so did I. But I can't do everything by myself. You are *so* inconsiderate!
Mark:	What . . . what have *I* done? I do all that anyone can expect from me!
Cleo:	What do you mean? You never, ever help me around here.
Mark:	Now you're exaggerating—I cooked last week!
Cleo:	You think that's fair?
Mark:	Look, I do what I have to—and you should do the same.

After a day of sulking, one of them would clean the kitchen, make breakfast, and promise to start again "with a more positive attitude."

What are the chances of Mark and Cleo resolving this conflict to *both* parties' satisfaction? Do you know people who appear to have different blueprints?

According to Fitzpatrick (1988a) people have different relational models—or schemata. You will recall that schemata work like blueprints, and relational schemata outline how relationships should be built. Unfortunately, people often do not realize that these different models exist and they may instead presume that others should follow their model. Unfortunately, this is often not the case. Fitzpatrick's (1988a) summary of research indicated that almost half of marital partners do *not* share in the partner's blueprint; that is, they had different models of relating. As Fitzpatrick documented, these "mixed" types had the least relational satisfaction and the most problems.

In sum, the development of a relationship occurs in two senses: as people get to know each other to develop their associations, and as these associations change over the life span. Of course, these findings are qualified by the fact that different kinds of relationships develop and are maintained.

CHARACTERISTICS OF DEVELOPED RELATIONSHIPS

How would you respond if you believed that a friend of yours was trying to steal your boy- or girlfriend? (This is one of those hypothetical situations we mentioned at the beginning of the chapter.) How you respond would depend on the nature of the relationship as seen in its feature characteristics, including how satisfied you are, how much you trust your friend and your partner, whether you cooperate or compete with each other, and how committed you are to each other. Since such features represent aspects of developed relationships, we will discuss them at this point. Specifically, relational satisfaction, trust, mutuality, and commitment provide a relational context that both defines the nature of the relationship and affects how people manage conflict.

Relational Satisfaction. Much research on marriage and the family has concerned whether conflict behavior corresponds to how satisfied couples are. This research as a whole reflects one simple principle: Conflict both reflects and affects relational satisfaction more dramatically than any other type of interaction.

Gottman (1994), for example, reviewed the literature on marital satisfaction and conflict observational studies, and he offered two conclusions that distinguish satisfied from dissatisfied couples. First, *satisfied couples engage in more constructive conflict behavior relative to destructive conflict behavior.* Gottman reported the ratio of positive to negative conflict behavior in satisfied couple discussions as 5:1. In other words, for each negative conflict behavior, the satisfied couple would enact five positive behaviors. However, in dissatisfied couple discussions, the ratio is 1:1; for every negative statement only one positive statement is offered. According to Gottman, satisfied couples more effectively "balance" their conflict interactions. For example, Noller, Feeney, Bonnell, and Callan (1994) found that satisfied couples were much less likely to engage in coercion, manipulation, or threats compared to dissatisfied couples.

Second, Gottman (1994) reported that *satisfied couples (versus dissatisfied couples) do not reciprocate negative emotion.* In the typical satisfied relationship, when a partner said something negative, the other person would avoid exchanging the insult, complaint, or show of anger. However, in the dissatisfied relationship, couples would often engage in exchanges of negative statements that would last several turns. For example, Ting-Toomey (1983) found that low satisfied couples would engage in reciprocation patterns of attack-defend and attack-attack messages, whereas high satisfied couples did not engage in these patterns whenever such behaviors emerged. Instead, satisfied couples reciprocated confirming or other integrative messages (chapter 3). In the next chapter, we show how the partner's behavior and escalation of emotion act as immediate, proximal factors that affect behavior. For now, we want to stress that reciprocating negative conflict appears to reflect an unhappy relationship, and it adversely affects the relationship.

Trust. Trust refers to the degree to which you are willing to make yourself vulnerable to someone. Most people require that the person they trust is both benevolent and honest—that is, the person cares about your welfare and means what s/he says (Larzelere & Huston, 1980). Research indicates that trusting a person has a distal effect on managing conflict (Canary & Cupach, 1988). More precisely, we are more likely to act in a cooperative manner with those we trust than those whose intentions we doubt or whose words have proven unreliable.

Cloven and Roloff (1993) have argued that people experience a "chilling effect" due in part to a lack of trust in the partner. More specifically, Cloven and Roloff stipulated that people who feel low in power and who are afraid of their partner are inhibited from raising their concerns. Of course, we can imagine how withholding information from the partner would increase one's sense of powerlessness and perhaps lead to the partner engaging in forceful behaviors. One implication of this research is that one should feel a sense of relief when one's partner feels comfortable enough to present his or her complaints—if they are presented in a cooperative manner. Regardless, a lack of trust appears to "chill" the relational environment and conflict interactions.

Control Mutuality. According to Morton, Alexander, and Altman (1976) every "viable" relationship requires that partners agree on who has rightful influence power. If parties cannot agree who has the right to lead, whether it be one person or both persons, then the relationship lacks control mutuality. For example, if a mother and her 17-year-old son do not agree that the mother has the right to discipline the son (e.g., to use "grounding," to prohibit use of the family car, or to require housework), then a lack of mutuality on the control issue can lead to many difficult conflicts between them (Morton et al., 1976).

Kelley (1979) has argued that control issues concern both outcomes regarding goals (or what he called "fate control") and how parties go about living their daily lives (or what he called "behavioral control"). Kelley (1979) also noted that relational partners differ in their mutual fate and mutual behavioral control—some people are very cooperative in how they define who influences whom in terms of goals and everyday actions, whereas other people are very unilateral in their controlling behaviors. In general, people dislike unilaterally defined relationships—with their partner using threat, intimidation, ridicule, and the like to get their way (Falbo & Peplau, 1980). Instead, productive conflict behavior has been positively associated with the extent that both parties agree on who has control over whom and in which areas that control may exist (Canary & Cupach, 1988).

Commitment and Exit-Voice-Loyalty-Neglect Responses. Another relational feature relevant to conflict is commitment. "Commitment" refers to the extent that one wants to remain in the relationship indefinitely. Commitment serves two important relationship functions. First, it acts to protect the relationship from outside forces (Lund, 1985). Second, it motivates couples to behave in constructive ways to manage relationship problems, an issue worth developing.

Rusbult and colleagues (e.g., Rusbult, 1987; Rusbult, Drigotas, & Verette, 1994; Rusbult, Johnson, & Morrow, 1986) have argued that one's commitment to the relationship determines how cooperative one is in responding to relational problems. Rusbult and colleagues have presented four primary responses, which are based on active versus passive and destructive versus constructive dimensions. The responses are *exit, voice, loyalty,* and *neglect.* Figure 4-1 presents these four responses (adapted from Rusbult, 1987; Rusbult et al., 1994).

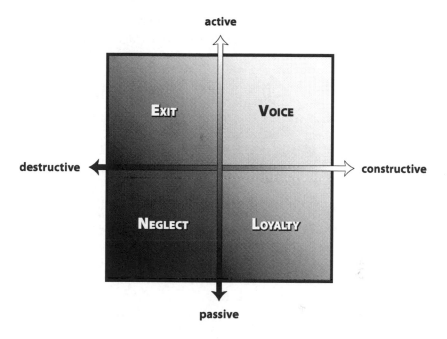

Source: From Rusbult (1987). Used by permission.

Figure 4-1   Exit, voice, loyalty, and neglect responses.

Exit represents an active, but destructive tendency to hurt the relationship through such behaviors as threatening to leave the partner, shouting, and abusing the partner. *Voice* is an active and constructive response to improve the relationship by talking things out. *Loyalty* presents a passive, though constructive way to manage relational problems. Loyalty can be seen in people's willingness to "put up and shut up" and to wait and see in order to accommodate the partner. Finally, *neglect* behaviors reflect a desire to see the relationship deteriorate by avoiding the partner, ignoring the partner, and the like. As Rusbult et al. (1994) summarized, commitment is *macromotive*; that is, commitment promotes the use of voice and loyalty, and commitment is negatively associated with the use of exit and neglect.

Summary

In this chapter, we examined several distal influences on conflict interaction. These influences do not exhaust the number of background factors. However, the ones selected have been explored in research and provide background to how conflicts unfold. We stressed both individual and relational difference factors that contextualize conflict interaction.

People vary in their individual personalities, and some personal properties appear to affect conflict management behaviors. For example, individuals with a secure attachment style tend to respond to conflict in more constructive ways. Two other salient individual difference factors concern the tendency of people to approach or avoid disagreements (i.e., variations in argumentativeness) and the tendency of people to believe that conflict outcomes depend on their own ability and effort (or internality) *or* on chance, fate, or powerful others (or externality). Those who would rather deal with disagreement and believe they can bring about positive outcomes are more likely to enjoy positive, productive conflicts. Those who avoid arguments or who see their conflict outcomes outside of their personal control are more likely to enact avoidance or distributive conflict behaviors, which in turn tend to bring about perceptions of incompetence and poor outcomes (chapter 6).

Much has been said regarding sex differences, though the research points to more similarities than differences when one considers the factors that predict conflict behaviors. In social relationships, we can reliably predict that people behave in stereotypic fashion. However, in close, personal relationships, where people have lots of information about the partner, sex roles may actually reverse themselves and women often take control of discussing issues under dispute.

The development, type, and character of one's relationship also set the stage for conflict. Relationships that entail high satisfaction, trust, control mutuality, commitment, and intimacy provide a rich background and appear to promote direct and cooperative conflict. As we have suggested, researchers know relatively little about how adult friends or parents with adult children manage their conflicts. Nevertheless, we can speculate that the baseline information gained from increased intimacy would provide a distal context for understanding these conflict interactions as well.

DISCUSSION QUESTIONS

1. What attachment style do you have? What reason(s) do you have to believe that is your style? How might your attachment style affect the levels of trust and cooperation you give to other people? Has your attachment style changed much since your early childhood (that you can recall)?

2. Have you ever known someone who was dogmatic—that is, the person disagreed about an issue even though they were clearly wrong? Is it possible to be argumentative and not dogmatic?

3. Should people believe that they have control over their conflict outcomes? Why or why not? In addressing this discussion question, please offer examples of people who might blame others for the conflict versus those who tend to take responsibility for conflicts.

4. Do you think that men and women are fundamentally similar or different? Does a person's biological sex affect his or her conflict behaviors in close relationships? Do you think that people with traditional ideologies hold onto sex role stereotypes more than those with nontraditional beliefs?

5. We have argued that satisfaction, trust, control mutuality, and commitment define the nature of the relational context. Can you think of other factors that might be just as important to how couples manage conflict? Do these characteristics apply universally to all relationship forms, including friendships and relatives?

6. Have you ever been really jealous in a relationship or have you known of someone who has been very jealous in a particular relationship? What might explain that jealousy? Do you think if the relational features we discussed were all positive in the relationship that the jealousy would disappear, or is jealousy more of an individual trait?

7. What type of marriage do you imagine you might someday have—*traditional, independent, separate,* or *mixed* (a combination)? Why? Do you expect your partner to share your blueprint of marriage? Why or why not?

chapter 5

PROXIMAL INFLUENCES
SPONTANEOUS REACTIONS TO CONFLICT

CHAPTER OUTLINE

Anger and Anger-Like Responses
    Causes of Anger
    Types of Anger
    Emotions Associated with Anger
Initial Reactions to the Conflict Situation
    Physiological Reactions
    Temporary Response Modes
    Scripts
Higher-Ordered Thoughts
    Attributions about Causes of Conflict
    Expectations for Achieving Goals
The Dyad as a System That Affects Each Person's Behavior
    System Properties
    System Dysfunctions
Summary
Discussion Questions

People are sometimes amazed by the way they respond to a conflict. Normally rational and self-controlled people can become highly emotional perpetrators of conflict escalation, and aggressive people at times behave timidly. Such unpredictable responses cannot be adequately explained by background relational and personality factors alone. In addition, we must examine influences on behavior that come into play immediately before and during conflict. Before we begin that examination, we present two observations that guide this chapter.

First, the unexpected emergence of conflict requires immediate, spontaneous reactions. By "reactions" we mean thoughts and emotions as well as behaviors. Rarely do people plan conflicts extensively in advance, although people may well benefit from planning to discuss problems at established times and places (Bach & Wyden, 1968). Conflict surprises people, arising most frequently while individuals are involved in an activity other than talking, such as balancing the checkbook, driving through heavy traffic, or making dinner (Sillars & Weisberg, 1987). This feature of conflict, that it often comes as an unexpected surprise, can compel people to feel as though they are unwitting parties to or even victims of a situation thrust upon them. People sometimes plan conflicts, such as when to initiate a breakup of a relationship, but more often, conflicts tend to occur with some degree of surprise.

Second, and closely related to the first assumption, as chapter 3 indicated, conflict interaction involves the behavior of both people. Part of the reason conflict surprises us is that we can rarely predict another's specific behavior with very high accuracy, even when we know the person well. Together, the parties to a conflict create a *system* through their patterns of interaction. Over time, partners, family members, friends, and others have a hard time interacting in ways that do not maintain the system. Accordingly, we should stress at the outset that although we focus on individual factors, these processes are jointly constructed and defined by evolving interaction over time.

Discussing proximal influences on conflict helps us become more aware of the processes of conflict interaction. In this chapter we discuss several proximal factors that occur almost at the same time. Because they are almost simultaneous, we argue no causal order among them. First, we discuss initial emotional responses to conflict. The role of anger and associated experiences are stressed. Next, we discuss people's *modi operandi* for the initial processing of conflicts, including physiological reactions and scripts that guide the expression of anger. A discussion follows, examining higher-ordered thoughts that affect behavior, including people's attributions, expectations, and goals. We conclude by discussing how relational systems constrain individuals' conflict behavior.

Anger and Anger-Like Responses

By definition, conflicts involve situations in which we perceive another party interfering with our ability to achieve a preferred outcome. Having our preferred outcomes blocked tends to be a source of frustration, and in such encounters anger is often a natural response. Given the ability of anger to fuel the initiation and escalation of conflict, it deserves extended consideration.

Anger is a natural and fundamental coping response to negative events in one's social environment (Berkowitz, 1993). By one estimate, 25% of people are "generally at least somewhat angry at work" (Gibson & Barsade, 1999). It is considered relatively normal for teens to express anger toward their parents, although such anger tends to decline in early adulthood (Galambos, Barker, & Krahn, 2006). People who cannot adequately express anger or who are overly expressive of anger may be at a somewhat elevated risk of physical problems (Everson-Rose & Lewis, 2005; cf. Myrtek, 2007) and devastating social effects (Tangney et al., 1996), especially among already vulnerable people such as victims of relationship aggression (Taft, Vogt, Mechanic, & Resick, 2007). As a rule, conflict is a negative event and often yields anger-like responses. To understand how we might respond to conflict, we need to understand how people in general experience and express anger.

CAUSES OF ANGER

Researchers have uncovered many causes of anger (Cupach & Canary, 1995; Harris, 1993; Turner, Russell, Glover, & Hutto, 2007), ranging from specific behaviors of others (e.g., hurling insults) to the view that anger is a fundamental orientation to your world (e.g., as a coping mechanism). Table 5-1 suggests some causes and subcategories of anger. In general, anger is triggered by the perception that another person frustrates you from achieving an important goal, questions an aspect of your integrity, or engages in some other reprehensible behavior such as rule violations, unfair behavior, infidelity, or betrayal. At some level, all sources of anger reflect some aspect of goal frustration. For example, discovering a partner's infidelity frustrates a person's goals to have a trusting relationship, to be seen as a person deserving of a faithful partner, and of seeing oneself as a person smart enough not to be surprised by such unfaithfulness. Not surprisingly, it is the people we are closest to and most interdependent upon who are most likely to be able to frustrate our goals and make us angry (Tafrate, Kassinove, & Dundin, 2002).

Table 5-1   Causes of Anger

Cause	Sample Subcategories	Examples
Identity management	Integrity threat	A classmate questions your ability to read.
	Condescension	A coworker acts superior and talks down to you.
	Insult	An acquaintance makes fun of your new dress, attributing the choice to bad genes.
	Blame/reproach	You are accused of being self-centered because you did not buy a wedding present for an acquaintance.
Aggression	Physical threat/harm	Your roommate threatens to punch you out if you don't leave the apartment.
	Sexual aggression	Someone you don't like keeps trying to seduce you.
	Verbal abuse	Your stepfather constantly intimidates you with threats, swearing, and demeaning comments.
Frustration	Goal interference	Your roommate watches TV all the time, making it hard to study.
	Expectation violation	Your daughter comes home for a short visit and never spends any time with you. Instead, she visits with all her friends.
	Thwarting of plans	Someone calls you an hour before a date and cancels, without a good reason.
	Impotence	You cannot convince the video store clerk that you returned the video on time, so you must pay a fine.

Lack of fairness	Inequity	Your brother expects you to call him all the time, though he never calls you.
	Blameworthiness	Your friend gets drunk and picks a fight with your new neighbor.
	Hurt feelings	Someone has just left your best friend for another person.
Incompetence due to ignorance	Incompetent others	The service station attendants cannot find out what is wrong with your car, and they've had it for a week.
	Thoughtless actions	You receive the same present from your brother that you gave him last year.
Incompetence due to egocentric motives	Self-centeredness	Your friend turns every topic to something that interests him.
	Opinionatedness	A classmate offers an opinion on every topic discussed in class.
Relationship threat	Jealousy	You are extremely jealous in a particular relationship.
	Unfaithfulness	You discover you have good reason to be jealous, since your partner admitted being unfaithful most of last year.
Predispositions	Predisposition due to experiences	Someone who was raised in an abusive home tends to display aggressive behavior.
	Predisposition due to drug dependence	A friend of yours acts edgy when he can't get a drink, and he gets aggressive when he does drink.
General learned reaction	Coping processes	An acquaintance gets angry at the slightest change of the weather.
	Response to aversion	You become angry whenever you experience negative feelings.

Source: Adapted from Canary, Spitzberg, and Semic (1998).

TYPES OF ANGER

Clore and colleagues (1993) have specified types of anger by delineating what people focus on when experiencing anger: Anger-like emotions can be separated in terms of (1) whether someone's action is blameworthy and (2) whether the consequences of the other's action are undesirable. Imagine that your roommate has borrowed your car and is supposed to return it by 1:00 PM, but doesn't arrive until 2:00 PM. Your roommate's behavior may be irresponsible but does not cause any serious consequences. If you had a job interview across town at 2:00 PM, however, then you probably would be more upset, given the negative consequences of that person's behavior (i.e., a job opportunity probably lost). Combining assessments of blameworthiness and consequences suggests some likely emotional reactions, four of which are anger-like responses: frustration, reproach, anger, and resentment (see table 5-2). We will elaborate on this analysis briefly.

First, you would feel a response of *frustration* if you experienced a negative outcome that wasn't necessarily linked to a reproachable behavior. For example, performers sometimes become ill and can't perform, which is frustrating for ticket holders. Frustrating anger is experienced in feelings such as displeasure, sadness, and even grief.

Reproach might be your response if the action of another person was blameworthy but did not have a negative consequence for you. For example, assume that you catch a fellow classmate obviously cheating on a major exam. If the instructor does not grade on a curve, then the cheater's score will not affect yours. You may thus feel reproachment anger toward this person—that is, anger in terms of contempt, indignation, and disdain, but not personal distress.

"Pure" *anger* arises from both a negative outcome and blameworthy behavior. Restating the examples already given, if you discovered that a performer faked an illness for publicity reasons or if your grade was lowered because of someone else's cheating (and raising the curve), you would experience pure anger; that is, you feel exasperated, offended, indignant, and perhaps outraged.

Finally, *resentment* arises when the outcomes for someone else are positive, but undeserved. For example, you might know someone who unjustly gets ahead in this world for no good reason, perhaps because of how they look or who they know. You may feel resentment anger in terms of envy or jealousy, and that the world does not give you a fair opportunity to be judged by your abilities.

Categorizing anger into types helps reveal alternative responses when the outcomes for you are positive or when the outcomes for the other person are negative. For example, table 5-2 indicates that if you were rewarded despite the reproachable behavior of others, you would experience *relief* (for example, you got the job even though your roommate did not return your car on time). Likewise, you might feel like *gloating* over someone who acted in a reproachable manner and who experienced a negative outcome (for example, a cheater who failed the test). And you might be *proud* of someone who

Table 5-2   Types of Anger and Related Emotions

Blameworthiness of	Outcomes for Self		Outcomes for Other	
other's actions	**Negative**	**Positive**	**Negative**	**Positive**
Blameworthy	"Pure" anger	Relief	Gloating	Resentment
Not blameworthy	Frustration	Joy	Pity	Pride

Source: Adapted from Clore and colleagues (1993).

obtained a positive outcome by acting in a just manner (for example, a relative who was promoted because of hard work).

EMOTIONS ASSOCIATED WITH ANGER

People can feel anger in conjunction with other kinds of negative, aversive feelings (Tafrate et al., 2002). Berkowitz (1993) showed that people act aggressively when they experience sadness or pain. For example, in two studies women were either subjected to pain (by having a hand kept in very cold water) or not subjected to pain (by having a hand kept in room-temperature water). In one study the women were then asked to evaluate another person's ideas and to reward or punish the other person. The women whose hands were in cold water gave out fewer rewards and more punishments than the women whose hands were in room-temperature water. There was no apparent anger-provoking event—only pain. In a second study, women exposed to pain recalled more conflict interactions with their boyfriends than did those who were not exposed to pain (Berkowitz, 1993).

Why should pain and sadness bring about anger-like responses? Berkowitz (1993) observed that "any given emotional state is best regarded as an associative network in which specific types of feelings, physiological reactions, motor responses, and thoughts and memories are all interconnected" (p. 9). Thus, almost any negative arousal can elicit angry responses. Environmental factors such as stressful environments, heat, pollution, foul odors, and cigarette smoke (Berkowitz, 1993) can cause aggression simply because negative experiences are associated with the expression of anger. Living in a polluted, crowded city during hot summer months sets the emotional stage for aggressive responses. For example, research indicates that these kinds of factors play a role in predicting the extent to which aggression is experienced in bars. When bars are rated higher in smokiness, crowdedness, loudness, darkness, and warmth, patrons are generally more likely to have experienced and observed violence in that bar (Leonard, Quigley, & Collins, 2003; Roberts, 2007). In short, people tend to become angry more easily as their comfort level decreases and might lash out at someone, regardless of any anger-provoking behavior on the part of the partner.

A related and important emotional predictor of how people manage conflict is *stress*. Among undergraduate students, stress has been associated with physical aggression toward one's partner (Makepeace, 1983). When people undergo pressure to meet deadlines and they are highly motivated to meet those deadlines, obstacles or distractions can trigger indifference to others' needs, as well as anger-like responses (Darley & Batson, 1973; Zillmann, 1990). Married couples experiencing greater stresses at work tend to carry over that stress in the form of anger in their relationships (Story & Repetti, 2006). Furthermore, chronic stress appears to play a role in predicting intimate violence in married couples (Hellmuth & McNulty, 2008). Recall the roommate who returned your car late when you needed to get to a job interview. Not only would you be angry at your friend, but you would be anxious and primed for anger by the stress of running late. So, you might act in anger at other drivers in front of you who simply obey the speed limit: You might tailgate, honk your horn, and curse at them. These drivers have done nothing reprehensible; they just happen to be in the way. People who chronically experience stress are handicapped in terms of meeting deadlines and in their emotional reactions to others.

Anger-like responses are not the only types of reactions to conflict. People also respond to negative experiences with *fear* (Winstock, 2007a). Berkowitz (1993), for example, argued that in aversive or threatening situations, people seek to escape or avoid the issue confronting them. Alternatively, people may respond to their fear in an angry manner, trying to regain control of the situation (Hocker & Wilmot, 1995). They may rely on defensive behaviors that evaluate the other, control communication, show indifference, dominate the partner, and the like (Gibb, 1961). People who are afraid and who choose not to use integrative behaviors may accordingly *act as if they are angry.*

Negative emotions of many forms provide a proximal context for conflict (Tangney et al., 1996). Thus, although you may do nothing that is sufficient in and of itself to cause a conflict, your partner's negative emotional state may trigger his or her angry response (and vice versa).

Box 5-1   Planning a Romantic Evening: A Case Study

Jack was looking forward to Saturday evening with Jill. He was going to prepare Jill's favorite dish, Cajun chicken. He bought the groceries and planned to clean his apartment. It was going to be a romantic night.

Jill was supposed to arrive at 7:00 PM, and Jack was still busy cleaning when the doorbell rang at 6:45. Jill had come early to see if Jack wanted any help.

"No, I don't want you to do anything. I'm running a bit behind though, so please have a seat and make yourself comfortable. I'll be right with you."

Jill sat in the living room and turned on the TV.

Jack finished cleaning about a half hour later and realized that he had forgotten to buy the red peppers. "Honey, I need to get something. Just keep relaxing—I'll be right back." On his way home, Jack thought to get some dessert, so he went to a bakery to get the chocolate cream pie that Jill liked so much. Jack returned a little after 8:00 PM, and in need of a shower.

Jill looked at him with hungry eyes. "Are you *sure* there isn't anything I can do, like wash the vegetables?"

"No, *no—please* let me do this for you," Jack pleaded. He put away the groceries, grabbed a quick shower, and dressed. About fifteen minutes later, Jack returned to the kitchen and informed Jill that he was making Cajun chicken with "dirty" rice.

Jill was getting very hungry by now, but she remained very polite and even supportive. "Sounds great!" she said. She came into the kitchen and noticed that the chicken had a lot of fat on it. "Honey, would you mind if I trimmed the fat off the chicken?"

Jack felt the screws tighten a bit. "You don't want fat on your chicken? OK ... fine! I'll trim the fat—you just get out of here and let me handle this!"

Discouraged, Jill returned to the living room. She could hear cupboard doors slamming and pots banging and occasional cursing. It was almost 9:00 PM.

Then Jack had another setback. He had begun the vegetables too far ahead of the chicken, which he was still trimming, and the rice wouldn't be ready for another fifteen minutes. Jack threw the chicken in with the vegetables and hurriedly began setting the table. A couple minutes later, he returned to the kitchen and decided that the vegetables were getting too cooked and that everything needed to be served immediately. He called to Jill, "Dinner is served!"

Jill sat down at the table, though she knew that Jack hadn't cooked the chicken more than a few minutes. "Honey, this smells great. But how long did you cook the chicken?"

"Long enough," Jack replied flatly. He was still feeling frazzled and just wanted to get on with the damn dinner.

"I don't mean to complain, but you know that we can die if this isn't properly cooked," Jill informed him.

Jack replied curtly, "We won't die, I promise. Let's just eat."

Jill was not convinced. "Do you mind if I cook it a few minutes longer?"

Jack was offended. "Of course I mind! I spend all day preparing this evening for you and unless it's done *your* way you don't want any! OK . . . fine. Go ahead and finish the cooking. *I'll* go watch some TV!"

Jill was offended at the implication that she was lazy. "Look, I offered to help! I knew you were having trouble in here!"

Jack felt that his competence was being directly attacked. He retorted, "No, that's not the issue. The issue is that everything must be done *Jill's* way or not at all!"

Jill shot back, "I wish I had a video camera! The issue is *not* things being done my way. The issue is whether the chicken is safe for us to eat! I don't want to die from salmonella poisoning!" Just then, the timer buzzer went off, indicating that the rice was ready.

Both Jack and Jill were disappointed; "romantic" was not a term either of them would use to describe that evening. The vegetables were soggy and the chicken was cold. Dessert would have to keep for another time.

Discussion Questions

1. What emotions or experiences were associated with Jack's anger? With Jill's anger?

2. How might Jack or Jill have shown more grace under pressure?

Initial Reactions to the Conflict Situation

There are a variety of feelings associated with the experience of anger. Among these feelings are changes in how the body reacts—we think of becoming "red-faced," "seeing red," feeling our "blood boil," and speaking through "clenched teeth." These expressions are not merely colorful metaphorical expressions. We tend to feel conflicts in our body, and our bodies feel our conflicts.

PHYSIOLOGICAL REACTIONS

One of the most intriguing features of one's immediate response to conflict is physiological reaction. Research indicates that people respond with excitation to discussions of problems. Gottman and Levenson (1988) summarized people's physiological responses in this way:

> Within the autonomic nervous system (ANS), the classic "flight-fight" . . . pattern is well known, consisting of such changes as increases in cardiac rate and cardiac contractility, sweating, deepened breathing, redirection of blood flow toward large skeletal muscles, and release of catecholamines (i.e., epinephrine and norepinephrine) from the adrenal medulla. (p. 189)

In other words, when faced with a problematic situation (including stressful conflicts), your body responds to the brain's "fight" or "flee" signals to increase your energy. You experience this instinctive response by feeling your heart pounding, by sweating, and by being flushed and alert. At first you are startled (typified by a blink, a gasp, hunched shoulders); then you quickly focus on the situation as your heart pumps greater amounts of blood (Gottman, 1994).

Once people are aroused physiologically, they require time to return to a normal state—that is, for the arousal to dissipate. For most people, this takes a few minutes, or the time it would take to cool off after a workout (as the heart settles from about 100 beats per minute to about 75 beats per minute) (Gottman, 1994). However, interpersonal conflicts often involve more than one point of arousal. When people exchange messages—particularly negative messages—they also exchange stimuli that prevent physiological recovery. Zillmann (1990) summarized people's physiological reactions to interpersonal conflict accordingly:

> Escalating conflict can be conceptualized as a sequence of provocations, each triggering an excitatory reaction that materializes quickly and that dissipates slowly. As a second sympathetic reaction occurs before the first has dissipated, the second reaction combines with the tail end of the first. As a third reaction occurs before the second and first reactions have dissipated, this third reaction combines with the tail ends of both earlier reactions. In general, the excitatory reaction to provocation late in the escalation process rides the tails of all earlier reactions. (p. 192)

Because of this buildup of negative arousal, people experience excitation at levels that appear to be an overreaction to the initial cause of the conflict ("I don't know why you get so angry when I only want to talk with you!"). In addition, Zillmann showed that too much excitation prevents people from thinking clearly and efficiently about the issue under discussion—a state Gottman (1994) called *flooding*.

These general patterns of physiological response may reflect universal tendencies, but they also are influenced by a variety of interpersonal factors. One of the important moderators of physiological reaction to conflicts is gender.

During conflict men, compared to women, appear to experience more physiological flooding that takes longer to dissipate; that is, men show stronger signs of negative physiological arousal for longer periods and tend to be more aware of their body's "fight" versus "flight" orientation (Levenson et al., 1994). Gottman (1994) explained this sex difference as stemming from the fact that men are not accustomed to exploring relational issues, since most of their childhood time involved sports and games, instead of playing house and similar relationship-oriented activities. Accordingly, men want to "flee" conflict situations because of their negative arousal, whereas women tend to ignore their physiological reactions in order to confront the relational problem.

These patterns of physiological response appear also to be influenced by the particular type of conflict interaction involved (Fehm-Wolfsdorf, Groth, Kaiser, & Hahlweg, 1999). "Specific patterns of interaction during conflict, most notably escalation of the conflict, withdrawal from the interaction, and attempts to exert control over the partner, have been linked to greater physiological reactivity in endocrine, immune, and cardiovascular domains" (Whitson & El-Sheikh, 2003, p. 289). Those who desire greater change from their partners may be more physiologically reactive to negative conflict than those relatively less desirous of change (Newton & Sanford, 2003). Satisfied couples seem capable of achieving a moderate balance of engagement and disengagement of physiological arousal during conflicts, whereas dissatisfied couples seem to be either too disengaged or overly engaged physiologically (Thomsen & Gilbert, 1998).

The impact of such physiological reactions may be substantial. Negative conflict behavior such as hostility and criticism in marriages is associated with indicators of poorer health (Robles & Kiecolt-Glaser, 2003), especially among individuals who are predisposed toward hostility (Miller, Dopp, Myers, Stevens, & Fahey, 1999). Research indicates that "negativity (such as criticism, interruption, blaming, or withdrawal) during conflict is associated with pronounced cardiovascular reactivity" and diminished immune response, especially among men (Whitson & El-Sheikh, 2003, p. 289). Men are not the only ones at risk from the link between conflict and physiology. In one 10-year community-based study, "women who 'self-silenced' during conflict with their spouse, compared with women who did not, had four times the risk of dying" (Eaker, Sullivan, Kelly-Hayes, D'Agostino, & Benjamin, 2007, p. 509). Men reported self-silencing more than their spouses, but it had no effect on their mortality.

Finally, understanding the role of physiological reactions in conflict has begun to provide key insights into a particular type of conflict: intimate violence (see chapter 10). Gottman et al. (1995) found that there were two types of violent men in relationships—those who experience relatively high levels of physiological reactivity during conflicts with their partners, and those who experienced diminished reactivity. Those who actually seemed to become more calm during conflicts were the more severely violent. Research has not fully supported this typology (Meehan & Holtzworth-Munroe, 2001; Meehan,

Holtzworth-Munroe, & Herron, 2001), but does indicate that a low resting heart rate may be particularly predictive of highly antisocial and aggressive men (Babcock, Green, Webb, & Graham, 2004; Babcock, Green, Webb, & Yerington, 2005). Contrary to what might be expected, the most dangerous partner may be the one who doesn't "feel" the conflict physiologically.

TEMPORARY RESPONSE MODES

Besides having physiological reactions, people develop initial appraisals and response modes to react to the conflict situation. *Temporary response modes* are immediate cognitive reactions that occur during the particular conflict episode and are not necessarily linked to one's general personality (Frijda, Kuipers, & ter Schure, 1989; Zillmann, 1988). For example, one morning you may feel strong and self-confident—willing to confront anyone who gets in your way—whereas usually you feel physically weak or too distracted to assert yourself.

These response tendencies may lead to *action readiness plans,* or your inclination to use different forms of interaction behavior (Frijda et al., 1989). Such plans may also be based on one's state of health, familiarity with the social situation, whether the company is friendly or hostile, and cues given from the partner (Schacter & Singer, 1962). Box 5-2 shows how emotional cues from one person can affect the behavior of another.

Response tendencies may translate into one or more of three response modes in a given encounter: *moving toward, moving against,* and *moving away* from others (Davitz, 1969). That is, you might be inclined in a given situation to respond in a cooperative, competitive, or avoidant manner. For example, if you experience "Monday blues," you might feel inclined to avoid others until the caffeine kicks in at 10:00 AM, after which time you become mostly competitive. But on Tuesday, you feel ready to work with others and maintain a cooperative response mode all day. Many people refer to response modes as "moods." The term "response mode," however, emphasizes a mental state of readiness to implement different strategies.

SCRIPTS

Recall from chapter 4 that people have blueprints to outline their relationships. Similarly, people have scripts for how conflicts should progress and for how they should handle anger when they experience it. As Russell and Fehr (1994) observed, "To know the concept of anger is to know a script (to be able to simulate a scenario) in which prototypical antecedents, feelings, expressions, behaviors, physiological changes, and consequences are laid out in a causal and temporal sequence" (p. 202).

A typical anger script among college students appears to have three general acts. In act 1, social actors see themselves as *reactors* to negative events that somehow violate their rights, expectations, and the like (Shafer, Schwartz, Kirkson, & O'Connor, 1987). In other words, people identify a cause for their anger (see table 5-1). This act could be titled "The Scene of the Crime."

Box 5-2   Emotions Are Contagious

In the early 1960s, an important study showed that people interpret their own emotions on the basis of the behavior of the other person (Schacter & Singer, 1962). Schacter and Singer held that people attempt to label their emotions given the information available to them. If people do not have a reasonable explanation for their emotions, they rely on situational cues—including the other person's behavior.

Schacter and Singer observed participants' reactions and survey responses regarding a fictional new vitamin, Superoxin. Superoxin was actually epinephrine, which causes feelings of excitation—mild increases in heart rate, blood pressure, muscle and cerebral blood flow, blood sugar, lactic acid, and breathing rate. Following the injection of the epinephrine, participants (who were male students) experienced different experimental conditions.

The first condition concerned the explanation for their physical reactions to Superoxin. Participants were informed in one of three ways: (1) they were accurately told about the physical symptoms they would experience because of Superoxin; (2) they were misinformed about their reaction to Superoxin (for example, that their feet would feel numb, though they never did); or (3) they were told nothing about physical changes.

The second condition involved another person's behavior. Once the physician had left the room, a confederate (someone who the experimenter has trained to behave a particular way) was brought in. The participant was told that the confederate was, like him, participating in the study. The participant did not know that the confederate had been told to act in a joyous and euphoric way *or* in an angry manner. Euphoric behaviors included playing "basketball" with crumpled paper and playing with a hula hoop. Angry behaviors were complaining about the experiment and showing increasing rage at the study.

The authors hypothesized that the confederate's behavior would affect participants' emotion and behavior, but only when participants lacked a reasonable explanation for their emotions. And that is exactly what Schacter and Singer found.

Participants who were informed accurately about their physical reactions to the epinephrine were not affected by the behavior of the other person in the experiment. Participants who were ignorant of the causes for their physical symptoms relied much more on the behavior of the confederate to understand their own emotions. These participants mirrored the behavior of the confederate. Those in the euphoria condition acted significantly more joyous, and those in the angry condition acted significantly angrier. Of course, those in the euphoria and anger conditions in reality had the same physiological reactions. The only difference between groups was in the behavior of the partner, the confederate.

Discussion Questions

1. Have you ever had such an experience?

2. Have you ever not known you were in a conflict until someone else indicated that a disagreement was taking place?

3. How is it possible to diffuse an angry situation, knowing that other people rely on you to discover their own feelings?

In act 2 of the anger script, the participants react negatively. Shafer and colleagues (1987) reported several alternative scripted reactions that people have to anger: (1) various kinds of verbal attacks, yelling, and complaining; (2) physical attack threats, such as clenched fists and threatening nonverbals, and physical attacks on objects (breaking things); (3) nonverbal ways of showing protest and anger, including slamming doors, stomping around, frowning, and being flushed; (4) feelings of anxiety and discomfort, which may be revealed in crying; (5) internal escape responses, including brooding and focusing on one's anger; and (6) avoidance, by suppressing one's outrage or defining one's feelings of anger as inappropriate. The second act could be titled "The Hero Confronts the Villain."

Act 3 shows how people recover from their anger. Like the previous acts, act 3 has alternative scenes that conclude the play: (1) The participants realize that if the anger continues, one or both parties and the relationship will certainly be hurt. In this version, the parties attempt reconciliation by taking a moment to collect themselves, "making up," and reaffirming each other. (2) One or both parties decide that the best way to reduce tension requires further distance or time apart. (3) Neither party knows how to manage conflicts productively, so they enact the script of aggression. Here, violence is seen as the preferred mode for reducing anger and rectifying the partner's reproachable behavior. Each of these versions of act 3 could be titled "The Aftermath."

Let's focus on the script alternatives in act 2. Note that the second act has no productive behaviors associated with it, simply because people typically do not see productive behavior as part of their anger script (Shafer et al., 1987). However, other scholars have questioned whether the behaviors in act 2 portray the various ways that people manage their anger (e.g., Clore & Ortony, 1991). There is no doubt that people follow other scripts besides the anger script for managing problems, since people report more self-control in real situations than they might expect of themselves in a typical anger script (Fitness & Fletcher, 1993). Nevertheless, the research on anger scripts is important, because people sometimes rely on them to enact their roles during conflict. The educational task, then, is to identify any scripts you rely on when managing conflict, including the anger scripts we have mentioned here.

Higher-Ordered Thoughts

In addition to your first inclinations to respond, you can rely on higher-ordered thoughts, or thoughts that involve central memory processing. Such thoughts permit one to gain self-control (Feshbach, 1986).

People who have cognitive deficits, however, have difficulty using self-controlling thoughts. For example, intoxicated individuals cannot prepare rational responses, do not clearly process their partners' cues, and do not attend diligently to social expectations for behavior (Zillmann, 1990). Likewise, people who take in high levels of caffeine (more than two cups of coffee or 36 ounces of cola) may be too excited to think clearly, whereas people using marijuana may feel entirely unmotivated to work at solving problems interpersonally (Lubit & Russett, 1984). In addition, people who become overly excited or "flooded" by the conflict find it very difficult to reappraise the situation in rational terms (Zillmann, 1988). It may be better for either or both parties to avoid the conflict discussion until people with cognitive deficits can re-collect themselves (Tavris, 1984).

Nevertheless, most people in most situations can use two kinds of higher-ordered thoughts directly relevant to conflict interactions: the attributions you have about the cause of the conflict and the assessments of probable outcomes of your behavior (Berkowitz, 1993). We wish to point out our use of the word "can," which implies that people have the ability to think before acting.

ATTRIBUTIONS ABOUT CAUSES OF CONFLICT

Communication is not simply a process of the raw sensory input of information from the environment and one's physiology. For communication to occur, there must be some translation of sensory input into meaningful interpretations. One of the most fundamental ways in which we make sense of our senses is through the process of attribution (Weary & Reich, 2000).

Attribution Dimensions. Attributions are explanations that people have for the causes of social events. Several dimensions characterize people's explanations for conflict situations (Spitzberg, 2001). The dimensions most important to conflict appear to be globality, stability, locus, intent, selfishness, and blameworthiness (Fincham, Bradbury, & Scott, 1990). *Globality* refers to whether the cause of the event is seen as specific to the situation or as something that explains many situations. A partner's excessive drinking might occur across a *variety* of situations, or only when the in-laws come over. *Stability* concerns whether the cause occurs reliably over time; stable causes last a long time and unstable causes apply only for a while. A partner's drinking problem might be seen as a temporary or episodic problem, or as a disease that will always be with the partner. *Locus* refers to where the problem lies, whether internal or external to the person and/or relationship. A partner's drinking problem could be considered sympathetically as a disease inherited from the partner's family of origin, or as a weakness of the partner's character. *Intent* concerns whether the cause indicates a conscious decision for the event. We might blame a vicious comment by our partner on the alcohol, or on our partner's actual thoughts about us. *Selfishness* refers to whether the cause suggests a person's motive as self-serving. A partner who seeks to excuse his or her drinking seems self-serving, but a partner who admits to the problem and the need for intervention is providing a more altruistic explanation. Finally, *blameworthiness* assigns responsibility for a failure (in contrast to *praiseworthiness*, which is responsibility for a success). Such attributions are to some extent a synthesis of the previous attributions, such that an individual's *responsibility* is perceived or communicated. Perceiving a partner's drinking behavior as being global (cross-contextual), stable (a continuing cause of conflicts), internal (part of who the partner is), intentional (a product of the partner's choices rather than disorder), and selfish (explained by blaming other people or events rather than oneself) will tend to lead to blaming the partner, and thereby to a less forgiving response.

Which attribution dimension most directly affects conflict behavior is not altogether clear, because these dimensions overlap when discussing a single event. Research suggests, however, that people who tend to see the causes of conflict as global, stable, internal, and selfishly motivated have dissatisfying and turbulent relationships (Bradbury & Fincham, 1990; Fincham et al., 1990; Vangelisti, 1994). People who view the cause of their conflict as reflecting global, stable, internal, and selfish dimensions are more likely than those who do not make these attributions to engage in negative behavior and less likely to experience positive relational outcomes. For example, in a study of roommates, Sillars (1980a) found that those who viewed the cause of conflict as stable and internal to the partner were more likely than others to engage in distributive conflict behavior (for example, threats, sarcasm). Ironically, since *both partners can simultaneously make attributions,* both people simultaneously may view the cause of conflict as the partner's fault (Schütz, 1999). Other research, however, indicates that given the opportunity, we are often inclined to attribute relational problems to the "relationship" itself, or the communication in the relationship, rather than exclusively to the partner (Berscheid, Lopes, Ammazzalorso, & Langenfeld, 2001; Manusov & Koenig, 2001).

People who accept some responsibility for a conflict tend to respond in a positive manner—for example, by focusing on what they can do to remedy the situation. In addition, people who refrain from generalizing from the conflict interaction itself to broader issues and who explain their partners' behavior in unstable, external, and unselfish terms are less likely to use distributive, negative behaviors.

People might generalize from the conflict behaviors themselves to assess relational issues (Gottman, 1994). For example, you might attribute the cause of your partner's negative behavior to thoughtlessness. From there you might generalize that you are unhappy in the relationship because you cannot be satisfied with an inconsiderate person.

Attribution Biases.   People not only vary in their attribution dimensions, but they also have biases. One of the most important biases is the *actor-observer bias*—that is, the tendency to link the partner's behavior to the partner's internal dispositions ("She didn't return my phone call because she is *rude"*) while linking our own behavior to external factors ("I couldn't return his phone call because I was *very busy* with clients"). Because of actor-observer bias, we quickly attribute motives to others (but not as quickly to ourselves) *during* conflict because we can see their physical features and expressions, but we cannot see our own physical expressions of dismay, disapproval, and the like (Storms, 1973).

The actor-observer bias has been differentiated into specific types of bias (Malle, Knobe, & Nelson, 2007). The first type of asymmetry is the *reason* bias. In most contexts, we have greater access to our own reasons for doing things than observers have, and in accessing such awareness, we are likely to account for ourselves as having more reasons for our actions than observers can spontaneously derive, which in turn portrays us as more active and rational. The second bias is the *belief* asymmetry. Because we have greater access to the specific types of information involved in our beliefs, as opposed to the more generic and universal notions of needs and wants, we often construct our reasons on such specific or unique information in beliefs, compared to observers, who consider our behavior based more on easily generalized wants. A third bias is reflected in how attributions are linguistically constructed with *belief markers*. In explaining our own behavior, we can easily invoke our beliefs (e.g., "I was late picking you up because I believed helping my boss out was more important under the circumstances"), but this kind of attribution might be more difficult for the observer (e.g., "You were late because you're thoughtless"). Thus, across a variety of conflict encounters, we are likely to be able, and inclined, to provide and make attributions in very different ways than those with whom we are having the conflict. The asymmetric explanations that arise often then become a focal point of the conflict in addition to the original event trigger itself.

A second attribution bias—the *activity bias*—is the tendency to make quicker attributions for extraordinary behavior (rather than for ordinary, normative behavior). Because people expect others to treat them with general respect and positivity, people more readily notice behaviors that are less positive, such as avoidance and negative messages (Canary & Spitzberg, 1990). This is one of the reasons people cannot simply "balance" a negative comment with a positive one (Gottman, 1994); people are more sensitive to others violating the norm of cooperation. If you recall some of your recent conversations, you probably will recall a higher proportion of negative behaviors, because these are more salient to you. This is consistent with research indicating that although we have far more positive than negative experiences in our everyday interactions (Zelenski & Larsen, 2000), it is the negative interactions that appear to disproportionately influence our well-being (Rook, 1998).

Attributions can be seen in the everyday discourse that occurs during conflicts. For example, accusatory "you" messages, as opposed to "I" statements, illustrate different linguistic forms of attribution. The difference between "I'm angry" and "You're making me angry," and "I'm really pissed" and "You're pissing me off," represent a potentially different attributional locus. Using the accusatory language appears to be more destructive to a relationship (Kubany, Bauer, Muraoka, Richard, & Read, 1995). Similar findings arise when considering the use of profanity during conflicts (Young, 2004). The relationship between attributional communication and relational satisfaction, however, may not be quite so simple. Some research indicates that high trust couples exchange very positive attributional messages, moderate trust couples exchange a relatively higher proportion of negative attributional statements, and low trust couples exchanged less negative and more neutral attributional messages (Rempel, Ross, & Holmes, 2001). It may be that when couples become dissatisfied or distrustful they settle into a more comfortable neutral pattern of everyday communication so as to avoid more serious conflicts.

The power of understanding attribution differences can be seen starkly in a research study where couples were videotaped interacting about their differences; afterward they were separated to view the videos; and then each partner provided both a description of what they *meant* or were thinking by their comments, and what they thought their *partner* meant by his or her comments (Sillars, Roberts, Dun, & Leonard, 2001). When presented in parallel, as in table 5-3, the differences in attributions are both obvious and suggestive of the complexity of the communication that would be necessary to manage these real-time disparities of the construction of meaning.

Another powerful role that attributions play in conflict can be seen in a theory of responsibility attributions (Weiner, 1995). In this theory, attributions essentially combine to determine the extent to which a person is judged

Table 5-3 Parallel Thoughts and Meanings in Couple Interaction

She thinks . . .	He thinks . . .
As far as most of the work goes, when I do ask for help, he refuses. Oh, it's "Yeah, I'll help you in a few minutes," but then he's too busy playing his Nintendo or super-graphics, listening to the radio, calling in for a contest. . . .	There **she's trying to lie** to get out of doing house cleaning because this is the way I was feelin'. . . that she doesn't want to do it. She's too lazy. She'd rather just lay around and watch TV all day and all night, and that's it . . . do nothing else.
I feel that if I have to clean up he really should help, workin' or not. Many men do help their wives and they don't complain, but **he always seems to find a complaint.**	Here she's makin' me angry because after I had done the attic she goes and redoes it and makes it worse. . . . It's just too much sometimes for me to handle. She expects me to handle everything.
Here **he uses the excuse** that the child walks all over me, when in fact, the only reason the child does anything when he's there is because he's afraid of him.	**. . . she's just saying this so she don't have to listen to it so she can ignore it** so it don't bother her and she knows it's bothering me.
Here **he acts as if he is the boss with me,** and I have no bosses as far as I'm concerned and I don't see any reason why . . . I have to do what he wants and **he just comes right out of the blue with it.**	There I was feelin' like I never do something for her and how **she's throwing stuff up in my face**, and it was hurtin' me. It hurts and makes me angry because **she says one thing and she totally does another.**

Source: Adapted from Sillars, Roberts, Dun, and Leonard (2001, p. 205).

as "responsible" for behavior (figure 5-1). When a person engages in some social action, we make judgments about what caused that action. To the extent we perceive the action as having been controllable, intentional, and consensually distinctive in its association to a perceived cause, the more we hold that person responsible for the action. In contrast, to the extent we view a behavior as uncontrollable, unintentional, and consensually or consistently indistinct in relation to the cause, we tend to absolve the person of the action. For example, if you pass a man on the sidewalk panhandling for change, you could make attributions along the following lines: People who are out of work are just lazy (controllable), having decided (intentional) that begging is an easier path. Everyone knows (consensus) that panhandlers like this are always (consistency) going to waste any money I give them on drugs (distinctiveness). Your response, if these were your attributions, would likely be quite unsympathetic, and perhaps even antagonistic. In contrast, if you judge that this person must have fallen on hard times (uncontrollable) due to hard economic times or policies (unintentional), from which people sometimes just need a temporary handout to get back on their feet (distinctiveness), as some have in the past (consensus), and as you and your friends or family may have observed (consensus), then your response might be far more sympathetic and cooperative.

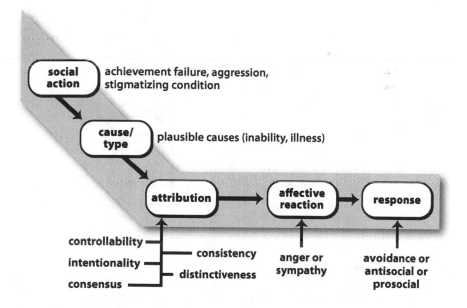

Source: Adapted from Weiner (1995).

Figure 5-1   Model of responsibility attribution, appraisal, and response.

EXPECTATIONS FOR ACHIEVING GOALS

Expectations you have for achieving goals affect your choice of conflict strategies. Expectations can be categorized according to the kinds of goals that people seek. This classification of expectation types helps us understand the kinds of higher-ordered thoughts that individuals engage in before acting. After discussing the nature of expectations, we will examine specific interaction goals.

Expectations.   By "expectations" we mean the likelihood that acting in a particular way will bring about particular consequences (Sillars, 1980b). Since many consequences represent positive as well as negative outcomes, or "prospects" (Kahneman & Tversky, 1979), researchers often assess the perceived value of the consequences (Eagly & Chaiken, 1993). Such expectations, sometimes called *expectancy-value* assessments, can be represented by a simple mathematical formula:

Behavior = Likelihood of Consequences × Value of Consequences

You may calculate this formula so often that it has become almost automatic. Every day you decide the likelihood that cooperating with, competing against, or avoiding others will bring about desired consequences and prevent undesired consequences.

The more important the conflict consequences are to you, the more careful you become in your calculations. For example, imagine that a teaching assistant (TA) appears to grade papers using subjective impressions, and he gives you lower grades than you usually earn. When going over the most recent assignment, the TA states simply that he "did not care for your word choice." If you needed an A in the class to qualify for graduate school, you might give a lot more thought to your response than if you just wanted to pass the course. Should you confront the TA and, if that doesn't work, complain to the department chair? Should you present your honest feelings of surprise and show how you fulfilled the assignment? Or should you act likeable and thank the TA for his honesty? If you needed only to pass, there would be little need to think about your response, and you probably would turn your attention to something else more important to you. But if you needed an A, you would carefully consider your response. You might even brood about the event all day, reconstruct the TA's weak answer, and rehearse a carefully crafted reply ("I'll show *him* word choice!").

Decisions are not simply a product of the expected gains relative to losses and their respective probabilities—this would be (too) purely rational. Instead, it appears that we have certain fundamental biases in the ways in which we approach situations. Prospect theory proposes that we often make choices less on the final expected outcome and based more on changes from our current situation.

Imagine you are given $1,000, and then you are presented with a choice between two alternatives: (a) a 50% chance of winning an additional $1,000, or (b) gaining a certain $500. Over two-thirds appear to prefer the sure thing (i.e., choice b). In an alternate description of the problem, however, you are given $2,000, and must choose between (c) a 50% chance of losing $1,000, and (d) a certain loss of $500. In this case, over two-thirds choose the risky alternative (i.e., choice c). Rationally, these two decisions are equivalent, since (a) and (c) both provide a 50% chance of ending up with $1,000 (or $2,000), and (b) and (d) both provide a result of $1,500. When the problem is framed as a certain gain of $500, we prefer it, and when the choice is a possible larger loss rather than a certain modest loss, we prefer to bet on the possible larger loss. Thus, we appear to exhibit "risk aversion for positive prospects and risk seeking for negative ones" (Kahneman & Tversky, 1979, p. 273). Another way of thinking about this is that we tend to view losses as twice as undesirable as we find gains desirable.

There are other types of asymmetries of choices that reflect our basic tendencies in evaluating prospects. The most famous examples are the "trolley" and "footbridge" moral dilemma problems. The trolley situation places you in a trolley station, in which a trolley is barreling down the tracks where five people are conversing and oblivious to the trolley that is about to run them over. You see a lever that you can quickly pull that will divert the trolley onto another track, where only one person is attending to something, and will certainly be killed as a result. Do you let the trolley kill the five, or do you actively pull the lever, saving the five but killing the one? Once you have decided your choice for this situation, consider the same trolley station, with five people at peril from the oncoming trolley. You are on a footbridge overseeing the impending accident, and realize that if you push a very obese person onto the track, it will certainly kill the person but stop the trolley before it can reach the other five people. Do you push the fat person onto the tracks, killing this person but saving the five? Online surveys indicate that well over two-thirds of people choose to pull the lever in the first situation, sacrificing the one for the five (with four net lives saved), but about two-thirds refrain from sacrificing the large person (which would have netted the "same" four lives saved). Thus, despite these situations being identical in prospects, people are relatively accepting of an impersonal approach to sacrificing another person to save others, but when it becomes more personal, we become more cautious (e.g., Greene & Haidt, 2002). Again, from a purely rational perspective, the two decisions offer the same types of choices, but there is a significant tendency for people to prefer one over the other.

Conflicts frequently are likely to involve such decisions. If you have cheated on a partner (a decision likely to reflect risk seeking), the decision of whether or not to tell your partner (a decision likely to reflect risk aversion) involves both judgments about the likely outcomes, such as whether or not the partner will leave you, and how valuable the relationship currently is with the partner. You are also likely to factor into such a decision judgments about the value of reducing your own sense of guilt, the morality of your original action, and the morality of the decision to keep it a secret. Finally, there are the costs and benefits that not telling your partner or telling your partner entail, such as the conflicts that may be foregone by not disclosing, and the improvements that might occur from attempting to build from a cleaner slate in the relationship. Collectively, therefore, it is not just the prospects that your decisions produce, but also a set of biases that reflect overweighting of costs (such as the ensuing conflicts), and the morality of one's own actions in the situation.

Instrumental, Relational, and Self-Presentation Goals.   No one calculates expectations for consequences in a social vacuum. According to theory and research, people have three types of general goals they pursue on a routine basis: instrumental, relational, and self-presentation (Canary & Cody, 1994; Clark & Delia, 1979; Newton & Burgoon, 1990). These goals help clarify the kinds of consequences that you seek. (Instrumental, relational, and self-preservation goals were introduced in chapter 2.)

Instrumental goals are objectives for personal advancement. As such, these goals are often concerned with obtaining resources or favors (Roloff & Janiszewski, 1989), and they are task-related. For example, you may need someone to take notes for you, to loan you money to cover a bill, or to babysit your kids so that you can study without distractions. In the United States, instrumental goals appear to be a primary concern (see chapter 7); that is, people often approach others for their own personal gain in order to accomplish a task.

Relational goals are objectives to develop, maintain, or de-escalate relationships (for example, as professional associations, as friendships, as uncommitted romantic interludes). The goal of maintaining a close relationship exerts a powerful influence on your choices of communication strategies to influence another person to obtain an instrumental goal (Sillars, 1980b). Concerns about maintaining relational goals increase the tendency to be solution-oriented and decrease the tendency to use verbally aggressive tactics in conflicts with a partner (Rogan & La France, 2003). On the other hand, if your partner in conflict is a stranger or an acquaintance, your concern for the relationship diminishes in the face of your instrumental objectives (unless, of course, you anticipate seeing this person again and routinely). In addition, when two people disagree about the nature of their relationship, relational goals in conflict can preoccupy the minds of communicators (for example, one person wants to remain friends, whereas the other person wants to terminate the relationship completely).

Self-presentation goals focus on how you want to be seen. Your public image is important to you for many reasons, including the fact that you present your own understanding of who you are in your self-presentation messages. People typically want to be seen as competent and likable (so they smile and make witty comments), although sometimes people want to be seen as weak (to achieve help) or dangerous (so that people respect them) (Canary & Cody, 1994). When a person's presentation of self is questioned, confrontation likely follows. Indeed, some scholars hold that self-presentation goals are most important in anger-provoking situations (Ting-Toomey, 1988) (see also table 5-1).

All three goals operate to some degree during conflict discussions. When you disagree with your supervisor, for example, you want to fulfill an instrumental goal, such as obtaining a particular work schedule or pay raise. You also want to maintain a positive and appropriate work association (relationship goal), and you want to be seen as responsible and fair (self-presentation goal).

To the extent that these three goals remain in operation during conflict, you and your interaction partner may not agree on the issue at stake. Recall the subjective TA. You enter his office to obtain an instrumental objective (grade change); however, the TA may view this confrontation as your doubting his authority over you (a relationship issue) and his ability to grade fairly (a self-presentation and identity issue). So, he responds abruptly by claiming that he did not like your word choice and, not only that, did not make your work a priority, given other "more important obligations." You then would likely become offended at the relational level ("He doesn't care enough about me to read my work") and self-presentation level ("He thinks I'm stupid"), forgetting for the moment your instrumental goal (the grade change—why you went to see the TA in the first place).

Expectancy Value and Goals. In our experience, people roughly calculate expectancy value in terms of their goals. That is, before people enact conflict strategies, they assess the likelihood that those strategies will achieve their salient instrumental, relational, and self-presentation goals. Research indicates that, in the United States, communicators usually value primarily their instrumental goals; relational and self-presentation goals are secondary (Dillard et al., 1989; Sillars, 1980b). In our earlier example, if the instrumental goal to earn a higher grade outweighs relational or self-presentation goals, you might discuss the issue with the TA in a clear manner, becoming more assertive if the initial attempts at achieving the goal have failed ("If you don't raise my grade, I'm taking my case to the department chair").

People shift focus from instrumental goals to other goals in two important ways. First, people seek their instrumental goals within the context of other goals, and these other goals constrain how people pursue their instrumental goals (Dillard et al., 1989). For example, you would not simply be clear with the TA about your desire for a higher grade; you would also likely be careful to show respect (to verify your relationship and to maintain the image of a "nice" person). Second, and perhaps more critically, conflict often escalates not because of the instrumental goal in question, but because the people involved feel that their public identities are at stake. Thus, the focus of conflict shifts to self-presentation issues (Schönbach, 1990). At times you may have felt that someone who disagreed with you did so to increase his or her public image at the expense of yours. For example, men who want to appear strong cannot easily back down from an argument (or they risk the perception of being weak), and the conflict topic itself becomes less relevant than who acts more "manly." Or you may have heard someone explain her rude behavior with the cliché, "It's not the issue, but the principle of the thing that matters." A closer look reveals that the "principle" in question most often concerns the person's self-presentation goal.

In sum, before people respond, they assess the causes of conflict in terms of attributions based on the information directly in front of them and in terms of how particular communicative behaviors would likely work to achieve their goals. Although people may often seek instrumental goals, their relational and self-presentation goals should not be underestimated.

The Dyad as a System That Affects Each Person's Behavior

Emotions are contagious. One person's feelings tend to bring about similar emotions in the other person. In our view, *emotional contagion* is the product of people interacting with each other. That is, your "catching" someone else's emotions during a conflict episode depends on the verbal and nonverbal behaviors of the other person. Consider the following three observations:

1. In several studies, the most powerful predictor of one's conflict behavior was the partner's immediately preceding behavior. For example, Burggraf and Sillars (1987) found that the partner's preceding behavior predicted one's own behavior and "swamped" any influences due to biological sex.

2. People often engage in patterns of interaction that they do *not* want to use. For example, Pearce and Conklin (1979) found that people engage in "unwanted repeated patterns" of behavior. Pearce and Conklin showed that these patterns are unpredictable in part because rules defining these episodes are difficult to discern.

3. Dissatisfied couples are "stuck" in rigid patterns of negative affect, whereas satisfied couples more quickly get out of negative patterns when they do occur (see chapter 4).

From a systems view, conflict (like all other forms of interaction) requires not only that we take into account the individual's internal wiring, but that we focus on how the *dyad* interacts over time (Fisher, 1978). Pragmatically, the individual's thoughts, emotions, and motives may even be irrelevant to understanding the individual's behavior (Watzlawick, Beavin, & Jackson, 1967). In other words, interaction itself matters more than thoughts and plans for interaction.

SYSTEM PROPERTIES

One of the steps in becoming an adult is realizing that interpersonal conflicts are the product of a dyadic system and not only the result of one person's violation of another's rights (Selman, 1980). To understand how people interact in conflict, we should examine properties of this dyadic system (Hocker & Wilmot, 1995).

First, human relationships are open, living systems. By "open" we mean that external sources of information affect the relationship. For example,

Bandura (1973) stressed that people learn aggressive behavior not only from experience, but also from observing and then modeling examples in their family, subculture, and media. Accordingly, external sources of information affect the dyad when each person models others' responses to conflict. Moreover, the influences from the external world continue. For example, observing how your sister and her husband communicate during conflict can affect your proclivity for managing conflict a particular way ("Ridicule is not cool"). A "living system" refers to any living and organized entity with a subsystem, including individuals, groups, subcultures, and nations (Miller & Miller, 1992). In this light, a relationship contains two individuals as subsystems and is itself a subsystem of a larger group (e.g., friends, family network) or organization.

Second, human relationships seek *equifinality*, which is the ability of systems to move through multiple pathways that end up at the same place. You may find that you and your partner may have a variety of discussions and use a variety of tactics of influence regarding where to spend your weekend time, and still end up doing the same thing most weekends. In contrast, *multifinality* refers to the ability of systems to pursue a given pathway, and yet end up in very different places. An argument that you use to influence your partner may work one time, but not another. The recognition that different types of communication sometimes result in the same outcome in a conflict (equifinality), and that despite the attempt to try multiple approaches to conflicts, the same result may occur (multifinality), is one of the most fundamental realizations practiced conflict managers and counselors achieve. Trying everything may not work, and trying anything may work. Competent conflict management requires a realization that there are multiple paths to an appropriate and effective outcome, and likewise, that any given approach may be competent in outcomes in some instances, and not others.

Third, systems often seek *homeostasis*, or a state of relative *equilibrium*. Like a house with a thermostat, the heating and cooling system systematically monitors the temperature and if it gets too high the air conditioning is increased, and if too low, the heating is increased, so as to keep the system within a comfortable range of preferred operation. Robin and Foster (1989), for example, argued that families are "homeostatic systems," and that biological changes to children undergoing adolescence disrupt the system. Accordingly, parents increase their control to compensate for the adolescents' increased demands for personal independence. A converse concept is *entropy*, adapted from one of the most fundamental laws of physics, the second law of thermodynamics. Entropy is the total decay of a system. A living space tends easily toward clutter—but it does not by itself get neater, cleaner, or more organized. Physical systems tend always toward chaos. Open or human systems can engage in activities to counteract entropy, which is what prompts the establishment and function of culture, government, laws, and social traditions such as marriage and family—the control of entropy by developing systems for maintaining homeostasis. So, for example, a rule such as "count to 10 before saying anything when you are angry" may be adopted after realizing how dangerous angry statements may be to preserving the system (in this case, the relationship or family). Physical systems cannot simply adopt such rules to stop forces such as erosion, decomposition, or loss of heat, but open systems can adapt to their environments by resisting the move to chaos.

Fourth, subsystems are interdependent in a way that makes obsolete any ideas of cause and effect. In a relational system, both parties affect each other simultaneously. Selman (1980) has shown that a critical step in an individual's personal development is coming to an understanding of conflict as one way that systems must be adjusted instead of one's rightful response (effect) to an anger-provoking event (cause). In addition, disagreement about how to "punctuate" behaviors in terms of who caused what and who is responding to whom lies "at the root of countless relationship struggles" (Watzlawick et al., 1967, p. 56).

Finally, human relationships are characterized by *nonsummativity*, the idea that the whole is different than the sum of its parts. One cannot dismantle the relationship and discover its "meaningfulness" in the personalities of the two people. The relationship requires both parties and is composed of the connections between them. A simple and common analogy of nonsummativity is obvious to anyone who follows sporting teams. A given football team may have great individual players, and yet still not perform well. Likewise, a given football team may have relatively mediocre individual players, and yet still outperform its constituent roster. Similarly, a decision-making group in an organization may be comprised of members who are all experts in their own areas, and yet the group may not interact very competently due to the particular mix of personalities and behaviors enacted. Another group in that organization, comprised of people who ordinarily might not be considered particularly well-suited to be in the same group, may produce excellent outcomes through their interaction. Systems can be both more, or less, than the sum of their individual parts.

SYSTEM DYSFUNCTIONS

Human relationship systems can be dysfunctional in several ways. We discuss three widely recognized system dysfunctions.

Transactional Redundancy. In systems characterized by transactional redundancy, there is little behavioral variation (Millar & Rogers, 1987). For example, people in dissatisfied relationships engage in negative reciprocations for long periods of time. People can also quickly agree with each other, not allowing partners to present their reasons for believing the way they do; they can avoid each other; or be so vigilant about maintaining a positive tone that any conflict appears extraordinary and "unnatural." People in these systems appear to be caught *inside* their patterns of interaction.

People can also be caught *between* patterns of interaction. That is, dyadic systems may have a routine that exists across episodes (Sillars & Wilmot, 1994). A couple might have the same fight pattern; for example, jealous couples who cannot get over a transgression may reenact a conflict they've had before, conclude it the same way, and then start again a few weeks later. Or a couple may have a pattern in which they have a "big fight" on Tuesday, do not see each other until the weekend, make up by Sunday, and fight again on the next Tuesday.

Dyadic partners may not realize that behaviors are being constrained by the system they themselves perpetuate. Members of the system understand their role relationships to each other by the very action of the system. Behaving as expected lends credence to the behavior and perpetuates the system, making it even more difficult to change. Such affirmation is given despite how undesirable the behavior may be to the partners. In fact, partners can prevent deviations from the system pattern by negatively sanctioning the deviations (Shimanoff, 1980). People outside the system often can see how rigid this interaction is and may attempt to offer advice ("Just avoid getting into a competitive shouting match when you're both stressed"). However, chronic transaction redundancy makes it difficult for parties to adjust readily to new information.

Subsystem Breakdown.   Most people realize that our bodies are composed of complex subsystems that are interdependent such that a breakdown in one subsystem threatens the entire organism. For example, if we do not exercise our muscular subsystem, our respiratory and cardiovascular subsystems become inefficient. In personal relationship breakdowns, one person becomes inefficient, ineffective, or otherwise unable to function as a healthy individual (for example, that person develops physical illness, chronic depression, or drug dependence) (Miller & Miller, 1992). How can the breakdown of individuals reflect a system problem? Several situations come to mind: verbal and physical abuse may harm one of the parties, avoidance may cause one party to feel isolated, or couples may treat each other unfairly such that one person suffers while the other benefits from the inequity. An example of the last point illustrates subsystem breakdown.

Hochschild (1989) reported that some women attempt to fulfill roles both as career women and as traditional housewives; that is, they work fifty hours a week and remain responsible for cooking, cleaning, and caring for children. Many of these women collapse under the strain of too many obligations (also called *role strain),* and they must choose one system over the other (career or family). Hochschild concluded that such role strain results from marriage systems that are *transitional*—that is, a system in which both partners agree that the woman has the right to do whatever she wants as long as she fulfills her obligations at home. This means, of course, that the man does none of the traditionally female chores. Hochschild reported two other, more personally rewarding, couple systems: *traditional,* in which the woman works only at home and does all of the household chores; and *egalitarian,* in which the man accepts the changing roles of women and does his share of the household chores.

Exceeding Roles. Partners may exceed their roles in the relationship to the detriment of both parties and the system. Nervous uncles who advise their sisters about raising nieces and nephews, friends who repeatedly set up other friends on blind dates, and coworkers who desire romantic relationships with colleagues illustrate how the primary relational function might suffer when people act in ways that exceed their roles.

One of the most critical findings regarding this system dysfunction concerns children who intervene in their parents' conflicts (Robin & Foster, 1989; Stafford & Bayer, 1993). Such interventions include giving less affection, less obedience, and more disruptive behavior to the parent who the child perceives as having shown less love to the spouse. In addition, the child may assume a parental function by giving one parent more support than his or her marriage partner does. This *parentification* of the child may give the child a sense of power in the short term, which would be witnessed in one-sided coalitions during conflict, with one spouse and the "parentified" child fighting against the other spouse (Stafford & Bayer, 1993).

Systems have an immediate and ongoing impact on people's interaction behavior. Once established, rigid systems are difficult to change, and couples in such systems may have a difficult time adjusting to new information from external sources. Although people outside the system may clearly see how the system is dysfunctional and provide advice, it can be difficult to follow others' advice for how we should act within our own relationship systems.

Summary

This chapter has described various kinds of proximal influences on conflict behavior. In our view, each of these factors can be salient in any conflict situation. Therefore, it is important for you to know the various kinds of spontaneous reactions that you might have to conflict. These factors act in combination, directly affecting your conflict behavior choices:

1. Anger-provoking events *and* other aversive emotions (such as depression) can bring on anger-like responses.
2. Physiological reactions and initial cognitions point to preferred responses.
3. Higher-ordered thoughts consider causes for conflicts and consequences of behavior in terms of desired goals.
4. Decisions are often based on biased ways of perceiving situations.
5. The relational system constrains behavior.

We stop short of presenting these factors as a causal progression for two reasons. First, we believe that these events happen so quickly that they all represent features of the same transactional process. Second, because people are reflective, they might consider the latter points before getting angry; that is, anger-provoking actions can be a product of attributions about the partner's behavior. People can recollect and "stew" over an event that occurred a long time ago, making themselves angrier and angrier at the different attributions they construct for the event.

Higher-ordered cognitions can moderate initial reactions, such as "fight" or "flight" physiological reactions and response readiness modes, assuming that the reactions do not flood the individual and that the person has the mental capacity to deliberate the causes and appropriate response alternatives to maximize his or her goals. One's personal system of ethics undoubtedly guides higher-ordered thoughts about how to respond to conflict. We want to underscore that people are ultimately responsible for their own behavior, and that our selection of key scientific factors does not excuse individuals from making sound and promotive choices for action. We believe that knowing the processes we are prone to as humans allows us to be more circumspect and competent in our conflict interactions.

The discussion of goals suggests that people assess the extent to which particular conflict strategies will yield positive outcomes in terms of obtaining their primary (instrumental) goal; then they modify their plans on the basis of how much damage the strategy might do to relational and self-presentation goals. Of course, people may operate with other priorities: considering self-presentation goals first and then other goals ("Whether or not I am right, I must look good to others"), or considering the relational consequences of behaving a particular way and then thinking about instrumental objectives won or lost ("I don't care if he wins this argument, I don't want him to be upset with me"). The priorities one places on goals are a personal decision, but regardless of such preferences, the resulting conflict behavior reflects those goals.

Finally, seeing that you are part of a system may help you pause for a moment to determine how the system needs to be changed, perhaps by a concerted effort to negotiate functions that allow both parties to function as individuals. Systems that do not reflect each person's values may require a closer look and modification to reach a more satisfactory steady state. In the next chapter, we discuss selected consequences of the conflict behaviors we have seen in this chapter.

DISCUSSION QUESTIONS

1. Examine table 5-1. On the basis of your experience, rank the top two or three causes of anger. (Recall that some researchers emphasize that anger stems from one cause more than others.) Why did you rank the anger causes the way you did? Compare your ranking to someone else's in class.

2. Recall experiences you have had with the emotions listed in table 5-2 in response to another person's reproachable behavior. Discuss how the person's behavior was reproachable and how you responded in terms of both your feelings and your actions. Do you think that table 5-2 provides an insightful way of looking at the emotional context of conflict? Offer reasons for your assessment.

3. If you had to write a short play entitled "A Day in the Life of My Family's Conflict," how would it read? Discuss the major parts of the script (the acts) and the roles of your family members in the play. What is your role? If you could revise the script so that you liked it better, what would you change?

4. Think about an ongoing problem you have had in a relationship, whether in a parent-child, sibling, friendship, or romantic involvement. Write down the cause for the problem. Discuss the kinds of attributions your cause implies: Is the cause global or specific? Stable or unstable? Internal or external? Selfishly or unselfishly motivated? Blameworthy or praiseworthy? What attributions do you think the other person is making? Discuss how both of you might be right *and* wrong in your explanations.

5. Examine the following scenarios. Discuss the kinds of goals being pursued and whether confronting the person or avoiding the person (for example, by changing the topic) would more likely lead to desired consequences. You may want to act out these situations in class.

   a. You need your 14-year-old daughter to help clean the house for a family holiday party. Your daughter, whose only weekly chore is to clean her bedroom, gets upset and tells you she is unfairly treated.

   b. Your brother is upset with you because he wants to borrow money that you simply do not have. He tells you that he doesn't believe you, and he takes it personally that you do not want to help him.

   c. A coworker constantly likes to talk about herself. Whenever you relate a story, she seems to need to offer a better (and longer) one about herself. You tell her you got to work late because of a huge traffic problem. She replies, "That's nothing—I had to drive through much worse conditions this morning."

6. Do you believe that relational systems constrain behavior more powerfully than do individual response tendencies or attributions? Provide reasons for your view. If your instructor is willing, you might use this question to have a timed, in-class debate between two groups, each group representing one view (system versus individual).

chapter 6

CONFLICT OUTCOMES

CHAPTER OUTLINE

Proximal Consequences
    Attributions
    Emotions
    Judgments of Competence
    Communication Satisfaction
    Face Threat and Restoration
    Physical Health
    The Cumulative Nature of Proximal Consequences
Distal Consequences
    Relationship (Dis)Satisfaction and (In)Stability
    Effects of the Demand-Withdraw Pattern
    Positive Consequences Involve More Than Simply Avoiding Negative
      Behaviors
    Conflict Combines with Positivity to Predict Divorce
Summary
Discussion Questions

The model we presented in chapter 2 (see figure 2-2) showed two types of consequences associated with interpersonal conflict, proximal and distal. Proximal outcomes are the immediate consequences of a conflict interaction. Such consequences include the thoughts and feelings that occur during and shortly after a conflict interaction. We can usually describe how a conflict episode has affected us in the short term.

Distal consequences are long-term effects of conflict. In particular, the management of conflict episodes that recur over time between two people can affect the durability and climate of their relationship, as well as their individual well-being. Proximal outcomes are more salient to us because they occur in proximity to the conflict episode. Our awareness of distal consequences, in contrast, is somewhat dim because the effects are delayed and (usually) somewhat removed from specific occurrences of conflict. We will first discuss proximal consequences because they can accumulate over time to produce distal ones.

Proximal Consequences

ATTRIBUTIONS

In chapter 5 we described how attributions about behavior directly can shape the course of conflict. Actually, the connection between making attributions and enacting conflict behavior is reciprocal (Gottman, 1994). Attributions both precede and result from conflict actions. In fact, most research on attributions and communication is correlational, making it difficult to specify which comes first—attributions or communication. Since conflict episodes unfold in time, both attributions and communication behaviors have the opportunity to affect each other.

The attributions you make are integral to your interpretation of a conflict situation, and they consequently influence how you behave during conflict. As discussed in chapter 5, when you infer that the cause of another person's behavior is global, stable, internal, and that the behavior is blameworthy, intentional, and selfishly motivated, then you are more inclined to enact distributive conflict behaviors (e.g., Fincham & Bradbury, 1992; Sillars, 1980a, 1980b). At the same time, the likelihood of making these negative attributions is greater when the person you disagree with engages in distributive behaviors. So the association between negative attributions and distributive behavior during conflict is actually reciprocal. Negative attributions both engender and result from distributive behaviors.

As the intensity of conflict increases, attributions become more biased and more polarized (Sillars, 1981). With increasingly defensive behavior, conflict escalates and attributions become more rigidly negative and critical regarding others. Negative behaviors lead to negative attributions, which create further negative behavior, which leads to more negative attributions, and so on.

Whatever attributions we make, they contribute to our understanding of a conflict episode. In this sense, attributions are cognitive outcomes. Depending on the intensity and importance of the conflict, these attributional outcomes may be relatively strong or weak, enduring or fleeting. Enduring attributional outcomes will more likely surface automatically as proximal influences in the next episode of conflict between two parties. If at the end of a conflict discussion, Ken perceives Emma's behavior as internally motivated and malevolent, then Ken may anticipate that Emma's behavior in their next conflict also will be internal and malevolent. The attributions at time 1 (a proximal outcome) emerge to "frame" the interpretation of later conflict at time 2 (as proximal influence). Research indicates that as individuals become less satisfied in a relationship, attributions become more rigid and biased in a negative direction (Baucom, Sayers, & Duhe, 1989). Both positive and negative behaviors are interpreted in a skeptical way.

For example, one study (Sanford, 2006) found that people's attributions for the conflict affected their own conflict behavior within the same day as well as two weeks later. Importantly, Sanford found that a person's attributions affected that person's communication behavior within a given sequence. In addition, a person's attributions predicted their partners' general behavior over time. This study confirms that one outcome of conflict concerns how one's own thoughts mostly affect one's own behavior, with the possibility that such behaviors then affect how one's partner behaves—either in a positive or negative way. Sanford concluded that if people could change their expectations and attributions about their partners' behaviors, then they could change their own conflict communication for the better.

EMOTIONS

The role of emotions in conflict runs parallel to the role of attributions. Hence, as with attributions, emotions are as much consequence as they are antecedent to a conflict episode. Emotions provide a context for performing and interpreting behavior. At the same time, however, the conflict behaviors enacted during an episode of conflict exert a potent influence on the nature and intensity of your feelings.

The feelings we experience during and after a conflict are themselves emotional consequences. A disagreement may cause you to feel anxiety, anger, hurt, frustration, relief, sadness, excitement, guilt, and many other emotions. The intensity, complexity, and duration of your feelings in the aftermath of a conflict episode depend (among other things) on the intensity and importance of the conflict itself, and the overall climate of your relationship. When the feelings endure, particularly if they are negative, they probably will emerge in subsequent conflicts as part of the proximal context.

A person's attributional and emotional outcomes stem, in part, from the behavior of the partner. At the same time, one's behavior stimulates the attributions and feelings held by the partner. This interdependent association between one person's thoughts and feelings and another person's behavior is depicted in figure 6-1.

Suppose Jeff confronts Steve in a belligerent and blaming way. Steve is likely to see Jeff's behavior as unreasonable and perhaps irrational, and Steve probably feels hurt, maybe a bit angry. These thoughts and feelings may lead Steve to respond to Jeff in a defensive and aggressive manner. Steve's behavior is then interpreted by Jeff as being selfish, intentional, blameworthy, and internally caused, which leads Jeff to become angry. Jeff's thoughts and feelings about Steve's behavior may lead Jeff to respond to Steve in an increas-

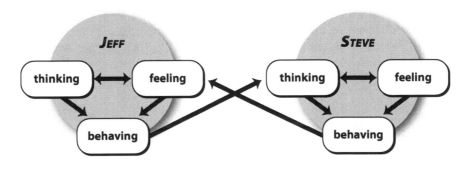

Figure 6-1 **The interconnectedness between one person's behavior and another's cognitions and emotions.**

ingly defensive and aggressive manner. And so it goes, a negative escalating spiral of conflict ensues, fueled by interlocking feelings and thoughts that lead to behaviors in one person, that in turn, produce feelings and thoughts in the other person, which affect the other person's behavior, and so on.

JUDGMENTS OF COMPETENCE

Although we are not always mindful of it, we make judgments about our own communication competence and the communication competence of others with whom we interact. In chapter 2 we argued that assessments of competence are particularly relevant to situations involving conflict. It is reasonable to assume that the immediate outcomes of conflict are tied to the quality of communication.

Two essential criteria for assessing communication competence, as we noted earlier, are *effectiveness* and *appropriateness*. Research consistently demonstrates that conflict communication strategies correlate with judgments of communication effectiveness and appropriateness, as well as overall, global perceptions of communication competence. In general, integrative conflict behaviors are seen as relatively more effective, appropriate, and hence competent, compared to distributive behaviors (Canary & Cupach, 1988; Canary & Spitzberg, 1987, 1989).

Effectiveness. Sometimes we initiate conflict when there is no clear goal, or we are only dimly aware of any goal. We all have created trivial disagreements simply because we are in a grumpy, disagreeable mood. We may simply need to cathart. Most of the time, however, the desire to achieve our own goals motivates us to initiate and to escalate conflict. In other words, people tend to fight for issues important to them, including their salient goals and values, more so than for trivial concerns (e.g., arguing about how many inches of snow fell last night).

Communication is judged to be effective when individuals fulfill their objectives and achieve their goals. If the outcome of an argument between Harry and Sally shows that Harry wins and Sally loses, we might say that Harry was effective and Sally was ineffective. Since each person has multiple goals, however, the issue of effectiveness can be complicated. Harry may be effective at achieving his instrumental goal with Sally (he got his way in an argument about how they should arrange the furniture in their apartment), but he may be totally ineffective at promoting the desired impression that he is a fair and sensitive partner. Indeed, Harry may "win the battle" by getting his way in this instance, but "lose the war" when Sally dumps him for a more compatible partner.

Since goals can be transactive and change during a conflict, the judgment of effectiveness may not always be obvious (as we indicated in chapter 5). Read box 6-1 for an example of how it is possible to be effective, even when your original goal is not fulfilled.

Box 6-1   Effectiveness Takes into Account All of Your Goals

June was an industrious and productive employee for eight years in the management information systems division of a large company. Frustrated with the manner in which policies were being implemented in her work division, June went to complain to her supervisor. She wanted to change certain procedures.

During their discussion, June learned how some of her ideas simply were inconsistent with the company philosophy, and were not likely to meet with the approval of higher management. June also discovered, however, that she could rotate into a different division of the company where she would be able to advance into a management position much more quickly than in her current division. June's supervisor, learning of June's dissatisfaction, was even willing to facilitate the transfer.

June's confrontation with her supervisor did not (at least in the short term) result in any policy changes. So June was ineffective if judged by her initial goal. It did alert June to desirable work opportunities of which she was unaware. June actually got more out of the confrontation with her supervisor than she initially imagined. Even though she did not anticipate the nature of the outcome of the discussion with her supervisor, she certainly felt that she was effective.

As it turns out, June's supervisor thought that her own conflict management behavior was effective too. She knew that June was a committed employee who possessed management potential. She was happy to work out a deal to keep June happy, even though she disagreed with some of her ideas about policy. June's manager felt that she was successful in facilitating the career development of a valued employee, which was very good for the company (despite the fact that she was losing the employee to another division).

You occupy the best position to judge your own effectiveness. You implicitly and explicitly know what your goals are, both prospective and transactive, and therefore serve as the most educated judge of the extent to which you achieved your various goals. But in order to be communicatively competent, as we contended in chapter 2, then you must not only be effective, but you must also be appropriate in the manner in which you pursue your goals. Lakey and Canary (2002) found that showing you are sensitive to the other person's goals during conflict increases the extent to which the other person perceives you as appropriate and effective.

Appropriateness. Appropriate communication meets your expectations for what behavior properly fits a given situation. Just as goals are used to determine effectiveness, *rules serve as our benchmarks for determining appropriateness.* Rules indicate what behaviors should or should not be performed in various situations. Although you are in the best position to assess the effectiveness of your own behavior, the opinions of others are probably more relevant when it comes to judging your appropriateness.

Rules vary in their level of *abstractness* or "crystallization" (Shimanoff, 1980). A rule of friendship, for example, might be that friends are loyal to one another. "Loyalty" is rather general, so individuals' ideas about what constitutes loyalty, and what constitutes an act of disloyalty, can be rather diverse. In comparison, the rule that you should not interrupt someone while they are speaking is more concrete and specific. Most people would agree on what constitutes an interruption; they may disagree on how important the rule is, however.

As we indicated previously, the violation of rules constitutes a source of interpersonal conflict. Indeed, the violation of a serious rule, or repeated violation of important rules, can be grounds for the termination of a friendship or romantic relationship (e.g., Argyle & Henderson, 1984; Baxter, 1986).

Where do rules originate? We are all familiar with social rules of etiquette and politeness (e.g., the advice given by Miss Manners), though by no means do people enjoy consensus regarding these rules. Social rules are heavily influenced by our culture, and operate most strongly in public settings or when communicating with nonintimate others. In more intimate relationships, partners determine for themselves the rules for appropriate behavior between them. That is, they develop their own rules regarding preferred or prohibited behaviors in the context of the relationship.

Unlike laws that officially stipulate regulations in writing, rules implicitly prescribe and proscribe behavior. We infer rules and take them for granted. In fact, we usually recognize a rule only after perceiving its violation and then wish to correct the transgression.

When one person directly accuses another of breaking a rule, conflict discussions often focus specifically on the nature of the rule and whether or not it was broken. Newell and Stutman (1988) call these discussions *social confrontation episodes*, and these researchers identified six questions that communicators might address in such episodes (p. 274). They are:

1. Is the implied rule mutually accepted as legitimate?

2. Is this a special situation?

3. If invoked, is the superseding rule mutually accepted as legitimate?

4. Did the accused actually perform the behavior in question?

5. Does the behavior constitute a violation of the rule?

6. Does the accused accept responsibility for the behavior?

People who discuss these questions contribute to the establishment and clarification of rules. Communicators use these discussions to negotiate mutual acceptance of rules, as well as when they apply, their exceptions, and their "meaning."

Assessments of conflict behavior appropriateness not only figure prominently in conflict discussions; they also represent proximal conflict outcomes. In other words, judgments of communication competence during conflict discussions are tied to the perceived appropriateness of conflict communication.

Among the rules that govern communication, there are rules regarding how to deal with conflict in particular. Table 6-1 illustrates some conflict rules commonly found in marital relationships (Jones & Gallois, 1989). Of course,

---

Table 6-1   Common Conflict Rules in Marital Relationships

Consideration
• Don't belittle, humiliate, or use character-degrading words about the other person.
• Don't dismiss the other person's issue as unimportant.
• Don't blame the other person unfairly or make unfair accusations.

Rationality
• Shouldn't get angry.
• Don't raise voice.
• Shouldn't be aggressive or lose your temper.

Self-Expression
• Should keep to the point and not get involved in other issues.
• Should get to the point quickly.
• Be honest and say what is on your mind.

Conflict Resolution
• Explore alternatives.
• Should make joint decisions.
• Should explain reasons for your point of view.

Positivity
• Should try to relieve the tension in arguments (e.g., make appropriate jokes, laugh together).
• Should use receptive body language (e.g., open body position).
• Should look at each other.

Source: From Jones and Gallois (1989).

---

not all marital partners subscribe to these rules. Relational partners negotiate rules to fit their particular relationship (Honeycutt et al., 1993). Some partners, for example, develop a norm for avoiding overt confrontation as much as possible. Others might share a rule that each person should honestly express anger during disagreements. This would weaken the "force" of rationality rules. Compatibility depends not so much on which rules each partner wishes to enforce, but rather on the extent to which partners share the rules. So if June's boss (box 6-1) believed that complaints about policies should be offered in writing, then June might never have learned about other advancement opportunities. But June and her boss shared the same rules and therefore perceived the management of the conflict to be appropriate, as well as effective.

COMMUNICATION SATISFACTION

Judgments of communication effectiveness and appropriateness represent cognitive proximal outcomes associated with communication competence. Concurrently, perceived communication competence associates with one's affective response of communication satisfaction. In particular, competent communication leaves communicators feeling satisfied with the process of interaction (Spitzberg & Cupach, 1984; Spitzberg & Hecht, 1984).

Research shows that behaviors generally perceived to be competent are also associated with communication satisfaction. In particular, your partner's use of integrative and supportive conflict behaviors is positively associated with your own communication satisfaction (Canary & Cupach, 1988; Canary & Spitzberg, 1987, 1990; Newton & Burgoon, 1990) as well as satisfaction with the outcome of the conflict (Sillars, 1980a). Emotional validation and problem-solving facilitation by the partner likewise positively associate with conflict interaction satisfaction (Haefner, Notarius, & Pellegrini, 1991). Moreover, responsiveness and lack of criticism positively affect satisfaction with the outcome of conflict discussions (Koren, Carlton, & Shaw, 1980).

FACE THREAT AND RESTORATION

One motivation that underlies all social interaction concerns the desire of communicators to have their identities confirmed. In other words, when you interact with others, there is a tacit agreement that you respect each other's face (Goffman, 1967). "Face" is the part of your identity that you present during interaction and expect that it will be accepted by others. This is part of the ever-present self-presentation goal we discussed in the last chapter.

Normally, face maintenance, or the presentation and confirmation of self, is taken for granted. We assume others will accept who we are (that is, who we present ourselves as), and others assume we will support who they are. The idea is that we can at least show respect for each other as persons, whether or not we agree with each other's ideas or behaviors. We maintain our own dignity by protecting our own face, and we show consideration when we protect the faces of others. Indeed, the ability to maintain face during an interaction and to successfully repair face when it has been threatened is a fundamental attribute of appropriate communication. Communication competence entails successful facework (Cupach & Metts, 1994; Oetzel & Ting-Toomey, 2003; Weinstein, 1969; Wiemann, 1977).

Conflict, by its very nature, creates circumstances that are inherently face threatening. First, when someone confronts you, they constrain your freedom by making you respond in some way to the issue, even if you prefer not to engage in conflict. Second, when someone disagrees with you or presents you with a complaint, you may take it as personal criticism. Disagreeing with your idea translates into an indirect disagreement with *you*. If the idea holds importance for you and if the person disagreeing is important to you, you may feel personally challenged. If someone complains about your behavior, you may feel that they disapprove of you. The experience of such disapproval threatens your face (Cupach, 2007). Of course, the manner of complaining or disagreeing has much to do with the degree of face threat we perceive. If your roommate constructively complains that you have not pulled your weight in cleaning up the apartment for an upcoming party, you might perceive the gripe as legitimate and not take it personally. However, if your roommate disdainfully refers to your "laziness" about cleaning up, you would probably feel unfairly attacked (Cupach & Carson, 2002).

Box 6-2 Events That Threaten Face	
You Can Threaten Your Own Face By:	**You Can Threaten Another's Face By:**
Losing an argument	Making personal criticisms
Losing your temper	Making them feel stupid or incompetent
Seeking forgiveness	Insulting or ridiculing them
Getting caught in a lie	Invading their privacy
Breaking a promise	Blaming them for causing a problem
Making a mistake	Pressuring them to do things they
Looking foolish or inept	don't want to do
Being disloyal	Devaluing your relationship with them
	Being disloyal

What other things can you think of that either create conflict or occur during a conflict discussion that can be face threatening?

Third, when conflict escalates in intensity, people tend to become closed-minded and defensive. Negative behaviors such as yelling, demanding, threatening, being rude and sarcastic, and making hurtful put-downs occur more frequently. Naturally, these behaviors can be employed intentionally to threaten face. Whether or not face threat is intended, as recipients we tend to perceive these negative behaviors as face threatening. In general, belligerent, antagonistic, and defensive behaviors undermine the expression and perception of respect and lead to feelings of contempt. Just as some people enact face-threatening behaviors more than others (i.e., they routinely try to bully and show disrespect), some people take disagreements more personally, even when confronted gently and politely (see chapter 4).

According to Goffman (1967), each of us is emotionally attached to our face; so when it is threatened, we must defend it. When face loss occurs, we usually attempt to restore or repair the damage done to face. Communication designed to prevent or counteract threats to face is called *facework* (Goffman, 1967; Tracy, 1990). We save face by couching potentially face-threatening behaviors in polite language (Brown & Levinson, 1987) and a respectful tone. If part of your performance appraisal includes criticism about the way you perform a certain task, your boss can minimize the face threat by praising your hard effort and by expressing understanding that you are new to the task (Carson & Cupach, 2000).

We also save face by actively repairing the damage done to face. If I insult you, I obviously have threatened your face. If I want to make up for the damage, I should sincerely apologize. If I get caught violating a mutually agreed upon rule, I should offer a credible explanation and promise not to repeat the inappropriate behavior. If we have a heated disagreement about what was said during a conversation a week ago, and it turns out I am wrong, I should admit it.

Saving face facilitates the management of conflict. Face threats complicate conflict and make the successful management of conflict more difficult. When someone threatens your face, you can interpret the threat very personally and respond defensively. Conflict gets bogged down and individuals become distracted when they feel compelled to defend their own faces instead of discussing the substantive issue of disagreement. When people maintain face and when parties to conflict remedy face threats with facework, individuals feel less threatened and more efficiently attend to resolving substantive issues. Face saving also enables partners to handle future conflicts more effectively. Conflicts are less likely to turn into destructive, negative cycles when individuals feel they can disagree without the conflict becoming personal and attack-oriented (Oetzel & Ting-Toomey, 2003).

Remember that face maintenance is a two-way street. It is a cooperative venture whereby each person depends on the other for face support. We must save each other's face if we are to save our own. When others apologize sincerely, they save your face at the expense of their own. In turn, your graceful and ungrudging forgiveness saves your partner's face. If one admits that he or she was wrong about a disputed fact, his or her admission helps save your face.

PHYSICAL HEALTH

Obviously conflict can harm your physical health if it escalates into violence. But can heated discussions and verbally aggressive debates adversely affect your physical well-being? We don't have a definitive answer to this question yet. But preliminary evidence suggests that some people may be affected physically by their conflict interactions.

In chapter 5 we discussed how an episode of conflict can be associated with anxiety and negative feelings such as anger, as well as physiological arousal. But what are the consequences of the arousal that can accompany conflict, particularly intense, escalated episodes? Research on the conflict interactions among newlyweds by Kiecolt-Glaser and colleagues (1993) showed that negative conflict behavior produced adverse effects on individuals' blood pressure and immune systems. The immune system changes were still apparent a full day after the conflict. Research also indicated that negative conflict may alter various hormone levels in the body (Malarkey, Kiecolt-Glaser, Perl, & Glaser, 1994). Clearly, there are potential proximal physical effects associated with conflict and its management.

Researchers have increasingly linked conflict to physical health. They show that competitive communication and anger can affect three important physical systems—the endocrine system, the cardiovascular system, and the immune system (Robles & Kiecolt-Glaser, 2003). Because we focus in this book on the relational implications of conflict management, we advise the reader interested in the links between interpersonal conflict and health outcomes to see the following reviews: Kiecolt-Glaser, McGuire, Robles, and Glaser (2003); Kiecolt-Glaser and Newton (2001); Robles and Kiecolt-Glaser (2003). Such effects are both short- and long-term, and they show that the way in which people manage conflict can help them live stronger and longer *or* can deteriorate their bodies and lead to early death.

THE CUMULATIVE NATURE OF PROXIMAL CONSEQUENCES

When negative behaviors become routine and repeated during conflict interactions with a certain individual, negative attributions and negative sentiments regarding that person may become habitual. The repeated and cumulative effect of proximal consequences can create proximal influences for future conflict episodes. These proximal influences may facilitate or undermine conflict management.

In chapter 2 we cited research to support the idea that perceptions of competence *mediate* the connection between conflict communication and distal relational features. In other words, conflict communication eventually affects distal relational outcomes by first influencing proximal outcomes. When a partner uses integrative conflict strategies, you tend to perceive that partner as communicatively competent and you feel satisfied with the conflict communication. It is these outcomes—your feeling of satisfaction and your judgment of the partner's competence—that translate over time into constructive relational qualities such as trust, mutuality of control, intimacy, and relational satisfaction (Canary & Cupach, 1988; Canary & Spitzberg, 1987, 1990; Lakey & Canary, 2002). So competent conflict management is constructive in the sense that it fosters relational growth and solidarity.

Similarly, when your partner uses distributive strategies, you tend to perceive the partner as being *less* communicatively competent and you feel *less* satisfied with the interaction. These negative proximal outcomes, in turn, undermine positive relational qualities over time.

Research on attributions in marital relationships also supports the mediational role of episodic or proximal outcomes (Epstein, Pretzer, & Fleming, 1987). Again, the attributions that spouses make regarding each other's behavior act as filters through which behaviors eventually influence marital satisfaction. When negative conflict behaviors are perceived to be due to the partner's malicious intent, for example, relational satisfaction diminishes.

Attributions, emotions, and judgments of competence and satisfaction of individual episodes of conflict translate into longer-term consequences that are somewhat removed from any specific instance of conflict, but are nevertheless significant. These distal consequences are considered in the next section.

Distal Consequences

RELATIONSHIP (DIS)SATISFACTION AND (IN)STABILITY

Perhaps the most robust generalization in the conflict literature is that frequent negativity in conflicts destroys relationships (e.g., McGonagle, Kessler, & Gotlib, 1993). In chapter 4 we discussed some of the copious research that distinguishes distressed from nondistressed marital couples.

The research consistently shows that, compared to satisfied couples, dissatisfied couples:

1. *engage in negative behaviors more frequently* (e.g., threats, demands, coercion, hostility, criticisms, put-downs, defensiveness, sarcasm, contempt) (Birchler & Webb, 1977; Gottman, 1979, 1994; Koren et al., 1980; Raush, Barry, Hertel, & Swain, 1974);

2. *rely on positive behaviors less frequently* (e.g., agreement, approval, humor) (Gottman & Levenson, 1992; Raush, Barry, Hertel, & Swain, 1974);

3. *engage in a smaller proportion of positive/negative behaviors, with the positive/negative ratios becoming smaller as the conversation continues* (Billings, 1979; Gottman, 1994);

4. *exhibit more frequent and lengthier patterns of negative reciprocation* (e.g., complain-complain, complain-defend, attack-attack, defend-attack) (Alberts, 1988; Billings, 1979; Gottman, 1979; Margolin & Wampold, 1981; Ting-Toomey, 1983); and

5. *entertain negative attributions about the partner's behavior* (e.g., attribute behavior to global, internal, and stable causes, and blame marital difficulties on the partner's selfishly motivated behavior) (Baucom et al., 1989; Fincham, Beach, & Nelson, 1987; Fincham et al., 1990).

In many of these studies it is difficult to separate causes and effects. Are unhappy couples more likely to engage in negative behaviors and thoughts because of their unhappiness (as we argued in chapter 4), or do the negative behaviors and thoughts lead to unhappiness? The answer, of course, is both. Relational climate and behaviors reciprocally influence each other over time.

Longitudinal research of married couples shows that negative behaviors during conflict discussions and negative attributions about the partner's behavior can predict subsequent dissatisfaction a year or more later (e.g., Fincham & Bradbury, 1987; Gottman & Krokoff, 1989). Moreover, the behaviors and cognitions that lead to dissatisfaction predict the likelihood of eventual marital separation and divorce (Gottman, 1994; McGonagle et al., 1993).

Although we can list many behaviors that can be considered negative, the extensive research on marital interactions by Gottman (1994) and his colleagues has identified four especially problematic types of behavior. When enacted frequently in a relationship, these behaviors undermine the climate of the relationship and contribute to its demise. Hence, Gottman refers to these behaviors—*criticism, contempt, defensiveness,* and *stonewalling*—as the "Four Horsemen of the Apocalypse." These four negative behaviors form a negative cascade, with one leading to the next, in relationships that are on a destructive path. Criticisms can eventually lead to contempt, which produces defensiveness, which invites stonewalling.

Criticism involves more than simply complaining. Rather than describing disagreeable behavior, criticism involves attacking the character or personality of an individual. This manner of complaining threatens the face of the recipient of the criticism. If Ray doesn't like Sarah's new green dress, he can criticize her poor taste or tell her she "looks lousy" in the dress. Sarah would likely take the complaint personally if Ray presented it in either of these ways. Alternatively, Ray could offer the less critical complaint that he prefers the red dress, or that he was really hoping she would wear the red dress tonight.

Contempt represents the flip side of respect. As such, exhibiting contempt for another shows a blatant disregard for that person's face. Insults, put-downs, sarcasm, mockery, derision, and the like illustrate various ways of showing contempt.

As indicated in the previous chapter, *defensiveness* represents one's attempt to protect oneself. You behave defensively when you feel victimized or unfairly attacked. People show defensiveness in numerous ways, among them, denying responsibility, making excuses, answering one complaint with another, and whining. Note the defensiveness of both Taylor and Joe in the following example. Each evades responsibility for the problem; each shows contempt, leading the other to be defensive:

> *Joe:* You forgot to call up the Smiths to tell them we weren't coming for dinner. Now we look like real jerks! How can you be so irresponsible?
>
> *Taylor:* You were supposed to call the Smiths, not me!
>
> *Joe:* So you think that falsely blaming me gets you off the hook?
>
> *Taylor:* You're the one doing the false blaming. We talked about this last week—it was your job to call.
>
> *Joe:* I should have called because I knew you would forget. Like you always do.
>
> *Taylor:* That's malarkey! *I* wouldn't forget something like that.
>
> *Joe:* Liar!

Stonewalling occurs when one completely withdraws during a conflict discussion. The stonewaller offers no feedback whatsoever, just cold silence and lack of expression. Stonewallers will claim that their behavior represents a neutral state. But as Gottman (1994) says, stonewalling conveys distance, smugness, and disapproval.

Of course, any of us, on one or another occasion of conflict, may engage in one or more of these behaviors. Yes, even happy and stable marital couples sometimes engage in negative behaviors. Two factors make these behaviors corrosive to a relationship: (1) when the behaviors become habitual, that is, they are more common than uncommon; and (2) when the occurrence of negative behaviors is grossly disproportionate to positive behaviors. As Gottman's (1994) research demonstrates, satisfied couples balance negative behaviors with positive ones, regardless of the couple's style of managing conflict. In satisfied couples, the ratio of positive to negative behaviors is roughly 5:1. The occurrence of positive and negative behaviors over time in a distressed relationship is closer to a 1:1 ratio.

EFFECTS OF THE DEMAND-WITHDRAW PATTERN

Earlier we referred to the "demand-withdraw" pattern (chapter 3). In recent years, the demand-withdraw sequence has received much attention, in part because it clearly affects relationships and the people in them. This pattern tends to occur between partners who are dissatisfied with one another. And most scholars concur that increasing demands that are met by the partner's avoidance negatively affect both parties' relational quality.

In close relationships, women tend to take on the role of the person wanting change (e.g., Christensen & Heavey, 1990). For example, women tend to perform the vast majority of household chores and sometimes need more help, so they approach their husbands and are often quite assertive about their helping (Gottman & Carrere, 1994). Husbands tend to avoid such talk (e.g., "Honey, it's the weekend—can't we discuss this later?" or "Honey, I just got home from work and need some down time"). However, men also engage in demand behavior if they want to change the status quo (e.g., Caughlin & Vangelisti, 1999; Christensen & Heavey, 1990).

Still, the tendency is for women to demand change and men to withdraw, and these demand and withdraw roles occur most often in dissatisfied couples (Eldridge, Sevier, Jones, Atkins, & Christensen, 2007). Eldridge and colleagues found that highly dissatisfied couples and moderately dissatisfied couples engaged in significantly more wife-demand/husband-withdraw behavior than did satisfied married people. However, Eldridge et al. found that when the husband wanted change, there was no significant gender difference—that is, both men and women engaged in demanding behavior when the husband sought change in the status quo. One reason why both partners engage in similar demanding behavior is that they reciprocate, or mirror, one another's behavior (Caughlin & Vangelisti, 2000). Interestingly, however, Eldridge et al. also found that, among highly dissatisfied couples, wives engaged in more demanding behavior even when the issue discussed was the *husband's* desire to change.

You probably have had a relationship with someone who does not do their fair share of the work—whether that person is/was a roommate, a romantic partner, sibling, or coworker. Thoughts about the unfairness of the situation can drive a person crazy, which would lead them to engage in demands for change. Engaging in such demands can affect you afterward. Malis and Roloff (2006), for example, found that people who initiated a confrontation with a partner self-reported that after the confrontation they had more unexpected intrusive thoughts (e.g., thinking about the conflict when they were thinking about other issues), more hyperarousal, and fewer activities when compared to their partners. Malis and Roloff also discovered that the demand-withdraw pattern affected the person who withdraws—they obviously engage in more avoidance of the partner and their stress about the situation increased.

Although the above paragraphs might suggest that not demanding anything from your partner but instead avoiding your partner might be a better strategy, early and recent research indicates that *a lack of conflict discussion can ruin a relationship* (e.g., Raush et al., 1974). Afifi, McManus, Steuber, and Coho (2009) summarized the literature regarding chronic avoidance accordingly:

> In sum, it is probable that the association between verbal conflict avoidance and dissatisfaction is bidirectional. That is, when people avoid talking about conflict inducing topics, it makes them dissatisfied in their relationships. At the same time, when people are dissatisfied with their relationships, they likely engage in greater avoidance with their partner. The emotional wedge that is created by the avoidance probably fosters even greater dissatisfaction. (p. 360)

The key to avoidance and being direct no doubt involves perceptions of relative power and other perceived constraints (e.g., Solomon & Samp, 1998). Also, people have other reasons for avoidance, for example, to prevent damage to the relationship or to avoid a conflict (Caughlin & Afifi, 2004). However, continual avoidance prevents one from improving his or her lot in life and from changing the partner's annoying behaviors, among other problems (for a review, see Afifi, Caughlin, & Afifi, 2007). Yet continual demands would likely push the partner into an avoidant reactionary mode, which could make one even less satisfied with the relationship because perceptions of partner avoidance are even more dissatisfying than one's own avoidance (Caughlin & Golish, 2002). Accordingly, we believe that being direct but cooperative (i.e., integrative) with one's partner often remains the best long-term strategic choice for managing conflict.

POSITIVE CONSEQUENCES INVOLVE MORE THAN SIMPLY AVOIDING NEGATIVE BEHAVIORS

Our emphasis so far regarding distal consequences has been on negative behaviors and patterns. But it would be misleading to conclude that competent conflict management merely forestalls negative distal outcomes. Indeed, *constructive conflict management over time is constructive for relationships.* Just as incompetent conflict management leads to relationship dissatisfaction and instability, competent conflict management promotes relational satisfaction and stability. First, conflict serves as the impetus to solving problems. When conflict management is competent, problems are more clearly identified and more often resolved, which prevents smaller disagreements from turning into larger, more serious disputes. Since problems are resolved more often than not, you feel happier. Second, conflict energizes relationships. Boredom and predictability in the extreme can actually destabilize intimate bonds. Conflict affords stimulation and challenge, thereby producing needed novelty and vitality for relational partners. Third, being able to overcome disagreements produces a feeling of mutual accomplishment, and strengthens the connections between relational partners. The mutuality of the process and the positivity of the outcomes associated with competent conflict foster interpersonal solidarity. Finally, conflict offers opportunities for personal exploration, understanding, and growth. Deutsch (1973) indicates that "conflict is often part of the process of testing and assessing oneself and, as such, may be highly enjoyable as one experiences the pleasure of the full and active use of one's capacities" (p. 9). Thus, competent conflict contributes to an individual's mental hygiene, which is likely to facilitate one's competence as a relational partner as well.

CONFLICT COMBINES WITH POSITIVITY TO PREDICT DIVORCE

Although we have stressed the outcomes of conflict on relational satisfaction, we must note here that conflict combines with other forms of communication behavior to predict whether or not a couple remains satisfied and/or together. Recent research suggests that negative conflict and positive messages predict whether married partners stay together. Even couples in their first year of marriage must balance their negative conflict statements with supportive and positive statements to affect relational satisfaction negatively (Pasch & Bradbury, 1998). Recall that satisfied couples engage in a ratio of about five positive comments for every negative comment, whereas dissatisfied couples "balance" each negative comment with only one positive comment (Gottman, 1994).

Moreover, the timing of divorce is predicted differently by negative comments and positive communication. For instance, Gottman and Levenson (2000) examined various factors that predicted divorce during the first seven years of marriage and during the subsequent seven years of marriage. They found being direct and negative with one's partner during conflict primarily predicted divorce the first seven years of marriage. After seven years, however, a *lack* of affection and other positive expressions of emotion were the more powerful predictors of divorce. These authors concluded, "Intense marital conflict likely makes it difficult to stay in the marriage for long, but its absence makes marriage somewhat more acceptable. Nonetheless, the absence of positive affect eventually takes its toll" (p. 743). In a similar manner, Caughlin and Huston (2006) presented evidence that two factors predict divorce—affection and antagonism. Couples who show each other much affection but little antagonism tend to remain stable. However, couples who display much antagonism and little affection tend to divorce within two years. As with Gottman and Levenson's research, couples who had declines in affection and only moderate conflict either divorced after seven years or reported that they were in unhappy marriages (Caughlin & Huston, 2006). In sum, the key to understanding how conflict affects your personal relationships is linked to how much you express positive emotion and affection toward each other, both verbally and nonverbally. In our final chapter, we will provide other guidelines for managing conflict in a competent manner.

Summary

Many potential consequences to conflict exist. This chapter discussed only some of the more important ones. It turns out that some of the same factors that affect how we conduct ourselves during conflict, namely attributions and emotions, also emerge as proximal conflict outcomes. Not surprisingly, positive feelings and relationship-enhancing attributions are more likely (1) when the relationship in which the conflict takes place is congenial and satisfying and (2) when conflict is managed with integrative strategies.

The attributions we make and the feelings we have during and after a conflict are interesting in their own right. They take on greater significance when we realize that they mediate the association between conflict behavior and relationship outcomes. Our attributions and feelings operate as interpretive filters that subtly translate the effects of individual conflicts on the overall relationship over time.

Similarly, judgments of communication competence influence the connection of conflict behaviors to relationship qualities. Communication satisfaction and successful facework are two proximal outcomes associated with communication competence. Effective communication leads to satisfaction and appropriate communication entails mutual face saving.

In discussing distal outcomes, we noted that conflict episodes can have cumulative effects on the relationship. We do not wish to leave the impression that the connection of conflict to distal outcomes is only negative. Indeed, integrative conflict management can be relationship enhancing, personally rewarding, good for your mental hygiene, and stress reducing. Relational bonds are strengthened when conflict is competently managed. To routinely avoid serious disagreements is just as problematic as overly aggressively confronting them. Interestingly, those married couples who have the greatest number of serious disagreements report the highest levels of avoidance of conflict discussion (McGonagle et al., 1993). Competent conflict engagement is constructive and highly positive in its consequences.

DISCUSSION QUESTIONS

1. Recall an incident where you violated a rule and were called upon to account for your behavior. What kind of excuse did you offer? What did you say? Did you give the true reason for breaking the rule, or did you withhold the real reason and provide an excuse that was more "acceptable"? What kind of attributions do you think others made about you on the basis of your excuse? How would their attributions be different if you gave a different excuse? Explain.

2. We are sometimes unaware that our own behavior influences our feelings as much as the behavior of someone else. During conflict, what behaviors of your own contribute to your feelings of anger? Guilt? Hurt?

3. Why are you in a better position than other people to judge the effectiveness of your own conflict communication? Why are you *not* in the best position to judge the appropriateness of your own conflict behavior?

4. Think of a friend or acquaintance and how that person usually manages conflict. Does this person follow the general rules of *consideration, rationality, self-expression, conflict resolution (problem-solving)*, and *positivity*? Do you two share other rules that may supersede these rules? What are they?

5. What is the connection between saving your own face and saving the face of the person with whom you disagree? When does saving your own face threaten the other person's face? How does saving the other person's face threaten your own? How do you reconcile the situation where saving your own face seems to conflict with saving the other person's face? Whose face takes precedence? Why? Does threatening another's face ever simultaneously threaten your own face? Give an example.

6. Does a demand-withdraw pattern exist in any relationship you have or know of? If so, what is your typical role; that is, do you tend to demand or withdraw? What frustrates you the most about this pattern? Can you think of ways to break out of this pattern?

chapter 7

INTERCULTURAL CONFLICT COMPETENCE

Stella Ting-Toomey
California State University, Fullerton

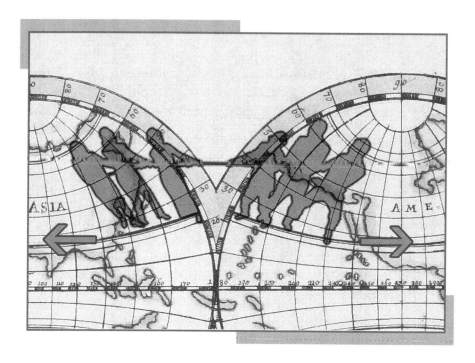

CHAPTER OUTLINE

Intercultural Conflict Competence: Criteria and Components
    IC Conflict Competence Criteria: Appropriateness and Effectiveness
    IC Conflict Competence Components: Knowledge, Mindfulness, and
       Skills
Intercultural Conflict: Antecedent Factors
    Culture-Based Value Dimensional Patterns
    Understanding the Complexity of Cultural Values Grid
    Individual Personality Tendency Patterns
Intercultural Conflict Communication: Process Factors
    Cross-Cultural National Conflict Communication Styles
    Cross-Ethnic Conflict Communication Styles
Developing Intercultural Conflict Competence: Process and Outcome
    IC Code-Switching: Communication Adaptability
    Mindful Transformation
Summary
Discussion Questions

Intercultural (IC) conflict frustrations often arise because of our lack of necessary and sufficient knowledge to deal with culture-based conflict communication issues competently. Our cultural ignorance or ineptness oftentimes clutters our ability to communicate appropriately and effectively across cultural and ethnic lines. As the global economy becomes an everyday reality in most societies, individuals will inevitably encounter people who are culturally different in diverse workplaces. Learning to manage such differences competently, especially in IC conflicts, can bring about alternative viewpoints and expanded visions to an existing problem.

IC conflict is defined in this chapter as the perceived or actual incompatibility of cultural values, situational norms, goals, face orientations, scarce resources, processes, and/or outcomes in a face-to-face (or mediated) context (Ting-Toomey & Oetzel, 2001). IC conflict competence refers to the mindful transformation of knowledge, attitudes, and skills from an ethnocentric lens to an ethnorelative lens. We engage in an ethnocentric perspective when we view our own cultural way of communicating as the most proper and correct way of communicating, and we view the unfamiliar communication practices of other cultural groups as improper and incorrect. Ethnorelativism, on the other hand, means the capacity to view communication behaviors from the other person's cultural frame of reference and understand why people behave the way they behave from their cultural values standpoint (Bennett & Bennett, 2004). The greater the cultural distance between the two conflict parties, the more likely the assessment of the conflict interaction process will be miscon-strued. The cultural membership distances can include deep-level differences such as historical grievances, cultural worldviews, and beliefs. Concurrently, they can also include the mismatch of applying different normative expecta-tions in a particular conflict episode.

This chapter is organized in four sections: First, the criteria and compo-nents of IC conflict competence are reviewed. Second, the distal factors of culture-based value dimensions and individual-based personality traits are introduced. Third, relevant research findings on cross-cultural national con-flict styles and domestic diversity cross-ethnic conflict styles are presented. Fourth, the chapter will end with a discussion on IC conflict competence out-come issues.

Intercultural Conflict Competence: Criteria and Components

Drawing from Spitzberg and Cupach's (1984) original conceptualization of interpersonal communication competence and also research in the IC communication competence domain, Wiseman (2003) conceptualizes gen-eral IC communication competence as involving the "knowledge, motiva-tion, and skills to interact effectively and appropriately with members of different cultures" (p. 192). Deardorff (2006), in interviewing 23 scholars and trainers in the IC communication field, identifies the most preferred defini-tion of IC competence as "the ability to communicate effectively and appro-priately in intercultural situations based on one's intercultural knowledge, skills and attitudes" (p. 249).

Canary and Lakey (2006) argue for the importance of the twin criteria of "appropriateness" and "effectiveness" in assessing conflict competence. They comment that "communication can be judged as competent only within the context of a relationship or situation because the context determines the stan-dards of appropriateness that must be met" and that "communication can be appropriate without being effective and effective without being appropriate" (p. 187).

IC CONFLICT COMPETENCE CRITERIA:
APPROPRIATENESS AND EFFECTIVENESS

The criteria of interactional appropriateness and effectiveness can serve as the evaluative yardsticks of whether an IC communicator has been perceived as behaving competently or incompetently in a conflict situation (Spitzberg & Cupach, 1989). *Appropriateness* refers to the degree to which the exchanged behaviors are regarded as proper and match the expectations generated by the insiders of the culture. To behave appropriately in any given cultural situation, competent communicators need to have the relevant value knowledge patterns of the larger culture that frame the particular conflict situation. They also need to apply the specific situational knowledge schema of what constitutes proper or improper, and respectful or disrespectful, communication patterns that promote optimal constructive outcomes. Thus, the criterion of "appropriateness" is conceptualized as a culture-sensitive application process in which individuals have mastered the deep knowledge structures of the culture-based values and the situational norms of the conflict context and that they are able to apply the knowledge schemata properly and respectfully.

The criterion of *effectiveness* refers to the degree to which communicators achieve mutually shared meaning and integrative goal-related outcomes through skillful interactional strategies in the various IC negotiation phases. To be perceived as effective IC communicators, individuals need to have wide-ranging verbal and nonverbal repertoires to make mindful choices and cultivate creative options. Interactional effectiveness has been achieved when multiple meanings are attended to with accuracy and in an unbiased manner, and mutually desired interaction goals have been conjointly worked out in a strategic and inclusive manner.

More important, appropriateness and effectiveness criteria are positively interdependent. When one manages a problematic situation appropriately, the "good faith" proper and respectful behaviors can induce interaction effectiveness. Likewise, when one promotes an integrative-inclined, mutual-goal outcome, the integrative posture can maximize the perceived effectiveness criterion and further induce cooperative interaction responses from the other cultural party.

IC CONFLICT COMPETENCE COMPONENTS: KNOWLEDGE, MINDFULNESS, AND SKILLS

Individuals from contrasting cultural communities often bring with them different value patterns, verbal and nonverbal habits, and conflict interaction scripts that influence the punctuation points of competent versus incompetent conflict behaviors. Sharpening the knowledge, motivation, and skills of IC conflict competence can simultaneously enhance general competence tendencies and situational-specific competence issues. Culture, from this backdrop context, is defined as a learned system of traditions, symbolic patterns, and accumulative meanings that fosters a particular sense of shared identity-hood, community-hood, and communication rituals among the aggregate of its group members. Both cultural and individual conditioning factors in conjunction with situational parameter factors shape the IC conflict competence outlook. Culture clash or conflict oftentimes entails the clash of group-membership identity values and vested personality traits.

According to the conflict face-negotiation theory (Ting-Toomey, 2005b), culture-sensitive knowledge, mindfulness, and constructive communication skills constitute the key features of IC conflict competence. Of all the components, knowledge is the most important component that underscores the other components of competence. With *culture-sensitive knowledge,* communicators can learn to uncover the implicit "ethnocentric lenses" they use to evaluate the "bizarre" behaviors in an IC conflict scene. With culturally grounded knowledge, individuals can develop an accurate culture-sensitive perspective and learn to reframe their interpretation of a conflict situation from the other's cultural frame of reference. Knowledge enhances cultural self-awareness and other-awareness. Knowledge here refers to developing an in-depth understanding of relevant IC concepts (e.g., cultural value patterns and preferred conflict communication styles) that can help to manage the conflict scene appropriately and effectively.

Knowledge and an open-minded attitude are closely intertwined and reciprocally influence one another. To be an astute decoder of a complex conflict situation, one must develop a mindful, layered systems outlook in assessing the macro- and micro-level features of a culture clash episode. *Mindfulness,* from the IC conflict competence framework, means the willingness to attend to one's internal cultural and personal communication assumptions, cognitions, and emotions and, at the same time, becoming exquisitely attuned to the other's communication assumptions, cognitions, and emotions (LeBaron, 2003; Ting-Toomey, 1999). Mindful fluency requires us to tune into our own cultural and personal habitual assumptions in scanning a problematic interaction scene. It also refers to the willingness to learn from the unfamiliar other. To be mindful of IC differences, individuals have to learn to see the unfamiliar behavior from multiple cultural angles (Langer, 1989, 1997), which means understanding the underlying value dimensions of the unfamiliar culture *as a starting point.*

Constructive communication skills refer to our operational abilities to manage a conflict situation appropriately and effectively via skillful verbal and nonverbal behaviors. Many communication skills are useful in enhancing IC conflict competencies. Of the many possible operational competence skills (see, e.g., Ting-Toomey, 2004), skills such as deep listening, mindful reframing, de-centering, face-sensitive respectful dialogue skills, and collaborative conflict negotiation skills (e.g., the skill set of the "A.E.I.O.U." negotiation, which stands for "attack, evade, inform, open, unite," developed by Coleman & Raider, 2006) across cultural and ethnic/racial lines are critical practices. With discussion of the criteria and components of IC conflict competence as the backdrop, I now turn to a review of the core value dimensions that can assert a profound influence on IC communicators' conflict styles and responses.

Intercultural Conflict: Antecedent Factors

IC conflict often starts off with diverse expectations concerning what constitutes appropriate or inappropriate verbal and nonverbal behaviors in a conflict encounter scene. Violations of expectations, in turn, often solidify the attributional biases and subsequent communication responses that individuals use in their conflict interaction process. Both cultural value patterns and individual personality tendencies serve as antecedent, distal factors in shaping one's conflict responses. In addition, situational norms and conflict goals serve as antecedent, proximal factors that frame one's conflict communication styles and outcome.

Let us look at the following two interaction episodes in example 1 and example 2. Example 1 takes place between two European American neighbors and example 2 takes place between two Japanese neighboring housewives.

Example 1

Deidra (knocks on her neighbor's screen door): Excuse me, it's past 11 o'clock already, and your loud music and dancing around are really disturbing my sleep. Please stop your jumping and banging around immediately! I have an important job interview tomorrow and I want to get a good night's sleep. Some of us do need to pay rent!

Kaitlyn (resentfully): Well, this is the only time I can rehearse! I have an important audition coming up tomorrow. You're not the only one that is starving, you know. I also need to pay rent. Stop being so petty!

Deidra (frustrated): I really think *you're* being *very annoying* and *intrusive*! There is an apartment noise ordinance, you know. And if you don't stop banging around immediately, I'm going to file a complaint with the apartment manager and he could evict you. . . .

Kaitlyn (sarcastically and turning up the music even louder): Whatever! Do what you want. I'm going to practice as I please. Don't bother to ask for my autograph when I become a big-time Hollywood star!

Example 2

Mrs. Atsumi: Hello, Mrs. Enomoto. . . . I heard your son Toji is entering his high school karaoke contest, isn't he? I envy you, because you must be so proud of his talent. You must be looking forward to his future as a pop singer. . . . I'm really impressed by his enthusiasm and dedication—every day, he practices so hard, for hours and hours, until late at night. . . .

Mrs. Enomoto: Oh, I'm so sorry. . . . Toji is just a beginner in karaoke singing. We don't know his future yet. . . . He is such a silly and inconsiderate boy singing so late. We didn't realize you can hear all the noise next door. I'll tell him to stop right away. I'm so sorry about all your trouble, it won't happen again.

CULTURE-BASED VALUE DIMENSIONAL PATTERNS

While the conflict communication mode in example 1 reflects an individualistic, direct way of approaching conflict, the conflict interaction mode in example 2 reflects a collectivistic, indirect way of engaging in problematic talk. A direct, up-front way of approaching conflict is labeled as low-context communication interaction, and a tactful, diplomatic way of approaching conflict is labeled as high-context communication interaction (Hall, 1983; Ting-Toomey, 1999). Low-context communication generally refers to a direct verbal style, up-front verbal engagement, explicit expression of emotions, and meanings that are often located via transparent talk. Comparatively, high-context communication generally refers to an indirect verbal style, understated verbal engagement, the use of hints and nonverbal subtleties (including silence), and meanings that are often located in the embedded situational-role contexts. The larger U.S. culture, German culture, Swiss culture, and many Nordic cultures, for example, have been identified as subscribing to a low-context communication outlook. Comparatively, Chinese culture, Japanese culture, Mexican culture, and many Middle Eastern and African cultures, for example, have been identified as subscribing to a high-context outlook. While the low-context communication style is reflective of individualistic value tendencies, the high-context communication style is reflective of in-group-based, collectivistic, or communal value tendencies.

As cultural beings, we are socialized by the values and norms of our culture to think and behave in certain ways. Our family, peer groups, educational institutions, mass media system, political system, and religious institutions are some of the forces that shape and mold our cultural and personal values. Two such primary value patterns are individualism-collectivism and small-large power distance (Hofstede, 2001). Indeed, in the recent GLOBE (Global Leadership and Organizational Behavior Effectiveness) empirical research project, researchers (House, Hanges, Javidan, Dorfman, & Gupta, 2004) have provided additional evidence that the foundational constructs of individualism-collectivism and small-large power distance permeate 62 countries (with a sample size of 17,370 middle managers from three industries) at the societal, organizational, and individual levels of analysis. Basically, *individualism* refers to the broad value tendencies of a culture in emphasizing the importance of the "I" identity over the "we" identity, individual rights over group interests, and individuated-focused emotions over social-focused emotions. In comparison, *collectivism* refers to the broad value tendencies of a culture in emphasizing the importance of the "we" identity over the "I" identity, in-group interests over individual desires, and other-identity concerns over self-identity concerns. Individualistic and collectivistic value tendencies are manifested in everyday interpersonal, family, school, and workplace social interactions.

Beyond individualism-collectivism, another important value dimension that is critical in understanding workplace conflict interaction is the value dimension of power distance (Carl, Gupta, & Javidan, 2004). *Power distance*, from the workplace values analysis standpoint, refers to the way in which a corporate culture approaches and deals with status differences and social hierarchies. Individuals in *small power distance* corporate cultures tend to value equal power distributions, symmetrical relations, a mixture of positive and negative messages in feedback sessions, and equitable reward and cost distributions based on individual merits. Individuals in *large power distance* corporate cultures tend to accept unequal power distributions, asymmetrical relations, authoritative feedback from the experts or high-status individuals, and rewards and sanctions based on rank, role, status, age, and perhaps even gender identity.

UNDERSTANDING THE COMPLEXITY OF CULTURAL VALUES GRID

In combining both individualism-collectivism and small-large power distance value patterns, we can discuss four predominant corporate value approaches along the two grids of the individualism-collectivism continuum and small-large power distance continuum: impartial, status-achievement, benevolent, and communal (Ting-Toomey & Oetzel, 2001). The *impartial approach* reflects a combination of an individualistic and small power distance value orientation; the *status-achievement approach* consists of a combination of an individualistic and large power distance value orientation; the *benevolent approach* reflects a combination of a collectivistic and large power distance value orientation; and the *communal approach* consists of a combination of a collectivistic and small power distance value orientation (see figure 7-1).

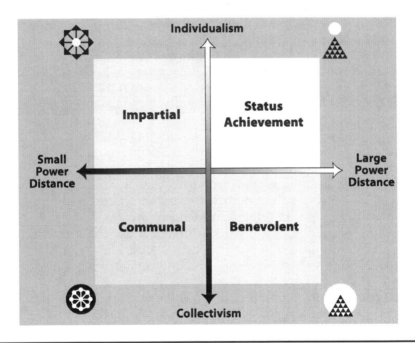

**Figure 7-1   Culture-based corporate values grid: Four conflict
           approaches.**

Case Study: An IC Conflict Critical Incident.   Let us take a look at the background information in the following case study (adapted from Clarke & Lipp, 1998, pp. 232–233). A Japanese multimedia subsidiary in the United States had just completed a very successful year. All of the company goals were met or surpassed. As a result, the annual sales conference was held at the Disneyland Resort in California. Many of the salespeople brought their spouses to the conference, to celebrate and enjoy a well-earned vacation. The audience at the dinner celebration consisted of mostly American salespeople and their spouses, and some Japanese technical support personnel. The Japanese president gave a brief welcome speech in halting English, but the audience appreciated his remarks.

Next, the American director of sales, William Bates, got up and introduced the Japanese vice president, Satoshi Ota-san. They had planned ahead of time to give two short motivational speeches to kick off the conference. Ota-san was about fifty years old, and he had used the last two weeks to memorize his carefully prepared speech in English. When Ota-san stood up, his posture was rigid, his face was serious, and his tone sounded harsh. Here is what he said:

> Thank you for your hard work this fiscal year. We have broken many records, *but* . . . we need to be careful and not to settle down so easily. We need to keep up our fighting spirit! Our competition is working to defeat us at this very minute while we are celebrating. You have done a good job . . . but you must do more and aim higher. There is no time for frivolous activities. You must prepare yourselves to work twice as hard this coming year. The company has invested a lot of money in new manufacturing facilities. These facilities are producing our new product lines. It is your duty and loyalty to this company to sell these products as efficiently as possible. You must not fail! You must not let your guard down! You must not be content! I hope you will do a better job in the new fiscal year. Thank you.

The American audience sat in stunned silence during most of Satoshi Ota-san's speech. The American director of sales, William Bates, stood up quickly, physically backed away from the Japanese vice president of sales, and with an awkward smile said:

> Disregard everything he just said. We are here to celebrate your fantastic achievements this year! We have out-performed all our competitors this past year and your success is far beyond expectations. So give yourselves a big round of applause, and, let the festivities begin!

The audience applauded. William gave the signal to the hotel staff to serve the dinner. For the rest of the conference, the tension between Satoshi Ota-san and William Bates was palpable, and most of the other Americans were irritable.

What went wrong here? Why did Mr. Bates physically back away from Mr. Ota? How do you, the reader, think Mr. Ota reacted to Mr. Bates' comment ("Disregard everything he just said")? Can you identify all the culture-based collision bumps in the above critical incident? Can the conflict clashes between the two key characters be reconciled? What corporate conflict approach did Mr. Ota practice? What conflict reactions did Mr. Bates exhibit?

Before I reveal the answers, let us explore more in-depth the conceptual frames of the four corporate conflict approaches. Overall, managers and employees around the world have different expectations of how a workplace conflict episode should be interpreted and resolved—pending on whether the workplace culture emphasizes impartial, status-achievement, benevolent, or communal conflict interaction rituals. More specifically, for example, in the *impartial approach* (a combination of individualism and small power distance) to workplace conflict, the predominant values are personal freedom and equal treatment (Smith, Dugan, Peterson, & Leung, 1998). From the impartial conflict approach lens, if an interpersonal conflict arises between a manager and an employee, the manager has the responsibility to deal with the conflict in an objective, up-front, and decisive manner. The employee is sometimes invited to provide feedback and reactions to the fact-finding process. He or she can also ask for clear justifications and evidence from the manager. In an equal-rank employee-employee conflict, the manager would generally play the "impartial" third-party role and would encourage the two employees to talk things over and find their own workable solution. Managers in large corporations in Denmark, the Netherlands, Sweden, and Norway appear to practice the impartial conflict communication approach (Hofstede, 2001).

Alternatively, from a *status-achievement approach* (a combination of individualism and large power distance) to conflict, the predominant values of this approach are personal freedom and earned inequality. For example, in France, employees often feel that they have the freedom to voice directly and complain about their managers in the workplace (Storti, 2001). At the same time, they do not expect their managers to change much because they are their bosses and, thus, by virtue of their titles hold certain rights and power resources. The managers, meanwhile, also expect conflict accommodations from their subordinates. When the conflict involves two same-rank coworkers, the use of up-front conflict tactics to aggression tactics is a hallmark of the status-achievement approach. Ting-Toomey and Oetzel (2001) also observed that the U.S. management style often follows a conjoint impartial approach and a status-achievement approach because the larger U.S. culture emphasizes that via individual hard work, personal ambition, and fierce competitiveness, status and rank can be earned and status cues can be displayed with pride and credibility.

Based on the empirical work of the GLOBE project (Carl et al., 2004), many managers in other parts of the globe also tend to see themselves as interdependent and at a different status level than others. That is, these managers think of themselves as individuals with interlocking connections with others and as members of a hierarchical network. They practice the *benevolent approach* (a combination of collectivism and large power distance value patterns) in approaching a conflict problem. The term "benevolent" implies that many managers play the authoritative parental role in approaching or motivating their employees. Two values that pervade this approach are obligation to others and asymmetrical interaction treatment. Countries and large corporate cultures that predominantly reflect the benevolent approach include most Latin and South American nations (e.g., Mexico, Venezuela, Brazil,

Chile), most Asian nations (e.g., India, Japan, China, South Korea), most Arab nations (e.g., Egypt, Saudi Arabia, Jordan), and most African nations (e.g., Nigeria, Uganda) (Hofstede, 2001).

For many of the large East Asian corporations, for example, Confucian-driven hierarchical principles promote a parent-child relationship between the manager and the subordinate. Under the benevolent conflict approach, while a manager can confront their employees in order to motivate them to work harder, it is very rare that subordinates will directly challenge the manager's authority during a conflict interaction process. However, they might opt for using passive aggressive or sabotage conflict strategies to deal with the workplace tensions or frustrations. In dealing with low-premium conflicts, managers would consider using "smooth over" relational tactics or subtle face-pressuring tactics to gain employees' compliance. However, in dealing with high-premium conflicts, benevolent managers could act in a very directive or autocratic and controlling manner. They might also practice preferential treatment or particularistic values by treating senior employees more favorably than junior employees, or family network friends more generously than peripheral workplace members.

Lastly, the *communal approach* (a combination of both collectivism and small power distance value orientation) is the least common of the four conflict workplace approaches. The values that encompass this approach are authentic interdependent connection to others and genuine equality via respectful communication exchange at all levels. Costa Rica is the only country found to fit this approach (Hofstede, 2001). Nonprofit mediation centers or successful start-up small businesses also appear to practice some of the communal decision-making behaviors and participatory democracy (where everyone has a say, and democratic leadership is achieved through rotation). In the communal approach, the importance of mindful listening skills, interpersonal validation skills, and collaborative dialogue skills are emphasized (Barge, 2006; Domenici & Littlejohn, 2006).

After reading the explanation of the four corporate conflict approaches, I hope you have increased your knowledge on these complex values issues. If you answered earlier that Mr. Ota used a benevolent approach to motivate his audience, your answer is correct. In addition, if you answered that Mr. Bates' conflict reactions reflected both impartial (e.g., based on objective facts, the American sales force had a banner year) and status-achievement (e.g., they all worked ambitiously to attain this well-deserved recognition event) conflict approaches, you also earn an "A" grade. Clearly, in this case study, the Americans and the Japanese carried different cultural assumptions about the meaning of a sales conference celebration event and the meaning of a motivational speech.

From the "status-achievement" corporate worldview, for example, Mr. Bates and the American audience were expecting an "individual status-recognition celebration" event. Many of them brought their spouses to mark the festivity and to enjoy a fun-filled vacation. They expected complimentary accolades and positive motivational messages. Instead, all they heard (or what seemed to them) were direct criticisms and insults. From the "benevolent" corporate worldview, Mr. Ota (and perhaps including some of the Japanese technical staff) viewed this context as another occasion to "motivate" the sales workforce to work harder and to plan productive sales strategies collectively. Mr. Ota had tried so hard for two weeks to memorize his motivational speech in English. He thought for sure that the celebration occasion in Disneyland itself sent a strong positive signal to the employees that the company already valued their hard work and dedicated effort. However, Mr. Ota was also looking forward to the special occasion to further motivate his sales employees to reach their highest professional potential and personal best. Mr. Bates' awkward smile and the cavalier phrase of "Disregard everything he just said" created enormous face loss for Mr. Ota and the Japanese president.

A knowledgeable, third-party IC consultant—either an individual or an IC consulting team who understands the deep societal and corporate cultures of both Japan and the United States—could perhaps help to bridge the widening chasm between the two cultural conflict parties. Understanding the underlying, unspoken value clashes and the misconstrued assumptions between the American and Japanese attendees would serve as a good first step to reconcile the cultural and corporate expectancy differences.

INDIVIDUAL PERSONALITY TENDENCY PATTERNS

Beyond group-based cultural conditioning value patterns, individuals within each culture also develop their own personality tendencies and traits via their distinctive life experiences and personal maturation process. This individual socialization process can include the study of the personality tendencies of independent self and interdependent self. Self-construal is one of the major individual factors that focuses on individual variation within and between cultures. *Self-construal* is one's self-image and is composed of an independent and an interdependent self (Markus & Kitayama, 1991, 1998).

The *independent construal of self* involves the view that an individual is a unique entity with an individuated repertoire of feelings, cognitions, and motivations. In contrast, the *interdependent construal of self* involves an emphasis on the importance of relational or in-group connectedness. Self-construal is the individual-level equivalent of the cultural variability dimension of individualism-collectivism. For example, Gudykunst and colleagues (1996) argued that independent self-construal is predominantly associated with people of individualistic cultures, while interdependent self-construal is predominantly associated with people of collectivistic cultures. However, both dimensions of self exist within each individual, regardless of cultural identity. In individualistic cultural communities, there may be more communication situations that evoke the need for independent-based decisions and behaviors. In collectivistic communities, there may be more situations that demand the sensitivity for interdependent-based decisions and actions.

The manner in which individuals conceive their self-images—independent versus interdependent selves—should have a profound influence on the expectancies of what constitutes appropriate or inappropriate communication responses in a wide variety of interactional situations across a diverse range of cultures (Kim & Leung, 2000). For example, in a cross-national conflict study in four nations, Oetzel and Ting-Toomey (2003) found that independent self-construal is associated positively with self-face concern (i.e., self-voice assertive focus) and the use of dominating/competing conflict strategies. Interdependent self-construal, on the other hand, is associated positively with other-face concern (i.e., relational harmony focus) and the use of avoiding and integrating conflict tactics. *Self-face concern* is the protective concern for one's own identity image when it is threatened in the conflict episode. *Other-face concern* is the concern for accommodating the other conflict party's identity image in the conflict situation. In addition, *mutual-face concern* is the concern for both parties' images and the image of the relationship (Oetzel et al., 2001). It would appear that independent self-construal fosters the use of self-face concern, and the use of direct, low-context assertive to aggressive communication responses. Interdependent self-construal, on the other hand, emphasizes other-face and mutual-face concerns, and the use of indirect, high-context accommodating to avoiding conflict interaction patterns. Ting-Toomey, Oetzel, and Yee-Jung (2001) also found that biconstrual individuals (those who are high on both independent and interdependent traits) tend to have more diverse conflict repertoires to deal with a conflict situation compared to independent, interdependent, and ambivalent (low on both independent and interdependent traits) personality types. However, as mentioned earlier, the nature of the conflict, whether the conflict takes place between unequal status individuals or same-status individuals, and the cultural workplace setting greatly influence individuals' expectancies concerning appropriate and effective conflict competence processes and outcomes (Kaushal & Kwantes, 2006; Merkin, 2006).

Intercultural Conflict Communication: Process Factors

Drawing from the conceptual explanations of the conflict face-negotiation theory (Ting-Toomey, 1988, 2005b), I will now present some summary research findings concerning conflict communication styles in diverse cultural and ethnic groups. *"Face"* is essentially about identity respect and other-identity consideration issues within and beyond the actual communication encounter process. On a deeper level, it is tied to the emotional significance and estimated appraisals that we attach to our own social self-worth and the social self-worth of others (Ting-Toomey & Kurogi, 1998). When our face image is being threatened in a conflict situation, we would likely experience identity-based frustration, emotional fragility or fear, hurt, anger, pain, guilt, shame, insult, or even vengeance. Whether we choose to engage in or disengage from a conflict process often depends on our ingrained cultural conflict habits, personality tendency, and how we negotiate various face concerns. Face concerns are expressed via a variety of conflict communication styles. Conflict communication style refers to patterned verbal and nonverbal responses to conflict in a variety of frustrating conflict situations (Cai & Fink, 2002; Ting-Toomey & Oetzel, 2001).

There are three approaches to studying conflict styles: dispositional, situational, and systems (Ting-Toomey & Chung, 2005). The *dispositional approach* emphasizes that individuals do have predominant and stable conflict style tendencies in handling a wide variety of conflict situations in different cultures. Conflict style is learned within the primary socialization process of one's cultural or ethnic group. It also depends highly on one's dispositional or personality traits. The dispositional approach emphasizes the distal factors in shaping our conflict styles. The *situational approach*, on the other hand, stresses the importance of the proximal factors that shape one's conflict approach and responses. Thus, the use of a particular conflict style varies across situations—depending on many role-context factors. Some of these proximal situational factors, for example, can include an individual's ethnocentric or ethnorelative lens in viewing a conflict episode, plus the weighing of various conflict goal types, the importance of the relationship, the interaction climate, time pressure, and the context in which the conflict occurs. All these composite situational factors have a strong influence on whether individuals will actively engage in the conflict or avoid the conflict altogether (for a recent review, see Nicotera & Dorsey, 2006). A third approach, the *systems approach*, integrates both dispositional and situational approaches (Wilmot & Hocker, 2007). It recognizes that for most individuals, they do have predominant or prototypical conflict style profiles because of strong cultural socialization, family socialization, gender socialization, and personality-based influences. However, the systems approach also recognizes the adaptable nature of humans when confronting different situational or role relationship conflict features. For the purpose of learning about IC conflict competence issues, a systems' approach offers both "macro" and "micro" views concerning how we can flex our communication muscles to adapt to different types of conflict situations. A systems approach emphasizes that individuals do strive for change and adaptation when being hit by repeated disorienting dilemmas and that the experience of repeated personal dissonances can propel us to move forward to discover new patterns of thinking and readjusting (Kim, 2001, 2005).

CROSS-CULTURAL NATIONAL CONFLICT COMMUNICATION STYLES

Individuals in different cultures use different conflict styles to approach a conflict situation. Many conflict communication researchers conceptualize conflict styles along two dimensions (for a recent critique, see Putnam, 2006). For example, Rahim (1992) bases his classification of conflict styles on the two conceptual dimensions of concern for self and concern for others. The first dimension illustrates the degree (high or low) to which a person seeks to satisfy her/his own conflict interest or own face need. The second dimension represents the degree (high or low) to which a person desires to incorporate the other's conflict interest. When combined, the two dimensions result in five styles of handling interpersonal conflict: dominating, avoiding, obliging, compromising, and integrating (see chapter 3).

Briefly, the *dominating* (or "competitive/controlling") style emphasizes conflict tactics that push for one's own position above and beyond the other person's conflict interest. The dominating style can include aggressive, defensive, controlling, or intimidating conflict tactics. The *avoiding* style involves eluding the conflict topic, the conflict party, or the conflict situation altogether. The avoiding style can include glossing over the topic, denying that conflict exists, to exiting the conflict scene. The *obliging* (or "accommodating") style is characterized by a high concern for the other person's conflict interest above and beyond one's own conflict position. Individuals tend to use an obliging style when they value their relationship more than their personal conflict goal. The *compromising* style, on the other hand, involves a give-and-take concession approach in order to reach a mid-point agreement concerning the conflict issue. It is an intermediate style resulting in some gains and some losses for each party. Finally, the *integrating* (or "collaborative") style reflects a commitment to find mutual-interest solutions and involves a high concern for self-interest and also a high concern for the other person's interest. In using an integrative style, individuals tend to use neutrally toned descriptive statements, self-disclosure sharing statements, qualifying messages, and probing questions to understand the other person's position and to arrive at a mutual-interest solution. The integrating style is also the most time-consuming, effortful style of all five conflict styles. It should be noted here that, in the U.S. conflict research literature, obliging and avoiding conflict styles often take on a Western slant of being negatively disengaged (i.e., "indifference" or "fleeing" from the conflict scene). However, collectivists do not necessarily perceive obliging and avoiding conflict styles as negative. These two conflict styles are often used by collectivists to maintain mutual-face interests and in-group harmony.

Research across cultures (e.g., in France, Germany, and the United States versus China, South Korea, Japan, Taiwan, and Mexico) clearly indicates that individualists tend to use more self-defensive dominating and competitive conflict styles in managing conflicts than do collectivists. In comparison, collectivists tend to use more compromising give-and-take conflict styles than do individualists. Research also indicates that collectivists tend to use more obliging and avoiding conflict styles in a wide variety of conflict situations more so than do individualists (Oetzel & Ting-Toomey, 2003; Oetzel, Garcia, & Ting-Toomey, 2008). Both groups also tend to perceive themselves as using an integrative, problem-solving conflict style in trying to resolve the conflict issue. Interestingly, whether the conflict interaction is with members of the in-group (i.e., members with strong affiliation and interdependent fate) or out-group (i.e., members with no emotional ties) also clearly influences how collectivists manage conflict. Chinese and Japanese, for example, are more likely to pursue a conflict with peripheral out-group members and less likely to pursue a conflict with familiar in-group members than U.S. Americans. They also use a stronger win/lose competitive process when competing with peripheral out-group members to win a reward versus when competing with familiar in-group members (Leung & Bond, 2004; Ting-Toomey & Takai, 2006). Meanwhile, U.S. Americans tend not to draw a sharp distinction between the boundary of in-group and out-group conflicts in comparison to Asian collectivists.

On the personal attributes level, independent-self individuals tend to use more competitive and dominating conflict styles than interdependent-self individuals, while interdependent-self individuals tend to use more avoiding, obliging, integrating, and compromising styles than independent-self individuals (Oetzel, 2001). Thus, to gain an in-depth understanding of an individual's conflict styles, we have to understand both his/her cultural conditioning process, his/her personality attributes, and the in-group/out-group conflict boundary in a particular cultural setting.

CROSS-ETHNIC CONFLICT COMMUNICATION STYLES

In terms of different ethnic conflict styles within the multicultural U.S. population, distinctive and similar conflict style patterns do exist in different ethnic groups in the United States. According to Orbe and Everett (2006), the following factors greatly shape the use of particular conflict styles among coculture group members (i.e., interactions among underrepresented and dominant group members) in the diverse U.S. society: social inequality, in-group/out-group tensions, perceptual differences, rigid stereotyping, media influence, and the lack of contact or exposure to cocultural membership differences (e.g., ethnic minority group members, gays and lesbians, people with disabilities, etc.). I will first address the African American conflict styles, and then Asian American, Latino(a) American, and Native American conflict style orientations.

African American conflict styles are influenced simultaneously by both individualistic and collectivistic value tendencies, and also by both small and large power distance value patterns. At the same time that traditional African values are collectivistic (e.g., community, interdependence, being one with nature, and church/religious participation) and large power distance based (e.g., respecting grandparents and pastors), African Americans are also in constant struggle against the power dominance of whites in the white privileged U.S. society (Asante & Asante, 1990). The white privileged social position refers to a general favored state of whites holding power over other minority group members in key decision-making roles in major policy-making institutions (Orbe & Spellers, 2005). There is also a general tendency for European Americans or whites to view racism episodes as individual acts rather than as part of a truncated, power-imbalance institutional package.

Thus, assertive and emotionally expressive conflict styles may be one method for African Americans to uphold self and in-group membership solidarity and dignity.

Research has also revealed that African Americans (in particular, African American women) tend to be more emotionally engaging in their conflict approach, whereas European Americans tend to be more emotionally restrained in their conflict discussions (Shuter & Turner, 1997; Ting-Toomey, 1986). The "black mode" of conflict is high-keyed: energetic, nonverbally engaging, and emotionally expressive. In comparison, the "white mode" of conflict is low-keyed: dispassionate, nonverbally muted, and emotionally restrained (Kochman, 1981). African Americans also emphasize the importance of "realism" in everyday interaction, while European Americans emphasize "honesty" (Martin, Hecht, & Larkey, 1994). For African Americans, being "real" means being authentic and asserting your sense of true self. For European Americans, they may prize verbal honesty but not necessarily "realism" in terms of letting their authentic feelings be known or experienced. In another study on interethnic conflict competence (Collier, 1991, 1996), African American interviewees reported the importance of sharing information, credible opinions, and assertiveness as part of an effective conflict style, while European American interviewees reported the use of directness, taking responsibility for behaviors, rational decision making, and shared control as effective conflict strategies.

According to a cross-ethnic conflict style research project (Ting-Toomey et al., 2000), African Americans who identify strongly with the larger U.S. culture also tend to use a more give-and-take compromising style in conflict than African Americans who identify weakly with the larger U.S. culture. As a complex diverse group, many African Americans have an integrative system of individualism-collectivism and small-large power distance value tendencies. Their conflict pattern is strongly influenced by ethnic/cultural values, social class issues, in-group/out-group demarcation, situational goals, and reactions to negative stereotypes and racial oppression features.

In terms of Asian American conflict orientations, it has been found that the philosophy of Confucianism strongly influences proper facework rituals and conflict interaction performance. Confucianism remains the fundamental philosophy that underlies many Asian cultures (e.g., China, Taiwan, Singapore, Korea, and Japan). Confucius was a Chinese philosopher of practical ethics who lived from 551–479 BC. His practical code of conduct emphasizes hierarchical societal structure (i.e., large power distance) and appropriate family role performance. Some core Confucian values include: a dynamic long-term orientation, perseverance, ordering relationships by status, having a sense of shame, and emphasizing collective face saving (Gao & Ting-Toomey, 1998). An interdependent sense of shame includes the constant awareness of other people's expectations of one's own or in-group performance and the particular sensitivity for mutual face-saving, face-losing, and face-giving (i.e., give-and-take face-enhancement process) behaviors.

Asian Americans who adhere to traditional Asian values (e.g., recent Asian immigrants) tend to use avoiding or obliging conflict styles to deal with the conflict at hand. They sometimes also use "silence" as a powerful high-context conflict mode. They may also resort to familiar third-party help—especially from trusted family members or networks to mediate the conflict situation (Sue & Sue, 2003). Asian Americans who identify strongly with the larger U.S. culture also tend to use an integrative conflict style to find substantive solutions to address a conflict problem more so than Asian Americans who identify weakly with the larger U.S. culture (Ting-Toomey et al., 2000). Given the diversity of the Asian American population, we should also pay close attention to the country-of-origin, immigration experience, acculturation pattern, generational level, language mastery, family socialization norms, and ethnic identity salience factors that create tremendous distinctions between and within these multiple groups.

In the context of traditional Latino(a) Americans' conflict practices, tactfulness and consideration of others' feelings are deemed to be important face-sensitive conflict norms. Tactfulness and considerateness are conveyed through the use of other-oriented facework behaviors such as the use of obliging or "smoothing over" conflict styles and the use of the avoidance conflict style (Garcia, 1996). They also tend to seek out trusted third-party help more so than the European American group (Ting-Toomey et al., 2001). More specifically, in the traditional-based Mexican American group, for example, the term *respeto* connotes honor, respect, and "face" that individuals accord to listeners in accordance with their roles and hierarchical statuses. Thus, diplomatic and circumspective face-sensitive behaviors, especially in dealing with unequal-status family conflicts, are critical in promoting competent conflict communication. In addition, since Mexican American facework is closely related to family loyalty, honor, name, respect, and extended family approval issues, family members are expected to uphold their family dignity at all times and not to bring shame into their extended family unit. However, in dealing with close friendship conflict, while the Mexican American interviewees believe that the conveyance of empathy for the other person's feelings is critical, they also endorse an emotionally expressive, confrontational conflict style in dealing with friendship problems (Collier, 1991).

Overall, collectivism and large power distance values are the underlying value patterns that undergird Latino(a) American conflict expectations. Research also revealed that Latino(a) Americans who identify strongly with their traditional ethnic values tend to use more emotionally expressive conflict styles than Latino(a) Americans who do not strongly identify with their traditional ethnic values (Ting-Toomey et al., 2000). Thus, under the broad category of "collectivism," while the Latino(a) group tends to endorse an emotionally expressive norm in some conflict situations, the Asian group tends to emphasize an emotionally restrained view in some conflict contexts. With the tremendous diversities under the "Latino(a) American" label, we will do well to increase the complexity of our understanding of the values and distinctive conflict patterns of each group (e.g., Puerto Rican, Cuban, Mexican, El Salvadorian, etc.).

Collectivism and larger power distance values also permeate traditional Native American tribes. Overall, Native Americans tend to prefer the use of verbal self-restraint and a verbal self-discipline mode in uncertainty conflict situations (Basso, 1990). Some of the value patterns of Native Americans that have been identified by researchers are:

1. *Mutual sharing:* honor and respect is gained by sharing and giving;

2. *In-group cooperation:* the family and tribe take precedence over the individual;

3. *Noninterference:* they are taught to observe and to not react impulsively, especially in meddling with other people's affairs;

4. *Time orientation:* they tend to be more present oriented rather than future oriented, and life is to be lived fully in the present;

5. *Extended family orientation:* there is a strong respect for elders and their wisdom and generational knowledge; and

6. *Harmony with nature:* they tend to prefer to flow with nature rather than controlling or mastering their natural environment (Sue & Sue, 2003).

Given these value patterns, we can infer that in terms of conflict styles, Native Americans tend to be more understated and emotionally restrained in dealing with conflicts in their everyday lives. Out of consideration for the other person's face or in-group face, they tend to use a more subtle, high-context conflict style in trying to resolve their conflict peacefully. They are also likely to go to a third-party elder in soliciting her or his wisdom in resolving the conflict issue and, thus, helping each other to maintain face. They also tend to use more deliberate silence in conveying their displeasure. However, given the fact that there are over 500 Native American groups, any ethnic-based generalizations should only serve as a starting point to go more in-depth to understand the complexity of each interethnic conflict scene. We should realize that, for example, Native Americans who live on or near reservations are more likely to subscribe to traditional values, while other Native Americans may adhere to predominant, mainstream values or maintaining a set of bicultural values (Ting-Toomey & Oetzel, 2001).

More empirical studies are needed in the future to investigate the conflict communication patterns within the broad umbrella groups such as the diverse African American, Asian American, Latino(a) American, and Native American populations. More ethnic-comparative studies are also needed to compare the different forms of collectivism and large power distance that exist, for example, in the Mexican American community versus the Vietnamese American cultural community. Of course, variations within the broad label of the "European American" cultural group should also be sought in terms of, for example, ethnicity-of-origin, immigration status, social class, gender, generational, religious, and regional diversity issues.

Developing Intercultural Conflict Competence: Process and Outcome

Arasaratnam (2006, 2007), in reviewing research in IC communication competence in the last 20 years, locates IC competence via five facets: empathy, positive attitude towards people from other cultures, ability to listen, experience/training in IC communication, and motivation to interact with people from other cultures.

More specifically, Ting-Toomey (2005b) views IC conflict competence as the optimal integration of knowledge, mindfulness, and communication skills in managing vulnerable identity-based conflict situations appropriately, effectively, and adaptively. In this final section, I will address two issues that facilitate IC conflict competence: IC code-switching and mindful transformation.

IC Code-Switching: Communication Adaptability

A competent IC communicator, regardless of cultural origin, can move beyond the original trappings of her or his culture and can negotiate her or his multifaceted identity fluidly in view of the communication situation at hand. They can do a figure eight dance—swinging adaptively from low-context communication style to high-context communication style, and from high-context communication movement to low-context communication steps.

According to Ting-Toomey (2005a), for example, as individuals cross cultural boundaries from a familiar turf to an unfamiliar environment, five dynamic identity change dialectics await them: identity security-vulnerability, inclusion-differentiation, predictability-novelty, connection-autonomy, and identity continuity-change. These five themes form the basic building blocks of the identity negotiation adaptation process. There are maximum and minimum thresholds for identity dialectics enactments. For example, too much security can bring tight ethnocentrism and complacency, and too much emotional vulnerability can bring intergroup fear and isolation. Thus, individuals often need to swing between the various dialectical poles depending on relative and summative circumstances.

Keeping the thresholds as backdrops, Molinsky (2007) fused some of these core identity negotiation ideas with the social psychology literature (e.g., Fredrickson & Branigan, 2005; Ward, 2004) and the cultural intelligence literature (Earley & Ang, 2003; Earley & Peterson, 2004), and developed what he labeled the "cross-cultural code-switching" model. The model emphasizes the identity and behavioral change challenges of the IC communication adaptation process and focuses on communication code-switching competence within and across interaction episodes. These ongoing, day-to-day interaction episodes form the basis of long-term, dynamic IC identity adjustment processes.

Cross-cultural or, more precisely, "intercultural" code-switching is conceptualized as "the act of purposefully modifying one's behavior in an interaction in a foreign setting in order to accommodate different cultural norms for appropriate behavior" (Molinksy, 2007, p. 624). In order to qualify as an IC code-switching situation, a situation must have norms that are either unfamiliar to the switcher or in conflict with values central to the switcher's identity. Central to Molinsky's (2007) model are two psychological challenges that need to be met: code-switchers need to execute the new behavior in such a manner that insiders of the culture judge the task performance and behavioral performance dimensions as appropriate to the context; and second, the code-switchers are eventually able to form a coherent sense of "identity dimension" via seeing the meaningful relevance of the behavior-in-context.

In sum, IC code-switching refers to the intentional learning and moving between culturally ingrained systems of behavior relevant to the situation at hand. Thus, individuals who have mastered the deep value structures of a culture (such as individualism and collectivism and other core culture-specific values) and the situational norms of an IC conflict episode can code-switch adaptively via an astute culture-sensitive situational analysis. To extend this line of thinking, there are two possible modes of code-switching. *Behavioral or functional code-switching* refers to surface-level verbal and/or nonverbal code-switching, especially for multicultural workplace survival and adaptation. In contrast, *dynamic or integrative code-switching* is an internal and external synchronized dance of fluid figure eight movements in which the dialectical tensions of individualism-collectivism (or any other seemingly contrastive value dimensions) within oneself are resolved or harmonized. Externally, the communication styles of this hybrid individual are also assessed as adaptive, appropriate, and effective. Lengthy foreign living experiences, bicultural and multicultural individuals growing up in a diverse household, third culture kids' adaptation experiences, and a willingness to encounter differences have been found to enhance creative tendencies of individuals (Leung, Maddux, Galinsky, & Chiu, 2008; Maddux & Galinsky, 2009).

MINDFUL TRANSFORMATION

According to Langer's (1997) concept of mindfulness, mindfulness can include the following characteristics: (a) learning to see behavior or information presented in the conflict situation as novel or fresh, (b) learning to view a conflict situation from several vantage points or perspectives, (c) learning to attend to the conflict context and the person whose behavior we are perceiving, and (d) learning to create new categories through which conflict behavior may be understood. Applying this Western mindfulness orientation to IC conflict, the perspective suggests a readiness to shift one's frame of reference from an ethnocentric lens to an ethnorelative lens, and the possibility to see things from the other person's cultural frame of reference.

On the other side of the spectrum, mindfulness, from an Eastern Buddhist orientation, means "emptying our mind-set" and learning to listen deeply without preconceived notions, judgments, and assumptions. Through an Eastern philosophical lens (Chogyam, 1976; Kabat-Zinn, 1994; Thich, 1998), mindfulness means learning to observe an unfolding conflict episode with one-pointed wakefulness and watchfulness. It means being fully present—attending fully to our own arising emotions and our conflict partner's conflict assumptions, worldviews, positions, interests, and arising emotions. It also means listening deeply with all our senses open and all our perceptual filters unclogged.

In fact, the Chinese character for *"listening"* refers to the term *"ting,"* which means "listening with one-pointed attention with our ears, eyes, and a focused heart." Thus, mindful listening in any conflict situation means listening to the hidden value assumptions, expectancies, words, tones, nonverbal nuances, multilayered meanings, and contexts that underlie the symbolic exchange messages. This layered way of listening is of great benefit in an IC tug-and-pull conflict episode. It slows down the antagonistic, polarized conflict process. It increases the chance of mutual, authentic understanding. It essentially involves a gradual shift of worldview or cultural perspective as viewed from an alternative lens. It takes into account not only how things look from my cultural identity perspective, but how they look and feel from my conflict partner's identity perspective. It also displays respect that allows the conflict storyteller to tell a complete conflict story without interruptions and judgments.

IC conflict competence is really about the mindful management of emotional frustrations and conflict interaction struggles due primarily to cultural or ethnic group membership differences. It means having the necessary culture-based knowledge, open-minded attitude, and operational skills of mindfully "minding the mind" and making the commitment to see things from a different light. *Mindful transformation* is the incremental awakening process in understanding how our own cultural worldviews and value system shape our conflict responses and gut-level reactions, and simultaneously, realizing that there are alternative worldviews and value systems that frame our cultural partners' conflict lens and meanings.

According to Senge, Scharmer, Jaworski, and Flowers (2004), to engage in transformative change, individuals need to practice a "U-movement," where the downward swing is characterized by "transforming our habitual way of seeing" and the upward swing is characterized by "transforming the source of our awareness" (p. 224). To transform "our habitual way of seeing," competent communicators need to intentionally shift their frame of focus from their habitual angle of seeing things to seeing things from another viewfinder. In committing to transform "the source of our awareness," competent communicators need to intentionally examine the grounded assumptions and premises that drive their opponents' conflict meaning-making process within embedded historical and immediate cultural contexts.

We can also use some critical reflective questions to guide our conflict transformative "U" learning process (Fisher-Yoshida, 2005; Mezirow, 2000). For example, if my IC conflict partner was using "silence" or indirect response to every question I asked during the conflict negotiation phase, the mindful transformative questions that I can process internally are: First, what are my cultural and personal assessments about the use of "silence" in this particular conflict scene (a content reflection question)? Second, why do I form such assessments and what are the sources of my assessments (a process critical reflection question)? Third, what are the underlying assumptions or values that drive my evaluative assessments (a premise-value question)? Fourth, how do I know that they are relevant or valid in this conflict context (a premise-self-challenge question)? Fifth, what reasons might I have for maintaining or changing my underlying conflict premises (an identity transformation question)? Sixth, how should I shift my cultural or personal premises into the direction that promotes deeper IC understanding (a mind-set transformation question)? Seventh, how should I behaviorally swing adaptively to the other person's preferred conflict competence responses in order to facilitate a productive mutual-interest outcome (a behavioral transformation question)? The first three questions are based on Fisher-Yoshida's (2005) work concerning the importance of engaging in deeper double-loop thinking in analyzing the role of self-in-conflict context. The last four questions are an extension of Ting-Toomey's (1999) mindful transformation work. Concurrently, these questions can also be extended to include your cultural partner's viewpoint in terms of his or her lens in viewing the ongoing IC conflict episode.

The mindful IC conflict negotiator is one who is nimble and flexible enough to engage in a figure eight dance during a protracted conflict situation. She or he can integrate the best practices of both individualistic and collectivistic value tendencies, and the equality treatment and respect-humility attributes of both small and larger power distance value tendencies. This creative, hybrid individual can also do multiple U-swing loops in learning to let go of some of his or her previously ingrained cultural habits and to recrystallize some of the newfound knowledge repertoires into his or her mindscape. Mindful reflexivity means digging deep into our own retinas to truly understand why we see what we see, and simultaneously, mindful transformation also means stretching our imagination and making a strong commitment to really see the holistic conflict meaning-making process from our cultural partner's field of experience and multifaceted vision.

Summary

Competence in IC conflict requires that we communicate appropriately and effectively in different IC conflict negotiation situations. To engage in appropriate conflict responses, we need to understand the worldviews and the value premises of a culture as a starting point. To communicate effectively to achieve mutual-interest conflict goals, we need to first truly understand why our conflict partner holds such a strong position concerning his or her conflict goal. Both criteria call for a mindful transformational process of our own value assumptions, affective reactions, and behavioral tendencies in approaching an IC conflict scene.

A mindful transformation process entails a deep process of listening—that is, mindfully listening to the cultural premises, personal expectancies, situational dynamics, and unmet interpersonal conflict needs of the other conflict party. It also requires us to code-switch adaptively in order to communicate elastically in the unfolding IC conflict drama. By understanding some of the value patterns such as individualism-collectivism and small-large power distance in a flexible manner, and by appreciating some of the shared common human emotions in any conflict, such as anxiety, fear, pain, anger, and hurt, we are on the road to practicing IC conflict competence.

IC conflict competence is an intentional commitment in viewing a frustrated conflict episode from an ethnorelative perspective. It is also an affective commitment in trying to approach our cultural opponents as copartners from whom we are willing to learn, with a sense of respect and mutual interdependence.

DISCUSSION QUESTIONS

1. Among the components that facilitate communicative competence, knowledge is the most important for managing IC conflict. What is meant by knowledge? Do you agree or disagree? Why or why not? Can knowledge about another person's culture ever lead you to be incompetent? If so, how? (Hint: If you meet a Japanese man and presume he possesses collectivistic values and treat him accordingly, do you run the risk of unduly stereotyping him?) Enter a debate with your classmates in terms of the pros and cons of understanding various cultural value patterns.

2. Low-context and high-context communication styles promote two rather different communication orientations to conflict. How are these differences reconciled in an IC conflict? Who should code-switch or adapt to whom? Identify all the factors that should influence your decision in terms of whether you should adapt to the other person's conflict style or he or she should adapt to your style?

3. Review the case study in this chapter. Identify all the distal and proximal factors that shape the conflict lens of Mr. William Bates and Mr. Satoshi Ota. If you are the IC consultant to this organization, what IC conflict competence guidelines would you offer to the two conflict parties? Can you offer an alternative follow-up script for Mr. Bates in terms of how he could have responded more productively to Mr. Ota's "motivational speech"? Can you offer some concrete tips to both Mr. Bates and Mr. Ota so that they can both approach each other in a follow-up conversation with an ethnorelative mind-set?

4. Cultural and personal habits are hard to break. What are some communication strategies you can use to motivate your friends or workplace peers to change some of their conflict habits and patterns? What are some self-motivational strategies you can use on yourself to experiment with some different ways of thinking about conflict and reacting to conflict? Identify some obstacles that prevent such change and pinpoint incentives or rewards that follow such change.

chapter 8

COMPETENCE IN ORGANIZATIONAL CONFLICTS

Wendy H. Papa, Michael J. Papa, and Rick A. Buerkel
Central Michigan University

CHAPTER OUTLINE

Case Study: Grameen Bank versus Moneylenders
Organizational Conflict Viewed from a Competence-Based Approach
Organizational Conflict and the Explanatory Model of Interpersonal
  Conflict
    Distal Context
    Proximal Context
    Conflict Interaction
    Proximal Outcomes
    Distal Outcomes
Phases of Conflict
    Differentiation
    Mutual Problem Description
    Integration
Applying the Phase Model to Organizational Conflict
    Interpersonal Conflicts in Organizational Settings
    Bargaining and Negotiation
    Intergroup Conflict
    Interorganizational Conflict
Summary
Discussion Questions

Case Study: Grameen Bank versus Moneylenders

The Grameen Bank in Bangladesh has become an international "icon" of organizations that focus on empowerment of the poor. Over the past 37 years the Grameen Bank has successfully mobilized more than seven million poor people in Bangladesh into an organizational framework in which they interact, generate income through self-employment, and improve their socioeconomic status (Auwal & Singhal, 1992; Fuglesang & Chandler, 1988; Papa, Auwal, & Singhal, 1995, 1997; Papa, Singhal, & Papa, 2006). However, as the Grameen Bank has expanded its offices throughout rural Bangladesh, its workers have come into increasing conflict with an organized group of moneylenders. These moneylenders have become an accepted part of Bangladeshi society, even though they charge very high interest rates that trap the poor into an economic relationship from which they can rarely exit. When a landless, poor family is denied access to conventional bank loans, the moneylenders surface as the only available source of credit. Although the Grameen Bank has successfully undermined the power base of this corrupt group in certain areas of Bangladesh, numerous conflicts have surfaced between moneylenders and Grameen Bank workers.

One story illuminates how a group of Grameen Bank workers managed a conflict with a group of moneylenders (Shehabuddin, 1992). Three moneylenders threatened to break the legs of a Grameen Bank worker who walked each day along a path in front of their office on her way to work. When the thirty women members of the local bank heard about this threat, they showed up at the office of the moneylenders. They told the moneylenders that they could threaten the bank worker only if they were prepared to lend the local poor the money they needed on the same terms as those of the Grameen Bank. The moneylenders were not willing to give up their exorbitant interest rates, but they promised to stop harassing the bank workers as well as the members of the local community who no longer came to them for money.

The Grameen Bank story gives us some insights into the management of conflict between members of two different organizations. The members of the Grameen Bank recognized that in Bangladesh no government regulations would help them manage their problems with the moneylenders. Furthermore, the moneylenders have become an established part of Bangladeshi society, despite their unfair treatment of the poor. The bank members realized that the moneylenders were confident in their ability to continue business, so they adopted a specific goal that addressed their immediate concerns. The bank members wanted to prevent the moneylenders from threatening and harming bank workers and local community members who were the recipients of bank loans. The conflict management strategy of the bank members was to confront the moneylenders directly in an organized group of thirty women. As Shehabuddin (1992) observed, "There is power in numbers: Thirty women can intimidate wealthy men if they join forces to show their collective strength" (p. 83). Their affiliation with the Grameen Bank empowered these women to oppose an oppressive force. Although moneylenders continue to operate in the local community, the Grameen Bank members established their right to receive loans at reasonable interest rates.

Organizational researchers have long recognized that conflict is an inevitable and pervasive part of organizational life (Baron, 1984, 1985; Fisher, 1993; Jones & White, 1985; Katz & Kahn, 1978; Morrill & Thomas, 1992; Papa, Daniels, & Spiker, 2008; Papa & Pood, 1988a, 1988b; Perrow, 1979; Pondy, 1967; Putnam & Poole, 1987; Tjosvold & Chia, 1989). In this chapter the term *conflict* refers to any incompatibility between people or other organizational units (Deutsch, 1973), especially incompatibility regarding valued goals (Wilmot & Hocker, 2007). As the Grameen Bank case study shows, incompatibilities often arise because of differences in orientations (for example, what sort of loan programs should the poor be offered, or what means of persuasion are acceptable to manage conflict) as well as in goals. Once orientations are clarified, conflict can be managed productively.

Putnam and Poole (1987) observe that organizational conflict occurs in primarily four arenas: (1) interpersonal (e.g., coworkers involved in a dispute, or a superior and a subordinate in confrontation); (2) bargaining and negotiation (e.g., labor versus management, sales representative versus buyer); (3) intergroup (e.g., departments fighting over scarce resources); and (4) interorganizational (e.g., organizations competing for market share). Each of these areas is important to explore for a comprehensive understanding of organizational conflict. In this chapter, we rely on *phase theory* (described shortly) for insight into how individuals or other organizational units can communicate competently during conflict episodes.

More precisely, this chapter outlines what we mean by competence in organizational conflicts. Following our clarification of competence, we discuss how individuals or other organizational units within organizations manage conflict, relying on phase theory.

Organizational Conflict Viewed from a Competence-Based Approach

A number of researchers have explained what is meant by a "competence-based" approach to the study of conflict (Canary, Cupach, & Serpe, 2001; Spitzberg et al., 1994). First, a competence-based approach examines the *impressions* of a person's communication behavior, not just the behavior itself. Second, a competence-based approach utilizes criteria that are often equated with communication quality. Two criteria that have been applied to conflict episodes are appropriateness and effectiveness (Canary & Spitzberg, 1987, 1989). Communication is *appropriate* when it does not violate relationally or situationally sanctioned rules, and *effective* when it achieves the valued objectives of the interactant. Thus, the more appropriate and effective an interactant is, the more that person optimizes the possible outcomes of conflict (Canary et al., 2001; Spitzberg et al., 1994).

The applicability of appropriateness and effectiveness (see chapter 2) to organizational conflicts is linked to the fact that most of these conflicts are between parties (individuals, groups, departments, organizations) that have a relational history and expect to have a relational future. For example, when two employees come into conflict over a work task, their relationship will probably continue after the dispute is managed. Since most organizational relationships do not end at the conclusion of a conflict episode, the balancing of appropriate and effective behavior becomes important. Each party in the conflict needs to engage in behavior that is viewed as effective, because such behavior increases the probability that each party will obtain valued objectives. However, each party also needs to engage in behaviors that are viewed as appropriate, given the nature of the relationship between parties, so that future problem solving can be productive (Gross, Guerrero, & Alberts, 2004). With its focus on a competence-based approach, the explanatory model of interpersonal conflict (see chapter 2) can also be applied to organizational conflicts.

Organizational Conflict and the
Explanatory Model of Interpersonal Conflict

The explanatory model of interpersonal conflict presented in chapter 2 identifies key components of conflict that are relevant to organizational conflicts as well. If organizational members understand these components and how they relate to one another, they will be more likely to manage their conflicts competently. So, we will look at each of these components.

DISTAL CONTEXT

As explained in chapter 2, *distal context* refers to "background" characteristics that exist prior to a specific conflict episode. Among the factors related to distal context are: culture, individual dispositions, relationship history and definition, prior conflict outcomes, and knowledge and skill. Let's consider each of these factors as they pertain to organizational conflict.

With respect to culture, the national cultural environment in which workers are embedded may influence how they socially construct conflict. For example, Kim and Leung (2000) note that American culture promotes individualism that results in the desirability of direct confrontation in conflict. Conversely, in many Asian countries where collectivism is cultivated, avoidance is used regularly to preserve relational harmony and to save others' face. So, the cultural environment in which one lives influences the type of social construction that unfolds with respect to particular communication processes such as conflict management. In addition, in our increasingly global environment challenges may arise in situations where workers from different national cultures must work through a conflict with one another. Specifically, what is seen as competent from the perspective of one cultural environment will not be perceived as competent from another.

Individual dispositions can also impact the course of conflict in organizations (Nicotera & Dorsey, 2006; Oetzel, 1998; Shuter & Turner, 1997). For example, Shuter and Turner (1997) focused on gender and race by studying conflict narratives used by African American and European American women in managerial and nonmanagerial roles. They discovered that African American women value more direct approaches to conflict than European American women. Shuter and Turner also asked their respondents to describe their perception of workplace conflict behaviors for African American women, for European American women, and for themselves personally. In providing their responses the women were asked to focus on four behaviors: avoidance, maintenance, reduction, or escalation. They found that European American women were viewed as more likely to avoid conflict in comparison to African American women. Also, in comparison to European American women, African American women viewed all women as more likely to choose escalation, were more likely to see themselves as reducing conflict, and were less likely to see European Americans as maintaining conflict. These findings show clearly that race influences perceptions of women in organizations concerning conflict.

Relationship history and definition also constitute part of the distal context. If two coworkers have developed a relationship where they trust one another, the conflict is likely to unfold productively. Conversely, a relational history replete with trust violations may result in each party viewing one another suspiciously during a conflict (Jameson, 1999; Papa et al., 2008).

Finally, prior conflict outcomes as well as knowledge and skill may impact how organizational members manage a conflict. For example, Jameson (1999) argues that a high record of success in managing conflict creates a more productive environment for discussion than does a low record of success. In addition, the more knowledge coworkers have about one another's views on issues and each other's personality characteristics, the more capable they will be in adapting to their partner in ways that produce positive outcomes.

PROXIMAL CONTEXT

Proximal context refers to the perceptual environment that is immediately attached to a specific conflict. Among the factors relevant to proximal context are goals, rules, emotions, and attributions. With respect to goals it is important to note that organizations have many goals. Some of these goals are clear, others are ambiguous, and some contradict one another. Many stakeholder groups also have goals that impact organizational functioning, ranging from employees and managers to consumer groups and regulatory agencies (Hodge, Anthony, & Gales, 2003). In fact, the multitude of goals that exist in and are connected to organizations creates many opportunities for conflict. For example, Song, Xie, and Dyer (2000) observe that incongruent goals are one of the leading causes of conflict in organizations. Furthermore, a high level of goal incongruity generally leads to a high level of cross-functional conflict and open hostility (Pinto, Pinto, & Prescott, 1993). This does not mean that incongruent goals prevent productive conflict management, however. Through competent communication, organizational members may clarify one another's goals and perhaps identify new goals that build on mutual interests.

Rules are necessary in any complex organization to allow for the coordination of effort among people and departments. The impact of these rules on conflict varies, however. On the one hand, rules may advantage some groups while disadvantaging others. Workers who believe that certain rules are unfair may use conflict as a means of challenging those rules and creating new ones. Conversely, in bargaining, parties may negotiate rules to structure deliberations in ways that create the grounds for productive conflict (Putnam & Poole, 1987).

When workers within organizations discuss issues that are of great importance to them personally and/or professionally, strong emotions can surface. Because conflicts over such issues may lead to a worker's needs not being met, the emotions that attend the conflict (e.g., anger, fear, etc.) might interfere with managing it in a productive manner (Burrell, Buzzanell, & McMillan, 1992; Papa et al., 2008).

Attributions occur when people attempt to explain behavior in terms of causality and responsibility. When attributions are positive (e.g., Jim always acts in the best interests of our department), the conflict has a greater chance of unfolding smoothly. However, in some workplace conflicts each party may attribute "the causes of negative events to internal and stable features of their partner" (Papa & Canary, 1995, p. 166). In such instances the motives and actions of each party are viewed negatively and with suspicion, creating a potentially destructive environment for conflict.

CONFLICT INTERACTION

Conflict interaction concerns what occurs during the process of the conflict episode. Here, the focus is on message tactics, strategies, and patterns. The tactics and strategies selected by conflict participants may create patterns that are constructive or destructive in managing disputes between parties. For example, Fisher and Ury (1981) contend that during a negotiation participants need to separate people from the problem. This separation is necessary because negotiators often become personally involved with the issues they are discussing and with their group's positions. When this occurs negotiators will perceive a response to their positions as a personal attack. This ensures a quick downward spiral in the ensuing discussions with each side perceiving that they are being attacked personally and then responding in kind. Conversely, when you effectively separate people from the issues under discussion you may address the issues without damaging the relationship between sides. Simply stated, the focus of the negotiation session should be on the problem and how to solve it.

PROXIMAL OUTCOMES

Proximal outcomes are the immediate consequences of a conflict episode. For example, Weider-Hatfield and Hatfield (1995) found that there was a strong relationship between the use of integrating strategies to manage conflict and five organizational outcomes: job satisfaction, perceptions of workplace equity, system outcomes, job and performance outcomes, and interpersonal outcomes. Integrative strategies during conflict have also been associated with more effective decision making (Kuhn & Poole, 2000). Finally, integrative conflict strategies have been found to promote the development of innovation in organizations (Song, Dyer, & Thieme, 2006).

DISTAL OUTCOMES

Distal outcomes refer to the delayed effects of conflict that emerge over time. For example, when two employees work creatively to manage a conflict that has created significant problems for both of them they may develop a stronger relationship with one another that eventually becomes a social relationship as well. At a broader level, consistently engaging in competent communication during conflict may, over time, impact the culture of an organization. Barge (2006) develops this perspective when he explains that a commitment to dialogue as a means of managing conflict in organizations could lead to a dialogic culture, "a way of being and living together that recognizes the differences that exist among members of a community and highlights possibilities for collaboration" (pp. 520–521). A dialogic culture recognizes and encourages multiple points of view, values otherness, encourages the pursuit of a rich understanding of the complexity of problems, and generates new possibilities for meaning and action.

In this section of the chapter, we linked the explanatory model of interpersonal conflict to organizational conflict. Next, we turn to phase theory to describe a general model that depicts how organizational conflicts can be managed in a competent manner.

Phases of Conflict

Phase models describe the sequences of behaviors that interactants display as conflicts unfold over time. For example, Walton (1969) characterizes conflict in terms of two broad phases: differentiation and integration. During *differentiation,* positions and differences are clarified. *Integration* is the convergence on agreement between positions. To move from differentiation to integration, we believe, requires another phase: *mutual problem description.* In this phase the conflicting parties describe the problem they are confronting in mutual terms (i.e., a problem that requires the efforts of each party to reach an acceptable solution). Thus, in this section we consider the behaviors that appear to be optimizing—that is, behaviors that should lead to appropriateness and effectiveness evaluations—during the differentiation, mutual problem description, and integration phases of organizational conflict.

DIFFERENTIATION

During *differentiation*, interactants raise the conflict issue, clarify positions, pursue the reasons behind those positions, and acknowledge the severity of positional differences (Folger, Poole, & Stutman, 1993). The importance of differentiation to conflict management is perhaps best summarized by Deutsch (1973), who notes that without differentiation, the probability of finding a solution—"one in which the participants are all satisfied with their outcomes—is a hit or miss venture" (p. 17).

Although differentiation represents an essential part of conflict management, it is difficult in the context of an ongoing conflict. When two people recognize that a conflict exists between them, often each person initially perceives his or her partner as a barrier or stumbling block to obtaining the desired goals or rewards (Wilmot & Hocker, 2007). How can the potential problems of differentiation be avoided? In the differentiation phase, communication behaviors are optimized through *information sharing* (explaining your perspective on the issue of dispute) and *information seeking* (soliciting the other person's perspective). Information sharing is crucial to each party's understanding of the perspective advanced by his or her partner. In this discussion the primary purpose of information sharing is to enable the other person to understand your position for joint advantage (Putnam & Jones, 1982). Research suggests that sharing information during a conflict increases the likelihood of reaching a creative solution that meets the needs and goals of each party (Papa & Pood, 1988a, 1988b).

Information seeking is important because it allows interactants to confirm the accuracy of their perceptions of a partner's views on the conflict issue. Without seeking information, each conflict interactant would experience difficulty attaining a clear understanding of his or her partner's views on the conflict. Furthermore, as Fisher and Ury (1981) argued, when people seek information during a conflict, the likelihood of understanding increases because "questions generate answers" and, therefore, lead to insight. Information sharing and seeking require that each party to the conflict explain his or her perception of the conflict issue. This exchange entails defining the problem that is creating the dispute, and in the process, each side may discover that different perceptions of the problem exist. Any perception that is different should be discussed, since it represents a starting point toward eventual management of the conflict.

Once the conflict participants agree on a definition of the problem (and each person accepts responsibility for his or her role in creating and maintaining the problem), they can identify their individual positions on the dispute and, importantly, their reasons for those positions. In explaining the reasons supporting a position, an interactant supplies his or her partner with insight into what is important about this particular conflict. Moreover, the strength of the commitment to the position becomes clear.

How do people share and seek information during differentiation? Each party to a conflict clearly explains his or her position on the issue of dispute, and the reasons underlying that position. After party A describes his or her position and the underlying reasons for that position, party B must seek clarifying information to make sure that B understands A's position and reasoning. The two parties to the conflict should then switch roles so that A can gain a clear understanding of B's positions on the conflict and the reasons supporting them.

MUTUAL PROBLEM DESCRIPTION

The *mutual problem description phase* is a bridge between the differentiation and integration phases. It can be considered competent for two reasons. First, in describing a conflict in mutual terms, each party accepts responsibility for the conditions of the conflict and socially constructs the conflict in understandable terms. Second, the problem is described as one demanding the efforts of each party to identify a solution that achieves the goals of each party. Thus, through mutual problem description, each party becomes invested in obtaining an optimal outcome.

Differentiation highlights the importance of presenting personal positions during conflict. When presenting positions and defining the conflict issue, each person should acknowledge his or her mutual role in creating and sustaining the conflict, thus contributing to a mutual problem description. Unfortunately, such mutuality is not always acknowledged. The feelings of anger that sometimes simmer before an individual expresses his or her opinions about a problem with a coworker, for example, might prevent the logical reasoning necessary to cast a problem in mutual terms (Freud, 1900/1953, 1949). Such a person can feel justified in pointing a finger of blame at the coworker and simultaneously see no contradiction in absolving him- or herself from any involvement in the creation or maintenance of the problem.

The first step toward mutual problem description when conflicting parties are stuck defining the problem from their individual perspectives is *recognizing relational interdependence.* As Papa and Canary (1995) observed:

> When two parties are involved in an open struggle and each perceives the other as a stumbling block to personal goal attainment the two parties are *interdependent.* So, the issue becomes how to get each party to recognize what is already present in their relationship. Competence in communication then is reflected in the actions of the person (or persons) who makes the move to define relational interdependence. (p. 163)

Even when conflict interactants accept the fact that it is in their best interests to negotiate an outcome that is mutually satisfactory, deadlocks can obstruct problem description. One way to remove such deadlocks is to *restructure the problem.* As Sycara (1991) observes, "problem restructuring is the process of dynamically changing the structure of the conflict problem to achieve momentum towards agreement" (p. 1248). The first step in restructuring the problem is for each side to put all of their desired outcome goals (both short-term and long-term) on the table. Once these goals are known, the parties can search for relations among the goals that indicate a dovetailing of interests. According to Sycara, "by having access to information concerning goals and relations among them, [conflicting parties] can produce promising problem reformulations" (p. 1249).

Mutual problem description can be considered an optimizing response to conflict because it ensures that the needs of each party are addressed. Thus, each party has the potential to be effective in obtaining his or her objectives when the final outcome is negotiated. Mutual problem definition also forces each party to be attentive to the needs of his or her partner. When party A focuses on the needs of party B during problem description, party A is being attentive to their relationship and thus is behaving appropriately.

INTEGRATION

After defining their problem in mutually constructed terms, conflict participants are prepared to move toward integration. During the integration phase, competent communication behaviors include: (1) displaying cooperative tactics, (2) generating alternative solutions, (3) evaluating the positive and negative aspects of each solution, (4) selecting and clarifying the solution to be implemented, and (5) establishing a monitoring system to determine if the solution is being implemented correctly. Such communication behaviors help the conflicting parties remain focused on the problem and commit to identifying a solution that meets the goals of each party.

Displaying Cooperative Tactics.   Various conflict strategies and tactics have been identified in the literature (see chapter 3). A strategy is the general approach a person takes to manage conflicts; tactics are the specific behaviors that institute the strategy (Newton & Burgoon, 1990). Three general strategies identified by communication researchers are *integration, distribution,* and *avoidance* (Putnam & Wilson, 1982; Sillars et al., 1982). In the integrative strategy (not to be confused with the integrative *phase* we are now discussing), parties unite resources to manage the conflict. Integrative tactics include behaviors such as considering a full range of alternatives, seeking a mutually beneficial solution, and compromising after a period of competition. The distributive strategy is competitive and includes behavioral tactics such as criticizing the partner, shouting, and using threats and sarcasm. Finally, the avoidant strategy seeks to distract attention from the conflict by denying the presence or severity of the conflict or by shifting the partner's focus to another issue. As a rule, the more cooperative behaviors are those that seek to integrate resources. In addition, such behaviors have been positively associated with perceptions of appropriateness and effectiveness (Canary & Spitzberg, 1990). Using integrative, cooperative tactics helps align, instead of malign, orientations to the problem (Papa & Canary, 1995).

Generating Alternative Solutions.   Solutions should not be advanced until both parties agree on the nature of the problem (Graham & Papa, 1993; Graham, Papa, & McPherson, 1997). One reason for withholding solutions is that standards for evaluating the effectiveness of the solution are based on meeting all exigencies presented by the problem. Two strategic approaches to generating solutions are collaboration and compromise. *Collaboration* involves seeking a solution that satisfies both parties' goals, whereas *compromise* refers to splitting the difference between parties' goals. Collaboration is often held as the preferred approach for problem solving; by definition, it is an optimizing response to conflict. As Wilmot and Hocker (2007) observed, however, collaboration is also costly in terms of time and energy. Not all conflicts merit the investment of energy required to collaborate. On the other hand, although compromise may be seen as cooperative and appropriate, the solutions reached through compromise may be temporary. Compromise also precludes the emergence of creative alternatives.

Solutions to problems should satisfy standards agreed to by all parties. Papa and Canary (1995) offered six such standards, describing the optimal *solution* as:

1. *Feasible:* The solution should be both doable and desirable.
2. *Ethical:* The solution should not violate standards for personal conduct.
3. *Fair:* Neither party should take advantage of the other.
4. *Efficient:* The solution should reduce the amount of work currently done to manage the problem.
5. *Permanent:* The solution should be effective over the long term as well as in the immediate present.
6. *Inexpensive:* The solution should not cost the company more money than it will receive in long-term benefits.

Standards that guide choices of solutions can also be used to monitor the effectiveness of solutions.

Evaluating, Selecting, and Monitoring. Hirokawa (1985, 1988) argued that solutions should be evaluated for both positive *and* negative consequences. Although employees might be eager to offer supporting arguments for solutions, they should also consider the possible negative ramifications of *alternative* solutions, including relational outcomes. To accomplish this task practically, parties to the conflict can write the positive and negative consequences separately and then jointly discuss their lists, or the parties can exchange their assessments orally. In either case, this activity can optimize the conflict situation. Although one cannot identify all the merits and problems associated with a solution before it is implemented, one may minimize hardships by anticipating negative as well as positive consequences of solutions (Graham et al., 1997).

After discussing both positive and negative aspects of alternative solutions, the parties need to select one solution. If the parties have engaged in the phases of differentiation, mutual problem description, and integration, the selection of a solution should be relatively straightforward.

Finally, the conflict parties should establish a monitoring mechanism to ensure that the solution selected continues to operate over time. Two obvious criteria that can be used to assess the efficacy of the solution are appropriateness and effectiveness. Accordingly, we can assess how optimizing the solution is by determining whether it has promoted the fulfillment of organizational expectations. In addition, the solution can be assessed in terms of its effectiveness; that is, one can ascertain whether the solution accomplishes both parties' goals.

The implementation of a monitoring system can prevent conflicting parties from reverting to prior destructive behaviors. Old ways of thinking and behaving are difficult to abandon. Some individuals even seek information that convinces them that the new idea should never have been adopted (Rogers, 2003). Thus, one purpose of monitoring is to ensure that each side follows the agreements that were part of the solution.

Applying the Phase Model to Organizational Conflict

Having identified conflict behaviors that are optimizing within the general framework of phase theory, in the following sections we examine how conflicting parties can display competence in the four main arenas of organizational conflict: (1) interpersonal, (2) bargaining and negotiation, (3) intergroup, and (4) interorganizational. In each of these contexts we demonstrate the utility of phase theory with examples. However, these examples do not exhaust how phase theory can guide other types of conflict.

INTERPERSONAL CONFLICTS IN ORGANIZATIONAL SETTINGS

Within organizational settings, interpersonal conflict arises primarily in two types of dyadic relationships: (1) superior-subordinate and (2) coworkers. The literature on the behaviors that surface in these conflicts suggests that when superiors are in conflict with their subordinates, they tend to use forcing or competitive strategies that rely on their power within the organization (Howat & London, 1980; Kipnis & Schmidt, 1982; Morley & Shockley-Zalabak, 1986; Phillips & Cheston, 1979; Putnam & Wilson, 1982). Conversely, subordinates tend to avoid, compromise, or smooth over issues when in conflict with their superiors (London & Howat, 1978; Putnam & Wilson, 1982; Renwick, 1975).

The literature regarding conflict between coworkers does not reveal as clear a set of behavioral tendencies. When positional power is removed from an organizational relationship, a wider range of behaviors seems to emerge. Researchers examining coworker conflict have focused more on how perceptual issues or informational and organizational environments influence behavioral choices. For example, Papa and Pood (1988a, 1988b) observed that when organizational actors enter a conflict with accurate knowledge of one another's views on the issue of dispute, they are more likely to enact friendly influence strategies (for example, "Larry can you help me understand why we should target this consumer group next month?"). Less knowledge is more likely to engender assertive behavior (for example, "Look, Larry, these figures make no sense whatsoever"). An organization's history or "conflict management culture" can also influence employee behavior. For instance, Tjosvold (1982, 1983) observed that when an organization has developed a problem-solving history, members are more likely to ask questions and integrate issues when involved in disputes. Conversely, organizations could endorse avoidance between coworkers.

We apply the phase model of competence in conflict by closely examining an organizational conflict at the interpersonal level. Box 8-1 presents an extended research example to illustrate this application. Interested readers should read box 8-1 carefully, to obtain a complete sense of phase theory in action.

Box 8-1   Phase Theory Application in an Interpersonal Context

As part of their research program examining organizational conflict, Papa and Pood (1988a, 1988b) videotaped 54 dyads who were involved in a dispute over their company's proposed plan to adopt a participative decision-making system. In these dyads, one person supported the company's proposal to adopt the system, and the other person opposed the system. Presented below are specific statements from a conflict in which the participants reported satisfaction with the outcome of their discussion.

> *Manager:* I like the proposed system because it includes input from more employees about how we get things done around here. Managers aren't the only ones who know how to get things done. People like you know as much about how things are done around here as anyone else.

> *Subordinate:* I haven't liked the system since I first heard about it. We're overworked now, and this new system will increase our workload. Plus, I don't think that many of the managers around here are going to back down and listen to one of our suggestions. What makes you think things will get better if we implement this system?

> *Manager:* I've heard some of the other people in our unit ask the same question. I know you all feel overworked, but if we could all start talking more about how work is accomplished around here maybe we could improve our efficiency and make things a little less hectic. We just keep plugging away on a day-to-day basis and never take the chance to think about whether there is a better way. Do you at least think that the people in our unit can put our heads together to improve things?

> *Subordinate:* I know you've been sympathetic to our workload in the past, and I appreciate that. I also know you're optimistic that if we put our heads together we can figure out a way to sort through all the craziness of juggling twenty different cases every day. I guess I'm just tired of listening to management talking about how things are going to get better, when they only seem to get worse. But we do help each other out, at least in our department. Maybe there's some hope. I'm just not sure.

In the preceding dialogue, the manager and the subordinate successfully work through the differentiation phase of their conflict by engaging in the optimizing behaviors of information sharing and information seeking. Both the manager and the subordinate state their positions on the issue of dispute (the proposed participative decision-making system) and the reasons for their positions. Both interactants ask questions of one another. These questions help each person to understand a little bit more about their partner's perspective on the conflict issue. We return to this discussion as the interactants begin to frame a mutual problem:

> *Manager:* You know I'm getting pressure from the regional manager to move this system along. But I know you're hesitant to spend time you don't have on a system you're skeptical of. Isn't there some way we can work together on this?

Subordinate: Well, I just want to feel that we're really going to be given a voice on this. I don't want to waste time talking about how we're going to participate, when nothing really changes. Can we get together and talk about how we're going to *share* responsibility to get things done? I think some of us in this department have some good ideas about how to streamline some procedures, but we have to be given the chance to try these ideas out without having to go through five levels of management to get the OK.

Manager: I think you're right. I want to be an equal partner with the rest of you in deciding how to improve things. I don't just want to be a gatekeeper who gets the OK for our group from upper management. I also don't want to stand in the way of what you and the others think is a good idea. We just have to try some new ideas first and see what happens. Of course, I think my opinions deserve to be considered like everyone else's. How does that sound?

Subordinate: I think we're going in the right direction here. If you're willing to listen to us and give us the chance to try some different things, maybe this participative decision-making plan will work. If we're really a team here and you aren't going to stop what the rest of us think will work, I'll feel more positive. I guess we can at least talk about what some first steps will be.

In the preceding dialogue, both interactants talk about how they have to work together if the new system is to be effective. From the subordinate's viewpoint, the manager's statement about wanting to be an *equal* member of the department on discussions of work changes is important. This statement helps meet the subordinate's concern that potentially good ideas can be vetoed by the manager. However, the manager also emphasizes that his opinions on new ideas deserve to be considered. Thus, in this short dialogue, the manager and the subordinate merge on the description of the problem that confronts them. These two people perceive themselves to be part of a work team. They are considering a shift in how decisions are made, and they need one another's help for the system to work. Let's return to the conflict as it approaches the integration phase:

Subordinate: How about we start by talking about increasing our financial authority to negotiate settlements with claimants? It's really a problem when we have to have so many of our decisions okayed by management.

Manager: I think that may be a good idea, but let's not rush things. How about we get everyone together to talk about the things that are causing the greatest problems and address them one at a time?

Subordinate: I don't know; that may just be a gripe session. What if we all write down the things that we'd like to change first, and then we can figure out what we can tackle first?

Manager: That sounds more organized. Everyone can give their list to me.

Subordinate: Wait a minute, how about everyone submit their ideas to me? That will show me and the others that you are trying to be a

(continued)

> team player. Maybe I can get together with the other seven people in our unit and we can prioritize the list.
>
> *Manager:* That sounds good, but shouldn't I be part of that meeting too? I won't be there to say yes or no to each idea, but I should have input too.
>
> *Subordinate:* Oh yeah, of course.
>
> In this portion of their conflict discussion, the interactants generate alternative ideas for establishing a participative decision-making system. As the alternatives are discussed and evaluated, the coworkers eventually arrive at one that is mutually acceptable. These statements meet the problem-solving criteria of evaluating and selecting solutions (Hirokawa, 1985, 1988). Now let's move to the final part of the integration phase—monitoring:
>
> *Subordinate:* I'm still worried that we're going to wind up spinning our wheels. What can we do to make sure that we keep on track? You know, so we know we're making progress.
>
> *Manager:* How about we get together once a month to talk about how our new ideas are working? That way we can keep track of what's going right and what problems need to be worked out.
>
> *Subordinate:* Maybe we can work this out. Have you talked to the others in the department yet?
>
> *Manager:* You're the last one. I think this program is finally going to get off the ground.
>
> In this final part of the discussion, the manager and the subordinate agree on a monitoring system. Establishing such a system helps ensure that enacted changes continue to be implemented correctly. By taking this step, the manager and the subordinate help prevent old problems from resurfacing.

BARGAINING AND NEGOTIATION

In bargaining and negotiation, parties exchange proposals as a means of reaching mutual agreement. *Bargaining* means negotiating for someone else; *negotiation* means arguing for your own outcomes. One type of bargaining that is receiving a great deal of attention in the literature is the collective bargaining process between labor and management. The agreements reached through collective bargaining can have a strong impact on the economic profitability of an organization, as well as influence the nature of the relationship between labor and management. In this section we discuss collective bargaining as it relates to labor and management.

Walton and McKersie (1965) first identified a distinction between distributive and integrative bargaining. *Distributive bargaining* typically involves the division of resources. The parties exchanging proposals believe a fixed supply exists of some resource, so one party's gain is the other party's loss. *Integrative bargaining* refers to situations in which the bargainers cast the issue(s) as a common problem that they should cooperatively face. In integrative bargaining, the parties search for solutions that meet the needs of all the participants (Andes, 1992; Mumpower, 1991; Nunamaker, Dennis, Valacich, & Vogel, 1991).

During the differentiation stage of negotiation, the parties need to clarify their positions on the issue in dispute. Integrative bargaining involves the most sharing of information and an accurate disclosure of each party's needs and objectives (Walton & McKersie, 1965). Through information sharing and information seeking, each side comes to a clear understanding of the issues that need to be negotiated.

Another key component of successful negotiation is arriving at a mutual definition of the problem. The first step in this process is to discuss differences in each party's initial perceptions of the problem (Walton & McKersie, 1965). Next, the parties need to separate and prioritize the subissues of the conflict so that they can redefine and clarify the problem (Putnam & Bullis, 1984). This process might result in a restructuring of the problem as the parties recognize relationships among their goals. Ultimately, the parties must determine how they are interdependent so that they can identify superordinate goals that unify them in the search for mutually acceptable solutions.

During the integration stage of negotiation, alternative solutions are identified that meet the goals of each party. To be effective, negotiators must drop their defensive barriers and listen carefully to their opponents' affective and substantive meanings (Lewicki & Litterer, 1985). Once solutions that meet the needs of each party are identified, a means of implementing the solutions should be discussed. Finally, a monitoring mechanism should be identified so that the groups can ensure that the solution remains intact as they continue to work with one another.

To assess the relevance of our phase model to collective bargaining situations, we examine an example that was discussed extensively in the media in 2007: the collective bargaining agreements reached between the United Auto Workers (UAW) and the top three automobile manufacturers in the United States (Ford, General Motors, and Chrysler). Box 8-2 (on pp. 180–181) provides this analysis. And, again, the reader should examine this box to obtain a clear understanding of how bargaining and negotiation competence is portrayed using our phase model.

INTERGROUP CONFLICT

The study of intergroup conflict requires a focus on aggregates rather than on individuals. In this approach, the group is most often viewed as a homogeneous entity. Since groups are composed of independent members, however, many views toward a given conflict issue can exist within the group. Thus, one key issue in intergroup conflict concerns "how groups become and remain homogeneous in order to present a coherent voice and to engage in unified action" (Putnam & Poole, 1987, p. 574).

The development of a coherent voice within a group is linked to the processes of social categorization and group differentiation as well as to the

Box 8-2   Bargaining between the Big Three and Auto Unions

In 2007, top management and owners of the Big Three U.S. automakers were locked into the age-old labor-management dispute over wages and benefits. Management believed that worker wages and benefits had escalated to a level that threatened the survival of the U.S. automobile industry and they appeared to have the financial figures to support their claim. In 1996, Ford, General Motors (GM), and Chrysler sold 73% of all automobiles and trucks purchased worldwide (their market share). With increased competition from foreign automobile manufacturers, the combined market share of the Big Three fell to 53.5% in 2006 (U.S. Department of Commerce, 2007), and projections indicated that market share may decrease to 48% in 2010. These significant reductions in sales have cost the U.S. auto industry billions of dollars a year since the mid-1990s. In fact, in 2007 alone GM lost $38.7 billion (Bunkley, 2008), Ford lost $2.7 billion (Durbin, 2008), and Chrysler lost $1.6 billion (Higgins, 2008). The workers countered by arguing that the losses were due primarily to management decisions, not worker performance, and their arguments were persuasive as well. Specifically, productivity in the auto industry has been rising rapidly, with real output per worker more than doubling since 1987, largely eliminating the productivity gap with the Japanese (Gindin, 2008). Furthermore, union leaders claimed that U.S. auto industry losses were linked to management's determination to stick with larger vehicles and their larger short-term profits when the public was demanding smaller, more fuel-efficient vehicles to cope with rising gasoline prices (Gindin, 2008).

During the early stages of this conflict in the summer of 2007, each side defined the conflict from its own perspective. Workers felt they deserved higher wages and a continuation of benefits (such as health care) because of their high levels of productivity. The owners felt that concessions were needed to reduce costs or the survivability of the U.S. auto industry would be threatened. A deadlock appeared inevitable as negotiations continued into the fall of 2007.

UAW members initiated a strike at GM in September and at Chrysler in October (Carty, 2007). Fortunately, these strikes were short lived as the UAW and management of the Big Three engaged in creative problem restructuring and the introduction of new goals. After carefully analyzing financial data for the U.S. auto industry over the past decade, both groups of negotiators realized that a new superordinate goal existed—industry survival. Without controlling escalating labor and health care costs, the U.S. auto industry was going to continue to lose billions of dollars per year, threatening not only worker jobs but also the entire industry. The agreement contained many components but the two that were most critical and controversial were a two-tier wage structure and a shifting of health care benefits from the automakers to the UAW. What did these two agreements mean for the automakers and UAW workers?

The two-tier wage structure retains wages for current union members at approximately $28 per hour. All future hires, however, will receive wages of approximately $14 per hour. Solidarity, a national labor organization promoting the interests of union workers, predicts that within four years 33–40% of all U.S. autoworkers will occupy this second tier, saving the Big Three billions of dollars per year (Solidarity, 2007).

The second major part of the agreement involved the UAW assuming responsibility for health care benefits for more than 1 million active and retired autoworkers (Ostroff, 2007). In exchange, GM, Ford, and Chrysler agreed to provide approximately $62 billion, collectively, to fund a UAW-run Voluntary Employees' Benefits Association (VEBA) that will pay its members' health care costs (Carty, 2007).

What are the advantages of this historic agreement to both labor and management? From the standpoint of labor, some experts argue that by helping preserve the companies its members work for, the union has a better chance of preserving jobs. "The only real strength of the UAW is sustainably profitable companies. Absent that, the UAW is toast," says David Cole, chairman of the Center for Automotive Research (Carty, 2007, p. 1). The fund also will make the UAW a more powerful force in Washington, where the union has been lobbying for nationalized health care for years. "This agreement is going to help push health care reform in the country," says Jane Lauer Barker, a labor attorney at Pitta & Dreier in New York (Carty, 2007, p. 1).

Management also expects to reap benefits from this labor agreement. First, the deal with the UAW should save the automakers approximately $1,000 per vehicle, making the Big Three more price competitive with foreign automakers. Second, by reducing their liability for providing health care coverage, the automakers will help improve their credit ratings, lowering future borrowing costs (Ostroff, 2007). Finally, some of the cost savings per vehicle can go into designing and building new products (UAW, 2008).

Of course, there are also critics of the labor-management agreement. Some question whether the newly established VEBA will really be able to cover future health care costs (Solidarity, 2007). For example, if returns on the fund are lower than expected or health and drug costs rise faster, the VEBA will either need to make cuts in coverage or increase worker/retiree co-pays (Gindin, 2008). Responding to such concerns, UAW President Ron Gettelfinger stated that he is fully confident that the union will be able to provide retiree health benefits for 80 years (UAW, 2008). So, the success of the agreement remains to be seen.

Looking at this historic labor agreement in the U.S. auto industry, there is one thing that is certain. Labor and management needed to find a way to work collaboratively to solve financial problems so critical that industry survival was a real issue that could not be ignored. This most recent labor-management agreement gives the U.S. auto industry some breathing room to face the challenges of surviving and thriving in the globally competitive environment of the early twenty-first century.

emergence of group ideologies (Folger et al., 1993). *Social categorization* is the process by which people determine membership in different groups. For example, a worker may view herself as part of the "labor" group, which views itself as distinct from the "management" group. Many different social categories are possible in a large organization. Social categories not only create a sense of identification for group members, they also determine which groups oppose others (for example, male versus female, blue-collar versus white-collar, Caucasian versus African American). Social categorization creates communication barriers as in-group members develop perceptions about other-group (or "out-group") members that are never tested. For instance, men develop perceptions about women by talking with other men. However, men are not as likely to test perceptions about women by talking to women about them. As Folger, Poole, and Stutman (1993) concluded, when people accept social categories, they are likely to act toward others on the basis of attributions developed within in-groups, reducing the likelihood of competent organizational conflict management.

Group differentiation refers to polarization between groups. This polarization usually results from group stereotyping. Furthermore, when groups compete with each other, member expressions of loyalty to their group tend to increase. Eventually, a self-reinforcing cycle of polarization and hostility develops between the competing groups. As Coser (1956) explained, in-group members begin to believe that the other group is responsible for their problems. These in-group members will attend primarily to information that portrays the other group as negative, and they do not test their perceptions through interaction.

For example, during a period of economic decline, an organization may have limited resources to increase worker pay. Conflict can develop between Caucasians and African Americans who view themselves in competition for scarce economic rewards. Caucasians may argue that affirmative action programs unfairly compensate African Americans for *who* they are rather than how productive they are. Conversely, African Americans may point to the Caucasian male power structure that dominates top-level decision making and the distribution of economic rewards in most organizations in the United States. Such finger pointing only weakens the relationship between the opposing groups and minimizes their ability to work together productively.

Concerning the practice of affirmative action, U.S. companies have a long way to go to ensure that workers of all races and ethnicities are treated equally. Box 8-3 illustrates such an instance of organizational policy. As before, the reader should examine this case study to obtain a good understanding of how the phase model can depict conflict in context—this time, intergroup conflict.

INTERORGANIZATIONAL CONFLICT

Interorganizational conflicts typically arise in the marketplace as "organizations attempt to carve out and maintain niches or domains" (Putnam & Poole, 1987, p. 581). One way to examine such conflicts is to focus on economic variables (percentage of market share, net profits/losses, and so on). Another way to learn about conflict between organizations is to examine how these disputes are managed by public or private regulatory agencies. For example, a company may be required to address charges that it has violated the provisions of the Antitrust Act. However, when examining interorganizational conflicts over market share, the adoption of a communication perspective is somewhat restrictive. The competing organizations view one another

Box 8-3   Application of Phase Theory to Intergroup Conflict

In 2005, the claims administrator in the *Gonzalez v. Abercrombie & Fitch* discrimination lawsuit sent award checks totaling $40 million to over ten thousand present and former employees of Abercrombie & Fitch (A&F) who were discriminated against for their race or ethnicity. Specifically, the claims administrator found evidence that the company purposefully targeted white employees for both entry-level employment and advancement opportunities in the company. In fact, A&F was found to target fraternities, sororities, and specific colleges for recruitment purposes. This method of recruitment purposefully excluded Latino, African American, and Asian applicants. Among the provisions in the settlement of this case are: (a) "benchmarks" for hiring and promoting Latinos, African Americans, and Asian Americans[1]; (b) advertising of available positions in publications targeting minorities; (c) a new office and vice president of diversity, responsible for reporting to the CEO on A&F's progress toward fair employment practices; (d) equal employment opportunity and diversity training for all employees with hiring authority; (e) revision of performance evaluations for managers, making progress toward diversity goals a factor in their bonuses and compensations; and (f) a new internal complaint procedure (Lieff, Cabraser, Heimann & Bernstein, LLP, 2006). Of course, A&F is just one company, but one can understand how many minority group members harbor suspicions about other organizations that engage in similar practices. These suspicions create barriers to interaction among workers of different racial and ethnic groups and make productive problem solving and conflict management difficult.

Once two groups have been in conflict for a prolonged time period, intergroup ideologies surface. *Intergroup ideologies* are organized belief systems that "describe the differences between groups in terms that present the in-group in a favorable light and explain the conflict from the in-group's perspective" (Folger et al., 1993, p. 37). Once intergroup ideologies develop, the opposing groups feel justified in displaying aggression toward each other. For example, a Caucasian supervisor may purposely give an African American worker unfavorable work assignments, offer only negative feedback on performance, and encourage others in the work group to sabotage this worker's work efforts. The supervisor justifies these behaviors because of ideologies formed with other Caucasians about African Americans and because of the corporate affirmative action program that he believes places him at a disadvantage.

Given such deep-rooted animosities and the emergence of intergroup ideologies, is it possible for competing groups to manage conflict with each other? To address this question, let's turn to our phase model of conflict management. The first step in managing an intergroup conflict is to initiate differentiation by sharing and seeking information. Groups that have formed ideologies of one another on the basis of stereotypes developed within in-groups need to separate fact from fiction by talking with one another.

As different groups come to terms with the thoughts and behaviors that distinguish them from one another, they can begin to focus on mutual problem description. One way to create a mutual problem definition is to *identify a superordinate goal*. However, unless groups "develop a culture of understanding each other and a different set of communication patterns, superordinate goals are not

(continued)

likely to work" (Putnam & Poole, 1987, pp. 578–579). Given the changing demographics of the American workplace, workers will need to adapt to people with many different ethnic and racial backgrounds. In addition, workers will need to adjust to men and women who work in nontraditional positions for their gender. Part of this mutual adaptation can be facilitated if people of different groups work together on common tasks. Thus, it is critical for human resource departments to develop training and education programs for employees to facilitate the transition to a culturally diverse workplace that do not tolerate discrimination based on gender, ethnic or racial heritage, religion, or physical disability.

How can the members of different social groups reach a point of integration in managing their conflicts? Fine (1991) proposes a framework for creating multicultural communication within the workplace that is based in feminist theory and includes two processes: (1) resisting privileged discourse and (2) creating harmonic discourse. *Privileged discourse* involves language that oppresses people and separates the power holders from those who are subject to their control. To create *harmonic discourse* means first to recognize language differences and then to integrate these differences for the good of the group. Again, this is not a simple process. The creation of harmonic discourse requires widespread organizational support. Finally, as noted by Thalhofer (1993), management must clearly indicate through behavior that different languages and behaviors are equally valued throughout the organization.

The final step of conflict management is the establishment of monitoring mechanisms to prevent old prejudices from surfacing and once again dominating intergroup relations. The members of different social groups should meet periodically to share success stories as well as talk about the problems associated with working together. These discussions should center on how to repeat successes and avoid the problems of the past. Group members need to receive reinforcement for disallowing discrimination and for striving for superordinate goals. Such a monitoring mechanism will minimize the reemergence of conflict between members of different social groups within an organization.

Note
[1] These benchmarks are goals rather than quotas and A&F is required to report on its progress toward these goals at regular intervals.

as adversaries, and any action allowed by private and/or public regulatory agencies will be pursued.

One area of interorganizational conflict that includes a mixture of motives to compete and cooperate is strategic alliances. *Strategic alliances* are "relatively enduring interfirm cooperative arrangements, involving flows and linkages that utilize resources and/or governance structures from autonomous organizations for the joint accomplishment of individual goals linked to the corporate mission of each sponsoring firm" (Parkhe, 1991, p. 581). The reason we focus on these alliances to depict interorganizational conflict is that alliances have become an integral part of contemporary corporate strategic thinking (Kale & Singh, 2007). IBM, for example, has entered more than

3,800 strategic alliances with companies in the United States and abroad (IBM, 2007). Furthermore, Lavie (2007) reports that the rate of strategic alliance formation between U.S. companies and international partners increased steadily during the 1990s and the early years of the present decade. In the software industry, for example, the percentage of publicly traded firms that engaged in alliances increased from 32% to 95% between 1990 and 2004 (Lavie, 2007).

The phase model advanced in this chapter clearly applies to the conflicts that surface during strategic alliances. These partnerships offer a mixture of motives to cooperate and compete. Cooperation is relevant within the context of the agreement reached between the two organizations. For example, a computer manufacturer may enter into an alliance with a firm that specializes in marketing computer systems. However, the two firms remain in competition with one another regarding the marketing of other high-technology products. The mixture of motives to cooperate and to compete in strategic alliances is analogous to the tension that exists between the appropriateness and effectiveness dimensions of competence during conflict. Appropriateness involves attending to the needs of the partnership—for instance, addressing the issue of how the two firms can combine their resources to produce and market a product more effectively. Effectiveness involves attending to self (organizational) needs such as survival and profitability. Thus, members of both management teams recognize that an important part of their job is to withhold certain proprietary information from their partners because such information could reduce their organization's competitive advantage. Of course, the two sides must disclose relevant information concerning the specific products or services that are marketed under the terms of the alliance, but information about organizational functioning that is beyond the terms of the alliance must be protected.

In the beginning stages of establishing a strategic alliance, management team members from each organization need to work through the differentiation process by seeking and sharing information. Why is information exchange so important? Consider Lei and Slocum's (1992) observation that the most productive alliances are between firms that have different core competencies. For example, one firm is more adept at manufacturing, while the other excels at product marketing. Building a strategic alliance requires that each side gain information about their potential partner's core competencies and motives for seeking the alliance. Furthermore, Lei and Slocum (1992) contend that if each party understands the other's strengths and weaknesses, an initial balance can be achieved that facilitates the eventual structuring and development of the alliance.

In working through the differentiation process, each party to a strategic alliance must acknowledge that mutual cooperation is not automatic. Although the members of an alliance must cooperate with one another for the alliance to succeed, the members of each organization are also motivated by self-interest. For example, by providing one another with access to organizational resources and personnel, each organization sets up the possibility that their partner will uncover proprietary information or technology that is not linked to the alliance.

One type of information sharing that must be part of differentiation in forming strategic alliances is a discussion of the risks of the alliance. As Lei and Slocum (1992) observe, without clearly "identifying the risks inherent in alliances, collaboration may unintentionally open up a firm's entire spectrum of core competencies, technologies, and skills to encroachment and learning by its partners" (p. 82). For example, in the consumer electronics industry during the 1980s, U.S. manufacturers ceased production of their own color television sets, VCRs, stereo equipment, and compact disc players. All electronic products sold under U.S. brands (Kodak, General Electric, RCA, Zenith, and so on) were made by foreign alliance partners and imported into the United States. In most instances the U.S. firms lost their competitive edge in manufacturing by unwittingly letting critical technology flow out of their corporations through poorly implemented alliance mechanisms (Lei & Slocum, 1992).

To lessen the risks associated with alliances, the alliance agreement must be carefully crafted from the outset. During differentiation, the potential partners should discuss their mutual incentives for opportunism. In addition, prospective punishments that are applied after the fact can be instituted. "These ex post deterrents consist of contractual safeguards, or stipulations in a formal partnership agreement, that inflict penalties for the omission of cooperative behaviors or commission of violative behaviors" (Parkhe, 1993, p. 804).

During differentiation the partners to a strategic alliance must come to terms with the mixture of motives to cooperate and compete. This process is facilitated when each party clearly communicates its goals for the alliance in the short and long term. A mutual discussion of goals helps the partners understand what each is supposed to contribute and learn from the alliance. As Lei and Slocum (1992) conclude: "The process of thinking through this duality of simultaneous collaboration and competition provokes questions that need to be raised before the alliance can be structured and the reward system fashioned" (p. 96).

A discussion of the goals of the alliance brings the parties to the mutual problem description phase of their conflict. In framing a mutual problem description, the parties to the potential alliance need to focus on the competitive advantages of forming a partnership. Ultimately, competing firms form strategic alliances when they perceive that such a partnership will enhance each firm's competitive position against *mutual* rivals (Shan, 1990). One part of the mutual problem description process, then, is to identify how the proposed alliance will benefit the competitive position of each partner.

During mutual problem description, potential partners need to compare the immediate gains that each side can receive from cheating with the possible sacrifice of future gains that might result from violating an agreement. By talking about the relative advantages of maintaining the partnership, each side begins to recognize the value of cooperating rather than competing. Part of this discussion should include a specific list of expected economic benefits from the partnership and a description of punishments linked to agreement violation (Lavie, 2007; Wahyuni, Ghauri, & Karsten, 2007).

When the proposed partners of a strategic alliance agree that there are specific advantages to the partnership and that there is a stronger mixture of motives to cooperate than to violate the agreement, they are prepared to move on to the integration phase of conflict. In establishing the alliance, the members of each firm must set up a communication system that allows for frequent communication between the organizations (Wahyuni et al., 2007). A system in which there is frequent interaction allows the partners periodic assessments of the outcomes of the alliance. In addition, Parkhe (1993) recommends promoting high behavioral transparency between the partners. *Behavioral transparency* refers to the speed and reliability with which alliance partners learn about each other's actions. Behavioral transparency is thus a means for each organization to monitor the other's actions.

To deal with the possibility of agreement violations, each party to a strategic alliance may wish to absorb bonding costs when they enter the exchange. Each partner must then set up monitoring mechanisms to detect any opportunistic actions that would require forfeiture of the bond. Although monitoring mechanisms are in the best interests of each partner, the cost of maintaining such mechanisms reduces the economic value of the alliance (Parkhe, 1993). Thus, each side should work toward the establishment of a trusting *relationship* that reduces the need for expensive monitoring mechanisms (Kumar & Das, 2007).

In the integration phase the potential partners can agree to commit nonrecoverable investments to the alliance. Nonrecoverable investments include special physical assets, such as buildings and equipment or human resources. The more nonrecoverable assets each side is willing to commit to the alliance, the more likely a trusting relationship will develop between the parties. Mutual investment of such assets exhibits commitment to the success of the partnership and reduces the likelihood that either side will engage in opportunistic behavior (Kumar & Das, 2007; Lavie, 2007).

One of the more fascinating recent examples of strategic alliance formation involves the Dell Corporation. Box 8-4 (on pp. 188–189) applies our phase model to the phenomenon of strategic alliances, using Dell and its partners. As you read this box, you might ask yourself whether you can identify other examples of interorganizational conflict that fit with the example we elaborate in box 8-4.

Although the behaviors identified in this chapter can contribute to effective problem solving and conflict management, there are limitations. First, the relational history (distal context) that social actors have established with respect to conflict management can impede their ability to display optimizing behaviors. For example, coworkers who have maintained an aggressive-defensive pattern of problem solving for years will find it extremely difficult to

Box 8-4   Interorganizational Conflict Witnessed in Dell's Strategic Alliances

Michael Dell, founding CEO of Dell Corporation, developed an innovative sales model in which Dell bypassed retailers by selling computers directly to customers by phone or the Internet. Furthermore, under Dell's build-to-order system, customer orders initiated the supplier's operations (Hulthén & Gadde, 2007). By ordering parts based on customer demands, Dell instituted a "just-in-time" inventory management plan and reduced its need for maintaining an inventory of finished computers (Byrnes, 2003).

Although they manufacture their computers at plants around the world, Dell outsources the assembly of component parts to various suppliers through a large variety of strategic alliances (Gandossy & Tower, 2005). In the United States, for example, Dell has formed partnerships with Sony for monitors, Intel and AMD for microchips, Microsoft and Linux for software, and UPS for logistics (Farhoomand, Lovelock, & Ng, 2002; Frei, Edmondson, & Hajim, 2003; Reimer, 2006). By ordering component parts to fill customer orders, Dell has successfully reduced its need to maintain an inventory of computers to meet customer orders.

Dell's innovative approach to manufacturing computers proved to be so successful that Dell maintained only six days' worth of inventory in 2000 (Holzner, 2006). By 2005, in its Austin, Texas, factory, inventory on hand was down to 5–7 hours, and, in some cases, 2 hours. Furthermore, this build-to-order model allowed Dell to maintain a huge negative cash conversion cycle. In most cases, payments were received from customers within four days while Dell took 45 days to pay suppliers for the manufactured components. During the 41 days before payment was made to the suppliers, Dell either reinvested the money in other operations or earned interest on it through certificates of deposit (Byrnes, 2003).

Dell's marketing innovations also proved to be very effective in reducing Dell's production costs. Michael Dell estimated that selling computers directly to the consumer saved his company 25–45% in markup on every machine made (Holzner, 2006). However, outsourcing through strategic alliances is not without its problems. Outsourcing can lead to a loss of long-run research and development competitiveness because it is often used as a substitute for innovation (Teece, 1987). Furthermore, outsourcing may shift knowledge to supplier organizations and destroy long-term competitive advantages (Bettis, Bradley, & Hamel, 1992; Kumar & Das, 2007). Finally, by relying too heavily on outsourcing through strategic alliances, firms can lose touch with new technological breakthroughs that could lead to new product and process innovations (Kotabe, 1992). Many believe that this is the case at Dell. In 2004, Dell's research and development budget was at 2%, while the industry average reached 5% or 6% (Aubert & Croteau, 2005). By outsourcing the manufacture of its component parts, Dell had lost its competitive edge in research and development and lacked cutting edge proprietary technology.

Hewlett Packard (HP) replaced Dell as the number one manufacturer of computers in the world in 2006. Although the computer industry grew by 7.9% for the year, Dell's growth was a meager 3.6% (Bangeman, 2006). By the first quarter of 2007, Dell's market share had dropped to 13.9% versus HP's 17.4% (Bangeman, 2007b). Due to these problems, Kevin Rollins, CEO of Dell since 2004, resigned abruptly as both CEO and as director, and Michael Dell returned to the CEO role (Bangeman, 2007a). However, Dell's slide continued and on March 1, 2007, Dell reported sales of $14.4 billion, down 5% from the prior year, and a net income of $687 million, down 33% from 2006 (Oreskovich, 2007).

As management at Dell reassesses the nature of how they do business, they may want to consider carefully the processes through which they establish and maintain strategic alliances. Although strategic alliances are becoming increasingly common, firms generally fail with roughly half the alliances they form (Kale & Singh, 2007). Dell created a successful business model during the 1990s and in the early years of the twenty-first century. In future strategic alliances, more attention should be given to managing the tension that exists between organizational incentives to cooperate and compete. Managing this tension more effectively could help Dell to improve its economic performance in a globally competitive industry.

change their behavior. Even if coworkers commit to change, entrenched patterns of behavior are very difficult to alter. Thus, in relationships where dysfunctional problem-solving patterns may become entrenched, a third party may be needed to help facilitate the shift toward more competent behaviors.

At a more general level than relational context is the organization's culture (distal context). Organizations establish cultures that influence the choices people make when involved in conflict. For example, one organization may develop a collaborative, problem-solving culture, whereas another could establish a competitive, win-lose culture. Individuals within organizational systems that do not support a competence-based approach to problem solving probably think it is impossible to obtain personal goals in conflict by displaying competent behavior. Thus, individuals need to make strategic choices regarding how to manage conflict that reflect the reality of their organization's culture.

Perhaps most important is the need to recognize that organizational conflicts may emerge that demand an approach very different from the competence perspective advanced here. For example, if an African American employee is subjected to racial slurs by coworkers, given the least favorable work assignments by supervisors, and ignored for promotions despite superior work performance, the approaches we have discussed appear naive. Such a person has the right to focus on self-oriented concerns. He or she should demand equal treatment from coworkers and superiors and insist that the racial slurs cease. This employee should also seek legal counsel to ensure that personal rights are respected and to obtain compensation for the injustices experienced on the job.

Summary

In the future, researchers need to scrutinize carefully the relevance of a competence-based approach to managing organizational conflicts. As explained in this chapter, this approach offers many opportunities for creative problem solving, but it also has limitations. In the final analysis, the more we learn about how to manage conflicts competently in organizational settings, the more we will know about how to sustain supportive and productive work environments.

DISCUSSION QUESTIONS

1. Information sharing is very important during the differentiation phase. People can become more accurate in understanding each other's positions through information sharing. Have you experienced a conflict at work or elsewhere that was never resolved in part because people simply did not understand each other? Are there special instances where understanding someone might hurt the relationship or company? Elaborate on your answers.

2. How might you bring about—through communication—differentiation, mutual problem description, and integration? Should one do this informally, without relating what one is doing, or should one begin these phases more formally, with an explicit agenda? Give examples to illustrate your opinion.

3. Compare the example of the UAW–Big Three negotiations discussed in this chapter with others that have not worked as well—for example, the 2007–2008 negotiations between the Writer's Guild of America and the Alliance of Motion Picture and Television Producers, or any other negotiation that you understand. In your opinion, what is missing from the "failed" negotiations?

4. An effective way to achieve mutual problem definition within intergroup conflict (for example, between departments) is to identify a bigger, superordinate goal that the two groups share. Discuss this idea in terms of groups that appear to be opposed to each other, but who actually share a common, superordinate goal. What might you recommend to these groups in terms of mutual problem description and integration?

5. Strategic alliances are ways that organizations differentiate themselves, for example, by noting how their resources can complement one another. However, organizations using strategic alliances must balance their need to compete with each other and their need to cooperate with each other. Does this tension between cooperation and competition also apply to interpersonal conflicts? Give examples to support your opinion.

chapter 9

FAMILY CONFLICT

Tamara D. Afifi, Desiree Aldeis, and Andrea Joseph
University of California, Santa Barbara

CHAPTER OUTLINE

Constructive versus Destructive Family Conflict

The Impact of Interparental Conflict on Children
   The Effects of Divorce and Conflict on Child Adjustment
   The Case of Triangulation
   Blended Family Problems

Parent to Child Conflict
   Adolescence and Family Conflict

Misunderstanding as a Source of Family Conflict

The Role of Parenting Style in Family Conflicts

The Effect of Children's Conflict/Aggression on Other Family
  Members
   Transition to Parenthood
   Sibling Conflict Effects on Parents

Examining Family Conflict in Families as a Whole

Conclusion: Competent Conflict Management in Families

Discussion Questions

The family has far-reaching implications for people's conflict tendencies. Even though individuals' conflict tendencies are generated from a variety of sources, the foundation for their conflict management skills begins with their family. Our family is the origin of our deepest attachments (Bowlby, 1988) and where we learn our earliest social skills and conflict competencies (Caffery & Erdman, 2000). According to social learning theory (Bandura, 1977), children often model their parents' conflict behaviors, whether they realize it or not. They may then carry over these conflict tendencies into their own personal relationships later in life (Amato & Booth, 2001; Caffery & Erdman, 2000). In contrast, some adult children compensate for their parents' conflict tendencies by doing the opposite of what they observed growing up—in an effort to disassociate themselves from undesirable conflict behaviors.

This social learning takes place in a multifarious environment. Families are incredibly complex—complex in their structure, complex in their communication patterns, and complex in their emotions. From a family systems theory perspective, a family member's conflict tendencies can best be understood by examining them within the family as a whole (Bowen, 1978; Minuchin, 1974; Satir, 1964). The ultimate goal of systems theory is not to study one component in isolation, but to recognize the many forces exerting themselves upon each system part. As a result, looking at conflict competencies in families from a systems perspective involves examining families as a whole and the various subsystems (e.g., individuals, dyads) within them. There are most certainly conflict competencies that are unique to the individual apart from one's family, but many of the ways that people approach conflict reflect larger patterns of interaction in their family, as well as the environmental and social factors that influence them.

Employing a systems approach also means looking at how family members' conflict competencies influence one another. Indeed, conflict does not occur in isolation—it is an interactive process that transpires among people. Family members influence the way that each member responds to conflict (Cui, Donnellan, & Conger, 2007). For instance, research on spillover or contagion effects suggests that parents have a tendency to communicate their distress and preoccupation with their conflicts, either verbally and/or nonverbally, to their children in a way that hinders parents' ability to provide effective social support to them (see Afifi, Hutchinson, & Krouse, 2006; Gomulak-Cavicchio, Davies, & Cummings, 2006). Other research has found that children who have been exposed to marital violence differ significantly in their stress responses than do children who have not been exposed to marital violence (Saltzman, Holden, & Holahan, 2005). One's conflict tendencies, in general, are often shaped in response to one's current partner and family members. Thus, one's own personal conflict competencies are often restricted, maintained, enhanced, and "defined" by one's self, in conjunction with others.

The purpose of this chapter is to discuss the research on constructive and destructive conflict patterns in families from all angles within the family. Most of the research on conflict focuses on how parents' conflict management skills impact children. However, a growing body of research has examined the reciprocal nature of conflict, emphasizing the important influence that children's conflict skills have on the rest of the family. We argue that in order to truly understand family conflict competencies and their impact on family members, we need to investigate the competencies of all of the individuals and dyads within the family and the family as a whole. As such, we first briefly detail what constitutes constructive and destructive conflict in families. In that section we outline some of the primary conflict skills that family members need to possess. We then investigate various conflict competencies of parents, children, siblings, and the family as a whole in more depth in the remaining sections. After reading these sections you hopefully will have a better understanding of what constitutes constructive and destructive conflict in families and its multifarious and interactive nature. You should also be able to think about, and apply, these skills to your own family and families you know.

Constructive versus Destructive Family Conflict

Researchers have had some difficulty distinguishing between constructive and destructive family conflict patterns (Grych & Fincham, 1993; Noller, Feeney, Sheehan, & Peterson, 2000). As Noller and colleagues (2000) have argued, "conflict has frequently been conceptualized in a unidimensional manner as inherently problematic, with no allowance made for effective resolution" (p. 80). Most of the research on family conflict focuses on problematic conflict patterns in families and their effects on health and relationship quality. Researchers often focus on problematic behavior patterns in families with the hope of being able to understand them and prevent them from recurring. However, the almost exclusive focus on problematic conflict patterns limits our understanding of effective conflict management in families. Just as researchers need to uncover the conflict patterns that inhibit family relationships, they also need to understand and report the conflict management skills that facilitate problem solving, cohesion, resilience, and other adaptive family dynamics.

Part of the difficulty of this task, of course, resides in determining what constitutes constructive versus destructive conflict. Destructive conflicts are often prolonged and recurrent, and involve coercive and avoidant strategies that undermine the purpose of the conflict and the ability to come to a mutually acceptable solution. Examples of conflict patterns that are often destructive include demand-withdraw patterns (e.g., Caughlin, 2002; Heavey, Christensen, & Malamuth, 1995); Gottman's four horsemen (i.e., criticism, contempt, defensiveness, and stonewalling, see Gottman, 1994); negativity (e.g., Huston, Caughlin, Houts, Smith, & George, 2001); and aggression and violence (e.g., Olson, 2002a, 2002b).

It is important for parents to model effective conflict competencies with their children. When children are exposed to ongoing conflict in their family that is hostile, aggressive, and emotionally and/or physically coercive, it has an adverse impact on their well-being (Noller et al., 2000). Children are especially vulnerable to the negative impact of conflict when it involves them directly, when it is intense and long lasting, and when they become intertwined in it. Whereas parents should not engage in negative conflict in front of their children, they should not completely avoid it either. If children have never witnessed their parents resolve a disagreement, they may learn to fear conflict and believe that it brings the demise of their own romantic relationships when they occur. Instead, parents need to show their children how they can communicate about their disagreements in a competent manner.

In addition to centering on problematic conflict patterns at the expense of productive ones, research also tends to be too simplistic in its view of conflict. Much of the research on conflict has focused on the sheer amount or frequency of conflict rather than on the types of conflict, intensity of the conflict, the topics of the conflict, or the duration of the conflict. For instance, much of the research on the impact of interparental conflict on children has examined the frequency of conflict between parents and its adverse effect on children. However, not all patterns of conflict should be treated equally because they likely have different implications for family relationships. More finite distinctions among the different types of conflict and their functions will help illuminate the conflict patterns that help versus hinder family development.

Conflict is constructive when people listen to each other's perspectives, reason, regulate their emotions, and create solutions that are mutually satisfying (Perlman, Garfinkel, & Turrell, 2007). This process often involves empathic understanding, effective social support (e.g., Burleson, Holstrom, & Gilstrap, 2005), problem-solving skills, affection, and authoritative parenting (Baumrind, 1991), and sometimes the use of communal coping or coping together as a group to solve a mutual problem (e.g., Afifi et al., 2006). In general, children need a loving and affectionate environment where there are clear standards and rules for behavior, while simultaneously feeling like they are autonomous individuals who can express their own opinions.

The Impact of Interparental Conflict on Children

THE EFFECTS OF DIVORCE AND CONFLICT ON CHILD ADJUSTMENT

Most research on family conflict has focused on how marital discord affects children. In fact, this is arguably one of the most important social problems that family scholars have faced in the past few decades. In particular, researchers have focused on how divorce, and the conflict that often exists as a result, impacts children's personal and relational well-being (e.g., Amato, 2001; Amato & Keith, 1991; Cummings & Davies, 2002). A profound finding from this body of research is that divorce has negative short-term and long-term effects on children, but it is not so much the divorce, per se, that affects children's health as much as the degree of interparental conflict (Afifi & Schrodt, 2003; Jekielek, 1998). In fact, as Amato (2001) and his colleagues (Amato & DeBoer, 2001; Amato & Sobolewski, 2001; Booth & Amato, 2001) have found, children whose parents stay married and who have a conflicted relationship may be *worse off* than children whose parents divorce. Unlike some children of divorce, children whose parents are still married and who engage in destructive conflict may be unable to escape their discordant family environment (Amato & Afifi, 2006). Some children also fare better after a divorce if they are removed from a highly conflicted environment. However, other children might not fare very well if their parents divorce from a low-conflict marriage (Booth & Amato, 2001).

Evidence exists for intergenerational effects of conflict skill deficiencies on children. As a whole, children whose parents divorce are more likely to get divorced themselves and have more difficulty maintaining healthy relationships with their own partners than do other children (see Amato, 2000; Amato & Booth, 2001). This intergenerational effect could occur for many reasons. One explanation is that children whose parents divorce fear commitment and/ or have less of a commitment to marriage than do children whose parents remain married (Amato & DeBoer, 2001). Another explanation, which most likely works in conjunction with the former explanation, is that children learn communication skill deficiencies from their parents that they then apply to their own relationships later in life (Amato & Booth, 2001; Caspi & Elder, 1988). Children whose parents divorce might have fewer opportunities than children whose parents remain married to witness constructive conflict management skills (Amato & DeBoer, 2001). For instance, Amato (1996) found that adult children whose parents divorced and who demonstrated interpersonal skill deficiencies, such as criticism, aggression, jealousy, dogmatism, and a lack of compromise, were more likely to develop these traits themselves, which increased the likelihood that their own marriages would end in divorce. Precisely how much conflict children were exposed to growing up and whether or not the children saw the divorce coming should be examined as well. As Amato and DeBoer (2001) discovered, the extremities of conflict for children of divorce—either an extreme amount of interparental conflict or the lack of a sign that anything is wrong—hurts children's psychological well-being.

Moreover, parental conflict can influence the sibling relationship. When parents are in conflict with one another or are experiencing divorce, siblings often turn to each other to buffer the stress (e.g., Feinberg, McHale, Crouter, & Cumsille, 2003). As a result, some sibling relationships become stronger when their parents' relationship is strained. On the other hand, other research suggests that children model their parents' conflict behaviors and become aggressive and more distant with their siblings (Igra & Irwin, 1996; Noller, 2005). Siblings probably engage in both modeling and compensation processes at different times or in different homes, which would explain why marital relationship qualities are inconsistently linked with sibling relationship qualities (Kim, McHale, Osgood, & Crouter, 2006).

Although research has tended to examine the impact of the amount of conflict that children witness on the children's well-being, researchers have begun to explore the features of conflict that are most harmful to children. For instance, some research points to the level of hostility in the conflict (Richmond & Stocker, 2006). For example, Grych and Fincham (1993) found that high levels of marital hostility negatively affect children. Specifically, Grych and Fincham discovered that hostile and angry marital conflict led to greater negative affect and more self-blame among children. This effect was particularly strong if the conflict was about the child, which led children to report feeling more shame and self-blame, as well as sadness and anger. This effect remained intact even if the children were told that the conflict was *not* their fault. Grych and Fincham concluded that both the nature of a conflict and the content of the arguments are unhealthy for children.

THE CASE OF TRIANGULATION

In addition, much of the research employing a systems approach has confirmed that the extent to which children become entrenched in interparental conflict affects children's health. In their seminal piece, Buchanan, Maccoby, and Dornbusch (1991) examined children's involvement in their parents' conflict. These authors found that the impact of parents' postdivorce conflict on their adolescent children's anxiety and depression was filtered by the degree to which the children felt caught in the middle of it. More recent research has confirmed that it is children's feelings of *triangulation*, or being put in the middle of their parents' conflict, that negatively impacts their well-being and not the divorce per se (Afifi & Schrodt, 2003). These feelings of being caught in the middle have also been shown to apply to children whose parents remain married or who are a part of "intact families" (Afifi & Schrodt, 2003; Amato & Afifi, 2006; Schrodt & Afifi, 2007). Afifi and Schrodt (2003) explored the factors related to parents' communication that contribute to children's feelings of triangulation. They found that adolescents and young adults whose parents engaged in demand-withdraw patterns (see chapter 3) and had less communication competence were more likely to feel caught. Moreover, even though children of divorced families reported greater feelings of being caught, these same patterns were experienced by children of intact families when their parents were in a conflicted relationship. In a similar study, Schrodt and Afifi (2007) found that parents' symbolic or verbal aggression, demand-withdraw patterns, and negative disclosures were positively associated with young adult children's feelings of triangulation. These feelings, in turn, were negatively associated with children's family satisfaction and mental health. Although the associations in the model were stronger for children of divorce, they held true for children from intact families as well.

Most of the research on the negative effects of children's feelings of being caught between their parents has assumed that parents do not like each other and do not effectively co-parent together. However, it might also be the case that parents who are divorced and trying to co-parent together and who see each other on a regular basis are more likely than parents who do not talk to one another to have children who feel caught between them. In this line of reasoning, parents who attempt to make joint decisions regarding their children fall into the trap of placing their children in the middle of their disagreements when making such decisions. They might ask for their children's feedback when they disagree and engage in more disclosures about the other parent because they are still very close to the other parent. As other scholars have noted (e.g., Emery, 1994), divorced parents who adjust their boundaries from being spouses to being co-parents is essential for children to adjust to the divorce.

BLENDED FAMILY PROBLEMS

The difficulties of redefining boundaries with a former spouse can become increasingly difficult when a new spouse or stepparent enters the scene. Loyalty conflicts or feelings of being caught also occur in stepfamilies. (In fact, some of the most visible research on family conflict that uses a systems framework is that of loyalty conflicts in stepfamilies.) Loyalty conflicts are often more complicated in stepfamilies because the relationships become more complex and the conflicts can assume multiple forms. For example, stepparents often feel like outsiders entering into a new family because of the preexisting emotional bond between the custodial parent and child (e.g.,

Braithwaite, Olson, Golish, Soukup, & Turman, 2001; Golish, 2003; Kelley, 1992). It is often difficult for stepparents to join this established coalition. On the other hand, sometimes stepparents form an alliance with one of the parents against the child in an effort to restore the power imbalance within the family. In addition, alliances can simultaneously form between the birth parents and the children.

Still, as other scholars (e.g., Coleman, Fine, Ganong, Downs, & Park, 2001) argue, researchers tend to assume that stepfamilies are rife with conflict and that conflict is always destructive. Coleman and colleagues found that conflict can be productive *and* destructive in stepfamilies; how the conflict is managed is essential to stepfamily functioning. They found that families that spent time together, had family meetings, and problem-solved through their conflicts successfully prevented them from escalating. In contrast, loyalty conflicts within the stepfamily, particularly when children felt caught between their custodial parent and stepparent, hurt stepfamily relationships. Most research (Afifi, 2003; Cissna, Cox, & Bochner, 1990; Kelley, 1992) suggests that to prevent such loyalty conflicts from occurring, many parents and stepparents form a united front by communicating the importance and permanence of the new marital bond to the children. Other research (Baxter, Braithwaite, & Bryant, 2006) has found that children find their relationships with their parent and stepparent to be the most fulfilling and the least conflicted when open communication occurs among all family members.

Parent to Child Conflict

In the prior section, we emphasized the effects of marital conflict on children. Another example that highlights the complexity of conflict in families is parent to child conflict. Similar to the research on interparental conflict, parents' conflict with their children has typically been studied from a unilateral approach—or how parents' behavior influences children but not how children's behavior influences parents and siblings (for reviews, see Sillars, Canary, & Tafoya, 2004; Wilson & Morgan, 2004). Much of the past research on parent-child conflict has illustrated the power differences in conflict between parents and their children (Eisenberg, 1992). Eisenberg highlights that the "traditional emphases in research on child development define conflict as 'parental discipline' or 'child non-compliance'" (p. 21). Although this perspective has been incredibly important for family scholars, it does not capture the interactive nature of family relationships (Canary et al., 1995). Studies involving the family unit as a whole further illustrate the nature of power in family conflict situations (Messman & Canary, 1998), as well as a way of conceptualizing conflict that extends beyond the parent-child dyad to the larger familial and social context (Caffery & Erdman, 2000).

When raising children, parents have the responsibility of teaching skills and controlling behavior to ensure the safety and well-being of their children and others (Roloff & Miller, 2006). In attempting to seek compliance, the child may resist, and a struggle for control could emerge. Thus, most research on parent-child conflict is conducted from a power or control perspective, with parents attempting to gain compliance from their children (e.g., Steinmetz, 1977; Wilson & Morgan, 2004). In addition, there is evidence that these communication patterns, such as parents asking/requesting things from their adolescents, often precipitate conflicts that escalate to adolescents psychologically and physically abusing their parents—most often the mother (Eckstein, 2007). Furthermore, not teaching children healthy conflict behaviors could have profound implications for the children's personal and social development. Based on this developmental argument, one particularly dark outcome of conflict in families occurs when children learn ineffective, inappropriate, dysfunctional, and even violent conflict interaction behaviors as part of normal conflict patterns and perpetuate these behaviors in later relationships (Messman & Canary, 1998).

ADOLESCENCE AND FAMILY CONFLICT

Adolescence, in particular, is a time of increased conflict in families. During this time, parents and adolescents often have different interpretations of the conflict, with parents seeing the disagreements arising from morality, personal safety, and conformity concerns and adolescents viewing them as issues of personal choice (Smetana, 1989). Additionally, adolescents report that about 40% of their daily conflict occurs with a sibling or parent (Jensen-Campbell & Graziano, 2000). Although conflict is high during this transitional phase, research also suggests that parent-child conflict tends to decline after adolescence (Noller, Atkin, Feeney, & Peterson, 2006; Roloff & Miller, 2006). However, parent-child conflict does not seem to entirely end at adolescence. Research indicates that adult children have conflict with their parents. For instance, Suitor and Pillemer (1987) found that the primary variable in explaining marital conflict in residence-sharing families is parent-adult child conflict.

Nevertheless, the public's perception about the amount and intensity of conflict during adolescent years is somewhat exaggerated (Steinberg, 2001). As Steinberg indicates, most parent-adolescent conflict is not as troublesome as the U.S. culture makes it out to be; approximately 75% to 85% of parents report that conflicts with their adolescents are not severe (Canary et al., 1995). Also, some conflict occurrences between parents and their children can be disguised as misunderstandings. Indeed, different communicative goals and perspectives can lead to conflicts that reflect simple misunderstandings. We now turn our attention to how such misunderstandings occur in families.

Misunderstanding as a Source of Family Conflict

The very nature of close relationships provides the source of persistent and troubling misunderstandings (Sillars, 1998). For example, understanding

can be affected by the emotionality and interdependence of close relationships, by the ambiguity and complexity inherent in communication, and by
communicative goals that influence the selectivity and structure of perception
(Sillars, 1998).

According to Sillars, Roberts, Leonard, and Dun (2000), the inability to
share another person's view increases with more intense arguments. In fact,
the more upset that people are with one another, the less likely their perspectives of the conflict are to be congruent with outside observers' views (i.e.,
parties amidst conflict do not perceive their own behaviors as well as objective coders do); intense anger makes it difficult for people to understand one
another. Controlled conflict in which people's emotions are regulated, on the
other hand, is more conducive to objectivity and shared perspectives. Misunderstandings occur for a number of reasons, but Sillars and colleagues (2000)
suggested that the self-serving bias may be to blame. That is, partners (and
other family members) tend to attribute constructive conflict acts to themselves, whereas they attribute negative intent and destructive outcomes to
their partners. Such self-serving perception likely leads to intensifying conflict, as responses from partners tend to follow in kind; positive affect or emotion tends to beget positive affect, whereas negative affect tends to beget
negative affect (Sillars, Pike, Jones, & Murphy, 1984).

Nevertheless, differences in perceptions about the frequency and type of
conflict in families can reveal important distinctions about family relationships. For instance, adolescents tend to have a more negative perspective
about their parents' relationship and their communication with them than do
parents (see Sillars, Koerner, & Fitzpatrick, 2005). Parents have a more optimistic perspective of their relationship with their children than their children
because to think otherwise might challenge their own identity as parents.
Adolescents are also at a point in their life when they are trying to separate
themselves from their parents and establish their own identity, which can
result in more negative evaluations of their parents. Children also often do
not tell their parents about their risky behaviors and a more accurate assessment of adolescents' problematic behaviors would come from a combination
of parents, teachers, siblings, and peers (Sweeting, 2001). Still, other research
has found that custodial parents tend to have a more optimistic view of the
conflict and problems in their stepfamily than do their children, with children's perspective, which is more negative, being more in line with that of the
stepparent (Golish, 2003; Kurdek & Fine, 1991). In some instances, parents
have a more hopeful view of their family in an attempt to prevent conflict or
to sustain their hope for a brighter future (Bray & Kelly, 1998; Ganong &
Coleman, 1994; Golish, 2003).

Taken together, interdependency among people's perceptions and their
subsequent conflict behaviors clearly are important to how family members
manage conflict. Conflicts are often seen differently from the perspectives of
different parties, and many times they depict entirely different conflicts from
either point of view (Sillars, 1998). Perspective taking requires a temporary

suppression of one's own perspective, which is especially difficult in a stressful and cognitively demanding environment (Ickes & Simpson, 1997). For example, a father may understand that his son does not want to spend time with the family (metaperspective), but he does not understand why (son's perspective). This lack of understanding can, predictably, lead to arguments. In this situation, maintenance of their relationship will depend on communication competencies. In fact, perspective-taking ability can also increase an individual's persuasive competence (see O'Keefe & Sypher, 1981). Theoretically, the father could gain an understanding of his son's perspective and convey messages that demonstrate their convergent thinking. However, because individuals often develop, defend, support, and refute messages based on their goals, which are at apparent odds with the other family member during conflict, the cognitive demands of communication limit one's ability to take the perspective of other people who appear to oppose them (Sillars, 1998).

The Role of Parenting Style in Family Conflicts

Parenting styles also contribute to constructive or destructive conflict patterns, and issues of control and misperception, between parents and children. Baumrind (1966) provides the following general definitions: *authoritative parents* balance high nurturance with high control and clear communication about what is required of the child. In contrast, *authoritarian parents* are dogmatic, strict, and lack warmth and reasoning with their children. *Permissive parents* typically lack control and effective monitoring by either neglecting or indulging their children. Baumrind's seminal studies demonstrated that children whose parents were authoritative showed higher levels of competence and psychosocial maturity than did their peers who had been raised by parents who were permissive or authoritarian. Later, Baumrind (1991) found an association between adolescent substance use and parenting styles. Adolescents with "neglecting and rejecting" parents were the most likely to engage in substance abuse. She further emphasized that adolescents' developmental progress (e.g., increased perspective taking) is stymied by authoritarian or disengaged practices, and facilitated by authoritative and democratic parents. Secure in their relationship with their parents, and with adequate protection from the instabilities present in the larger society, adolescents from authoritative homes can simultaneously individuate from their parents while remain connected to them (Baumrind, 1991). Children with parents who are warm and who demonstrate reasoning and problem-solving skills can help siblings effectively solve their disputes with one another (Brody, 1998). In contrast, authoritarian parents are likely to foster harsh discipline styles and unresolved anger that feeds into sibling conflict (Brody, 1998). Overall, children who grew up with authoritative parents learn effective conflict management skills and the social skills necessary to talk through their arguments with other people (Steinberg, 2001).

Larger family communication patterns can predict communication skills and/or deficits in parent-child conflict. In their work on family interaction patterns, Fitzpatrick and Ritchie (1994) noted that parents and children can have different family communication schemata or sets of underlying beliefs about the family. For family members with dissimilar schemata, Fitzpatrick and Ritchie believed that conflict can be avoided by suppressing unpleasant topics or by enforcing conformity. Some characteristics of these family types, where conformity is high and conversation is low, include situations where obedience is prized and little concern exists for conceptual matters. Children in these families appear to be underprepared for dealing with outside influences and tend to be easily influenced by others (Fitzpatrick & Ritchie, 1994).

Taken together, parenting styles and family communication patterns can play a formal role in the ways that families choose to handle conflict. Conflict can be managed several ways depending on the structure and hierarchy of family interactions. The families that are best able to deal with conflict are those equipped with communication skills to manage the conflict effectively. Although instances often arise where family conflict might never be resolved, communication skills and the ability to manage conflict are essential to building and maintaining satisfying family relationships. Family interaction provides an important context for individual development during the management of conflict, insofar as families have the most conflict of all social groups (Shantz & Hobart, 1989).

The Effect of Children's Conflict/Aggression on Other Family Members

A less commonly explored phenomenon of family conflict concerns the effect of children's behavior on their parents and other members in the family. From a family systems approach, the effect of children's behavior on their family members provides another piece to the complex family conflict puzzle. Typically, children's aggression and how it affects families uses adolescents' participation with risky behaviors or entrance into adolescence as an explanation of sources of conflict in families (Steinberg & Morris, 2001). There are also some instances where adolescents are intent to gain power and control over their parents (Eisenberg, 1992). For example, in research exploring adolescent abuse of parents, Eckstein (2007) acknowledged that both parents and adolescents contribute to the conflict process. However, she found that adolescents often controlled how and when three different types of abuse (emotional, verbal, and physical) ended after the adolescents requested something of their parents. When parents decided not to entertain their adolescent's requests by leaving the room, ignoring the adolescent, or not giving in to the adolescent's request, the adolescent often escalated the conflict from emotional and verbal abuse to physical abuse (Eckstein, 2007).

Also, children often initiate conflicts with their parents or respond to their parents' requests in ways that either ameliorate or exacerbate the intensity of the conflict in the family. For instance, O'Connor, Hetherington, and Clingempeel (1997) discovered that parental behavior toward an adolescent was reciprocated by the child, and often spilled over into behavior patterns with the other parent. Adolescent behavior toward parents was as strong as parental behavior toward the adolescent in determining healthy family functioning (O'Connor et al., 1997). In this sense, adolescents contribute just as much as parents to the overall "tone" and direction of the conflict between them. One parent's conflict with a child can also have a spillover effect with the other parent.

Some research has examined how children's behavior impacts their parents' marriage and other aspects of family life. For instance, children's externalizing behaviors (e.g., aggression, acting out, engaging in risky behaviors) corresponds with a decline in marital satisfaction, as well as a decrease in positive marital affect and an increase in negative marital affect (Hetherington, 1999). Similarly, parents with children who exhibit externalizing behaviors also experience a greater degree of marital conflict (Hetherington, 1999). In other words, there is a reciprocal relationship between parent marital problems and adolescent internalizing (e.g., low self-esteem or self-worth, depression, anxiety) and externalizing behaviors. In addition, greater interparental conflict can result in more problem behaviors from children, which in turn can increase interparental conflict (Cui et al., 2007). In this way, it becomes clear that looking solely at individual behaviors is often unsatisfactory for determining family outcomes; numerous family relationships must be studied in conjunction in order to understand the circularity of conflict in families.

TRANSITION TO PARENTHOOD

Research on the transition to parenthood also demonstrates that having children can increase the amount of stress and discord in marriage. Numerous researchers have found a curvilinear pattern between the introduction of children and marital satisfaction such that marital satisfaction decreases upon the arrival of children and only increases after children leave the home (Huston & Vangelisti, 1995). Indeed, children increase the level of stress and conflict in a couple's life by straining their amount of romantic time together, making it more difficult to balance work and family and distribute household tasks equitably, and making it harder to negotiate a sense of autonomy (Grote & Clark, 2001; Stamp, 1994). As Huston and Vangelisti (1995) noted, however, numerous critiques exist of the research on the transition to parenthood. For instance, couples who become distressed after they have children may not have had a solid foundation for their marriage before they had children. Other studies do not address changes in satisfaction over a long enough time period or do not use control groups of couples who do not have children (Huston & Vangelisti, 1995). Thus, although the introduction of children can be conflict inducing for couples, its impact on marital quality can only be discerned after considering the numerous factors that influence marital quality.

SIBLING CONFLICT EFFECTS ON PARENTS

The overall level of children's aggression and sibling conflict in the home can also have a rippling effect on the rest of the family. Some sibling conflict is inevitable and normal. However, prolonged aggressive and contemptuous sibling interaction can predict conduct problems in children and may be a reflection of larger marital and/or family coercive patterns (Garcia, Shaw, Winslow, & Yaggi, 2000). Sibling conflict and negativity have been shown to predict marital discord and distressed family relationships as a whole (e.g., Query, 2001). Garcia and colleagues (2000) also found that sibling conflict and rejecting parenting practices were associated with aggressive behaviors in 5-year-old children over time. Nevertheless, it is important to note that parents who intervene in their children's conflicts effectively can teach their children perspective-taking and problem-solving skills and reduce the amount of sibling conflict (Smith, 2005).

Research also suggests that conflict between siblings typically increases with the transition to adolescence, but decreases over time (e.g., Kim et al., 2006; Sillars et al., 2004). Presumably, once siblings are not forced to live together, their relationships become similar to voluntary friendships. The sibling relationship has been described as a love-hate or emotionally ambivalent one to reflect the observation that both intensely positive and negative exchanges often are evident within these relationships (Kim et al., 2006). Although early research focused on sibling rivalry as a cause of sibling conflict, recent research suggests that sibling conflict may simply reflect interdependency (Roloff & Miller, 2006). To gain a better understanding of sibling experiences, Kim and colleagues (2006) examined both parent-offspring and marital relationships. Some of their findings suggest sibling intimacy and conflict were linked more closely to fathers' than mothers' marital evaluations. Additionally, changes in mothers' and fathers' family relationships were linked to changes in sibling experiences. This finding suggests that dynamics in sibling relationships may serve as important sources of social comparison, with siblings evaluating one dyadic relationship by virtue of the level of harmony and discord they experience in other relationships (Kim et al., 2006). In fact, a growing body of literature illustrates that sibling relationships are most likely to nurture children's social, cognitive, and psychosocial development (see Brody, 1998). Interestingly, both conflict and supportiveness in sibling interactions have been linked to children's development of social-cognitive skills such as affective perspective taking and consideration of other people's feelings and beliefs (e.g., Brody, 1998). These findings suggest that conflict and support are not simply the opposite ends of a continuum but can coexist to give children a variety of experiences in learning to communicate with others. Such balance can provide a unique opportunity for children to develop social-cognitive and behavioral competencies that are linked to managing conflict and anger on one hand and providing support and nurturance on the other (Brody, 1998). In the end, this research suggests that positive and negative relationship experiences do not occur in isolation, but rather reverberate throughout other relationships.

Thus far, we have covered family conflict by examining the manner in which conflict between parents affects children. We also highlighted the effect of children's conflict and/or aggression on other family members. Next, we discuss findings regarding family conflict from a systems perspective.

Examining Family Conflict in Families as a Whole

The analysis of family conflict from a true systems perspective has increased dramatically in the last 20 years. Using this approach, scholars have studied many facets of family life from the relationship between family cohesion and adolescent externalizing behaviors (e.g., Richmond & Stocker, 2006) to families' perspectives on their own conflict (e.g., Smetana, 1989). Researchers who use this approach tend to examine conflict within multiple family relationships and the family as a whole. They also look at the interdependencies or "rippling effects" that conflict can have in families.

Despite the fact that there are proportionally fewer family conflict studies with triads and tetrads, there are some exemplar pieces of research that involve three or more members of a family. One such study was conducted by Rinaldi and Howe (2003). Using the systems perspective, the scholars surveyed 60 middle-class Canadian families to learn about their perceptions of the conflict patterns between the members of the families. Surveys were sent to 60 children in fifth or sixth grade as well as the sibling closest to them in age and both of their parents, resulting in data collection from four members of each family. Their results showed that both parents and children agreed on the types of conflict strategies often employed during marital conflict, but disagreed about sibling conflict tactics—except in determining the level of warmth in the sibling relationship. Also, little agreement was found regarding interactions between parents and siblings. For example, parents felt their actions during conflict with their children included more reasoning strategies than their children perceived. Children, on the other hand, felt their parents used more verbal aggression when in conflict with them than parents perceived.

In addition to finding differences in perceptions within dyads about the nature of conflict, Rinaldi and Howe (2003) found conflict within one subsystem can affect other subsystems in a family. For instance, siblings' perceptions of the interactions between them influenced their view of their relationship with their parents. Negative sibling interactions were associated with negative parent-child conflict, whereas positive sibling interactions were associated with positive parent-child relations. Finally, the authors found a positive correlation between marital conflict and parent-child conflict, whereby marital reasoning, verbal aggression, and avoidance tendencies were positively associated with parent-child reasoning, verbal aggression, and avoidance tendencies. This is similar to the study by Brody, Stoneman, and McCoy (1994), which found that less overt marital conflict led to less negative parent-child interactions.

One factor that may help promote resiliency in families (i.e., the ability for a family to overcome unusually hard times) during conflict is cohesion or solidarity/closeness. Caughlin (2003) argues that families are most satisfied, and thus, likely to display more functional communication patterns, when members are more cohesive. Families that value openness and the expression of affection, give emotional and instructional support, and interact regularly tend to function well. Not surprisingly, the presence of these qualities is associated with less externalizing behaviors by adolescents, even after controlling for parent-child hostility (Richmond & Stocker, 2006). Richmond and Stocker (2006) found that family cohesion negatively influenced adolescents' externalizing problems, independent of the variance explained by the hostility in the parent-child dyad. Parents who interact with their arguing children and encourage them to share their side of the conflict and consider both sides equally also tend to discourage dysfunctional sibling conflict (Brody, Stoneman, McCoy, & Forehand, 1992).

In contrast, one factor that can place families at greater risk for negative patterns of conflict is differential sibling treatment. In addition to interparental conflict, treating siblings differently can result in negative outcomes for families. Differential sibling treatment is associated with a more negative sibling relationship, even four years later (Brody et al., 1994). When mothers treat their children unequally, siblings tend to report less intimacy (Kim et al., 2006), whereas differential treatment by fathers is associated with more conflict and a greater sense of rivalry among children (Brody et al., 1992). Such rivalry occurs because fathers spend less time with their children than do mothers, which makes differential treatment more salient to the siblings (Brody et al., 1992). In the same vein, fathers' hostility toward their children explains the differences between adolescent externalizing behaviors, both within and between families (Richmond & Stocker, 2006). That is, fathers who are differentially hostile to their children promote more problematic behaviors by the sibling receiving the brunt of the destructive behavior. Moreover, when compared with other families, greater hostility within one family as a whole can lead to greater externalizing behaviors by siblings (Richmond & Stocker, 2006). Interestingly, Feinberg and colleagues (2003) found that siblings try to compensate for differences in parental warmth by differentiating themselves from one another. In this way, through interests and involvements in different activities, siblings avoid competition and conflict.

Certainly, not all families engage in conflict in the same way. As such, scholars have identified several dimensions of conflict along which family systems vary. For example, many scholars contend that it is not just the presence of conflict that causes harm to children, but rather the manner in which parents argue (e.g., Gottman & Krokoff, 1989). Jenkins (2000) found that anger-based parental conflict is associated with adolescent anger and aggression, as well as frequent and deviant outbursts of anger (as rated by the child's peers, teachers, and mother). The more anger-based conflict children are exposed to, the more relationships in which they also exhibited anger and aggression (Jenkins, 2000). Specifically, these children are more likely to engage in conflict with their siblings, parents, peers, and teachers.

One interesting question concerns how conflict patterns and generalized negativity can reverberate throughout a family and how "whole family functioning" influences family members. There is an association between conflict within one dyad and conflict within and among other dyads in the family—creating negative synergy in the family at a more general level. Perhaps not surprising is the finding that families with destructive patterns of marital conflict report greater negativity within the family (Noller et al., 2000). That is, marital conflict spills over into other relationships within the family and creates a negative environment for the family as a whole. In particular, marital conflict has a negative relationship with fathers' views of their children, whereby high marital conflict results in children being viewed negatively by their father (Noller et al., 2000). In the same vein, destructive marital conflict is associated with greater amounts of conflict between fathers and children, between siblings (Noller et al., 2000), and between mothers and children (Smith & Forehand, 1986).

Conclusion: Competent Conflict Management in Families

We conclude this chapter by reviewing the implications of our discussion for competent conflict management. That is, we use the research to point to ways that people can promote family functioning during times of conflict.

First, parents should remember that their own conflicts can dramatically affect their children. Sometimes parents think that their children are not paying attention to the way they communicate. But, children are extremely perceptive and can pick up on even the most subtle conflict cues like avoidance and silence. Parents need to be good role models for their children, which means demonstrating constructive conflict management skills. Some examples of constructive or effective parental conflict management skills for parents (and family members in general) include the following:

- Not putting their children in the middle of their disputes.
- Promoting individual and family problem solving.
- Managing extreme emotions, like intense anger or mood swings, that can inappropriately escalate the conflict and make it difficult for parents to think about each other's perspective.
- Refraining from criticism, defensiveness, prolonged avoidance, contempt (showing a lack of respect for someone or attacking another's personal character), and other destructive forms of conflict management.

- Talking about their feelings and how they approach conflict.
- Creating "ground rules" for their conflicts (e.g., deciding to "take a short break" when they feel themselves getting heated and agreeing to come back to calmly talk about the issue after a few minutes).
- Taking the perspective of the other.
- Developing creative solutions to problems.
- Collaborating (creating a solution that everyone likes) and compromising.
- Teaching children how to express their emotions when they are angry and problem solve through these feelings with their siblings and peers.

Second, children should not underestimate the effects of their own behaviors. Parents' conflict behaviors affect their children, but children's conflict behaviors also affect other people in the family. For example, when siblings engage in conflict, it has a rippling effect on everyone else in the family. It is normal for siblings to fight—but prolonged and destructive conflict can have an adverse effect on other siblings and the parents' marriage. Some tips for developing productive conflict management skills for adolescents and young adults are provided below:

- Remember that conflict is natural—it is how it is managed that is key.
- Many of the ways that we view and engage in conflict are a result of social learning or patterns that we have learned from our family members growing up. It is important to understand why you react the way you do in conflict, which often means reflecting back on your experiences with conflict as a child.
- If you do not like the way your parents manage conflict, remember that because communication is largely socially constructed or created through our interactions and experiences around us, we can "relearn" ways of engaging in conflict. How you manage conflict is a choice.
- Your conflict patterns may be modified depending upon your current romantic partner; understanding your own romantic partner's conflict management style can also help explain why you engage in conflict the way you do.
- You may have a tendency to fight the most intensely with siblings that are closest in age to you. However, siblings that are closest in age also then tend to grow to become the closest of friends later in life. Sometimes your intense feelings of love and hate toward your siblings are a reflection of your similarities and attempts at vying for resources (e.g., parents' attention, friends).
- Remember that your conflict behavior affects your siblings and your parents' individual and relational health. When you are angry or stressed, they often become stressed in return. Learning to moderate or manage intense emotions is important to everyone's health.

- Learning early on to talk through your conflicts and problem solve about them with others helps develop general social skills and friendships later in life.

- Engage in the same productive conflict management skills recommended for your parents.

Finally, we need to recall that families have subsystems that affect each other. When individual family members are stressed, it affects everyone else's mood. When parents are in conflict with each other, it spills over onto their children, even if they do not realize it. Similarly, children's moods and aggressiveness impact their siblings and parents. In order to truly understand family conflict and its effects on its members, we need to examine it from multiple angles and from a holistic perspective.

DISCUSSION QUESTIONS

1. How did your parents engage in conflict when you were growing up? How did your family, in general, engage in conflict? How do you think these patterns influenced your own view of conflict? How have these patterns influenced how you engage in conflict?

2. Complete the following sentence. Conflict is like a _____. Sometimes the use of similes or metaphors can help shed light on the way we view conflict. Most people view conflict negatively. For instance, someone might put down that conflict is like a war because they are used to conflict being heated and not having many positive results. However, it is how it is managed that is essential. Conflict is natural and important to family functioning. It can have numerous benefits when it is managed effectively.

3. What does it mean to engage in productive conflict in families? What does it mean to engage in destructive conflict in families?

4. What impact do you think interparental conflict and divorce have on children? Why? What are your own experiences with parental conflict? Divorce?

5. How would you describe your conflict management tendencies or "style(s)"? How would you describe your romantic partner's tendencies (or a previous partner)? How do your conflict patterns influence each other? How might these tendencies relate back to the conflict patterns in your own family?

INTIMATE VIOLENCE

Brian H. Spitzberg
San Diego State University

┌───┐
│   CHAPTER OUTLINE   │
├───┤

Myths and Maxims of Aggression and Violence in Intimate
  Relationships
    Myth 1: Violence Is Obvious
    Myth 2: Violence Is Gendered
    Myth 3: Female Violence Is Motivated by Self-Defense
    Myth 4: Intimate Violence Is Unilateral
    Myth 5: Intimate Violence Is Chronic
    Myth 6: Intimate Violence by Males Is about Power
    Myth 7: Intimate Violence Is Harmful and Traumatizing
    Myth 8: Physical Violence Is More Harmful and Traumatizing Than
      Communicative Aggression
    Myth 9: Intimate Violence Is an Incompetent Approach to Conflict
      Management
An Interactional Model of Intimate Aggression
    Intimate Violence Evolves from Intimate Conflicts
    Intimate Conflicts Are about Transgressions
    Transgressions Evoke Negative Emotions
    Negative Emotions Escalate Conflict Severity
    The Course of Conflict Depends on the Interactants' Competence
    Communicative Aggression Increases the Risk of Intimate Partner
      Violence
Refining the Interactional Model
Competent Violence?
Summary
Discussion Questions

When asked whether or not violence is a competent response to conflicts, most people, and especially most experts, are inclined to claim that violence is wrong and that better ways should be used to resolve conflict. Yet,
violence is a common response to a variety of situations encountered in society. The question has an air of something wrong about it, and even asking
such a question can arouse disapproval from many who seek to rid our relationships of violence. This chapter intends to take a very hard look at the uses
of aggression and violence in intimate relationships. It does so in two basic
sections. First, a number of myths or overly simplistic beliefs about aggression and violence will be examined, and for each myth, a set of maxims or
more valid claims will be specified. Second, a more communication-based
model explaining the use of aggression and violence in intimate relationships
will be developed, with attention to the role that competence plays in this
process. As a preview, the myths and their maxims are listed in table 10-1.

Table 10-1   Myths and Maxims of Intimate Violence

Myths	Maxims
1. Violence is obvious	a. Violence exists on a continuum. b. Violence is influenced by cultural interpretations. c. Violence is interpreted differently by people in relationships.
2. Violence is gendered	a. Males are victimized by violence more than women. b. Females engage in similar rates of violence in intimate relationships as males. c. Females experience greater harms from intimate violence than males.
3. Female violence is motivated by self-defense	a. Intimate violence by both males and females is complexly motivated. b. Self-defense is a motive for intimate violence for both males and females. c. There is substantial disagreement among those involved and those observing intimate violence as to who is to blame for intimate violence. d. Violence is often blamed on both partners. e. Who is to blame depends substantially upon who is asked to provide an account.
4. Intimate violence is unilateral	a. The violence that occurs in intimate relationships that experience violence is mostly reciprocal, both at the episodic and at the relationship level. b. When asymmetries are identified in these couples, it is not uncommon for the female-to-male violence to be as common or more common than the male-to-female violence.
5. Intimate violence is chronic	Although there are some people and relationships that are relatively stable over time in their experience of violence, most violence in relationships is unstable across episodes and over time.
6. Intimate violence by males is about power	a. All conflict is about power, regardless of gender. b. Power can be a motive to compensate or dominate. c. Both males and females report relatively similar motives for power, and this motive for power has a similar relationship to violence for both males and females. d. Both males and females report many motives in addition to, and instead of, power. e. The use of tactics of power and control often reflect emotional and expressive motives rather than, or in addition to, motives to establish power.

(continued)

Myths	Maxims
7. Intimate violence is harmful and traumatizing	a. A substantial minority of relationships with violence are satisfied. b. Most intimate violence is relatively minor (i.e., noninjurious). c. When injury does occur, the substantial majority of injuries are relatively minor.
8. Physical violence is more harmful and traumatizing than communicative aggression.	In general, communicative aggression has more damaging and long-term effects on quality of life than physical violence.
9. Intimate violence is an incompetent approach to conflict management	a. In general, violence is unlikely to be viewed as a competent approach to managing conflict. b. In certain contexts, intimate violence is viewed as ambivalent, rational, justified, functional, or competent.

Myths and Maxims of Aggression and Violence in Intimate Relationships

As used here, the term *myth* is used to refer to common and overly simplistic beliefs or assumptions. Myths tend to be both normal and normative. They are *normal* in the sense that they are common, popular, or widely accepted by people. They are *normative* in the sense that they usually imply some explicit or implicit judgment of what *should* or *should not* be. Thus, for example, if it is normally believed that men are far more violent than women in intimate relationships, there is an implicit normative belief that women suffer more than men and that male violence against women is a significant societal problem. It is important to recognize, however, that most myths exist because there is at least some degree of truth to them. The challenge, therefore, is to determine to what degree they are valid. To establish their validity, it is essential that careful attention be given to the scientific evidence on the matter rather than common beliefs. As such, this chapter will emphasize research and evidence in the examination of these myths and maxims.

MYTH 1: VIOLENCE IS OBVIOUS

Decades ago, Supreme Court Justice Potter Stewart ushered a now infamous statement commonly paraphrased as: "I can't define pornography, but I know it when I see it." Do you know violence when you see it? Table 10-2 includes several descriptions of behaviors. After reading each, indicate whether or not you consider it a form of "violence," and the extent to which you consider the action justified or unjustified.

To what extent did your beliefs about the appropriateness or inappropriateness of a behavior influence your labeling of the behavior as violence? Our

Table 10-2 Assessing the Existence and Justification of Violence

Instructions: Below is a list of scenarios—your task is (1) to decide whether or not the **bolded** behavior in each scenario constitutes a type of "violence" and (2) regardless of whether or not you defined the behavior within the scenario as violence, rate how "justified" or "unjustified" each behavior is in the situation using the following scale:

```
0    1    2    3    4    5    6    7    8    9    10
not at all              justified            completely justified
```

	Yes	No	
1. You **spank** your child after the child started to walk out onto a street with oncoming traffic.			0 1 2 3 4 5 6 7 8 9 10
2. A teacher **spanks** your child after your child insulted the teacher in front of a classroom of students.			0 1 2 3 4 5 6 7 8 9 10
3. A woman walks in on her fiancé in bed with one of her brides-maids a few days before the wedding and **slaps** him.			0 1 2 3 4 5 6 7 8 9 10
4. In a heated argument with your boyfriend or girlfriend, you **kick** the sofa you are standing next to.			0 1 2 3 4 5 6 7 8 9 10
5. In a heated argument with your boyfriend or girlfriend, you **pick up a kitchen knife and stab it into the table** next to you.			0 1 2 3 4 5 6 7 8 9 10
6. Your boyfriend or girlfriend is about to walk out the door in the middle of a heated argument and you grab them and **hold them against the wall** to finish something important you were saying.			0 1 2 3 4 5 6 7 8 9 10
7. During a heated argument with your boyfriend or girlfriend to get their attention and to get them to shut up you **hold up a fist** with a raised arm as if you are going to hit them in the face, but you just hold that position.			0 1 2 3 4 5 6 7 8 9 10

(continued)

	Yes	No	
8. Your beloved parent has been struggling with a devastating and painful prolonged illness, and you **help them take a lethal overdose** of medication.			0 1 2 3 4 5 6 7 8 9 10
9. You see someone flirting with your boyfriend/girlfriend at a party after you went to get some refreshments and you use your open hand to **shove** them away from your partner.			0 1 2 3 4 5 6 7 8 9 10
10. The same person from the party swings a punch at you but misses and you **hit** them hard in their face **with** your **fist.**			0 1 2 3 4 5 6 7 8 9 10
11. You arrive home to find a person leaving your apartment or home with valuable property and you **tackle** them **and hold them down** while your friend calls the police.			0 1 2 3 4 5 6 7 8 9 10
12. A hockey player on the team you are rooting for legally **checks** a member from the opposing team **into the boards**, causing the other player to lose three teeth in the process.			0 1 2 3 4 5 6 7 8 9 10
13. A 14-year-old teen gets pregnant and gets an **abortion** in a legal medical clinic during her first trimester.			0 1 2 3 4 5 6 7 8 9 10
14. A person who is convicted (through a confession and DNA evidence) of murdering one of your children is executed by **lethal injection after being found guilty** by a court of law.			0 1 2 3 4 5 6 7 8 9 10

	Yes	No	
15. You and an attractive person are driving home after a night of drinking. You show the person into his/her home, and s/he says, "I'm totally wasted." You start undressing the person, who says, "I don't want to do this," but you **persist and have sexual intercourse**, despite the person trying to push you away from time to time.			0 1 2 3 4 5 6 7 8 9 10
16. An American tourist steals an item in a marketplace in an southeast Asian country. He is caught, and administered what the law requires—20 **lashes by a cane.**			0 1 2 3 4 5 6 7 8 9 10
17. The parents of a young girl in a central African country decide that she should have a **clitorectomy** (surgical removal of the clitoris) as per tribal/cultural tradition, and have the operation performed on their daughter.			0 1 2 3 4 5 6 7 8 9 10

culture disapproves so much of violence in general that it generates language to refer to certain types of behavior that are viewed as justified. For example, some of the behaviors described in table 10-2 would be labeled as self-defense, as punishment, as justice, as discipline, as deterrence, as retaliation, or simply as accidents. But some of the behaviors seem to occupy some gray area. For example, kicking furniture seems violent against the furniture, but may not seem interpersonally or relationally violent. Self-defense and punishment seem somehow different from violence, but why? Furthermore, to what extent does the definition of capital punishment or abortion as violence depend on your religious or political affiliation, or the way you were raised?

A substantial percentage of the U.S. public approves of corporal punishment, abortion, and the death penalty (ABC News, 2002; DiCamillo & Field, 1997, 2002). A substantial percentage of school children have been in a fight at school (Astor, 1998), have received corporal punishment from their parents or caretakers (Straus, 1994), or experienced violence with their siblings (Wiehe, 1990), and even as adults in contexts such as barrooms (Graham et al., 2006). Violence in one form or another is common in the popular media, sports, and a variety of organized or institutional forms of violence, such as wars, terrorism, and "peace-keeping" activities. In the context of all this violence, it seems likely that the exact nature of violence has become blurred.

For the sake of this chapter, *violence* is defined as *any action intended to harm another person physically.* The question of *intent* is both crucial and troublesome at the same time. People differ in their interpretation of intent, and such differences are often at the center of conflict and aggression. The importance of including intent, however, is to distinguish accidental actions that may produce harm from those that intended harm. If you throw a pillow at a roommate and it hits a plate with a fork on it that incidentally pokes the roommate in the eye, this is clearly harmful but not intentional, and generally would not be viewed as either an act of aggression or violence. The qualifier *physically* is included to distinguish forms of physical contact from verbal and oral forms of communicative aggression. *Sexual violence*, including sexual assault, attempted rape, and rape, is a subset of all physical violence, but research often indicates that the process of sexual violence is distinct enough that it is valuable to study it as a separate type of violence. In this chapter, the general term of *intimate partner violence* (IPV) will often be used to refer to this range of physical violence in intimate relationships.

"*Communicative aggression* is defined as any recurring set of messages that function to impair a person's enduring preferred self-image" (Dailey, Lee, & Spitzberg, 2007, p. 303). Communicative aggression is often referred to as "psychological abuse." The *harm* of communicative aggression is more psychological than physical, although it can have physical side effects. For example, a parent may lovingly pressure a daughter to lose weight, and in the process facilitate the development of a body-image and eating disorder. The intent was actually one of caring, but had the harmful effect of both diminishing the child's desired identity and physical health. In defining communicative aggression the condition of *intent* is not required in part because "intent"

Box 10-1   Sexual Coercion as Violence

According to summaries of research, approximately 13% of females and 3% of males have been raped (Spitzberg, 1999). Males report lower levels of perpetrating rape than women report victimization from it (Spitzberg, 1999), so it seems likely that either a few males are very sexually aggressive and inflict such aggression across multiple victims, or males are unlikely to accurately report their perpetration of such acts. In contrast, many women have been raped, yet appear unwilling or ignorant about applying the label "rape" to their circumstances (Koss, 1989). When less violent forms of sexual aggression are considered, victim rates increasingly converge: (a) 18% of females and about 6% of males report experiencing attempted rape, (b) 22% of females and 14% of males report having been sexually assaulted, (c) about 25% of females and 23% of males report having experienced sexual coercion (Spitzberg, 1999).

The near equivalence of reporting sexual coercion suggests that it may be a gray area in the arena of intimate violence and aggression. Coercion refers to actions "taken with the intent of imposing harm on another person or forcing compliance" (Tedeschi & Felson, 1994, p. 348). Although bodily force is often counted as a form of coercion, as defined in this chapter, it would be considered a type of violence. The other forms of coercion are punishments and threats involving compelling another's compliance "under duress or threat" (Sidman, 1989, p. 31). Some threats are obviously connected to violence, such as when a person brandishes a knife or gun. Other threats may be more vaguely related to violence, but are just as effective (e.g., threatening to push someone out of a car and then leave that person stranded in an isolated place, threatening to spread rumors or ruin a person's reputation, threatening to reveal secrets, etc.).

Given the potential societal disapproval of sexual aggression, there is not a lot of definitive research on the motivations underlying sexual aggression in dating or intimate relationships. What evidence there is suggests that whereas stranger rapes tend to be the use of sex to get power, in contrast, most date rape and sexual coercion is the use of power to get sex (Spitzberg, 1998). Date rapists tend to report that they expected sex to occur, but not rape (Kanin, 1984). Beating, weapons, and other types of physical aggression are relatively rare in date rape episodes, and the most extreme force typically involves either the use of debilitating drugs or holding or pinning the female down, using the male's weight and strength to relative advantage (Spitzberg, 1998). These are clearly coercive and aggressive, but reveal little in the way of a directed drive for power per se.

In the stereotypical attitudes of both males and females of the past, research has indicated that there are circumstances in which people often consider sexual coercion at least moderately appropriate. These conditions include contexts such as: when a male has spent a lot of money on the female, when the couple have been dating for an extended time, when there has been prior sex or sexual activity in the relationship or when the female has had sex with prior partners, and when she has "led him on" or has gotten him very sexually excited (Goodchilds & Zellman, 1984). Other research indicates that factors such as alcohol consumption or drug use by either person, the female being dressed in a very sexually revealing manner, or when there has been advanced foreplay, may be seen as "excuses" for sexual aggression and coercion (e.g., Muehlenhard & Linton, 1987). It is perhaps not surprising, therefore, that as many as 40% of women who have experienced sexual coercion or aggression by a person continue to have sex with that person in the future (Koss, 1989; Stets & Pirog-Good, 1989). Similar to the situations in table 10-2, it may be useful for you to consider what effects such conditions have upon your own views of how appropriate it is to "demand sex" in a relationship.

The link between sexual aggression and competence is likely to be complex. One hypothesis predicts that most date rapists are seriously deficient in interpersonal skills. Their lack of competence in attracting partners through normal social interaction leads these socially unskilled persons to seek sexual intimacy with others through threats and violence. In contrast, an alternative hypothesis predicts that some sexually coercive persons are socially *hyperskilled*. These persons are so skilled that they can entice and beguile persons into compromising situations through lies, impression management, and subtle threats (Muehlenhard & Falcon, 1990). Of course, both types of persons may be populating the social environment, exploiting those who become available as targets for their sexual pursuits.

itself is often the focus of the negotiation and conflict that evolves from such actions (e.g., "I didn't *mean* to hurt your feelings"). In the most obvious cases of communicative aggression, however, it is relatively easy to discern intent, such as when someone yells or criticizes in an overly harsh manner.

Communicative aggressions are not considered a form of "violence" for a relatively simple reason—a person's nerve endings cannot choose to ignore physical injury. With sufficient mental confidence and training, however, communicative and symbolic forms of aggression can be ignored or managed. Along these lines of reasoning, the United States elevates "speech" to a very high level of protection, and as such, it is treated differently than physical actions of injury. We easily prosecute and imprison people for physical assault and violence, but very rarely consider that such punitive measures are appropriate for a person's words.

Physical violence, sexual violence, and communicative aggression are distinct processes, yet they are often used in conjunction. Furthermore, to say that someone has "experienced" one or the other is often an ambiguous statement, given that people who are victims of such behaviors are often perpetrators as well, and victims of one form of aggression may have experienced other forms as well. A nationally representative study, for example, examined the percentage of women who had been victimized in their current or most recent relationship by one of these types of violence but not the others. It found that 18% had experienced at least one form of aggression, 2–2.5% experienced more than one type of aggression, and another 2.3% had experienced psychological abuse, sexual assault, *and* physical assault (Smith et al., 2002).

Physical violence comes in many forms. The majority of research over the past several decades has tended to differentiate the following types: *severe physical* (e.g., beating, strangling, using a weapon, etc.), *minor physical* (e.g., shoving, kicking, slapping, etc.), and *sexual* (e.g., sexual assault, rape, sexual contact, etc.). Some studies are now including *stalking*, the unwanted and repeated intrusion into another's privacy in threatening ways (Cupach & Spitzberg, 2004). Not all stalking, however, involves physical violence, so it is only considered a form of violence when it involves intentional physical harm. Despite the relatively intuitive nature of these categories, there are plenty of gray areas. For example, a husband in an extremely traditional marriage might control their finances and the mobility of his wife by denying her money and access to a car, thereby isolating her from social relationships. Abusive parents might punish their children by denying them food or by locking them in a closet. Such actions may not fit the typical notion of "physical contact," but they clearly do represent actions that physically restrain a person in ways that constitute a form of contact. Then there are injuries to a person's property rather than his or her physical self. For example, an angry ex-partner might "key" your car, or kidnap or harm your pet.

Instead of thinking of violence as a relatively obvious experience, there are three maxims that provide a more valid way of thinking about the nature of violence. *First, violence exists on a continuum*. There are very mild forms of violence (e.g., a bump, shove, or slap) and extreme forms of violence (e.g., rape, attack with a weapon, strangling). This continuum might be thought of as ranging from relatively mundane or acceptable forms of physical harm, to highly disruptive, threatening, or damaging forms of harm. There are also qualitatively different forms of harm—a fist to the face is likely to be experienced in a very different way than incest or rape.

Second, violence is influenced by individual and cultural factors. There are countries and cultures in the Middle East and Asia in which a woman can be stoned to death for behaviors interpreted as infidelity or that would bring shame on the family. There are countries and cultures in Africa in which young daughters are given surgical clitorectomies presumably to manage their sexual promiscuity. A majority of adults in the United States support the death penalty and corporal punishment. These are clearly forms of intentional physical harm that are viewed as culturally acceptable.

Third, violence is understood, defined, and evaluated differently by different people. Although violence in general is conventionally viewed as inappropriate, "given the rules of Western culture, physical aggression has an appropriate place" (Harris, Gergen, & Lannamann, 1986, p. 254). For example, Arias and Johnson (1989) found that "both men and women evaluated female violence less negatively than male violence" (p. 303). In their study, violence by either males or females was approved of by at least 25% of respondents in each of four situations: "(1) slapping the partner in self-defense, (2) slapping the partner in order to protect your child, (3) slapping the partner because s/he has been sexually unfaithful, and (4) slapping the partner because s/he hit first" (p. 304). Although intimate violence is perceived as generally inappropriate, Bethke and DeJoy (1993) found that "a slap by a male was rated more negatively than the same action by a female, and slapping one's partner was considered less appropriate when the dating relationship was casual. . . . Similar effects in the same direction were obtained for pushing a dating partner" (p. 44). Simon and colleagues (2001) found that up to 15% of respondents endorsed that it is "okay" for a person "to hit his wife or girlfriend 'if she hits him first,'" and up to 9% if it was intended "to discipline/keep her in line." In contrast, up to 46% reported "that it is okay for a woman to hit her husband or boyfriend 'if he hits her first'" and up to 13% "to discipline him/keep him in line" (p. 118). In one study of Asian cultures, the approval of violence ranged between 24–54% if a wife "had sex with another man," 4–43.5% if she "refused to cook and keep the house clean," 5–34% if she "refused to have sex with him," 8–45% if she "made fun of him at a party," 12–38% if she "told friends that he was sexually pathetic," and 8–46% if she "nagged him too much" (Yoshioka, DiNoia, & Ullah, 2001, p. 912). Thus, violence is understood differently in different contexts, by different persons, and when judged by different people.

MYTH 2: VIOLENCE IS GENDERED

Violence is obviously gendered in certain ways. Males on average are larger and stronger. Boys are taught "not to hit girls." There are shelters for battered women, but this is almost unheard of for men. So this myth clearly has some basis in fact. The question is somewhat a "Mars and Venus" type of question—does the experience of intimate violence represent entirely different worlds for men and women? It is a question that has received an enormous amount of research and attention (Dutton & Nicholls, 2005; Richardson & Hammock, 2007).

There are at least two broad approaches to examining gender in intimate violence: biologically (i.e., males versus females) and socio-psychologically (i.e., masculine versus feminine), although these approaches clearly oversimplify the complex cascades of influences of sex and gender (Lippa, 2002). A starting point in any discussion of biological sex and violence is to recognize a more valid set of maxims.

First, males are far more likely to be victims as well as perpetrators of violence in society in general (Archer, 2004). Males' entire development relative to females reveals higher levels of antisocial and physically aggressive behavior (Moffitt, Caspi, Rutter, & Silva, 2001), and therefore, in interactions with either sex, males also experience greater risk of both aggression and victimization. Compared to females in society, males are more likely to be victims of violence by gangs, in the commission of crimes, and in everyday conflict encounters.

In the intimate and partner context, however, females are more likely to suffer the physically injurious consequences of violence (Phelan et al., 2005) and intimate homicide (Wilson & Daly, 1993). Women in general consider themselves at greater risk of intimate violence than men (Harris & Miller, 2000; Tjaden & Thoennes, 1998), and experience greater fear in the context of IPV (Felson & Outlaw, 2007). Compared to men, women's relationship satisfaction (Katz, Kuffel, & Coblentz, 2002; Williams & Frieze, 2005) and psychological health (Coker et al., 2002) appear to be more negatively affected by relational violence. Archer's (2000) meta-analysis found that "significantly more women than men were injured by their partners" (p. 657). In his study of college students in 32 nations, Straus (2008) reports that "although there may be symmetry in perpetration, at both the minor and severe levels, men inflict more physical injury than women" (p. 262). *Thus, the second maxim is that compared to men, women experience greater psychological and physical harm from intimate partner violence.*

Even this maxim, however, needs some qualification by types of violence. For example, a focused reanalysis of the large scale national study quoted above (Tjaden & Thoennes, 1998) found that women were more likely to receive a minor injury and men were more likely to inflict a minor injury, which is more common, but men were more likely to sustain types of serious injury (Felson & Cares, 2005). One possible explanation for these different views is suggested by a study of a domestic abuse helpline *for men* (Hines, Brown, & Dunning, 2007). The fact that it is the first such helpline available in the country is itself potentially telling. All of those calling "were primarily calling because their wives were physically abusive towards them, and 52.4% of males who were currently in an abusive relationship indicated that they were fearful that their female partners would cause a serious injury if she found out that they had called the helpline" (p. 72). Substantial percentages of the men who contacted the helpline complained of threats made by their spouse, whereby she would use their children in manipulating the justice system. The authors also examined narratives indicating that

> several men . . . were revictimized by a system that is set up to help female victims of IPV, and at times, may not even consider that men can be victimized. A number of male victims in the current study reported calling several different domestic violence help lines only to be turned away, laughed at, or accused of being a male batterer. (Hines et al., 2007, p. 69)

As Straus (2006) suggests, "male victims because of lack of fear of injury and ideas of chivalry . . . may be even more willing than female victims to tolerate being hit by a partner and even more reluctant to call the police" (p. 1089).

Even though women experience greater harm from intimate violence, it is not because they are less violent in such contexts. In Archer's (2002) meta-analysis of intimate aggression studies, females were more likely to throw something, slap, kick, bite, punch, and hit with an object, whereas men were more likely to beat up, choke, or strangle. Overall, the research on biological sex and violence reveals that despite some types of studies showing females as the more victimized sex, "there are more than 150 studies showing equal or higher rates of assault by women, and this now includes results showing approximately equal rates of assault against dating partners by university students at 68 universities in 32 countries" (Straus, 2006, p. 1086). As the information in table 10-3 (on pp. 224–225) illustrates, there are very few significant sex differences in the reported experience of relational violence, regardless of country. The evidence consistently shows that females are at least as violent as men, and they are at least as likely to initiate violence (rather than use it in self-defense). Furthermore, studies indicate that the factors that might explain or predict intimate violence rarely differ between males and females (Medeiros & Straus, 2006), indicating that men and women are far, far more similar than they are different in the way they respond to conflict or use aggression.

Thus, a third maxim under this myth is *females engage in at least as much violence in intimate relationships as males do.* To the extent that females are injured more than males in intimate relationships, it may be because of factors such as size and strength differences rather than psychological or cultural features of gender. "Men, having greater upper body strength use direct physical violence more than women. Women use weapons more often than men to generate an advantage" (Dutton & Nicholls, 2005, p. 707). Analyses such as these do not deny the existence of a male-dominated type of coercive violence. Feminist scholars, for example, have described a pattern of IPV referred to as *patriarchal (or intimate) terrorism* (Johnson, 2001), which is typified by a male unilaterally enforcing his power through psychological abuse and violence against a

Table 10-3   32-Nation Study Results for College Student Samples Reporting Perpetration of Assault on Dating Partners

National Setting	Minor Assault Only			Severe Assault			Any Violence	Any Violence Bidirectionality		
	M (%)	F (%)	F% of M	M (%)	F (%)	F% of M	Assault Rate (%)	M Only (%)	F Only (%)	(%) Both Violent
All (Median)	24	32	129	8	11	139	31	10	21	69
Australia	18	21	112	8	9	110	20	14	21	65
Belgium	29	35	120	7	12	161	33	11	20	69
Brazil	22	23	106	7	6	87	22	15	14	71
Canada	19	27	140	7	10	143	25	9	22	68
China	22	42	188	9	20	230	35	7	32	61
Germany	24	28	116	6	8	126	27	12	25	63
Great Britain	25	40	161	7	16	222	38	4	19	77
Greece	39	26	66	18	14	79	29	26	16	58
Guatemala	17	32	188	6	9	150	24	8	25	67
Hong Kong	24	43	182	7	19	285	37	8	37	55
Hungary	27	21	79	12	11	86	23	13	18	70
India	36	31	87	7	14	186	32	8	17	75

Iran	96	71	74	18	16	86	77	4	1	95
Israel	21	18	84	9	7	80	19	10	28	62
Japan	25	18	74	7	10	154	21	8	12	81
Lithuania	22	39	176	5	11	233	34	6	24	71
Malta	30	16	52	0	5	?	19	22	30	48
Mexico	27	47	177	13	17	129	44	7	16	78
Netherlands	31	32	101	8	5	54	32	5	24	71
New Zealand	14	22	221	4	13	348	28	9	28	63
Portugal	14	18	125	5	5	94	17	14	23	64
Romania	29	32	110	9	11	124	32	7	26	67
Russia	24	38	160	9	15	175	32	3	27	70
Singapore	10	28	282	0	7	?	23	10	32	58
South Africa	43	39	91	43	14	32	40	8	10	82
South Korea	24	37	153	8	19	238	32	8	19	73
Sweden	19	18	94	1	2	153	18	12	28	60
Switzerland	27	24	90	7	5	78	25	9	26	65
Taiwan	18	42	227	16	26	162	36	7	25	68
Tanzania	32	44	138	15	26	173	37	7	2	91
United States	27	32	118	9	12	136	30	10	21	70
Venezuela	25	24	93	15	10	66	24	17	19	63

Source: Straus (2008). Adapted from tables 1 and 2.

female partner. Yet, by one analysis, "about one in 200 men arrested of partner abuse would qualify for the patriarchal terrorist label" (Dutton & Nicholls, 2005, pp. 704–705). Biological sex alone does not seem to be a very sound basis upon which to distinguish the likelihood of using violence.

A second approach to explaining the role of gender in intimate violence is to consider *psychological* gender rather than biological sex. Research on sex role ideology shows mixed results. Sugarman and Frankel (1996) distinguished between gender *attitudes* (e.g., in a traditional framework, wives should be obedient to their husbands; in a liberal framework, husbands and wives should share in all family decision making) and gender *schemas* (e.g., within the feminine role, one would say, "I am a very expressive person"; within the masculine role, one would say, "I tend to control my emotions"). Schemas refer to a person's self-conception, or the extent to which a person describes self as embodying the appropriate characteristics of a particular gender. Sugarman and Frankel's (1996) meta-analysis found that assaultive husbands were higher in traditional gender attitudes, but also rated themselves *lower in both masculinity and femininity* schemas. In contrast, assaulted wives endorsed both higher feminine gender schemas *and* more liberal gender attitudes. Stith and colleagues' (2004) meta-analysis found a significant but moderate effect for traditional sex role ideology on male perpetration of intimate aggression. Thus, there appears to be some tendency for more traditional gender identities to be a factor that increases the likelihood of intimate violence.

Simple models of sex and violence, however, tend to fall apart when research demonstrates relatively comparable levels of intimate violence in lesbian and gay relationships as in heterosexual relationships (e.g., Moracco, Runyan, Bowling, & Earp, 2007; Tjaden, Thoennes, & Allison, 2000). If IPV is an extension of hypermasculine or biological gender-based control motives, it becomes difficult to account for in the context of lesbian relationships in particular, and in lesbian-gay-transgender-bisexual (LGTB) relationships in general (Dutton & Nicholls, 2005).

MYTH 3: FEMALE VIOLENCE IS MOTIVATED BY SELF-DEFENSE

If females engage in as much violence as males in intimate relationships, it could be that they are simply engaging in more self-defense at the hands of the larger, stronger, and perhaps more aggressive males. The evidence, however, does not consistently support this assumption. Fiebert and Gonzalez (1997) found multiple motives for college female initiation of violence in their relationships, including partner insensitivity to needs (46%), desire to gain partner's attention (44%), belief that violence could not harm the partner (38%), partner not listening (45%), and partner verbal abuse (38%). When the underlying motives were explored, additional supportive rationale included, "I have found that most men have been trained not to hit a woman, and therefore I am not fearful of retaliation from my partner" (19%), "I believe that men can readily protect themselves so I don't worry when I become physically aggressive" (24%), "I believe if women truly are equal to men then women should be able to physically express anger at men" (13%), and "I feel personally empowered when I behave aggressively against my partner" (12%). Studies tend to show that males and females initiate violence and claim self-defense as a motive at relatively low and comparable rates (Coker et al., 2002; Sarantakos, 2004). Swan, Gambone, and Fields (2005) concluded from their study of an ethnically diverse community sample of women that "women's motivations for their behaviors were complex and indicated that violence was often multiply determined by different motivations. Many women used violence in self-defense, but many also used violence to control their partners" (p. 18). In reviewing the existing evidence, as well as reporting newly collected data across 32 nations, Straus (2008) concludes that "self-defense explains only a small percentage of violence by either men or women" (p. 268). Collectively these studies suggest the following maxims: (a) *intimate violence by both males and females is complexly motivated* and (b) *males and females are similar in claiming self-defense as a motive for intimate partner violence.*

When blame and attribution of who *initiated* violence are considered, the picture continues to reveal complexity. In one of the most detailed analyses of initiation and motivation, Olson and Lloyd (2005) discovered that initiation is influenced by mutuality patterns of violence. Specifically, when both members of a relationship had been violent (i.e., mutual violence), women were more likely to be the initiator of aggression (66% versus 32%), but when only one of the members of a relationship had been violent (i.e., unilateral violence), men were more likely to be the person initiating that violence (68% versus 18%). Further, "for those conflicts wherein initiation of aggression was described in terms of the 'first act,' there was a nearly equal breakdown by gender" (pp. 609–610). They also found that despite an extensive qualitative focus of the interview, "for several of the participants, it was difficult to determine which partner initiated the aggression. Specifically, the women commonly described initiation in an *equivocal* way, going back and forth, talking about the role that each partner played" (p. 609). Overall, only 9% of their sample explicitly claimed self-defense or protection as their motive for aggression. Collectively, the evidence was mixed regarding the conclusion that women's use of violence in intimate relationships is primarily motivated by self-defense (Olson & Lloyd, 2005).

Research on the attribution of blame reveals similar complexity. Sarantakos (2004) found that whereas 47% of wives attributed self-defense as a motive for their use of violence, 88% of mothers-in-law, 95% of children, and 100% of husbands in these families explicitly indicated that self-defense was *not* the wife's motive for using violence. Cantos and colleagues (1993) found that

> the percentage of cases in which the husband blamed himself and only himself and his wife blamed him and only him for the violence were 8% for the first episode and 18% for the latest. The corresponding percentages for sole wife blame were 7% and 4%, respectively. The percentage of cases in which both husband and wife agreed that they were both to blame were 10% for the first and 12% for the latest episode. (p. 295)

Clearly, some of these discrepancies in attributing blame or responsibility of intimate violence can themselves be attributed to self-serving motives, but is unlikely to account for all of the discrepancies. It appears that more valid maxims regarding responsibility for intimate violence motivation are: (a) *there is substantial disagreement among those involved and those observing IPV regarding who is to blame* and (b) *responsibility for IPV is often accepted as mutual.*

Myth 4: Intimate Violence Is Unilateral

A common image of intimate violence is of a "batterer" or a "wife-beater," someone who initiates violence and terrorizes the helpless victim who does not dare attempt to fight back. Some IPV is unilaterally perpetrated (Olson & Lloyd, 2005). The vast majority (50–85%) of intimate violence, however, is reciprocal or bidirectional (Caetano, Ramisetty-Mikler, & Field, 2005; Kessler, Molnar, Feurer, & Appelbaum, 2001). Straus and Douglas (2004), for example, found that both relationship partners reported psychological aggression in 93% of cases, mutual assault in 63–72% of cases (46–51% of "severe assault" cases), and injury in 65–67% (79–90% of severe injury) of cases. Ridley and Feldman (2003) found that "84% of nonviolent women also had nonviolent partners, and 81% of the extreme violent women also had extreme violent partners" (p. 164).

In an attempt to disentangle the relationship between biological sex and reciprocity, Luthra and Gidycz (2006) found that female perpetrators of violence were 108 times more likely to have a violent male partner, whereas male perpetrators were only 1.5 times more likely to have a violent female partner. "The single largest predictor of female dating violence perpetration was a partner's use of aggression" (p. 725). In Straus' (2008) study of college students across 32 nations, he found that "regardless of whether the data were reported by male or female respondents, in over two thirds of the cases, both partners were violent, Female-Only violence characterized a fifth of the cases, and Male-Only violence was found in one out of ten couples" (p. 260). Indeed, much evidence indicates that female-only initiated violence is more common than male-only initiated violence in intimate relationships (Dutton & Nicholls, 2005).

"There are strong theoretical reasons to believe that relationships between communication processes and family violence are bidirectional" (Anderson, Umberson, & Elliott, 2004, p. 639). Violence emerges from an interactional environment in which action and reaction is sustained through mutual construction. Consequently, more appropriate maxims would be that (a) *most violence in most relationships that experience violence is reciprocal, both at the episodic and at the relationship level* and (b) *when asymmetries are identified in these couples, it is not uncommon for the unilateral female-to-male violence to be as common or more common than the male-to-female violence.* Thus, although women suffer more injury and trauma from violence in intimate relationships, the actual enactment of violence tends to be largely mutual, and self-defense cannot account for much or most of this violence for either males or females.

MYTH 5: INTIMATE VIOLENCE IS CHRONIC

The stereotypes of "intimate terrorism" and the "battered-wife syndrome" evoke notions of chronic, ongoing, repetitive, stable, or even constant exposure to violence. Whereas such chronically abusive relationships do exist, they appear to reflect a relatively small minority of all violent intimate relationships (Dutton & Nicholls, 2005). The research on intimate violence reveals considerable instability over time and interactant. To get some idea of the quantities of actual assault, Tjaden and Thoennes (2000) estimate that "female physical assault victims averaged 6.9 assaults," and "male victims of intimate partner physical assault reported 4.4 assaults by the same partner" (p. 39). Capaldi and Owen (2001) differentiated "frequently" from "infrequently" violent couples, and found that "the average number of physically aggressive acts for the infrequently aggressive couples was one or two per year" (p. 431). The rates of violence perpetration were considerably higher for the frequently violent couples, who averaged a little over one such act per week in the past year, but these couples represented between 9–13% of the couples studied.

As averages, some couples will be more violent more consistently than others. This raises the question of whether or not couples can experience violence "occasionally," or perhaps only once or twice. Several studies indicate that between half to two-thirds of couples who report some violence in a given year will not engage in any violence for up to two subsequent years of study (Jacobson, Gottman, Gortner, Berns, & Shortt, 1996; Straus, 2001). Other studies indicate that only 10–20% (Aldarondo, 1996; Riger, Staggs, & Schewe, 2004), or perhaps as much as a third (Caetano et al., 2005), of couples are "stably violent." Collectively, therefore, the more valid maxim regarding chronicity is that *although there are some people and relationships that are relatively stable over time in their experience of violence, most violence in relationships is unstable across episodes and over time.*

MYTH 6: INTIMATE VIOLENCE BY MALES IS ABOUT POWER

A centerpiece of most traditional feminist approaches to IPV is the assumption that "men use violence in intimate relationships as a means of exercising power and control over women. Violence does not 'just happen,' as many men insist. Instead, violence is purposeful and intentional and so are men's responses to it" (Cavanagh, Dobash, Dobash, & Lewis, 2001, p. 699). There are several reasons to doubt the validity of the claim that intimate violence is primarily "about" power.

First, a simpler maxim needs to be emphasized: at some level, (a) *all conflict is about power, regardless of sex or gender.* Conflict is a subset of power relations. To the extent that the vast majority of IPV emerges from conflict episodes, and that violence is a tactic used to influence others, it is obvious that all conflict, and therefore violence, is a form of power. Thus, as demonstrated above, if females use violence as often as males in their intimate relationships, it is *about* power for both sexes.

Second, if male intimate violence is about power, and power is about gender, again it becomes difficult to comprehend why intimate violence is at least as common in lesbian relationships as in heterosexual relationships (e.g., Tjaden et al., 2000). If violence is about power and power is about gender, there should be significantly less violence in female-only relationships, unless sexual orientation is unequivocally linked to gender asymmetric relationship structures.

Third, power can be understood in a multitude of ways; it can be conceptualized in psychological, behavioral, sequential, episodic, and relational ways (Stets, 1995). Across many of these approaches, neither males nor females appear to have a consistent gender-based power advantage or disadvantage (Dutton & Nicholls, 2005). One such study (Rudd & Burant, 1995), for example, found that women do use influence strategies, but tend to use more indirect forms such as aversive stimulation (pouting, sulking) or ingratiation (favors, affection). When "need to control" is measured as a trait, need for control (Winstock, 2006) and dominance and perceived power imbalance (O'Leary, Smith Slep, & O'Leary, 2007) contribute similarly to the prediction of aggression for both men and women. Ehrensaft and Vivian (1999) found that *both* males and females in aggressive relationships perceived their partner's use of controlling tactics as less controlling than those in nonaggressive relationships, suggesting the possibility that aggressive couples struggle more than nonaggressive couples with control tactics but rationalize them as relatively normative. Yet, using very different methodologies, Rosenbaum and O'Leary (1981) found that abusive husbands were less assertive with their wives, compared to nonviolent dissatisfied or satisfied couples, and Stets and Burke (2005) found that "wives report higher levels of control over their spouse than do husbands" (p. 170). In sum, aggressive couples do appear locked in power struggles, but the exact nature of that power struggle is not consistently determined by gender. Furthermore, it seems that not all uses of power "look like" power in the traditional and overt sense.

Fourth, when the concept of power is broken down into various potential motives for use of violence, studies tend to find that both women and men interpret multiple motives underlying their use of intimate violence. Studies tend to find that control and dominance are reported as a motive for intimate violence about a fifth of the time, whereas other motives, such as expressive action (e.g., anger, upset, hostility, jealousy, possessiveness), face or self-esteem preservation, or rejection, are also commonly reported (e.g., Gondolf & Beeman, 2003; Mouradian, 2001). Follingstad, Laughlin, Polek, Rutledge, and Hause (1991) found no sex differences for several motives, including: to feel more powerful, self-defense, to prove love, sexual arousal, or to get attention. Women reported more anger motives than men and more "retaliation for emotional hurt" motives, and men reported more "retaliation for being hit first." Olson and Lloyd's (2005) study found that of the aggressive conflicts studied, women attributed their motives most to psychological factors (46%), rule violations (36%), gaining attention and compliance (33%), and face restoration (23%). They concluded that a "glaring pattern" of the data "was how often the women explained that aggression was the only way to get their partners' attention or to get the men to listen or acknowledge the women" (p. 615).

Fifth, it is important to consider what is obscured by the claim that violence is about power. Does this mean that males use power because they *lack* power, or because they already *have* power? That is, is the claim that males use power to compensate or to dominate?

The answer to this question has many implications for how violence is understood. If males use violence because they feel they lack power in the relationship, this makes it difficult to claim that females lack power because of their sex or gender. Research that has attempted to address this issue reveals a complex set of relationships between perceived power imbalance and violence. Some studies have found that abusive men are more likely to perceive themselves, and be perceived by their partners, as lower in power in the relationship (Ronfeldt, Kimerling, & Arias, 1998; Sagrestano, Heavey, & Christensen, 1999). In contrast, other studies implicate the feeling of powerlessness in provoking violence for both men and women (Caetano, Vaeth, & Ramisetty-Mikler, 2008; Kernsmith, 2005). Complicating the picture further, one study found that "women with ongoing violence in a dating relationship report that they are more likely to allow control from the male and report stronger feelings of romantic love" (Follingstad, Rutledge, Polek, & McNeill-Hawkins, 1988, p. 180). The concept of "allowing" control presents an enormously complex problem in interpreting the concept of power in any relationship, much less violent relationships.

The 32-nation study of college students by Straus (2008) found little difference between male and female amounts of relationship dominance. He concluded that at least in more developed countries, increasing gender egalitarianism and equality is consistent with the empirical similarity of rates of violence. Furthermore, he points out that dominance is associated with relationship violence, but similarly for men and women—it is not an issue of gender per se, but about relationship dominance, which *can be achieved by either the male or the female in any given relationship context.* Indeed, in his large scale sample of university college students, dominance for males was more closely associated with bilateral violence than it was with unilateral male-initiated violence, contrary to a dominance-oriented interpretation. Female relationship dominance, in contrast, was substantially related to female-only initiation of violence.

Therefore, a more reasonable set of maxims about gender and power would include the following: (b) *power can be a motive to compensate or dominate,* (c) *both males and females report relatively similar motives for power, and this motive for power has a similar relationship to violence for both males and females,* and (d) *both males and females report many motives for their uses of violence in addition to, and instead of, power.*

Sixth, there is increasing evidence and theory supporting two relatively distinct motivations for violence across a broad spectrum of types of violence.

Violence can be affective/expressive, or predatory/instrumental (Babcock, Jacobson, Gottman, & Yerington, 2000; Meloy, 2002). This dichotomous classification finds support in clinical, forensic, and physiological literatures (McEllistrem, 2004). To the extent that intimate violence emerges from highly arousing contexts, expressive motives may better represent the nature of the violence than control motives. To the extent that violence is also closely associated with emotions such as anger, frustration, jealousy, and rage, it would reflect expressive motivations. Thus, a more complex understanding of the motives for male perpetration of intimate violence reveals that (e) *the use of tactics of power and control often reflect emotional and expressive motives rather than, or in addition to, motives to establish power.* Thus, more simply put, all intimate violence is a *form of power,* but this does not mean that all (male) intimate violence is *about* power.

MYTH 7: INTIMATE VIOLENCE IS HARMFUL AND TRAUMATIZING

There is no doubt whatsoever that there are many victims of IPV who are severely scarred physically and psychologically. Research is relatively definitive that exposure to family violence as a child (Anda et al., 2006), and as an adult (Coker et al., 2002; Smith et al., 2002) in general, has lasting harmful effects on victims' psychological, emotional, and physical health. "Battered women in shelters often tell incredible stories of beatings, rapes, torture, and constant terror" (Giles-Sims, 1998, p. 49). The question of whether or not all or most IPV is harmful, however, is a more complex question.

Out of all the violence that occurs in relationships, only a small percentage can be considered "severe." Across several large-scale studies, and across high school, college, adult, and international populations, rates of "severe" IPV in the population range from 1–11% (Kessler et al., 2001; Straus, 2008).

Given the many forms of harm that can be caused by interpersonal violence, there is no denying the seriousness of consequences for many victims. A common misconception, however, is that all violence is traumatic in its effects. Several studies, for example, have found one-third to two-thirds of people indicate their relationship stayed the same or improved after experiencing violence (Gryl, Stith, & Bird, 1991; Murphy, 1988). Other studies find that about the same proportion intend to continue the relationship, or even result in marriage (Dutton, Kaltman, Goodman, Weinfurt, & Vankos, 2005). In two samples of college students, Katz, Kuffel, and Coblentz (2002) found that violence showed only a small to moderate relationship with love, caring, and relational satisfaction, which did not differ for mutually or unilaterally violent couples, or by sex of the violent person. In summarizing such studies up to 1989, Sugarman and Hotaling concluded: "On average, the relationship has worsened because of the violence in about 40 percent of the cases, but in roughly six of every ten relationships that did not terminate, the violence is reported to have had no effect on, or to have actually improved, the relationship" (p. 14).

The occurrence of violence in relationships generally appears related to relational dissatisfaction, but it is not obvious that one leads to the other. Dissatisfied couples are more likely to engage in conflict, and may become more likely to use violence. In such cases, it is the dissatisfaction that may lead to the violence rather than the violence that leads to the dissatisfaction. Furthermore, several studies indicate that a fifth to a third of relationships that report violence also report that they are moderately to very satisfied with their relationships (Tonizzo, Howells, Day, Reidpath, & Froyland, 2000; Williams & Frieze, 2005). Thus, a more appropriate maxim regarding IPV and trauma is that (a) *a substantial minority of relationships that experience intimate partner violence are satisfied with their relationship.*

One of the more obvious forms of trauma is physical injury. Tjaden and Thoennes (2000) found in their large-scale study that *of those experiencing physical assault,* 41.5% of women and 20% of men report injury from the violence, and 28% of the women's and 21.5% of the men's injuries were reported to require medical care. Of the types of injuries reported, over three-quarters were reported as "scratch, bruise, welt"; with lacerations ($\cong$ 9%); broken or dislocated bone ($\cong$ 11%); head and spinal cord injury ($\cong$ 7%); sore, sprained, or strained muscle ($\cong$ 6.5%); broken tooth ($\cong$ 1%); burn ($\cong$ 1%); knocked unconscious ($\cong$ 1%); and internal injury (0.0%). According to a different large-scale U.S. study, of the 4.5% of women who experienced serious injury as a result of nonfatal intimate violence, .1% involved gunshot wounds, .6% knife wounds, 1% internal injuries, 1.8% broken bones, .8% were knocked unconscious, .2% received other serious injuries, and 3.4% were victims of rape or sexual assault without any additional injuries (Catalano, 2006). Thus, although injuries are unfortunately common, and more common among women than men, (b) *most intimate violence is relatively minor (i.e., noninjurious),* and (c) *when injury does occur, the substantial majority of injuries are relatively minor.*

MYTH 8: PHYSICAL VIOLENCE IS MORE HARMFUL AND TRAUMATIZING THAN COMMUNICATIVE AGGRESSION

Research is emerging to indicate that psychological abuse and communicative aggression have more durable and severe effects on desire to end a relationship (Gortner, Berns, Jacobson, & Gottman, 1997), psychological well-being, and quality of life than most types of physical aggression in intimate relationships (e.g., Basile, Arias, Desai, & Thompson, 2004; Rosen et al., 2002). Research also indicates that communicative aggression relates significantly to diminished health, psychological well-being, and relationship quality, even when controlling for the effects of physical violence victimization (Coker et al., 2002; Straight et al., 2003).

The explanation for the disproportionate impact of communicative aggression seems relatively straightforward. Almost everyone experiences physical injuries as a normal part of growing up. Scrapes, bruises, cuts, and worse are common. We learn that over time, these physical injuries tend to heal, and the scars they leave, if any, are often relatively minor. In contrast, we have no effective "first-aid kit" for psychological wounds. Being told that we are worthless, or that we are not loved, can represent a far more complex, long-lasting, and damaging blow to the ego than a physical blow to the body. We spend billions of public dollars to combat physical abuse in our society, and almost nothing to enhance the way we communicate with one another in our relationships, yet it is the latter that appears to be the more valuable and needed investment.

Communicative aggression can take an almost infinite variety of forms. In an attempt to understand its nature, Dailey, Lee, and Spitzberg (2007) examined hundreds of studies, dozens of existing measures, and identified over 1,000 statements potentially describing aspects of psychological abuse. Potential types of communicative aggression were also drawn from 25 different areas of research, including conflict, social rejection, bullying, criticism, hurtful messages, and so forth. When these items are systematically refined, 11 types of communicative aggression are found (see table 10-4).

Because these forms of communication often strike at vulnerable self-images, they are capable of affecting all of the other aspects of a person's quality of life. Thus, although physical aggression is likely to be harmful, it is

Table 10-4   Types of Communicative Aggression

Type of Communicative Aggression	Examples: "My partner..."
Verbal Aggression	"screams at me for no reason"; "is verbally aggressive toward me."
Freedom Restriction	"checks up on me"; "regularly monitors my behavior."
Risk Taking	"engages in offensive or illegal acts"; "drives recklessly when I'm a passenger in the car."
Degrading Dominance	"forces me to do things I don't want to do"; "treats me like a personal servant."
Threatening Valued Resources	"denies me money"; "threatens my family or friends."
Isolation	"isolates me from my friends or family"; "alienates those who care about me."
Humiliation	"spreads bad stories or information about me"; "insults me in front others."
Insecurity Induction	"threatens to have an affair"; "threatens to leave me."
Withdrawal	"does not respond to me or my attempts to talk"; "withholds affection from me."
Name-Calling	"uses profanity in reference to me"; "calls me negative names or uses insults toward me."
Dominance	"dominates me"; "controls who I can see or talk to."

Source: Hannawa, Spitzberg, Wiering, and Teranishi (2006).

not likely to be as damaging to quality of life in the long term as psychological abuse. Of course, psychological abuse and intimate violence often occur together (e.g., Henning & Klesges, 2003). When these processes are combined, the effects may be particularly toxic. Furthermore, communicative aggression may be used as a substitute for physical violence (Jacobson et al., 1996). For example, violence may be effective in the earlier stages of the relationship, but once it has effectively intimidated the person, all that may be needed is the *threat* of violence and abuse, which would be enforced through various forms of communicative aggression. A maxim of intimate aggression, therefore, is that *in general, communicative aggression has more damaging and long-term effects on quality of life than physical violence.*

MYTH 9: INTIMATE VIOLENCE IS AN
INCOMPETENT APPROACH TO CONFLICT MANAGEMENT

Intimate violence is undeniably harmful, and even fatal, in far too many cases in society. Violence evokes passion, requires considerable energy, and often makes things worse. But is it incompetent? As with the other myths, the answer to this question requires greater subtlety. As a first maxim, *in general, violence is unlikely to be viewed as a competent approach to managing conflict.* Given the potential destructiveness of violence, it is probably best viewed as either a "last resort," or something that should be used with extreme caution and moderation. Even this maxim, however, is likely to be difficult to understand without some careful explanation.

First, given that many relationships are satisfactory despite the use of occasional violence, that people intend to continue their relationships with partners who have engaged in violence, and that the vast majority of violence is relatively mild, it seems that violence itself may have relatively little impact on judgments of competence. Second, given that violence tends to be reciprocal, it may be perceived by both members of a relationship as an acceptable form of conflict.

Third, to the extent violence is treated as a "last resort" in managing relational conflicts, it may serve an important function as a *critical juncture* in both the conflict episode and in the relationship. It is entirely possible that violence represents a qualitative escalation of conflict that signals things are getting out of hand, resulting in cooling off periods, an unsettling of entrenched positions, or needed catharsis. These kinds of disruptions may help a couple move in a different direction. In essence, such escalation may serve as a shock to the relational system that requires the partners to pursue the conflict in a different, perhaps more competent, direction. It would be nice to think that there are always *more* competent ways of managing conflict in our relationships, and there likely are. But violence may serve a relatively unique function by representing a marker of seriousness, a warning system of sorts, that the very person and the relationship are at risk if deeper problems are not more competently addressed.

Fourth, although violence in general is conventionally viewed as inappropriate, there are various conditions in which large percentages of the public approve of violence (Funk, Elliott, Urman, Flores, & Mock, 1999; Johnson & Sigler, 1996). Alzenman and Kelley (1988) found that while 95% of college students disapproved of violence, 1% of women and 7% of men "indicated that violence can be helpful in a relationship" (p. 307). According to research by Koski and Mangold (1988), although 93–96% of respondents considered it always wrong to "slap spouse" or "hit spouse with fist," far smaller percentages of respondents say it is always wrong to "yell at a spouse" (28–32%), "slam a door" (29–36%), or "kick an object" (56–77%). Cook (1995) found that even though "more than 98% of all respondents stated that under *any* circumstances the use of force or threats is generally not acceptable" in attempting to obtain sex, when presented with a list of 14 scenarios (e.g., "she says yes then no," "they have had sex before," "he spends a lot of money on her"), the percentage who completely rejected verbal threats of harm across all situations decreased to about 81%, and decreased even more when attempting (71%) or in actually obtaining (76%) intercourse. Cauffman, Feldman, Jensen, and Arnett (2000) found that "although date violence was generally rated as unacceptable, . . . the most acceptable justifications were acting in self-defense, just being playful, and seeking revenge" (p. 661). Follingstad, Rutledge, McNeill-Harkins, and Polek (1992) found that "women who have been the victim of force tend to romanticize jealousy and possessiveness," and "believe that physical domination can be fun" (p. 133). In a qualitative study, Olson (2002a) found that "while many participants noted that the use of aggression was an incompetent form of communication, they also described many instances when employing aggression was appropriate and effective, allowing them to justifiably achieve their goals" (p. 185).

Fifth, violence has its own type of rationality, in which it can be viewed as justified, and therefore, appropriate and effective. James, McIntyre, Glisson, Bowler, and Mitchell (2004) have been investigating conditional reasoning processes that may underlie aggression. To the extent people can conceptualize a rationale for their aggressive actions, violence can be enacted within a social context of appropriateness. As the perception of violence justification increases, the perception of its competence is likely to increase relative to other forms or contexts of violence. Thus far, James and colleagues have identified *six attribution* biases in ways of thinking about violence that are used to justify the use of violence. A *hostile attribution bias* is a tendency to perceive others' actions as malevolently selfish. A *derogation of target bias* is a tendency to ascribe negative characteristics to another person, making that person more deserving of aggression. A *retribution bias* is a tendency to favor negative reciprocity or retaliation rather than reconciliation. A *victimization by powerful others bias* is a tendency to cast oneself as a victim of the other, thereby making the other person more deserving of aggression. A *potency bias* is a tendency to cast issues in terms of strength and weakness, within which aggression is perceived as a virtue. *Social discounting biases* represent a tendency toward cynicism regarding traditional cultural mores, which fosters insensitivity to the effects of aggression on others.

Such biases may enable aggression and enhance its evaluation in the eyes of those who reason in such ways. Research indicates that as perceived justification of aggressive anger expression increases, so do perceptions of its competence (Sereno, Welch, & Braaten, 1987). Whereas assertive and passive forms of anger expression appear to be more competent and satisfying, aggressive forms of anger expression are surprisingly not viewed as particularly *in*competent (Guerrero, 1994). A more valid maxim, therefore, is that *in certain contexts, intimate violence is viewed as ambivalent, rational, justified, functional, or competent.* An important qualification to keep in mind in regard to this maxim, however, is the importance of always considering whether or not alternative, more collaborative behaviors might be *more* rational, justified, functional, or competent. It seems reasonable to believe that they are.

An Interactional Model of Intimate Aggression

If violence and aggression in intimate relationships is less about power and gender, and more about how a relationship has developed over time to resolve its participants' conflicts, then a more interaction- and communication-based model of aggression is needed (Winstock, 2007b). Such a model would locate the causes of intimate aggression more in the emergent process of conflict, and less in trying to identify what kinds of people are aggressive or violent. This model will identify basic propositions that describe the process by which aggression and violence erupt in intimate conflicts, and the aftermath of these eruptions. Many of the conflict processes that lead to violence are likely to be relatively similar to everyday conflicts. The particular combination of these processes, however, may have a cumulative reinforcing effect, like catalysts, producing a particularly volatile conflict episode.

Conflicts involve interdependent goals that are perceived to be incompatible (Canary et al., 1995). One party is attempting to influence another party to do something the other party does not consider appropriate or effective. In such contexts, therefore, conflicts almost by definition threaten the face of the participants: both the appropriateness (i.e., positive face) and effectiveness (i.e., negative face) of interactants is threatened by conflict (see Canary et al., 2001; Lakey & Canary, 2002; Olson & Golish, 2002). When a person's face is threatened, unpleasant emotions tend to result, which complicate rational approaches to resolving the conflict. A complex entanglement occurs where (1) conflict threatens face, (2) face threat evokes defensive tactics, which escalate the intensity and now the mutual face threat of the conflict, and (3) the escalating emotions reach hazardous tipping points of rage and violence.

INTIMATE VIOLENCE EVOLVES FROM INTIMATE CONFLICTS

Intimate violence may occasionally emerge "out of the blue" (Dobash & Dobash, 1979), a phenomenon that might reflect the relationship between angry rumination and aggression. Even this relationship, however, appears to occur only in the face of presumed provocation (Bettencourt, Talley, Benjamin, & Valentine, 2006). Intimate violence almost always emerges out of verbal conflict (Feldman & Ridley, 2000; Katz, Carino, & Hilton, 2002). At least one study indicated that 98% of the time physical violence occurred it was in the context of verbal conflict (Stets, 1992). Another study (Medeiros & Straus, 2006) found that "low relationship conflict" persons were far less likely (men = 1%, women = 4%) to have engaged in a severe assault on their partner than "high relationship conflict" persons (men = 64%, women = 24%). If intimate violence is to be understood, the conflict processes that provide the context for such violence must be understood. Out of all the millions of interpersonal conflicts that occur each day on this planet, only a small percentage result in violence, so it is important to understand the characteristics of the types of conflicts that are likely to erupt in violence.

Qualitative studies of couples experiencing violence provide an overview of the process. A "verbal fight" is typically identified as the "prehistory" of a violent episode. Most of these verbal fights represent utterances about a common topic that is perceived by the other person as a challenge. The challenge often takes the form of a request that is perceived as illegitimate or that challenges the social status of the partner. The rejection of the implicit or explicit criticism or request then activates a struggle for face management, which often results in a pattern of verbal conflict between the partners (Hydén, 1995). The pattern that is emerging is similar to what is described by Zillmann (1990) as "aggravated conflict," in which insignificant disagreements escalate into acute conflict, which in turn escalates to intense emotions such as frustration and anger, stimulating outbursts of rage and violence.

INTIMATE CONFLICTS ARE ABOUT TRANSGRESSIONS

Conflicts that precipitate violence are likely to involve one or more perceived affronts, rule violations, or "noxious events" (Mack, 1989). Specifically, *rules* are followable prescriptions for behavior (Shimanoff, 1980). Rules generally develop because they help regulate behavior in ways that facilitate goal achievement in relationships with others (Argyle et al., 1981). "While we are having a sexual relationship, do not have sexual relations with anyone outside of our relationship" might be a rule partners are aware of, whether explicitly stated or unstated. If violated, at least two threats to face have occurred—first, the cheater has demonstrated through behavior that the relationship itself is not valued (Cupach & Metts, 1994), and second, the partner has shown disrespect to the rules by which the relationship was to operate. The partner feels betrayed on multiple levels, resulting in the perception that he or she has less ability to control his or her own feelings, the partner, or the relationship (i.e., negative face), as well as feeling less attractive to the cheater, who obviously chose someone else (i.e., positive face). Such violations, because they threaten individual valued goals, represent an *affront*, or challenge, to a person's sense of appropriateness and face. Such affronts are obvious flash points for conflict among people. As threats to appropriateness and effectiveness, conflicts tend to imply diminished evaluations of one another's competence. Further, to the extent conflict behavior can be performed in a manner that is perceived as higher rather than lower in competence, the less that face is threatened, thereby permitting more collaborative forms of management. Collectively, affronts, rule violations, and face threats tend to comprise perceived *relational transgressions*, or a violation of a valued relationship expectation.

To the extent that a person's comments in a conflict are perceived as implying criticism or rejection, the use of abuse or aggression to resolve conflict becomes more likely. There is ample evidence that intimate conflict is connected to perceived transgressions. Physically aggressive husbands tend to feel more attacked compared to only verbally aggressive or withdrawing husbands (Margolin, John, & Gleberman, 1988). When Stets (1988) asked people "what led to violent incidents" she found evidence of an impulse stage, in which a problematic situation is recognized. In the context of this problem, "when a woman's behavior was *perceived* by the man as challenging to his power, decisions, authority, or control, violence often erupted" (pp. 70–71). Graham and Wells (2002) inquired as to the perceived cause of violent incidents, and found that more men (76.5%) than women (49%) attributed the cause to "someone being obnoxious or annoying," "someone insulting someone" (men = 78%, women = 52%), "someone picking on or bothering someone" (men = 68%, women = 43%), and "someone feeling embarrassed or put down" (men = 50%, women = 31%). In another study, "women reported that various relational norms and expectations had been violated, implying that aggression was a viable means by which to correct the wrongs of the violations or to correct for unmet needs" (Olson & Lloyd, 2005, p. 614).

Qualitative studies continue to reveal the importance of perceived affront or rule violation in the attributed instigation of violence. Sarantakos (2004) concluded that

> in 64 percent of cases studied, prior to the wives' aggression, there was no aggression on the part of the husbands. In these cases, what triggered the aggression by the wife was violation of household rules or of personal expectations or demands of the wives on his part, such as disregard of the wife's wishes or instructions regarding child responsibilities, insulting one of her close friends, staying out longer than expected, gambling household money, forgetting to make the monthly mortgage payments, or being found to have had an affair with another woman. (p. 281)

So powerful is the perceived connection of affronts to violence that when observers view conflicts involving violence, if the observer perceives the victim as engaging in communicative aggression, the observers blame the perpetrator less for the violence. It seems that being nasty to someone, even toward the person who uses intimate violence, increases the extent to which observers accept that person's justification for using violence (Taylor & Sorenson, 2005; Witte, Schroeder, & Lohr, 2006).

This process of perceiving that a transgression *justifies* an aggressive or violent response suggests that the participants have very different interpretations of the situation. Those who break rules often are either not aware of their violation, or they disagree that such a violation occurred. Transgressions also represent actions that threaten a person's valued goals, and obstruction of goals is a primary element of conflict. Frustration of goals is also a cause of negative arousal and emotion.

TRANSGRESSIONS EVOKE NEGATIVE EMOTIONS

The collective effect of combining face threat, perceived affronts, and conflict is to precipitate an experience of unpleasant emotions (Carson & Cupach, 2000; Cupach & Carson, 2002). Frustration of goals is considered one of the fundamental causes of negative arousal and aggression (Bettencourt et al., 2006). Olson and Golish (2002) identified "problematic behavior of partner" as the most common topic of conflict co-occurring with aggression (22%), which elicited "feelings of jealousy, abandonment, insecurity, humiliation, disrespect, or the need to control their partners" (p. 187).

One of the most researched types of affront in relation to intimate violence is the attempt by one of the partners, most typically the female, to leave the relationship. In particular, there is now considerable research that has identified attempted and actual *relational separation* as a significant risk factor of both intimate violence and femicide (e.g., Shackelford, Goetz, Buss, Euler, & Hoier, 2005; Wood, 2004). Violent males react more strongly to abandonment scenarios than nonviolent males, suggesting an experience of "abandonment anxiety" (Dutton & Nicholls, 2005). The link between attempted or actual partner departure and violence is interpreted as a product of a proprietary culture in which men react violently to the prospective loss of their "property" (Serran & Firestone, 2004). Hannawa, Spitzberg, Wiering, and Teranishi (2006) found that the more people view their partners as "property," regardless of gender, the more likely they are to engage in violence. The intrinsically hurtful nature of personal or social rejection appears to be hardwired as part of our neurological experience (see Eisenberger & Lieberman, 2004). A potentially compelling explanation of this "estrangement" effect, therefore, is the shame, anger, and rage resulting from the implicit affront of someone denying the perpetrator's self-presumed rights of ownership, competence as a partner, and mating status.

NEGATIVE EMOTIONS ESCALATE CONFLICT SEVERITY

The collective effect of combining face threat, perceived affronts, and conflict is to precipitate an escalation of the conflict intensity. When interactants are asked to nominate the causes of their violence, emotions tend to arise far more often than explanations related to power or control.

Key among the emotions attributed to intimate violence are shame, anger, and jealousy (Marcus & Swett, 2003; Mullen, 1996). *Shame* is "the emotional signal of an impaired bond" with valued others, or a negative emotional experience of being viewed in an unfavorable way by others whose views matter (Retzinger, 1991, p. 55). To feel ashamed is to be conscious of oneself as an object of moral devaluation by others. Shame may be the trigger that transforms ordinary anger into violent *rage* (Retzinger, 1991). *Anger* takes many distinct forms, but typically represents a negative emotional state directed toward some object associated with the unpleasant emotion (Canary et al., 1998; Cupach & Canary, 1995). It encompasses such experiences as rage, hostility, irritation, exasperation, disgust, envy, and torment. *Rage* is a particularly intense form of anger, associated with terms such as outrage, fury, wrath, hatred, and so forth. "Flying into a rage" implies that a person has lost ordinary restraints, and is acting on pure emotion. One of the more exemplary experiences that can elicit rage is jealousy.

Jealousy is a combination of emotion, cognition, and behavior elicited by a perceived threat to a valued relationship (Guerrero et al., 1995). Jealousy is a common reaction to perceived forms of infidelity, which are examples of relational transgression, affront, and rule violation (e.g., Emmers-Sommer, 2003). Jealousy often overlaps with anger (Hupka, Otto, Tarabrina, & Reidl, 1993) and shame and guilt (Tangney & Salovey, 1999), and shame and anger are thought to be uniquely associated with rage and aggression (Retzinger, 1995). Narratives of jealousy in relationships indicate that the function of jealousy "is to signify a violation of the rights of ownership or entitlement to some desired object and to protest this violation" (Morgan, Stephens, Tuffin, Praat, & Lyons, 1997, p. 78). Abusive males are found to report "greater feelings of jealousy, rejection, and abandonment to provocative partner behavior" compared to nonabusive males (Moore, Eisler, & Franchina, 2000, p. 77).

To summarize, almost all violence emerges from conflict. Conflict tends to erupt from perceived transgressions. These sources of frustration evoke negative emotions, which fuel the escalation of conflict into more severe and intense forms. People often experience such negative emotions in conflict without resorting to violence. To understand why some of these conflicts continue the escalation to violence, it is important to look at several communication processes that turn mere conflict into aggression and violence.

THE COURSE OF CONFLICT DEPENDS ON THE INTERACTANTS' COMPETENCE

Some conflicts are negotiated more competently than others, and the use of some behaviors will be viewed as more competent than others. One of the most prevalent processes that contributes to escalation is an increasing divergence or separation between the interactants' views of one another. Specifically, interactants begin to regard their own views as more righteous and the other person's perspective as less justified. This is a process of attributional divergence.

Attributional Divergence Increases the Severity of Conflict Escalation. A transgression is a trigger of defensiveness in part because of what may be basic biases in the perception of the appropriateness of one's own behavior relative to the behavior of others.

One's own behavior is judged as more appropriate than the similar or identical behavior of the other person involved. This results irrespective of whether the person holds the position of initiator and reactor and thus whether one's own behavior takes place as an initiative action or a hostile action. . . . One's own critical behavior is always judged as more appropriate and less aggressive in tendency than the opponent's behavior. Courses of aggressive interactions thus can be considered as chains of segments in which the respective positions of actor and victim and the corresponding evaluations of the critical behavior change. (Mummendey, Linneweber, & Loschper, 1984, p. 98)

Interactants are less likely to recognize their own transgressions as much as their partner is likely to perceive such transgressions (Sillars, Leonard, Roberts, & Dun, 2002). This self-serving bias, working on both sides of the conflict, is likely to magnify the severity of the affront given one's own relative innocence in the predicament. These biases are common in conflict encounters (Weiner, 1995). To the extent participants blame each other for the conflict, such perceptions are likely to fuel an escalating spiral because each person feels justified in resisting compromise. Such biases are particularly pronounced in dissatisfied couples relative to satisfied couples (Bradbury & Fincham, 1990; Vangelisti, 1992).

Attributional differences are also likely to arise as the actual topic of conflict as well. *Attributional conflicts* are interactional struggles explicitly about who or what is responsible or to blame for a conflict. Attributional conflict is often implied by the topical conflict. A simple statement to a roommate such as "This place is a mess" often implies an accusation, which in turn implies responsibility. To the extent the roommates disagree about who is responsible for the mess, or whose responsibility it is to clean it up, a subsequent conflict may arise over "who's fault" it is. Such attributional conflicts can serve as additional sources of spiraling escalation.

As the intensity of the conflict escalates, the other person's resistance and perceived obstruction tends to increase frustration and leads to the interpretation of divergent narratives or explanations of each other's behavior. Such interpretations often involve irreconcilable views that the other person's actions involve unreasonable, inflexible, or selfish motives. The result is that in addition to the original issue of the conflict, there is now an additional layer of conflict over the interpretation of the causes and explanations of the conflict (Sillars et al., 2002). So complicated are such processes that attributional conflicts (arguments over who is to blame for a conflict) may not be resolvable in everyday conflicts (Orvis, Kelley, & Butler, 1976), especially when there is hostility involved (Epps & Kendall, 1995).

Weiner's (1995) theory of responsibility attributions proposes that judgments of another's intentional responsibility for one's own anger leads directly to anger and retaliatory responses. Research on aggressive or violent conflict largely supports these predictions (Betancourt & Blair, 1992). Partners in aggressive conflict tend to blame each other (Bryant & Spencer, 2003;

Schütz, 1999). Several studies indicate that in violent couples there is a tendency to blame the violence on the other person, and when blaming it on the other person, blaming the person's character (e.g., violent personality) rather than the person's situation (e.g., stress at work) or other cause (Tonizzo et al., 2000). Moore, Eisler, and Franchina (2000) found that compared to nonabusive males, abusive males made more negative attributions and perceived greater rejection, jealousy, and sense of abandonment in response to moderately provocative partner behavior. It is not surprising, therefore, that "conflict-promoting attributions may inhibit forgiveness processes" (Hall & Fincham, 2006, p. 518). Attributions of intent significantly influence both blameworthiness and the extent to which forgiveness for a transgression can be achieved (Boon & Sulsky, 1997).

If forgiveness is difficult to provide because the other person is believed to be to blame, then it raises an important question of whether or not there are communicative strategies that might manage the conflict more competently before it becomes aggressive and violent. The most common strategies for managing affronts and rule violations are referred to as accounts.

Incompetent Use of Accounts Increases the Severity of Conflict Escalation. Given the perceived disruption resulting from a perceived transgression, and the subsequent flush of jealousy, anger, shame, and strain of conflict, the source of the affront will be expected to make amends of some sort. The study of interactional repair and remediation tends to focus on *accounts*. Goffman (1967) conceptualized the accounting process as a "remedial interchange" involving some type of challenge, some type of offering or account, an acceptance (or nonacceptance) of the offering, and often a form of expressed appreciation for the offering or acceptance (e.g., thanks). Generally, the more severe the transgression, the more intense the challenge, and the more intense the challenge, the more defensive the accounting process (Metts, 1994). Typical aggressive episodes may well reveal a basic structure in which a precipitating incident produces an attempt to implement control, which often leads to noncompliance and an exchange of insults, which instigates a threat, which results in noncompliance with the threat, which is then followed by a physical attack (Newell & Stutman, 1988; Schönbach, 1990). An understanding of the role of accounts, therefore, provides insight into the process by which conflict escalates to violence.

Although numerous types of accounts have been investigated, the most common and relevant to the study of conflict include excuses (along with apologies) and justifications. *Excuses* tend to diminish the transgressor's responsibility, typically by externalizing the cause of a transgression (e.g., "I had a terrible day at work"), attributing the cause to an uncontrollable source such as an accident (e.g., "I didn't mean to throw the plate at you—I thought I was throwing it at the wall"), or applying a disinhibiting factor (e.g., "I was too drunk to know what I was doing"). *Apologies*, or statements of "sorry" in response to the transgression, may be used as part of, or independently of, excuses, but usually imply some degree of responsibility along with regret or sympathy for the victim of the transgression. *Justifications*, in contrast, accept responsibility, but attempt to provide a rationale for the legitimacy of the transgression (e.g., "You had it coming to you for flirting with that person"), or a devaluation of the extent of harm done (e.g., "Just get over it already—it's not that big a deal"). There is a third set of strategies, *contextualizations*, that broaden the frame within which the transgression is interpreted (Fritsche, 2002). For example, arguing that other people do it, that there is a grander scheme of things, or that there are more complex issues involved, offer ways of placing the violation into a broader context so that it does not seem quite as bad or quite as connected to the wrongdoer. *Denials* attempt to contradict the presupposition of transgression by claiming that no such rule or expectation existed, or that no violation or offense occurred. Finally, *refusals* represent a strategy of inattention or nonengagement in the topic, perhaps by avoidance, changing the topic, or leaving the scene.

Accounts generally vary along an aggravation-mitigation continuum. *Aggravation* refers to the extent to which the face threat in the encounter is escalated or intensified, whereas *mitigating* accounts tend to de-escalate or reduce the intensity of face threat. Justifications, denials, and refusals tend to be more aggravating because they imply the "aggrieved party" has no basis for complaint. Such a contradiction of claim tends to further threaten the face of the person, increasing defensiveness and the already escalating cycle. Contextualizations provide a way of deflecting personal responsibility and harm without being as directly face threatening to the aggrieved party (Fritsche, 2002). Excuses tend to be further along the continuum toward mitigation by implying some ownership of causation ("Yes, I threw the plate . . .") and yet diminishing blameworthiness (". . . but I didn't mean to hit you with it"). Apologies are likely to be furthest along the mitigation end of the continuum in that they support the aggrieved party's complaint, and thus, face, and offer a degree of relational repair (Ohbuchi, Kameda, & Agarie, 1989; Scher & Darley, 1997). Apologies also appear to help transform the conflict into a more integrative or collaborative pattern (Bachman & Guerrero, 2006).

If apologies are the most mitigating response to a perceived affront or transgression, it follows that they are underrepresented in violent episodes. Several studies indicate that within both verbally and physically aggressive interactions, only between 3–25% of people report having apologized, or that their partner apologized (Cascardi & Vivian, 1995; Mouradian, 2001). In a study that examined the use of accounts over the course of a relationship, Wolf-Smith and LaRossa (1992) found women in domestic violence shelters reported apologies were "offered 94% of the time after the first incident, 81% of the time after the middle incident, and 77% of the time after the last incident" (p. 326). Approximately three-quarters of abusers continued using apologies, but increasingly used a mix of strategies, "blending their apologies with other, more 'self-preservative' accounts" (p. 327). A small percentage of men (13%) shifted from using apologies to using excuses, and another 23%

used both apologies and excuses. Such shifts suggest an interactional effort to increasingly absolve the aggressor of responsibility or blame, and perhaps implicitly provide an excuse for future abusive behavior.

These findings indicate that although apologies may sound like a preferred interactional approach, there is an obvious potential dark side to their use in abusive contexts—they may be so effective that they extend an abusive relationship (Emmers-Sommer, 2003). In a study of battered women, when asked what persuasive messages were used to get them to stay or return, about a fifth reported the use of apologies (Schutte, Malouff, & Doyle, 1988). The irony of this is that the abuser often appears to comprehend that using strategies that appear more competent to a partner will preserve the relationship, but this competence of one partner works to the detriment of the other partner in the long run.

Apologies are often not used in response to using violence in a relationship, and even when they are used, they are often diluted by more defensive forms of accounting and remediation strategies. In many abusive episodes, it seems likely that partners in abusive relationships perceive the violence as resulting from factors that diminish the abuser's "capacity for self control: transient physical states owing to alcohol or drugs, transient psychological states such as loss of control, and external stresses such as job problems" (Bograd, 1988, p. 67). It is not surprising, therefore, that violent males appear generally to account for their violence with excuses, minimization, and denials (Stamp & Sabourin, 1995) or justifications (Bograd, 1988). Abusers' narratives often appear "riven with evidence of the ways in which they deny, minimize and blame others for their own use of violence" (Cavanagh et al., 2001, p. 696). Abusers' accounts are further characterized as paradoxical in nature by confusing responsibility and simultaneously seeking forgiveness.

When accounts fail, interactants may find themselves with "nowhere to go." In such situations, often the only place left to go is to go. That is, when the interaction begins to appear hopeless for achieving a desired goal, avoidance becomes the most obvious response. A particular pattern of avoidance that has been studied extensively is referred to as the demand-withdrawal pattern.

Incompetent Use of Demand-Withdrawal Increases the Severity of Conflict. In essence, a *demand* is typically considered a question or request that can be (or often is) interpreted defensively as a demand, or even a criticism or attack. *Withdrawal* represents a pattern of topic avoidance, evasion, silence, or departure that shuts off further interaction. Despite sounding like a passive or subordinate type of action, withdrawal is commonly viewed as a power move because it is relatively nonnegotiable, and leaves the conflict unresolved. Because demand-withdrawal patterns reflect dysfunctional patterns of communication that diminish problem solving and increase relational dissatisfaction, they are likely to set the stage for more explosive conflicts and subsequent violence.

Several studies have found demand-withdraw patterns among violent couples (Feldman & Ridley, 2000; Katz, Carino, & Hilton, 2002), although some of these studies found the pattern only based on gender and amount of power imbalance in the relationship. Overall, gender does not appear to influence who uses avoidance or accommodation more (Gayle, Preiss, & Allen, 2002). The dysfunctional aspect of demand-withdrawal patterns is suggested in Olson's (2002b) interviews of women in abusive relationships: "due to their partner's withdrawal, several females indicated they felt the need to use aggression to get the attention of their partner, but then, once the partners were engaged, the conflicts would often escalate" (p. 118).

COMMUNICATIVE AGGRESSION INCREASES THE RISK OF INTIMATE PARTNER VIOLENCE

As the interaction becomes more complicated, layers of incompatible and defensive interpretations are made by the participants, and increasingly hostile-sounding statements are made. Given the strong tendency for reciprocity, especially for negative actions or statements, the temptation arises to engage in communicative aggression. Communicative aggression threatens the face of the recipient and inflames the emotions of anger and shame. In this context, communicative aggression increases the risk of emotional rage, which in turn increases the likelihood that more rational cognitive control processes will prevail in limiting self and partner's behavior.

There is an axiom in social sciences that the best predictor of future behavior is past behavior. Yet, in a systematic examination of existing studies representing 26 variables, emotional/verbal abuse showed a relationship with IPV that was five times larger than the history of partner violence in the relationship (Stith et al., 2004)—in other words, communicative aggression is a better predictor of current violence than even past violence is. This relationship between psychological abuse and physical violence surprisingly holds for satisfied and dissatisfied couples alike (Katz, Kuffel, & Coblentz, 2002). Across a number of studies, 95–100% of episodes of violence co-occurred with communicative aggression (Cascardi & Vivian, 1995; Olson & Lloyd, 2005; Stets, 1990).

To summarize thus far, intimate violence co-occurs with conflict, and conflict tends to erupt when there are perceived transgressions. One of the more common forms of transgression is perceived relational infidelity or abandonment, which tends to elicit jealousy. Transgressions also elicit shame, and when shame is not acknowledged, it is likely to elicit anger. Anger, perhaps especially when combined with shame and jealousy, is likely to lead to defensiveness and a communicative attack on the attributed source of these feelings. Attributional divergence occurs, in which each participant tends to view him- or herself as blameless and the other as blameworthy. Defensive accounts are offered and negotiated without success. This divergence reinforces both the negative emotions as well as the escalation of the conflict episode. Withdrawal may be attempted, often running the risk of escalating the conflict further. As escalation increases, some emotional threshold is likely to be crossed into a state of rage, which tends to disable the more conscious and rational control and coping responses to the conflict.

Refining the Interactional Model

There are no doubt people in this world who are disturbed, violent, and even psychopathically aggressive. The vast majority of violence in our everyday relationships and interactions, however, emerges from normal processes occurring between "normal" people. A less "psychological" or gendered approach and a more "interactional" approach is needed. The model developed in this chapter is depicted in detail in figure 10-1 on the following page.

Most conflicts begin with an affront, rule violation, or face threat, or what collectively could be considered forms of perceived transgression (Metts & Cupach, 2007). These transgressions are perceived as a disruption of a partner's values or goals. The partner experiences a rush of negative emotion, and displays this unpleasant experience through behavior. The partner's behavior represents a reproach of the perceived transgressor, and can take forms that are relatively mitigating reproaches, such as a minor facial expression of disapproval or a mild comment (e.g., "That was *so* un-cool"). At this stage, the attributed transgressor will evaluate the competence of the reproach relative to the presumed transgression, and the reproacher will evaluate the competence of the transgressor's violation. The more either participant views the other's action as inappropriate, or the more one or both consider their own behavior to have been ineffective, the more negative emotion is likely to be experienced.

Threats to personal integrity and jealousy are common sources of anger and shaming, and both are obvious forms of affront and transgression (Fitness & Fletcher, 1993). People who respond to interpersonal conflict with anger tend to be more violence-prone (Bird, Stith, & Schladale, 1991). Conflicts in general and transgressions in particular are likely to evoke anger, yet the expression of anger may well violate another rule (e.g., "Don't use that tone of voice with me"). Both the actor (A) and the coactor (C) experience some negative emotions. The possible transgressor (A) may feel shame for having made some kind of mistake, or may feel anger for feeling unfairly reproached. The reproacher may feel anger for having been betrayed, ignored, or otherwise unappreciated, and shame for being unappreciated. These negative emotions may stimulate divergent perspectives toward the conflict to come.

A complicating factor in episodes of anger and violent transgression is that the two parties tend to have divergent and self-serving perceptions of the process (Andrews, 1992; Baumeister, Stillwell, & Wotman, 1990). As much as 75–100% of people in relationships who have experienced violence do not view themselves to blame (Sugarman & Hotaling, 1989). When attacked, or transgressed against, the most intuitive response tends to be defensiveness to preserve one's sense of face.

At this juncture, both interactants' *motivation* and *knowledge* come into play as determinants of their willingness to use their *skills* to pursue a conflict epi-

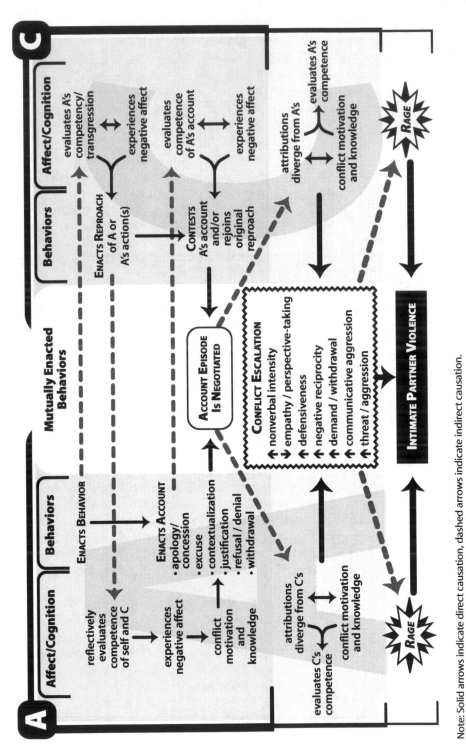

Note: Solid arrows indicate direct causation, dashed arrows indicate indirect causation.

Figure 10-1   Model of intimate partner aggression and violence.

sode regarding the transgression. Some transgressions (e.g., leaving an empty drink can on the table upon leaving the room) may be viewed as too minor to pursue a conflict. In contrast, other transgressions are more serious (e.g., forgetting an anniversary). Even if the participants are motivated to pursue an argument over whether or not a transgression occurred and how serious it was, they may not have sufficient knowledge about the situation, or about how to explore the issues. Assuming they have both the motivation and knowledge to pursue the negotiation of the presumed transgression, they may lack conflict management skills that would allow them to negotiate competently.

Assuming one or both interactants have the motivation, knowledge, and skills to pursue the interaction about the possible transgression, A will need to provide some form of account. This account, like the reproach, may be more mitigating (e.g., "I'm sorry. I'll try to be more careful in the future"), or more aggravating (e.g., "Jeez, get off my case, will you! What's wrong with you anyway—why do you have to take everything so seriously!"). The account is evaluated in terms of competence, and the extent to which the reproacher seems inappropriate in pursuing the situation leads A to evaluate C's competence as well. The more incompetent interactants perceive their respective actions to be, the more upsetting they will find their partner's behaviors, and the more their respective views toward the situation begin to diverge. This attributional divergence results from the interactants digging their heels in, perceiving their positions as further apart than they may actually be, and an emotional investment in "winning." Both members feel that their face is now involved, and that their partner has in some way threatened or disrespected their face.

Even at this stage of the conflict, which many couples experience, if the interactants have high levels of motivation to manage the conflict competently, and have the knowledge and skills for managing conflicts, the conflict may be resolved or managed with a relatively limited level of escalation. If motivation, knowledge, and skills are lacking for either or both participants, it increases the likelihood that the conflict will begin to spiral out of control, with expansion of the original issues into more face-threatening actions, more negative emotion, and at some point communicative aggression will be enacted. Such aggression will often trigger an escalation beyond some threshold of containment, wherein the *fight or flight* impulses of the participants take over, and physical pushing, shoving, or hitting of objects leads to an increased level of threat, and eventually, to actual violence.

Thus, conflicts tend to escalate into violence both because violent couples generally seem to lack communicative motivation, knowledge, and skills that might defuse the dispute (Holtzworth-Munroe & Anglin, 1991; Infante, Sabourin, Rudd, & Shannon, 1990), and because violent couples engage in fewer minor squabbles that might ease the tensions of relating to one another (Lloyd, 1990). Instead, violence seems to brew in the volatile conditions of transgression, intense emotions (i.e., shame, anger, rage), perceptual differences, and self-reinforcing cycles of conflict. In the midst of such storms the lightning and thunder of violence are played out.

The role of communication competence is integral throughout. Several studies indicate that violent couples often involve one or more members who lack communication, empathy, perspective-taking, assertiveness, or problem-solving skills (e.g., Hamilton & Mineo, 2002; Loudin, Loukas, & Robinson, 2003; Mehrabian, 1997). It is very important to consider, however, that there may be paradoxical effects of communication skills. For example, Babcock, Waltz, Jacobson, and Gottman (1993) caution that "if the wives of batterers are more adept at verbal arguments and the husbands are desperate to win those arguments, . . . [the husbands] may choose physical violence as their alternative" (p. 48). Minimally, a safe prediction is that negative or aggressive communication, negative reciprocity, the use of aggravating reproaches and accounts, divergence of perspectives, and demand-withdrawal patterns tend to increase the risks of violence, whereas positive (collaborative, mitigating) reproaches, accounts, and communication tends to decrease the risks of violence (Marshall, Weston, & Honeycutt, 2000; Sabourin, 1995). Interactants with high levels of communication motivation, knowledge, and skills have far less need to resort to violence to attain their goals in a relationship, and are far better equipped to de-escalate conflicts before they reach the level of violence (Roberts & Noller, 1998).

This model also provides a potentially important role for the strategic use of avoidance or withdrawal. The demand-withdrawal pattern is likely related to aggression and violence in part because the couple never returns to the issue to resolve it, so that it simply resurfaces in another conflict that degrades into another demand-withdraw pattern. The attempt at withdrawal may also appear to the partner like a unilateral attempt at control. In contrast, competent couples are likely to engage in more tactically appropriate withdrawals (Raush et al., 1974). The intense negative emotions evoked during "aggravated conflicts" may make ordinary approaches to conflict management less effective. "Aggravated conflict cannot be resolved by rational means—at least not by the parties in conflict" (Zillmann, 1990, p. 202). Instead, Zillmann recommends *cautious disengagement* or withdrawal to de-escalate aggravated conflicts that have already begun. To avoid the onset of aggravated conflicts to begin with, Zillmann recommends *passive inhibition*, in which aggressive acts are simply not performed, and therefore cannot reinforce or strengthen aggressive reciprocity. When withdrawal or avoidance is collaboratively pursued with the cooperation of the partner, it is likely to provide better future opportunities for competent conflict management.

This model identifies multiple stages that lead up to violence. If any of these stages can be understood and managed more competently, then the ultimate step of violence can be avoided. Traditional models indicate that some people are simply more violence-prone, and should be avoided. Such traditional models suggest avoiding types of people, whereas this interactional model suggests avoiding certain types of behavior, and when such behavior is encountered, to learn to move the trajectory of the interaction by the use of more competent means of conflict management.

Competent Violence?

Is violence ever justified in the context of an intimate relationship? It is a difficult question to ask, and an even more difficult question to answer. Clearly it is sometimes effective, and according to the research, it is even considered appropriate in many situations. I propose that violence should in general always be viewed as a tactic of last resort, and that other forms of conflict management are almost always going to offer a *more* competent approach to managing the conflict. But violence itself is one of many tactics available, and perhaps rarely even the worst of the tactics available. As such, in your own life you will be faced with situations in which the choice between violence and nonviolence, aggression and nonaggression, are choices you will need to make. An awareness of the complex role that violence can play in relationships, and the role that competence plays, will help avoid this last resort.

Summary

The phrase "red in tooth and claw," coined by Alfred Lord Tennyson, was echoed theoretically by Charles Darwin to provide insight into the essence of nature. The violence of nature is not a moral issue when viewed in the grand scheme, for violence both causes great individual suffering, and also functions to constrain the course of evolution and change. Had the dinosaurs not been extinguished through some form of violence, humans probably would never have evolved. However, viewed from the frames of human perception, society, and culture, violence *must* be a moral issue.

This chapter has attempted to view violence as an "objective" phenomenon. In this frame, violence is found to be commonly misconceived as more harmful, more individually based, more masculine, and more pathological than it actually is. From the strictly scientific frame, violence is often relatively harmless (even though it is also often very damaging, and often deadly), isolated, and coconstructed in the context of verbal conflict. But morally, it is important to ask such questions as, "How much violence is acceptable in society?" and "Even if both sexes are violent, how should our society cope with the fact that far more women are seriously injured in intimate conflict than men?" These are moral questions that science can illuminate, but not answer.

DISCUSSION QUESTIONS

1. Which is worse, in your opinion, verbal aggression or physical violence? Support your answer.

2. This chapter offers many interesting and controversial findings about violence. For example, about half of college students see slapping as acceptable in dating relationships, and 75% of college students report

having inflicted and received violence with their dating partners. Given these findings, discuss when you think slapping a dating partner is appropriate. What about other forms of violence?

3. Several studies have shown that men do not necessarily use violence more than women. Women might even use violence more than men. Discuss why sex differences may not be as large as people assume and provide personal examples (if you wish).

4. Which myth of violence is the most surprising to you? That is, which myth do you think is most reasonable to accept and why do people largely accept it? Can you disbelieve this myth, or do you need more evidence? Elaborate your answer.

5. Which maxim of violence is most insightful to you? That is, which maxim most increases your understanding of relational violence? Why?

6. Have you ever witnessed violence that emerges from an affront or a transgression? Describe the specifics of your experience to determine if the general progression discussed in this chapter applies to your experience. What insights does this description provide that could help you avoid violence in a conflict situation?

chapter 11

MEDIATING CONFLICT

Claudia L. Hale
Ohio University

Amy Thieme
Eastern Kentucky University

CHAPTER OUTLINE

What Is Mediation?
   Mediation and Other Forms of Dispute Resolution
   Principles of Mediation
   The Goals of Mediation
How Are Mediations Conducted?
   How Are Mediations Initiated?
   Stage 1: Introductions
   Stage 2: Telling the Story
   Stage 3: Identifying the Issues
   Stage 4: Generating Options
   Stage 5: Writing the Agreement
What Skills and Knowledge Contribute to Mediator Competence?
What Skills and Knowledge Contribute to Disputant Competence?
Summary
Discussion Questions

In an ideal world, if two or more parties found themselves in disagreement, they would confront each other in a constructive manner, talking through their individual perspectives and needs. As discussed in chapter 2, in this ideal world, the parties involved in the disagreement would communicate with each other in an effective and appropriate manner. Their conversations would continue until they managed, via joint negotiation and problem solving, to find a way of working together to address their disagreements successfully.

Obviously, we do not live in an ideal world. We live in a world where individuals vary widely in their skills as communicators and in their willingness to collaborate when faced with disagreements. Even individuals who are excellent communicators and problem solvers face situations that tax the limits of their abilities. Emotions might run too high or trust might be too low for the involved parties to communicate in the effective and appropriate manner described in chapter 2. Cultural and social differences can impose additional barriers to communication and conflict management efforts.

Left on their own, unresolved conflicts can grow until they eventually result in cases that unnecessarily clog our court system and even in outbreaks of violence. This does not have to be the end result, however, because a variety of *alternative dispute resolution* (ADR) mechanisms exist for people who want a constructive venue for addressing their conflicts. One ADR option is dispute mediation.[1] Dispute mediation is a unique conflict episode because it involves a neutral third party—the mediator. The inclusion of a mediator into the conflict process adds another layer of communication competence. Not only do we have to be concerned about the communication competence of the parties who are in the conflict (and their perceptions of each other's competence), but the communication competence of the mediator is also a point of concern.

Imagine Nick and Sara, who are in conflict concerning who should assume financial responsibility for a broken window in an apartment that they share with each other. Their attempts to resolve their conflict have been unsuccessful. Finally, they agree to have a neutral third party mediate the conflict. Success in the mediation (whether that is defined as reaching a mutually satisfying solution to a problem or as transforming a relationship and the ways in which two people communicate with each other [Bush & Folger, 1994, 2005]) will depend, to at least some degree, on the communication competence of all of the parties involved in the mediation—including the mediator—and on their willingness to expend the effort necessary to work with each other.

Typically, disputants enter mediation because they have been unsuccessful in reaching their goals (the outcomes they desire). Chapter 2 discussed three types of goals that are present in most communication situations: instrumental goals, self-presentation goals, and relational goals. We would like to add an additional goal that is often part of conflict interactions: *process goals* (Wilmot & Hocker, 2007). We will talk more about these goals in the next section but, first, a bit of history and background are needed.

Dispute mediation (even if unfamiliar to many readers of this chapter) is not new. Mediation has a long and rich history that crosses cultural, national, and religious boundaries. In their ADR timeline, Barrett and Barrett (2004) noted the use of mediation and arbitration by the Mari Kingdom in 1800 BC. Mediation was the principal means of dispute resolution in ancient China (Brown, 1982). Various forms of mediation and conciliation have rich histories within Japanese law and customs (Henderson, 1965), Native American tribes (LeResche, 1993), and African communities (Gulliver, 1979). In the United States, the American Jewish community established the Jewish Conciliation Board in 1920 (Yaffe, 1972), and the early Quakers practiced mediation to resolve commercial disputes and marital disagreements (Folberg & Taylor, 1984).

Today, people use mediation in a wide variety of contexts. Not only do we have the familiar use of mediation to address labor-management disputes, but some states (e.g., Alaska, California, Maine) mandate the use of mediation as an approach for resolving some of the controversies that emerge during divorce. By "mandate" we mean simply that the conflict parties must appear at a mediation session. It is impossible to require enthusiastic participation or to insist that agreements be reached. Many communities look to mediation as an approach for handling family disputes, neighborhood disagreements, gang-related conflicts, landlord-tenant difficulties, and customer-merchant problems. Mediation is one of the conflict management processes employed in tackling some of the most vexing environmental conflicts (O'Leary & Bingham, 2003) and intractable conflicts (Crocker, Hampson, &

Aall, 1999, 2005) that exist in contemporary society. In some communities, mediation programs bring together victims of crime and their victimizers to discover a form of restitution or reconciliation. These programs are typically referred to as victim-offender reconciliation programs, or VORP. (For more information about such programs, see Umbreit, 2001.) Also, an increasing number of school systems employ peer mediation programs to empower youngsters to manage their own conflicts and to teach problem-solving skills (see Jones, 2006).

Our objective in this chapter is to provide you with an introduction to dispute mediation that is in line with the competence framework of this book. We hope that the information we offer will help you to gain an understanding of both the process of dispute mediation and the constructive role that mediation plays in addressing interpersonal conflicts. Our discussion is organized around the following topic questions: (1) What is mediation? (2) How are mediations conducted? (3) What skills and knowledge contribute to competence on the part of mediators? (4) What skills and knowledge contribute to competence on the part of disputants? Our own backgrounds in mediation come not only from our activities as researchers but from training and experiences as participants in community mediation programs. That training and those experiences provide lenses through which we view both the promise and the problems associated with conflict management through dispute mediation.

What Is Mediation?

MEDIATION AND OTHER FORMS OF DISPUTE RESOLUTION

Simply put, *mediation* is a process involving two or more parties who are in conflict with each other and an "uninvolved" third party (the mediator).[2] Ideally, the mediator serves as a neutral and impartial guide, structuring an interaction that enables the conflicting parties to find a mutually acceptable solution to their problems. The mediator remains neutral to the extent that she or he does not have a personal or professional relationship with any of the disputants and thus, at least in theory, will not act in a way that gives advantage to one of the disputants over the other(s). Specifically, neutrality often applies to the proposed solutions and to whether those solutions seem fair to all involved parties. A mediator is considered impartial to the extent that he or she does not act as an advocate for one party or adopt an adversarial role (arguing against the position of one of the parties).

Although neutrality and impartiality represent fundamental ideals, they are not trouble free. Almost without exception, documents that describe ethical behavior for mediators caution the mediator to assume responsibility for ensuring that the final agreement by the disputants is fair. In at least some instances, this responsibility for ensuring fairness seems to call on the mediator to take a position, perhaps noting problems with or concerns about a proposal that is acceptable to one disputant but that significantly disadvantages the other disputant. Questions have also been raised about *how* a mediator acts neutrally and/or impartially (Cooks & Hale, 1994; Garcia, Vise, & Whitaker, 2002; Heisterkamp, 2006; Mayer, 2004; Rifkin, Millen, & Cobb, 1991). It is one thing to tell someone that they are to be neutral and impartial; it is another thing to explain exactly what that means in terms of that person's verbal and nonverbal communication.

Mediation can be easily distinguished from arbitration and adjudication (that is, decision making through the courts): During mediation, the people in conflict are the decision makers. The mediator serves not as a judge but as a *facilitator.* He or she tries to set the stage for conversation, encouraging the individuals in conflict to work effectively and appropriately with each other. One by-product of a successful mediation can be the discovery of new ways of communicating that are constructive and productive. Such skills can be especially important in an ongoing relationship, for example, between a landlord and tenants, between neighbors, within a family, between roommates, or between divorced parents who continue to share parenting responsibilities for their children.

Although a mediator does not control decision making with respect to issues of substance, the mediator attempts to control the communication process during the mediation. In direct negotiations, the disputing parties control both the process and the solution. When they enter into mediation, however, the disputing parties agree to relinquish to the mediator at least some control over the process.

PRINCIPLES OF MEDIATION

A wide variety of people in different professional organizations have been involved in efforts to define mediation. A partial list of those organizations would include the American Bar Association, the American Arbitration Association, the Association of Family and Conciliation Courts, the National Association of Social Workers, and the Association for Conflict Resolution. Despite the diversity of these groups, researchers and practitioners agree on the basic principles that define mediation. Primary among those principles is that *mediation is a dispute management process that attempts to promote self-determination.* That is, dispute mediation emphasizes that the conflicting parties reach *voluntary, uncoerced* agreements that reflect *autonomous* decision making on their part. Returning to our story of Nick and Sara, ideally, both of them would want to participate in the mediation and would be comfortable with the approach taken by the mediator. The mediator would guide the mediation process in an appropriate and effective manner, organizing a discussion that allows both Nick and Sara to express their points of view. Neither Nick nor Sara would feel "forced" into making a decision or agreeing to something that he or she thought to be a bad idea.

Another defining principle of mediation is that *disputants make informed decisions, both about their own participation in the mediation and about their commitments to (or rejection of) proposed solutions.* In some cases, mediators recommend that each of the disputants seek the advice of an attorney prior to making final commitments to the proposals that emerge during the mediation. The intent of this recommendation is to ensure that the disputants consider all options and make informed decisions concerning the proposals that have been put forward.

The final defining principle is that of confidentiality. Mediation is a confidential process, and the mediator typically reassures the parties that, at least as far as he or she is concerned, nothing said during the mediation will be communicated outside the mediation setting (at least not to inappropriate parties or in a way that would identify the mediation participants). There are limits to such a promise, however. Should information be revealed that points, for example, to possible child abuse or child neglect, the mediator is ethically bound to communicate that situation to the appropriate authorities.

THE GOALS OF MEDIATION

Although agreement exists concerning the basic principles that define mediation, the goal of the process is a matter of some controversy. Some practitioners believe that the primary goal of mediation is to resolve interpersonal conflicts by reaching agreement (Bannink, 2007; McIsaac, 1983). In this approach to mediation, any emotional or relational issues within the conflict are secondary concerns. Other practitioners believe that the primary goal of mediation is to assist disputants through the emotional issues, with resolution of substantive issues defined as a secondary concern (Milne, 1978). Campbell and Johnston (1986) note that the manner in which mediators allow emotional issues to enter the mediation process varies depending on the model of mediation used by the practitioner, and Schreier (2002) argues for the value of including work on emotional intelligence as part of mediator training. Moreover, at times there may even be a discrepancy between the mediator's and the disputant's perceptions regarding the "best" approach to use to manage the dispute (Jacobs & Aakhus, 2002). For example, a disputant might want more emotional work while the mediator might focus more on the substantive issues. Bush and Folger (1994, 2005) champion a form of mediation called "transformational mediation." As suggested by the title of one of the chapters in their book, transformational mediation focuses on "Changing People, Not Just Situations" (1994, p. 81). Bush and Folger (1994, 2005) hold that mediation should help empower individuals so they can manage conflict with others more productively. Indeed, Bush and Folger (1994) note that empowerment can emerge as a by-product of mediation, regardless of any instrumental goals. Winslade and Monk (2000) argue for an approach to mediation that emphasizes storytelling and helping disputants to craft a narrative that will transform their conflict in positive ways. The bottom line is that the mediator's own ideology regarding the goal of mediation will influence the methods (strategies and tactics) that the mediator uses. Figure 11-1 represents a spectrum of the goals of the mediation process.

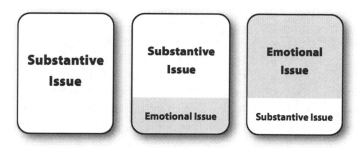

Figure 11-1   The range of mediation goals.

To the extreme left of the continuum are the practitioners who believe that mediation reflects a goal-directed, issue-oriented process aimed at achieving an agreement. This model assumes an orientation of humans as rational beings who can contain their emotions and proceed logically to resolve their disputes (McIsaac, 1983). Coogler (1978), the pioneer of this perspective, advocates a very systematic, structured approach to mediation that provides legally enforceable agreements between disputants. A mediation session will stop, at least temporarily, if the disputants need to work out emotional issues elsewhere (for example, in family counseling) before proceeding with substantive discussions.

The middle of the spectrum is occupied by a group of practitioners who recognize that feelings are not so easily separated from the conflict, and that, for an agreement to be reached, the mediator must address emotional issues (Bush & Folger, 1994, 2005; Folberg & Taylor, 1984). The mediator addresses these issues by using communication skills such as active listening, questioning, paraphrasing, and reflecting. The idea is to address the emotional issues and encapsulate them, after which the substantive issues can be tackled (Campbell & Johnston, 1986). According to Bush and Folger (2005), people need to feel empowered before they can understand what the other parties want. Accordingly, the mediator's role using this perspective means promoting behaviors that help people become empowered and help them to recognize the other person's perspective.

Finally, at the far right of the spectrum, a group of practitioners view mediation as a therapeutic event. This type of mediation is advocated for high-conflict cases such as divorce or child custody disputes. The primary goal of this type of mediation is to assist the disputants through the emotional issues that have divided them (Haynes, 1982).

A key question for anyone involved in a conflict is: Which dispute management procedure will best help me meet my objectives? Sander and Goldberg (1994) reviewed a variety of binding and nonbinding procedures in an attempt to answer that question. Dispute mediation is considered a nonbinding procedure because, with its emphasis on disputant self-determination, any proposed and accepted agreements are maintained *voluntarily* by the disputants. By contrast, litigation and, typically, arbitration provide binding decisions concerning how a conflict should be handled. Sander and Goldberg argue that if the disputants' objectives are to (1) obtain vindication, (2) obtain a neutral opinion concerning the merits of their individual positions within the conflict, (3) establish a formal precedent, or (4) maximize recovery and/or minimize loss, then mediation is probably not the best approach for resolving their conflict. However, if the disputants are interested in (1) minimizing the cost associated with managing their conflict, (2) having relatively speedy access to a conflict management process, (3) engaging in a process that will be private and confidential in nature, and perhaps most important, (4) maintaining or even improving their relationship with each other, then mediation is ideal. Sander and Goldberg also argue that, in comparison to some other dispute management processes, mediation is more likely to help disputants overcome barriers to settlement that might exist because of poor communication skills, the need to express emotions, or constituent pressures (that is, pressures exerted by individuals or groups who are being represented by the disputant). We could extend the idea of constituents to include friends of the disputants or other family members (that is, any individual the disputant views as an advisor or "opinion leader" with respect to the dispute in question).

How Are Mediations Conducted?

Mediations do not simply happen. A trained mediator follows an established set of sequential and developmental stages. The progression of these stages is important because each builds on the work accomplished in the previous stage. For example, in the initial stage of the mediation, a mediator typically explains his or her role to the disputants and establishes any ground rules that will guide the sessions. Mediation proceeds only after the mediator has obtained agreement from all disputants to the ground rules. Often, one of the ground rules concerns engaging in behaviors that exhibit mutual respect. An example of respectful behavior is to refrain from interruptions. During the mediation, if the disputants begin interrupting each other or displaying other signs of disrespect, the mediator can regain control by, in part, reminding the disputants of their earlier acceptance of and agreement to the ground rules.

To help illustrate the process of mediation and to accompany the remainder of our discussion, we have created a transcript for a prototypical mediation (contained in boxes 10-1 through 10-6). No two mediations are alike, and we have controlled the development of this one for our own purposes. However, this hypothetical case should provide at least a general idea of the various stages of mediation.

A mediator works at reducing tensions between the parties in conflict and at gaining trust and commitments to work together. Most mediation models are structured to move disputants from a "you-me" to an "us-we" orientation. This new perspective helps the disputants look for mutually satisfactory ways of resolving their conflict. If this change in perspective is not accomplished in the initial stages, the mediator runs the risk of having disputants polarize even further into their own positions. In the later stages, polarized disputants will have difficulty perceiving any areas of common ground and that difficulty, in turn, will affect their ability to reach an agreement. Therefore, an experienced mediator does not rush the process but, rather, takes the time needed to work through each stage. The amount of time spent in each stage depends on the intensity of the conflict, the type of conflict, and the negotiating skills of the disputants (Moore, 2003). As might be expected (because of space constraints), the example we provide here represents a mediation that moves relatively smoothly and quickly from one stage to the next. In the real world, the picture is often quite different.

One other disclaimer is warranted. We provide a very general description of the way in which mediation works at many community mediation centers; however, variations exist. Not all centers handle the intake procedures in the same way, nor do all mediators establish the same sets of ground rules. The mediation centers where we have worked have tended to prefer a comediator model, where two mediators are present to conduct any mediation session. For the sake of convenience, we describe our mediation as though only one person occupies the mediator role. Also for the sake of convenience, our discussion focuses on only two disputants, but it is certainly possible to have disputes that involve three or more parties (with almost any number of people making up a party). Despite these simplifications, we hope the description we provide will give you an adequate understanding of the way mediation works.

HOW ARE MEDIATIONS INITIATED?

Frequently, the disputing parties themselves initiate mediation. They can do so, either unilaterally or bilaterally, by seeking the assistance of a mediator or mediation agency. Although unilateral initiations are common, a dispute can be mediated only when at least two disputants agree to participate. It would be impossible, for example, to mediate a dispute between our apartment dwellers, Nick and Sara, if Sara refused to participate in the mediation process. By contrast, bilateral initiation can signal willingness on the part of both disputants to negotiate in good faith and to actively explore possible solutions to their problems. Although it is not possible to mediate a dispute unless all parties are willing to be involved, Jones and Brinkert (2008) champion the notion of "conflict coaching," which can involve working with only one of the parties and guiding that individual in terms of how he/she might appropriately and effectively address a conflict with another person.

In some situations, disputants will be referred to mediation by secondary sources, such as close friends, family members, social service agencies, police officers, or lawyers. Although secondary sources are not principal actors in the dispute, they are likely concerned about the consequences of the conflict, should it continue. In our example, the police officer could have referred the neighbors to mediation as a means of containing the conflict and prevented

---

Box 11-1   Zappia–Spriggs: A Hypothetical Mediation

Case History

Mike Zappia and Scott Spriggs are in conflict. They have lived next door to one another in a residential neighborhood for seven years. The conflict started (or escalated) between the two neighbors one afternoon when Mr. Zappia cut down some branches from Mr. Spriggs's maple trees. The branches were hanging over Mr. Zappia's property. When Mr. Spriggs learned about the destruction to his property, he stormed over to Zappia's house and declared that if Zappia ever did anything like that again he'd be sorry. Zappia responded angrily that if Spriggs had taken care of his own trees then Zappia would not have had to cut them in the first place. Spriggs, frustrated and angered by his confrontation with Zappia, called the police. The responding police officer warned Zappia not to cut down any more branches.

The conflict escalated the following week when Mr. Zappia was working in his yard. Still angry about the branches over his property, he raked up all the leaves in his yard and dumped them on Spriggs's front lawn. Spriggs decided he'd had enough and that the only way to settle this mess was to take Zappia to court. The judge assigned to the case noted that she could easily make a ruling that would solve the immediate problem but recognized that no court order could address the underlying conflict or necessarily help improve the long-term relationship between the two neighbors. Thus, the judge referred the case to mediation.

---

escalation. Referral also could have come from spouses or mutual friends. We have structured a scenario in which the dispute was referred to mediation by the courts (see box 11-1). If the dispute was not settled in mediation, it would be sent back to court for a ruling by a judge.

After parties to a conflict have been referred to a mediation center, an intake professional tries to educate the parties about the process of mediation and help them determine whether mediation is the most appropriate arena for resolving their dispute. Most mediation centers take a "multidoor" approach to case screening (Ostermeyer, 1991); that is, the intake professional not only determines if mediation is appropriate but also tries to determine whether other dispute management or support processes (such as family counseling) are necessary as well. To make this assessment, intake professionals ask parties about the history and nature of the dispute, whether or not violence or substance abuse is involved, what the parties hope to gain from mediation, and whether the parties are willing to resolve their dispute. If mediation is thought to be suitable for the situation (and the disputing parties agree to participate in the process), the intake professional tries to match the case with a mediator (or mediation team) and to schedule a mediation.

STAGE 1: INTRODUCTIONS

Although the individual who handles the intake process typically provides the disputants with information concerning the process of mediation, during the first meeting involving the mediator and the disputants, the mediator begins the session by taking a few minutes to give an overview of the process and to explain her or his role as mediator. Box 11-2 illustrates the introductory stage of the Zappia–Spriggs mediation. Mediators typically try to make clear that they are not judges and that, as mediators, they will not try to determine who is right or who is wrong, or dictate a solution. Instead, the determination of a solution is the responsibility of the disputants.

At the beginning of the initial mediation session, it is reasonable to expect that the disputants will be feeling angry and frustrated with each

---

Box 11-2 Zappia–Spriggs Mediation (Stage 1: Introductions)

Mediator: Good afternoon. My name is Chris Jones and I have been asked to assist you in discussing the issues that brought you to mediation. First, I'd like to congratulate you both on agreeing to try to negotiate a solution to an issue that might have been difficult for you to discuss in the past. What we will be doing in this mediation is talking through the problems that have brought you here today. Once we have a clear understanding of the issues of concern, then we will turn our attention to a search for solutions that will satisfy your needs and interests. It is important for you to understand that, as a mediator, I am not here to judge who is right or wrong, or to tell you how to resolve your differences. What I will try to do is to assist you in identifying any problems or issues you want to talk about, guide you through a problem-solving process, and, generally, help keep you on track and focused. It will be up to you to create and agree upon a solution that is right for both of you.

So that everyone can feel comfortable talking openly, I want you to know that I consider these mediation sessions to be confidential. This means that I will not discuss what occurs or what is said with anyone not directly involved in this session. You will notice that I will be taking notes during the mediation, but these are just to help me keep track of the concerns that you raise. I promise you that these notes will be destroyed following the mediation.

Before we begin, there are some ground rules that I would like each of you to follow. These ground rules focus on demonstrating civility and respect for each other while we are involved in this process. Civility and respect can be demonstrated in a variety of ways. At the most simple level, I would like one party to speak at a time. While that party is speaking, I ask that the other party listen carefully and not interrupt. If you have a question about what is said, I ask that you hold it until it is your turn to speak. Is this agreeable to each of you?

Zappia: Yes.

Spriggs: Yes.

Mediator: Are there any questions before we begin? If not, then let's get started.

other, and perhaps even distrustful of the mediator. As explained in chapters 1 and 2, disputants can bring a great deal of "baggage" to any conflict in terms of cultural norms, personal dispositions, relational history, and prior conflict outcomes (recall figure 2-2). In addition, mediators must keep in mind that individuals who have never experienced mediation can bring with them misconceptions (and even disappointments) not only about the conflict they are in but about the process of mediation. The first mediation that one of the authors conducted involved three current roommates and a former roommate. This mediation was particularly difficult at least in part because the former roommate wanted to be in a court of law rather than in mediation. She wanted a person in authority—a judge—to tell the other disputants that they had acted inappropriately. When we began the mediation session, she made her feelings known, stating in an angry tone of voice: "All we're going to do is talk. We've already tried that. I can't see what possible good this is going to do." Fortunately, we were able to get beyond that point and achieve an agreement on a number of problems the women had been experiencing with each other. However, this particular disputant remained disappointed at not having someone in authority tell the other young women that their behavior toward her had been wrong.

During the early stages of the mediation, it is imperative that the mediator begin the session on a positive note, gaining the trust of the disputing parties. To build this positive tone, the mediator might begin by congratulating the parties on their willingness to come to mediation and on their openness to work on the problems they have been facing. This approach can reinforce the disputants' commitment to work together. The mediator needs to establish his or her position as a neutral and impartial third party whose role is to facilitate discussions. Typically the mediator emphasizes that the disputants will share the decision-making process, and that the solutions they arrive at will be their own (as opposed to the mediator's). The mediator should also explain that the sessions are confidential and that anything discussed during the mediation will not be disclosed—at least by the mediator—to parties outside the mediation.[3] This reassurance is designed to encourage the disputing parties to speak freely. Creating a safe and open environment can be essential to effective communication during the mediation.

Finally, during the initial stage of the mediation, the mediator will establish the ground rules, or guidelines and expectations, for the mediation sessions. Typically, one rule will state that parties are expected to listen carefully to what the others say and not to interrupt while another person is speaking. Parties are asked to agree to these guidelines before the mediation continues.

Throughout the introduction, the mediator should attempt to build rapport and trust. Ideally, the physical setting will encourage open communication and mutual problem solving. The mediator should be courteous and professional toward everyone involved in the mediation sessions. Through careful attention to the nonverbal cues of the disputants, mediators attempt to determine the emotional states of the parties and to assess their willingness to negotiate.

Stage 2: Telling the Story

Once the mediator has finished the introductory comments, answered any questions, and obtained agreement to the ground rules, the mediation proceeds to the storytelling phase. During this stage, the mediator will ask each party, one at a time, to share his or her perspective concerning the problems that have brought them to mediation. As illustrated in the Zappia–Spriggs case (see box 11-3), usually the mediator begins with the "complaining party." This is the person who wants something to change, so beginning with him or her makes sense. However, during the mediation process, terms such as "complaining party" or "complainant" would not be used, since they might be perceived as insulting and could undercut any rapport that has been developed. In a similar sense, the mediator would never refer to the other party as the "defendant," since such a label would define that person's position as one of defending him- or herself rather than as sharing his or her perspective on the dispute. If the mediator believes that a power imbalance exists between the parties, he or she might decide to begin with the weaker party and thus enable that party to be at the table as an equal.

Box 11-3   Zappia–Spriggs Mediation (Stage 2: Telling the Story)

Mediator: Mr. Zappia, since Mr. Spriggs brought the matter to the attention of the courts, I'm going to begin by having him tell me his perspective on the issue. When he is finished, I will give you the same opportunity. Is this OK with you?

Zappia: Yes.

Mediator: Mr. Spriggs why don't you begin. Take a few minutes and tell me the concerns that brought you to mediation.

Spriggs: My family and I have lived in our house for twelve years. One of the reasons we moved into the neighborhood was that it was an older neighborhood in a wooded area and there were a lot of kids around to play with our children. We have always gotten along with all of our neighbors, and I just can't understand why Zappia keeps harassing us.

Mediator: Mr. Spriggs, please take just a moment and explain to me in more detail exactly what you mean by "Mr. Zappia keeps harassing us."

Spriggs: Well, it all started with trees. There are five maple trees that border the property between Zappia's house and my house. One day, I came home from work and found Zappia chopping the branches off my maple trees. I was shocked that he had done this and told him that he had no right to destroy my property. Zappia swore and threatened to continue cutting. So, I called the cops. I mean, what would you do if you were in this situation? He was destroying my trees.

Mediator: I'm not sure what I would have done, but if I'm understanding you clearly, you felt it was appropriate to call the police when you saw Mr. Zappia cutting down the branches on your maple trees. Is that accurate?

(continued)

Spriggs: Yeah, that's right.

Mediator: Mr. Spriggs, what do you mean when you say that the trees were "destroyed"?

Spriggs: Well, Zappia cut off all the branches on the side of the trees that borders his property. Not only do my trees look bald on one side, they will probably die from the shock of the slicing. Parts of the trees are open and exposed. I'm afraid all sorts of insects and other bugs will get in there and eat away at my trees. The trees will probably rot.

Mediator: Is there anything else you think I should know about this situation?

Spriggs: It just seems like this guy is out to get me. If it's not one thing, it's another. Just the other day I found the guy dumping leaves from his yard onto my yard. He told me he did that because they were the leaves from my trees. How can I be responsible for the leaves that blow into his yard? It's always something with him. The guy is nuts.

Mediator: Is there anything else you want to talk about?

Spriggs: No. I just want him to pay for the damages to my trees and leave me and my property alone.

Mediator: Let me see if I can summarize what your specific concerns are. First, you are worried about the health of your trees because some of the limbs were removed, and you believe Mr. Zappia should be responsible for the cost of their damage. Second, you are uncertain about who is responsible for the maintenance of the leaves from your trees. Is that basically the situation from your perspective?

Spriggs: Yes, and the fact that I don't know why he's doing all this.

Mediator: Thank you very much, Mr. Spriggs. Mr. Zappia, I appreciate your listening to Mr. Spriggs's statement. Now, I would like to have you take a few minutes and tell me about the concerns that brought you to mediation.

Zappia: Basically, I think this guy is full of it. He is acting like everything is my fault, and besides, he doesn't get along with any of his other neighbors.

Mediator: Is Mr. Spriggs's relationship with his other neighbors causing problems for you that you want to discuss?

Zappia: No. That's his problem, not mine.

Mediator: Mr. Zappia, why don't you give me your perspective about what brought you here today.

Zappia: It's like this: Spriggs doesn't care about anybody but himself. As long as his lawn and trees look all right, he's happy. He doesn't care what effect his stuff has on anyone else.

Mediator: Please be more specific; what do you mean by "his stuff"?

Zappia: His trees.

Mediator: What affect are Mr. Spriggs's trees having on you?

Zappia: Well, for one thing, they're too big. The branches are overtaking my driveway. Seedlings and leaves are always falling off all over my yard and my cars. They get stuck on the windows and make a big mess. Not to mention the mess the birds make on my cars.

Mediator: What do you mean when you say the leaves and the birds are making a big mess?

Zappia: Sometimes the leaves are sticky and they get the cars all sticky. Sometimes they get stuck on the car and leave leaf prints. The birds perch in the branches all day and night and leave droppings all over the cars and driveway. I told Spriggs that and he didn't do anything about it. So, I just trimmed the branches back a little. It was no big deal.

Mediator: Tell me about the conversation you had with Mr. Spriggs.

Zappia: I told him he had to do something about the trees. I told him that every morning when I come outside my cars are filthy from the leaves and birds.

Mediator: Did you discuss what you wanted Mr. Spriggs to do about the trees?

Zappia: Not in so many words. I guess I thought it was obvious.

Mediator: You assumed Mr. Spriggs knew you meant the branches should be trimmed and when he did not do it, you trimmed them.

Zappia: That's right. I just trimmed them a little, though.

Mediator: What do you mean by "trimmed them a little"?

Zappia: Well, the branches from his trees hung over my lawn and driveway, so I trimmed them back to his property line.

Mediator: Approximately how far would you say that was?

Zappia: Seven or eight feet. I didn't hurt the trees. I love trees as much as the next guy, but I would do something about them if they were interfering with someone's property. Then he goes and calls the cops. I told the cops the branches were on my property so I had every right to trim them. The cops told me not to trim anymore and to have it settled in court. Now I'm not allowed to cut the branches. He won't cut them so my family and I are forced to park our cars in the street so we won't have to keep cleaning them. On top of that, the darn leaves from his trees keep blowing into my yard so I just started blowing them back into his yard.

Mediator: Is there anything else you would like to discuss?

Zappia: No. I just want him to do something about those trees.

Mediator: What would you like to see happen?

Zappia: I would like him to cut them down.

Mediator: Let me see if I understand your concerns, Mr. Zappia. Some of the maple trees that border the property between you and Mr. Spriggs have branches that extend over your driveway. You are feeling somewhat frustrated when the leaves from those branches fall into your yard and on your car because it requires you to rake them up and spend time cleaning the outside of your car. You believed that trimming the branches was a way of solving the problem. Is this accurate?

Zappia: Yes.

Mediator: Thank you very much, Mr. Zappia.

Situations of power imbalance pose great challenges for mediators and provide the basis for many of the concerns voiced by individuals who are critical of the mediation process (see, for example, Grillo, 1991; Lerman, 1984). The assumption is that, in a court of law, the rules that guide the process and the knowledge and skills of the attorneys and judges involved will protect those who need protection. Mediations, however, rely on the intellects, communication skills, and decision-making abilities of the participants. What if one of the parties is significantly less skilled as a communicator or has less power (however that term might be defined) than the other disputant? In this case, we must rely on the ability of the mediator to (1) find an approach that balances the power of the disputants or (2) recognize that, because of the problems and risks created by the power imbalance, the conflict is not amenable to mediation.

The storytelling phase of the mediation allows the mediator to hear the disputants' explanations and to begin defining the issues that need to be addressed. In addition, the storytelling stage provides a structured arena that forces the parties to listen, without interruption, to each other's perspective regarding the conflict. To check for accurate understanding, the mediator might even ask parties to paraphrase what they hear each other saying. Understanding does not indicate agreement, but it does indicate that each party at least comprehends the other's perspective. After both parties have had the opportunity to tell their story, any differences between them are at least mentally noted by the mediator. The differences could indicate key areas of misunderstanding between the parties. The mediator might ask a series of close-ended or open-ended questions to clarify and correct misperceptions and inaccurate assumptions. The mediator must be careful in the phrasing of these questions so as not to imply judgment of either party. Remember that the mediator is supposed to behave in a neutral and impartial manner.

The storytelling stage also allows for the venting of emotions. The need to vent emotions in the beginning of the mediation is normal and should be expected (Moore, 2003). In fact, Moore argued that venting is almost a prerequisite for dealing with the substantive issues. However, intense emotional displays should be minimized, since they can be counterproductive to the mediation process. Such emotional displays might block a party's willingness to negotiate or interfere with a party's ability to reason. Moore suggested that mediators manage emotions by recognizing their existence, identifying them, and selecting appropriate interventions. If a mediator thinks that the expression of emotions will not be counterproductive to the mediation, she or he should let the party vent. In fact, the venting might help enlighten the other party about the intensity of the conflict. If the mediator believes that the venting will be counterproductive, he or she might decide to caucus (that is, meet separately with the parties) to allow each party to vent in a neutral environment, or the mediator might initiate a break in the proceedings, giving each party a few minutes to compose themselves and the mediator a chance to refocus the mediation process.

Another important goal of the storytelling stage is to help disputants identify their instrumental, self-presentation, relational, and process goals. As noted in chapter 2, competence in interpersonal conflict requires one to be knowledgeable about his/her goals and knowledgeable regarding how to achieve those goals productively. It is not unusual for disputants to be unable to articulate their goals, which might be one of the main reasons disputants might find themselves in mediation. Therefore, it is important for the mediator to assist disputants in identifying their goals.

For example, in the Zappia–Spriggs (see box 11-1) conflict, both Zappia and Spriggs say the conflict is about the trees, the instrumental goal. On the surface it is. It is our opinion that a mediator who only focuses on the instrumental goal is not gathering enough data about the conflict to help parties truly resolve the conflict. In other words, a mediator also needs to determine the self-presentation goals, relational goals, and process goals that are driving the conflict. An effective mediator helps disputants become knowledgeable about their goals as the goals relate to the situation, and she or he must also discover how each disputant perceives the other is blocking him/her from achieving her or his goal(s). Therefore, throughout stages 2 and 3, disputants' prospective goals often become transactive goals as the mediator gathers more relevant information. By "prospective" goals, we mean those goals that the disputants had prior to sitting down to talk with the mediator. "Transactive" goals are the goals that develop during the course of the conversation with the mediator and the other disputant. It is certainly possible that a disputant's prospective goals and his/her transactive goals will be exactly the same. However, in our experience, it is more likely that the questions posed by the mediator and the experience of the mediation process will result in changes to a disputant's goals.

In the case of Zappia and Spriggs, although both initially say that the conflict is about the trees, the possibility exists that the conflict really concerns perceptions of lack of respect (self-presentation goals) and/or there is a conflict in the definition each holds for the word "neighbor" and the kind of obligations that neighbors owe to each other (relational goals). They might also disagree with each other about the right approach for handling their problems and disagreements (process goals). Process goals also refer to the ways in which disputants have been communicating about the conflict. Are they avoiding? Competing? Accommodating? Is one person trying to collaborate while the other is trying to compete? As discussed in chapter 2, interpersonal competence involves making the appropriate choices in communication behavior to attain goals. Incompatible or destructive process goals sustain or escalate a conflict. Therefore, another role of the mediator is to discover how the disputants have been communicating about the conflict and guide them toward more productive communication strategies.

The main goal during the storytelling stage is for the mediator to create a sense of shared perceptions concerning the dispute. Often conflicts are struggles over misperceptions of differing sets of assumptions or goals. As explained in chapter 1, in addition to parallel conflicts (that is, conflicts that have an objective basis), the disputants within a mediation can experience displaced conflicts, misattributed conflicts, and/or latent conflicts. The role of the mediator is to help the parties reshape and relabel the language of the conflict to ensure that they are talking about the same issues (Evarts, Greenstone, Kirkpatrick, & Leviton, 1983; Kiely & Crary, 1986; Moore, 2003; Zaffar, 2008).

The mediator's role becomes one of translator of the disputants' messages: it is the mediator's responsibility to reshape the language in a form that makes sense and is acceptable to both parties. Terms that are unclear must be defined, and emotionally charged language must be reworded and neutralized. Throughout the process, the mediator should summarize important points in neutral, positive terms and continually emphasize areas of shared understanding and/or agreement. Looking back at the transcript in box 11-3, note the points at which the mediator engages in each of the activities indicated here, seeking clarification about what is being said and reframing the disputants' contributions in clear, less negatively charged language.

STAGE 3: IDENTIFYING THE ISSUES

The information gathered during the storytelling stage is used to define the problem or key issues that must be resolved. One potential difficulty for the mediator at this point is that the issues might seem completely different for each party. For example, in the Zappia–Spriggs case (see box 11-4), the issues for Mr. Zappia regard the mess the trees are making and his frustration at being ignored by Mr. Spriggs. Mr. Zappia would prefer the trees be cut down and wants his needs and perspective as a neighbor to be respected by Mr. Spriggs. The issues for Mr. Spriggs revolve around his desire for his trees to be left alone; he wants to collect for damages to the trees and he, too, is frustrated and wants respect from his neighbor. In essence, the parties argue from their own positions and world views. When parties argue from their

---

Box 11-4   Zappia–Spriggs Mediation (Stage 3: Identifying the Issues)

Mediator: As I understand it, the situation between the two of you centers on a need for mutual respect for each other's property. In this instance, it's the need for a leaf-free zone while protecting the health of the trees. Is that an accurate assessment?

Zappia: Yes. Definitely.

Spriggs: Yeah, that and the issue of who is responsible for paying for the damages to my trees.

Mediator: Okay. Do you both agree these are the issues to resolve?

Zappia: Yes.

Spriggs: Yes.

positions, how can a mediator help them find a satisfactory solution? The answer emerges from the dictates of principled negotiation (Fisher & Ury, 1981). The mediator must find a way to encourage the participants to focus on their underlying interests rather than on their positions.

Fisher and Ury (1981) argue that *interests* are the motivating force behind positions. In other words, our interests shape the positions that we claim. The mediator's task is to discover *why* a person has chosen a particular position, but strangely enough, that has to be accomplished without asking the specific question "Why?" since the word "why" implies judgment. The question, "Why did you say that?" can be heard as, "I don't understand you—I don't agree with you." Although their positions are different, Zappia and Spriggs do share common interests: they each want their property and needs to be respected by the other party. If the parties agree about the shared interests, the mediator has changed the focus of the session from arguing over *positions* to trying to find solutions that satisfy *shared interests*—showing respect for each other's property and personal rights.

Once the issues have been identified and agreed upon, the parties are ready to move to the solution stage. We emphasize, however, that the disputants must agree with the mediator's summary of the conflict. If one or more of the disputants indicates that the mediator's summary is in error, before moving on the mediator must spend the time and energy required to discover how that summary (and identification of issues) needs to be revised. This happened with one of the authors when mediating a family conflict. There were several issues separating a mother from her two daughters, including who was the rightful owner of a horse that had been given to the daughters by their father, but was stabled on the mother's property and cared for by her. When it was time for me to summarize and identify a key issue for our attention, my biases as a communication scholar kicked in and I identified "communication" as an area that needed attention. From both sides of the table, the disputants responded, "No, it's the horse." So, we focused, first, on the horse.

STAGE 4: GENERATING OPTIONS

With the issues identified and the parties in agreement concerning the importance of those issues, the disputants can begin to generate solutions (see box 11-5). The mediator encourages the disputants to offer several solutions and then evaluate them one by one as they try to find the best course of action. If the parties experience difficulty in this process, the mediator might offer some suggestions, but a great deal of care has to be exercised. As we mentioned earlier, the mediation process centers on the concept of self-determination. The parties produce the "best" solutions themselves since they are more likely to be fully committed to ideas (solutions) that they themselves developed. Huff-Arneson (1988) suggests that mediators pay particularly close attention to the wording of disputant proposals, especially in cases where the language and phrasing used is "if . . . then," since such phrasing usually marks a willingness to work collaboratively.

The mediator's responsibility during the option generation stage underscores that the solutions being proposed meet the disputants' criteria. That is, as they have talked through their perspectives on the problem, each of the disputants has described one or more "needs" that, if met, will result in a satisfactory agreement for managing the conflict. "Ideal" solutions address the needs of all parties, are practical, and are enforceable.

Unfair or unbalanced agreements present a difficult paradox for the mediator. On the one hand, *mediators are ethically bound to remain neutral and impartial throughout the process*; that is, the mediator should not act as an advocate for one party against the other or for one particular solution, even if that solution seems better in the eyes of the mediator. However, *mediators are also ethically bound to help disputants reach fair solutions* (often defined in terms of what would be acceptable within a court of law and/or as being responsive to the needs of each disputant). If, in the mediator's best judgment, the solution

---

Box 11-5   Zappia–Spriggs Mediation (Stage 4: Generating Options)

Mediator: I'd like to compliment you on the progress you have made so far. Now that we understand what the issues are, I'd like to talk with both of you in detail about the ways to handle this situation. Mr. Spriggs, since we started with you, I'd like to go back to you again and ask what, in your opinion, would resolve this situation.

Spriggs: I will agree with Zappia and say the branches on the trees did extend over his driveway. However, until now, I wasn't aware that the problem was that bad for him. He says he talked with me, but I don't remember his ever saying anything. Had I known, I would have had them trimmed. However, as sorry as I am about that, I still don't think he had the right to cut down the branches without my approval. And I don't think I should get stuck paying for a tree professional to come treat the trees so that they don't rot.

Mediator: So, you are saying that you are now aware that the branches on the trees were troublesome for Mr. Zappia, but you would prefer not to be responsible for the cost of the tree professional.

Spriggs: Right.

Mediator: How would you resolve this?

Spriggs: I think Zappia should pay for the treatment.

Mediator: Thank you. Let me take this proposal to Mr. Zappia. Mr. Zappia, Mr. Spriggs has indicated that he understands the branches created a problem for you. Nonetheless, he believes there is a need for a tree professional to treat the trees and he is asking that you pay for the cost of that professional.

Zappia: As I said before, since the branches extended over my property I thought I had every right to trim them. If I have to pay for the tree professional, then he should pay for my entire car washing bills and labor for raking his leaves over the years.

Mediator: Do I understand that you believe the expenses to wash your car and maintain your lawn will equal the cost of having a tree professional treat the trees?

Zappia: Right. I have my receipts from the car wash right here and they total about $25 a month.

Mediator: You propose that you pay for your car washing bills and lawn maintenance and Mr. Spriggs should pay for the tree professional?

Zappia: Correct.

Mediator: Mr. Spriggs, Mr. Zappia has indicated the expenses from washing his car and maintaining his lawn equal the cost of the tree professional. Because of this he believes each of you should be responsible for your own bills. What are your thoughts on this?

Spriggs: I have an estimate from a tree professional. He determined it would cost $150 to tend to the trees. I don't think it's fair to attribute all the dirt on Zappia's cars to my trees, and for several months of the year, there are no leaves on the trees. For the sake of settling this, I'd be willing to pay for $50 of the tree professional to even out some of his car washing bills.

Mediator: Mr. Zappia, you heard what Mr. Spriggs said. What do you think?

Zappia: I think $100 is too much for me to pay. I would like to have a breakdown of what the tree professional is going to do.

Spriggs: I have the form right here. $45 would be for three spraying treatments to prevent the openings on the trees from rotting or becoming infested with insects, $30 would be to even out the trimming, and $75 would be for labor.

Zappia: Since you said if you had known the effect the trees were having on us you would have had a tree expert come and trim the trees, you would have had to pay for that anyway. I would be willing to split the cost of the labor and the three spraying treatments if you pay for the trimming.

Mediator: You would pay for $37.50 for labor and $22.50 for the sprayings and Mr. Spriggs would be responsible for the trimming fee?

Zappia: Correct.

Mediator: Mr. Spriggs, what do you think of that proposal?

Spriggs: I guess that sounds fair.

Mediator: Mr. Zappia?

Zappia: Sounds OK to me.

Mediator: Great progress! Next you need to determine when the tree professional will come, who needs to be there when he does the work, and how the two of you will set up payment. Mr. Spriggs, do you have any suggestions?

Spriggs: I have already scheduled him to come this Saturday. I will definitely be there. I don't suppose Zappia needs to be unless he wants to. Zappia can pay me his share and I will give the man the check.

(continued)

Zappia: Saturday is fine, but I work that day so I won't be there. However, I'd prefer to be billed directly for my portion from the tree professional with a breakdown of the fee on the bill.

Mediator: Mr. Spriggs, how do you feel about that?

Spriggs: Fine with me.

Mediator: I think you have achieved a very positive resolution so far. Now, you need to discuss the issue of who will be responsible for the care of the trees and the leaves in the future. In other words, should the branches of the trees cause problems in the future, who will be responsible for tending to them and when the leaves fall from the trees, who will be responsible for raking them? Since I started with Mr. Spriggs last time, I would like to start with Mr. Zappia this time. What suggestions do you have Mr. Zappia?

Zappia: I'd like to see those branches kept trimmed at all times so this doesn't happen again. That will also keep most of the leaves out of my yard and reduce the problem with the birds.

Mediator: Define "trimmed" for me.

Zappia: I do not want the branches to cross into my property.

Spriggs: That's quite an expense, but I guess I won't have to trim them that often. I'll go along with that, but I also want assurance that he won't cut the trees again when he sees them crossing the property line. I think thirty days notice would be fair.

Mediator: How do you want Mr. Zappia to notify you if he thinks a problem is developing?

Spriggs: In writing.

Mediator: Let me check to make sure I understand you correctly. You will be responsible for trimming the trees. If Mr. Zappia notices the branches are beginning to cross over the property line into this yard, he should notify you in writing and give you thirty days to trim the trees.

Spriggs: Right. But I'd like him to notify me through certified mail to make sure I get the request.

Mediator: Mr. Zappia, what do you think of that proposal?

Zappia: Sounds fine to me.

Mediator: Very impressive work. One last issue to be discussed: what should be done about the leaves that gather in Mr. Zappia's yard?

Spriggs: I can't be responsible for all the leaves in the neighborhood that blow into his yard. I mean, who knows if they are from my trees or not. If he doesn't want leaves from other neighbors' trees blowing in his yard, he might consider putting up a leaf fence. They're cheap and they work.

Mediator: Mr. Zappia?

Zappia: To tell you the truth, I never thought of that. I guess a leaf fence would be a good idea.

Mediator: Is there anything else either of you would like to discuss today?

Spriggs: No.

Zappia: No.

being proposed and agreed to by the disputants does not meet the standards of fairness (as defined, admittedly, by the mediator), then most defined standards of practice for mediators indicate that the mediator should make his or her concerns known (refer to the guidelines in the following organizations: American Bar Association, Association of Family and Conciliation Courts, American Society of Professional Mediators, National Association for Community Mediation). This action on the part of the mediator might not keep the parties from going forward with their decision, however, it at least alerts the parties to the mediator's concerns. The mediator then needs to decide whether she or he should continue to be part of the mediation process.

The kinds of decisions we are discussing are not simple, nor are there always clear guidelines. Critics of mediation (especially Grillo, 1991) argue implicitly, if not explicitly, in favor of mediators assuming activist roles, ensuring that the rights and position of any disadvantaged participant is protected. At the same time, though, any attempt to define a single, "right" answer for all situations would ignore possible cultural differences or other factors that might argue for more sensitive attention to situational and relational distinctions.

Assuming that the disputants have been able to generate and come to agreement concerning an acceptable solution, the mediator will write up that agreement (see box 11-6 on p. 276).

STAGE 5: WRITING THE AGREEMENT

The agreement itself should be written in precise, positive, and balanced language. By "precise," we mean that the agreement should clearly indicate the who, what, where, when, and how of the actions the disputants will be taking. Also, most agreements contain a "what if" clause that specifies what will happen should one of the disputants violate the provisions of the agreement. The agreement should be phrased in a positive manner. That is, the agreement should focus on what the parties agree to do (e.g., respect each other's property) rather than what they agree not to do (e.g., not intruding on each other's property), and the agreement should not point a finger of guilt at any of the parties. Finally, the written agreement should be balanced. For example, to the extent possible, "we" language should be used, and if one of the disputants is going to do three things, then if at all possible the other party should do three things as well.

Once written, the agreement is reviewed by the parties and, if found acceptable, signed by all parties (the mediator may also sign as a witness to the agreement). Because of the confidential nature of mediations, the only document that results from the mediation is the written agreement. In the Zappia–Spriggs case, because the mediation was mandated by the courts, a copy of the agreement would typically be forwarded to the judge. Otherwise, the disputants and the mediation center (assuming that the mediation was conducted through a community mediation service) would be the only individuals or agencies to retain a copy of the agreement.

> ### Box 11-6 Zappia–Spriggs Mediation (Stage 5: Writing the Agreement)
>
> *Mediator:* Let me summarize what you have agreed to today. If I miss anything or if you have anything else to add, please feel free to let me know. Mr. Spriggs will have the tree professional come Saturday to spray and trim the trees. He will have the tree professional bill him for $30 for the trimming, $22.50 for half of the spraying, and $37.50 for half of the labor. Mr. Spriggs will have the tree professional bill Mr. Zappia $37.50 for half the labor and $22.50 for half of the spraying. In the future, if the branches from the maple trees begin to cross the property line, Mr. Zappia will notify Mr. Spriggs in writing and will have the letter sent to Mr. Spriggs by certified mail. Mr. Spriggs will attend to the problem within thirty days of receipt of notification. Finally, Mr. Zappia agrees to install a leaf fence. Is that your understanding of the agreement?
>
> *Zappia:* Yes.
>
> *Spriggs:* Yes.
>
> *Mediator:* Great! I would like to thank both of you for coming today and for all of your hard work. I think you have reached a very positive solution. Our mediation center will be contacting both of you in a few weeks to make sure this agreement is working for you. If you have any questions or concerns before we contact you, please feel free to call the center. Thank you for all of your hard work.

What Skills and Knowledge Contribute to Mediator Competence?

The model portrayed above might be referred to as the *interventionist,* or *control-based,* model (Burrell, Donohue, & Allen, 1990). The primary characteristic of this model is its highly structured process. The mediator facilitates discussion and seeks to empower the parties to address the issues under dispute rather than solve their problems for them. An interventionist mediator structures the interaction by controlling turn taking, equalizing talk time, balancing power, maintaining or changing the topic, and helping the disputants identify both the key issues involved and the potential solutions to their problems. Honeyman (1990) suggests that the best mediators are capable of (1) identifying and seeking out information relevant to the issues in dispute, (2) demonstrating empathy for all parties, (3) exhibiting ability at persuasion and presentation of ideas, (4) reducing tensions at appropriate times, (5) managing the interaction by coping with conflicts and developing effective strategies for the interaction, and (6) demonstrating expertise (as needed) concerning the issues in dispute.

Mediators are *not* some things. As indicated above, a mediator is *not* a judge. Some people mistakenly believe that mediators determine who is right and who is wrong, and that mediators hand down decisions. However, the role of mediator does not involve such activities. The rules of evidence and procedure that exist within a court do not exist within a mediation. Mediators do not (or should not) offer legal advice, represent clients, dictate courses of action, or champion the cause of one of the disputants against the other.

Nor are mediators therapists. Occasionally, people seeking mediation should really be seeking the help of family or personal counselors. While a mediator is not a therapist or a counselor, conversations during a mediation can help an individual or a couple decide whether counseling is needed. Many psychologists, social workers, and other counseling professionals are adding mediation to the list of services they provide. However, the professional associations that describe standards of ethics for these professionals (for example, see National Association of Social Workers, 1991) caution their members that any attempts to act *both* as a counselor for a client *and* as a mediator for a dispute involving that client will probably be viewed as a conflict of interest.

In a discussion of mediation ethics, Robert A. Baruch Bush (1992) outlined nine types of dilemmas faced by dispute mediators (see table 11-1 on the following page). We do not have sufficient space here to discuss each of these dilemmas in depth. However, as you examine them, you will discover that each calls for the mediator to monitor her or his behavior carefully within the mediation, and she or he should be aware of the definitions others might apply to the way in which the mediation was conducted.

Although it might be easy, in the absence of experience, to provide an answer for each of the dilemmas that Professor Bush's research identified, every mediation provides its own set of challenges. Mediators must learn from each of their mediations, being honest with themselves both about what they did "right" and areas where they should have responded differently (i.e., in a more appropriate and effective manner).

Occasionally, obstacles make it difficult for all the participants in a mediation to meet the criteria of appropriateness and effectiveness in their participation. One such obstacle is that of power imbalances. Power is the ability of a person to affect outcomes (costs or benefits) in an interpersonal context (Thibaut & Kelley, 1959). Power imbalances within a mediation mean that one party has more influence or control over the other party or over the outcome.

Davis and Salem (1984) argue that power imbalances within a mediation can have extreme adverse effects on the process. They argue that the mediator has a responsibility to interrupt intimidating behaviors within the mediation; otherwise, it will not be possible to reach a fair agreement. Whereas Davis and Salem believe that a mediator can equalize power within a mediation, Auerbach (1983) argues against mediation when a power imbalance is present. He believes that the only fair way to equalize power is to address the issue in a court of law.

Even though we are citing authors who were writing in the 1980s, this issue is still hotly debated and a focal area for mediation researchers (Brigg,

---

Table 11-1   Dilemmas for Mediators

1. *Keeping within the limits of competence.* Recognizing when either the mediator's own ability to diagnose a problem or a disputant's ability (skill) to participate in the mediation process is not sufficient.

2. *Preserving impartiality.* Recognizing when prior associations with or personal reactions to the parties during the mediation either impair the ability of the mediator to act impartially or create questions concerning the mediator's impartiality; exercising caution with respect to the development of any type of relationship (even a professional relationship) with the disputants *after* the mediation is concluded.

3. *Maintaining confidentiality.* With respect to outsiders, distinguishing between information that should be kept confidential and information (such as allegations of child abuse or criminal activities) that must be reported; with respect to the parties, determining how a confidential disclosure should be handled.

4. *Ensuring informed consent.* Recognizing when a party either does not possess the information necessary to make an informed decision or does not possess the ability (intellect) to make an informed decision.

5. *Preserving self-determination/maintaining nondirectiveness.* Determining how to respond to situations in which the parties want the mediator to make a decision for them; determining how to respond to situations in which the decision reached by the parties is illegal, unfair to a weaker party, unwise, or unfair to an outside party (for example, the children of a divorcing couple).

6. *Separating mediation from counseling and legal advice.* Recognizing when the parties need expert information or guidance, or therapy and counseling.

7. *Avoiding exposure of a party to harm as a result of mediation.* Recognizing when mediation might make a bad situation worse.

8. *Preventing party abuse of the mediation process.* Recognizing when a party is not participating in good faith (perhaps by concealing information, lying, or engaging in intimidation).

9. *Handling conflicts of interest.* Recognizing when relationships with the courts, referral agencies, lawyers, or other professionals might create the reality or the appearance of a conflict of interest on the part of the mediator.

Source: Adapted from Bush (1992).

2003; Garcia et al., 2002; Jacobs & Aakhus, 2002; Mayer, 2004), perhaps in part because there are various ways of defining power and because truly equal power between disputants is probably a false hope. It is the responsibility of the mediator not only to understand that power imbalances exist and to appreciate how such imbalances might affect the mediation, but also to be familiar with techniques for trying to balance power (such as having an advocate present for the weaker party) and be willing to call a halt to the mediation sessions should the situation be one in which the imbalance simply cannot be overcome.

What Skills and Knowledge Contribute
to Disputant Competence?

Many mediation practitioners assume that by providing the right structure and techniques, a mediator can help disputing parties reach mutually satisfactory agreements. The need for an effective performance of appropriate conflict management behaviors is not, however, limited to the mediator. Mediators garner the majority of research attention; however, much of the credit for the success—or failure—of any mediation rests with the disputants. In the same manner as the mediator, disputants must bring something to the mediation if the process is to achieve its desired goal.

No universally established and agreed-to disputant qualities or skills guarantee a successful mediation. However, characteristics (or capabilities) that typically contribute to the perception that someone is a competent communicator probably significantly increase the chances of a positive mediation experience for all involved. As a negative example, disputants who deviate from the established rules by refusing to negotiate in good faith, by breaking turn-taking rules or by refusing to listen to the contributions of the other disputant will probably be viewed not only as less competent but as less trustworthy by the others involved in the session (including the mediator).

Examination of each of the stages of mediation suggests different skills or abilities that might contribute to a successful mediation experience. The initial stage (the intake process) requires that the disputants be capable of explaining their problem to the intake professional, who will assess whether mediation is a suitable venue for talking through their conflict(s). During stage 1 of the mediation, the disputants must focus on the mediator's instructions and, again, make a decision about their willingness to commit to the mediation process. In stage 2 (storytelling), the disputants must possess the communication skills to share, in a coherent fashion, their perspectives on the issues in dispute. Although the mediator might assist in the development of the story (by asking questions, reflecting back on what he or she hears the disputant saying, helping the disputant clarify points that might be vague or select a more precise and effective way of phrasing his or her point), the mediator cannot tell the story for the disputant. At stage 3 (issue identification), the disputants must work with the mediator to define their underlying needs. In some situations, disputants should express disagreement with the mediator—for example, if the mediator misidentifies the key issues. Stage 4 (option generation) requires that disputants participate in creative problem solving, again expressing their needs and evaluating proposals in terms of those needs. Finally, stage 5 (the written agreement) requires that each of the disputants understand the nature of the commitments being entered into and that they have the power (or authority) to enter into those commitments.

At each stage, disputants are asked to listen (to the intake professional, to the mediator, to the other disputant). During all stages, disputants are encouraged to consider the point of view of the other party and to look at the dispute from a perspective different from their own. Clearly, disputants whose communication skills and cognitive capacities have not developed sufficiently to allow them to participate fully in the process should not be forced (or allowed[4]) to enter into mediation as the venue for handling their disputes. At the same time, we remind you that peer mediation programs have been introduced and are operating successfully in many elementary schools throughout the country. Nonetheless, mediators must help protect against situations in which an individual who is not capable of representing him- or herself—especially as an equal—is asked to take part in a mediation.

Summary

Out of necessity, we have presented a very general picture of mediation. In presenting this picture, we have only hinted at or given basic descriptions of the challenges that face mediators and disputants involved in dispute mediation. A variety of authors (see, for example, Bickmore, 2002; Brigg, 2003; Bush & Folger, 1994, 2005; Crocker et al., 1999, 2005; Jones, 1994; Mayer, 2004; Rule, 2002) have written about the potential of mediation to transform and/or reframe the relationship that exists between the disputants. In the picture that we have presented, we have not fully explored this transformative potential. Were we to do so, one of the things we would do in the Zappia–Spriggs case is spend much more time in the mediation exploring the disputants' understandings of what it means to be a neighbor and what is desired from the relationship. The mediator would work toward a situation in which the neighbors are capable of communicating directly as opposed to via registered mail.

Our decision to develop the Zappia–Spriggs case as we did does not repudiate the call for transformative mediations. Instead, acknowledging the imperfections of the approach presented, we hoped to convey in part the fact that mediators must deal with the solutions that the disputants believe to be best. It is the disputants—and not the mediator—who must live with the results of the mediation.

As mediators, we have experienced situations where we identified a particular issue as more important (central to the dispute) than did our disputants and where the disputants enthusiastically embraced courses of action that we would not have preferred for ourselves. We have tried to convey a sense of how such situations can be problematic for mediators. On the one hand, mediators should help disputants exercise autonomous decision-making ability. On the other hand, mediators should help establish a process in which the disputants act as equals, reaching agreements that are fair and responsive to their individual needs.

We began this chapter by referring to an "ideal" world. In such a world, individuals in conflict collaborate to find ways of managing their conflicts. When people lack the ability to collaborate, mediation is an important mechanism for trying to work through problems and, ultimately, finding the elusive solution to those problems. In comparison to other dispute management processes that rely on the involvement of a third party, the clear advantage of mediation is that the disputants retain decision-making power with respect to issues of substance. The process is not perfect—no process is. However, mediation offers realistic potential for transforming even the most stressful and contentious of conflict situations into a circumstance where collaboration and mutual problem solving are fully possible.

DISCUSSION QUESTIONS

1. The benefit of mediation, in comparison to other forms of dispute management, is that the disputants retain decision-making power with respect to issues of substance. Why is that desirable? Under what circumstances would it be undesirable for disputants to retain decision-making power?

2. Some mediators believe that the primary goal of mediation is to reach agreement regarding the substantive issues of dispute. Others believe that the primary goal is to help parties deal with the emotional and relational issues, and that resolution of substantive issues is secondary. Which approach to mediation do you favor? Explain why. What are the pros and cons of your preferred approach?

3. Mediators are supposed to be fair, neutral, and impartial. Does this imply that their mediation behavior is not influenced by distal and proximal influences? What are some distal and proximal factors that might influence the mediator's behavior?

4. In what ways does the behavior of a mediator affect the communication competence of disputants? How does it enhance disputants' appropriateness and effectiveness? How could it detract from the perceived competence of one or more of the disputants? Does a good mediator attempt to compensate for a disputant who is less communicatively competent than his or her adversary? How so? Would doing so violate the principle of being impartial? Explain your answer.

5. To be communicatively competent, mediators presumably need to possess knowledge, motivation, and skill if they are to be successful at helping disputants resolve their differences. What knowledge, motivations, and skills in particular does a competent mediator need to have? Are they any different from the characteristics that any of us should possess for managing our everyday (nonmediated) interpersonal conflicts? Please explain.

NOTES

1 As is true of most of our communication colleagues who work in the area of conflict management, we adhere to the position that no conflict is ever truly resolved. Rather, conflicts are

managed. Nonetheless, we might occasionally use the terms *resolve* or *resolution* at least in part because of the formal designation of mediation as an ADR mechanism. Even if "resolution" is a façade, the language of resolution is well established within the literature and the vocabularies of many individuals who work in the area of ADR.

2 What is presented here is a picture of mediation as it is generally practiced within the United States. Cross-cultural comparisons of mediation would reveal interesting variations. In some cultures, for example, the mediator is typically a well-known and respected community elder as opposed to the unknown, neutral third party that is common in the United States.

3 If the mediation is conducted through a community program or agency, agreements reached or difficulties experienced with the mediation process are often reviewed with the director of the agency but would not be discussed with outside parties. In court-connected programs, the court might need to review any agreements reached, or at least be apprised of the fact that the parties have been able to mediate their differences.

4 The word *allowed* is used here on purpose. At least within the private sector, mediators do not have to accept every disputant who crosses their doorstep. Even within the public sector, though, there are disputants whose situations are inappropriate for mediation.

chapter 12

LOOKING FORWARD
TO FUTURE CONFLICTS

CHAPTER OUTLINE

The Inevitability of Conflict

The Value of Competence in Managing Interpersonal Conflict

Guidelines for Managing Interpersonal Conflict

    The Question Is Not If, but How

    Avoid Reciprocating Negative Affect

    Respond Proactively to Your Own Anger

    Do Not Inadvertently Reinforce Aggressive Behaviors

    Discern Each Person's Goals in a Conflict

    Save Face

    Recognize the Systems You Create

Summary

Discussion Questions

We do not mean to imply with this chapter title that all conflicts should become enjoyable. Instead, now that interpersonal conflict has been described and reviewed in different contexts, we think it is necessary to conclude with a look toward future interactions. In doing so, we emphasize the theme of competence in managing conflict. We begin by discussing the implications of the inevitability of conflict. Then we summarize the value of a competence approach to interpersonal conflict and comment on the ethical ramifications of our approach. Finally, we synthesize some of the recurring suggestions in this text in the form of general guidelines for managing conflict.

The Inevitability of Conflict

As we indicated in chapter 1, interpersonal conflict is pervasive. From the time you are a toddler, you experience interpersonal conflict and its social functions. *Conflict enables people to understand their personal and social boundaries, to develop ideas, and to coordinate actions and activities.* Because no two people see the world identically, there will always be disagreements. Because people must rely on others in order to get what they want, and because people often see the goals and behaviors of others to be incompatible with their own goals, conflict is common. Although you may sometimes avoid direct confrontation, you cannot eliminate the experience of conflict.

Why is conflict so ubiquitous? Disagreement per se is not abnormal. Conflict is a natural ingredient of interpersonal interaction. Whenever you and someone else communicate, the two of you become at least partially interdependent. Moreover, you do not restrict your conflicts to dissimilar or disliked others. Ironically, the more you know and like another person, the *greater* the opportunities for conflict! Intimacy in relationships creates greater interdependence and, usually, more frequent interaction (Braiker & Kelley, 1979). These very conditions increase the propensity for disagreements, even between people who are generally compatible with one another. Whenever you interact with others, you risk the possibility of interpersonal conflict.

We usually think about conflict in terms of its overt expression—that is, the communication of disagreement. But conflict is not confined neatly to overt confrontation. If you feel dissatisfied with your roommate's behavior but avoid discussing it, your roommate may not realize that your anger and annoyance are escalating. On the other hand, confronting your roommate and negotiating an amicable agreement does not preclude the possibility that the issue of disagreement will crop up again later.

Some conflict issues are not easily "resolved"; they recur again and again, and you must manage them temporarily and intermittently over time (e.g., Roloff & Johnson, 2002). You and your close friends probably disagree in some irresolvable ways. In such cases, you will agree to disagree if the relationship can tolerate it. If the issue overshadows the relationship, however, the ongoing conflict can dissolve the relationship. If you have a disagreement with a coworker, you can either avoid the issue, agree to disagree, or work to resolve the dispute. If the issue is especially important and bothersome to you, you might seek a transfer or new employer.

The Value of Competence in Managing Interpersonal Conflict

This book has focused on how to respond in a competent manner during conflict interactions—that is, ways of appropriately and effectively managing disagreements with others. Throughout this book, then, competence has served as a unifying framework to discuss processes and products of conflict interaction. A critical underlying assumption is that people *should* behave in appropriate and effective ways, for ethical as well as practical reasons.

The competence approach to managing conflict does not specify a set of behaviors that invariably lead to positive outcomes (although the research indicates that certain behaviors are destructive, more often than not, when compared to alternative behaviors). No one can offer a magic formula that guarantees success. No single strategy or set of particular actions will be suitable for all the varied conflict situations you will face. Moreover, a highly competent performance on your part does not ensure a successful conflict outcome when your conflict partner is determined to sabotage the interaction. However, possessing knowledge about conflict management and developing communication skills that help you translate your goals into actions can increase your chances for managing conflict competently. Being motivated to handle conflicts competently also will help you realize success.

Competence implies an *ethic* for managing conflict—a set of principles regarding conduct that is considered preferable and good. Competent interaction involves appropriateness as well as effectiveness. Appropriateness *modifies* effectiveness. That is, *socially and interpersonally agreed-upon principles should guide the behaviors you employ to satisfy your individual needs and pursue your individual goals.* If effectiveness entails successful control of your environment (and hence others in that environment) so that you get your way, then appropriateness embodies the ethical means of exercising that control.

We do not presume to know what is ethical and what is unethical in managing every conflict. But we do believe that you should *approach conflict ethically;* that is, *you should have a sense of moral responsibility when dealing with conflict,* and that responsibility should be reflected in both your attitude and your behavior.

The standards for judging behavior vary considerably across individuals, communities, and cultures. Still, as Parks (1994) indicated,

> There is also a remarkable level of consensus about what constitutes incompetence. We can agree that it is a mark of incompetence when . . . self-esteem is damaged, and when physical health is threatened. We can also agree that socially inappropriate and violent behavior is usually undesirable. (p. 589)

Standards of appropriateness contribute to competent conflict management for several reasons. On philosophical grounds, we contend that appropriateness promotes social values of civility and respect. What constitutes respect is not universally held, but the human desire for it is. Regardless of cultural and social differences, people everywhere want to be treated by others with dignity, honor, and respect (Domenici & Littlejohn, 2006). Even in the face of serious disagreements, people expect to affirm these fundamental human values.

Fostering mutual respect and meeting minimal expectations for appropriate behavior promote collaboration that is necessary to sustain civilized interaction. By "civilized" we mean the coordinated efforts of individuals through communication (Pearce & Cronen, 1980). Without the ability to coordinate efforts through communication, social behavior would become anarchic and unpredictable—especially in situations where people disagree. People engaging in destructive or avoidant messages could understand the anarchy they could cause with messages, and they might purposefully create uncertainty to limit others' ability to coordinate actions.

Providing reasonable excuses for acting incompetently does not help much in coordinating future activities ("I didn't tell you the truth because I knew you would get angry with me"). Unreasonable excuses for incompetence during conflict provide even less confidence in coordinating future events ("I hit you because you wanted me to").

Competent communicators appreciate the fact that "there are limits to how much any given situation or person can be controlled. Expecting to influence others in unrealistic ways is a mark of incompetence" (Parks, 1994, p. 613). When your attempts to resolve disagreements become coercive rather than persuasive, you are seeking personal effectiveness at the expense of appropriateness. Wiemann (1977) explained that *"effectiveness* in an intrapersonal sense—that is, the accomplishment of an individual's goals—may be incompetent in an interpersonal sense if such effectiveness precludes the possibility of others accomplishing their own goals" (emphasis in original, p. 196).

Similarly, it is unethical to thwart the partner's goals or to hurt the partner because one is frustrated from obtaining rewards—that is, when one is ineffective. In the clearest form, this behavior involves physical aggression. But aggression often serves the simple purpose of venting anger: People sometimes feel better when they hurt others who frustrate them (Berkowitz, 1993). And people often do not know the source of their own ineffectiveness and frustrations and may be hurting someone without cause. For example, people with low self-efficacy and an external locus of control (see chapter 4) believe they cannot manage difficult problems. Such people may give up too soon and blame the partner for their task failures and relational frustrations, thereby justifying verbal or physical harm to the partner. In other words, people sometimes blame their own incompetence on their partners. Of course, few people would agree that being incompetent justifies punishing other people.

The criterion of appropriateness makes sense pragmatically as well as ethically. Codes of appropriate behavior not only constrain our pursuit of personal effectiveness; they also provide a means of being effective and they represent a product of effectiveness (Parks, 1994). As we have stressed throughout this book, you always possess multiple goals. Competence involves your ability to recognize and balance those goals. Pursuing one goal in a socially inappropriate manner is incompetent to the extent that you undermine your ability to achieve equally or more important goals. So, if you get your friend to loan you money by threatening to tell secrets about him if he doesn't comply, you may get the money, but you may also lose a friend and develop a reputation for being an unscrupulous bully. You have scored the classic *Pyrrhic victory:* You have won one battle, but with staggering overall losses.

Appropriate behavior is also desirable simply because it typically promotes the achievement of your own goals. Appropriateness *is* pragmatic. Competent communicators know that displaying appropriateness is often most effective. When you are engaged in interaction, particularly in conflict situations, your outcomes intertwine with the outcomes of others. In other words, each person has some degree of control over what happens to the other. Undermining the goal achievement of others to get your own way can easily backfire. "People who consistently fail to satisfy their goals are likely to display more anger, to be violent, to be more exploitative, to be less generous, and to be less cooperative" (Parks, 1994, p. 611). Thus, facilitating the effectiveness of others can enable your own effectiveness. Parks offers this summary:

> Competent communicators recognize that they usually have a vested interest in maintaining the rules of social conduct because they recognize, however dimly, that their ability to pursue their own goals often depends on the freedom of others to pursue their goals. (p. 613)

Guidelines for Managing Interpersonal Conflict

In this section, we offer some general guidelines for managing conflict. We do not believe in micromanaging conflict behavior. In our experience, students can quickly learn how-to formulas and forget them following an examination. More importantly, no one set of behaviors is suited to all the different conflicts you encounter. Competent communicators possess the ability to adapt their behavior to the unique circumstances of the situation at hand (Spitzberg & Cupach, 1984). Accordingly, we do not offer prescriptions of particular communication skills that you should employ whenever in conflict. Instead, we attempt to provide general guidelines that you can adapt to your own conflict encounters.

THE QUESTION IS NOT IF, BUT HOW

Believing that you can avoid conflict places blinders on your understanding of how people work and live together. The question is not whether you will have conflicts with others—you will. The question is *how* you manage your conflicts through communication.

If you wanted to bet on how you should manage conflict, you should bet on constructive messages. *People engage in constructive or destructive conflict* (Deutsch, 1973). Constructive conflict, as its name implies, focuses on reaching positive and creative outcomes for both parties. Some features of constructive conflict messages have been implied in previous chapters. The following features presume that the conflict interactions involve no serious, physically threatening circumstances:

1. *Combine the parties' resources to solve the problem.* Both parties' talents are maximized to achieve beneficial results instead of being used for combat. When both parties' talents are used to maximize each person's outcomes, we can see the conflict as a win-win situation, instead of a competitive win-lose situation.

2. *Free the avenues of exchange between parties.* Both parties share their thoughts about the causes, definitions, and solutions for the problem in a balanced manner, giving each the same opportunity to present views and to propose and evaluate solutions.

3. *If parties cannot agree, they should agree to disagree.* Compromise could be utilized if the parties cannot pool their resources and work together. Although compromise may not maximize what each party obtains, it can ensure at least some gain and can minimize losses. For example, couples who compromise during mediation do not have to sell their homes to pay divorce lawyers who litigated their cases.

4. *Adopt a nonviolent stance.* Once a person uses coercion, force, or violence, she or he loses the ability to use problem-solving communication to manage the conflict productively. By definition, aggression involves harming another person.

5. *Flee the scene of a crime before it occurs.* If you cannot engage in productive conflict, then at a minimum, refrain from engaging in destructive conflict. Such restraint may appear nearly impossible, but it is worth it in the long run. If only to preserve your sense of dignity, you should avoid doing things you will regret later.

Avoid Reciprocating Negative Affect

The reciprocation of negative emotion powerfully affects your relationships. Nothing appears to affect a relationship as adversely as the reciprocation and escalation of negative messages (see chapter 6).

The urge to respond in a like manner directly and powerfully affects people—especially in conflict episodes. Gottman (1994), however, argued that satisfied couples and dissatisfied couples appear to focus on different elements of the same message. Satisfied couples focus more on the content of the message and how to resolve the problem indicated by the partner, whereas dissatisfied couples tend to react to the negative features of the message, such as a disapproving and whining voice, a rejecting stare, or the inequity in a complaint. As chapter 6 showed, negative conflict behaviors (especially criticism, disgust, and contempt) appear to adversely affect people and relationships immediately as well as cumulatively over time.

How you choose to live your life is reflected in the way you manage conflicts with other people. Do you choose to remain patient, asking for the other person's view and reasons for their frustration? Do you routinely decide to avoid disagreement and accommodate other people whenever possible? Or do you seek an "eye for an eye" and meet aggression with aggression? If you selected the latter, understand that this response mode works *against* most people's goals. The reason is that people view others who engage in such negative behaviors as inept, both in terms of work and play, and as socially undesirable. Hence, although you should stand up for your rights, you can easily lose your objective if you use negative messages. Instead of reciprocating negative messages, you should consider unilaterally using more constructive or even avoidant messages to stop conflict escalation.

Respond Proactively to Your Own Anger

It should not be surprising that interpersonal conflict can provoke anger. People feel frustrated when their goals are thwarted or interrupted (Berscheid, 1983). Perceptions of being treated unfairly (Mikula, Scherer, & Athenstaedt, 1998) or hurt intentionally (Vangelisti, 2007) also tend to induce feelings of anger. It is precisely such feelings that can make it salient to you that you are in serious conflict with another. Competent communication requires that you restrain the impulse to reactively express your angry feelings in a destructive fashion. In planning how to express your feelings, consider the social expectations regarding anger. Averill (1993) provided the following rules for expressing anger:

1. One has the right to become angry at intentional wrongdoing and at unintended misdeeds—if those misdeeds can be corrected (for example, negligence).

2. One should direct anger at objects or people who are responsible for the action(s).

3. One should not vent anger on innocent third parties, "nor should it be directed at the target for reasons other than the instigation."

4. The objective should be to correct the problem and restore fairness—not to create a sense of fear in the other person.

5. One's response to anger should match the instigation; it should not "exceed what is necessary to correct the situation, restore equity, or prevent the instigation from happening again."

6. One's expression of anger should follow the provoking event as soon as possible; it should not last longer than the time needed to remedy the problem.

7. One's expression of anger should involve a commitment to solve the problem, including any necessary follow through (pp. 182–184).

"If you are patient in one moment of anger, you will escape a hundred days of sorrow," concluded Tavris in a review of the effects of anger (1984, p. 188). The saying was taken from a fortune cookie. Nevertheless, this quote represents more than conventional wisdom; it reflects a guideline that is supported by the research. Counting to ten (or even more) when you are very angry and want to crush someone you find extremely offensive can work to your benefit in the long run.

DO NOT INADVERTENTLY REINFORCE AGGRESSIVE BEHAVIORS

This is a tough guideline to adopt, for many reasons. For example, Bandura's (1973) analysis showed that people rely on aggression because over time they have learned to do so and that they view aggression as effective in obtaining rewards. For example, someone who has learned how to slander others continues to use slander to obtain goals. Over time, the aggressor stops feeling remorse for his or her actions by gradually becoming desensitized to the pain he or she inflicts. Sometimes the aggressor becomes desensitized by discounting the victim's feelings ("It's a cruel world, friend, so you better get used to this kind of treatment"). Bandura (1973) observed that one can stop aggression by modeling alternative behaviors, by providing positive rewards for different behaviors, and by punishing aggression. In this manner, the expectations for positive outcomes when using aggressive behaviors (such as slander) could be reduced. Accordingly, one way to discourage the use of slander and malicious gossip is simply not to say anything, thereby not providing any reward (such as laughter) for the behavior.

DISCERN EACH PERSON'S GOALS IN A CONFLICT

Conflict occurs when one believes that one's own goals are incompatible with another person's goals, and the other person's actions interfere with one's goals. In order to reconcile incompatible goals you need to know what the goals are. People's goals are not always obvious, however. The actual goals people possess do not always correspond to the issues overtly expressed in a conflict interaction. For example, Tasha complains to Tony that he spends too much time watching TV. This overtly expressed desire for Tony to watch less TV might reflect Tasha's hidden (unexpressed) goal of wanting more attention from Tony. Alternatively, Tasha may simply be venting at Tony, not because she wants Tony to watch less TV, but because she is in a cranky mood due to an unpleasant interaction she had with a coworker earlier in the day. Tasha may not even be consciously aware of the goal that motivates her complaining.

Each individual routinely pursues multiple goals simultaneously in any given encounter (see chapter 2). For example, suppose you lent your roommate some money and she has neglected to repay you as promised. Your primary goal is to get your roommate to repay the loan. At the same time you are likely pursuing other goals that will constrain the ways in which you pursue your primary goal. You will consider such goals as wanting to continue an amicable relationship with your roommate, not wanting to appear to be overbearing, unfair, or untrusting, wanting to ask your roommate for a big favor, and so forth. Your roommate will also have a set of goals when responding to your confrontation. In order to successfully manage your conflict, each of you needs to be able to prioritize your own goals and figure out what goals are motivating the other person.

Regardless of what overtly expressed instrumental goals drive a conflict, there are usually some relational goals that are latent, intangible, and perhaps unexpressed. These latent goals are quite important because they arouse emotions and motivate people's behavior. Fisher and Shapiro (2005), for example, refer to four "core concerns" that underlie people's interactions to varying degrees. These are:

1. *Appreciation.* We want others to see merit in our own point of view. Whether or not others agree with us, we want to feel that they understand us. We feel unappreciated to the extent others devalue what we think and do.

2. *Affiliation.* People want to feel connected to (some) other people. We feel disconnected when someone we care about treats us as an adversary.

3. *Autonomy.* We want the freedom to make our own decisions and we desire to be free from the imposition of others. Our autonomy is threatened when others are demanding, threatening, or constraining. The natural tendency to feel *reactance* in the face of threatened freedom leads us to attempt to reestablish our autonomy (Burgoon, Alvaro, Grandpre, & Voulodakis, 2002).

4. *Status.* People generally do not like to be seen as weak or to be treated as inferior. We want our legitimate social standing to be recognized, and we expect to be treated with courtesy and respect.

Fisher and Shapiro (2005) indicate that it is essential to recognize how these core concerns motivate our own behavior and others' behavior in a conflict. Failing to address these intangible goals can undermine the successful resolution of more tangible issues. In fact, satisfying another's core relational concerns by showing appreciation, expressing affiliation, respecting autonomy, and conveying status are among the ways you can support that person's face.

SAVE FACE

All people want to have their identities supported when they interact (see chapter 6). Unfortunately, and for various reasons, conflict situations are particularly ripe for face threats. As conflict escalates, we seem to worry more about protecting our own face and we exhibit less concern than usual with preserving the face of our disputant. Moreover, as people get more defensive during conflict, they are more likely to threaten the other's face through insult or imposition. Face threats are naturally provocative and further contribute to conflict escalation.

Face loss can make you feel awkward, confused, guilty, ashamed, embarrassed, angry, and defensive (Cupach & Metts, 1994). These feelings tend to interfere with the constructive management of conflict. Instead, they often lead to behaviors that exacerbate the loss of face. Ironically, the relationships with the greatest intimacy are probably the ones in which we display the least amount of tact, the greatest amount of impoliteness, and the most distressing forms of disrespect, particularly during episodes of conflict.

The key is to maintain your own face *and* the faces of others, even during disagreement. Saving the face of another promotes cooperation and helps to keep the conflict discussion focused on substantive issues of disagreement rather than making the conflict about the people having the disagreement. Saving face requires conscious effort during conflict, and it should be something you try to make habitual.

Notarius and Markman (1993) devised a "no-nonsense guide to politeness." They recommend that during conflict discussions, you imagine that you have a sack over your shoulder that contains all the infinitely different things you could say to your partner. The sack contains statements that can be divided into "zingers" or polite remarks. During conflict, imagine reaching into the sack for something to say. If you pull out a zinger, throw it back and keep reaching into the sack until you have something polite to say. (Remember, being polite does not prevent you from disagreeing.) Notarius and Markman (1993), on the basis of decades of research and clinical experience, offer seven specific guidelines for recognizing and eschewing zingers and finding politeness during conflicts with relational partners:

1. When asked to do something, say what you can or want to do rather than what you can't or don't want to do. For example, if your partner asks if you want to go to the movies and you are feeling tired, you might say, "I'd love to go to the movies tomorrow" rather than "I'm too tired."

2. When you first notice that your partner has done a chore, always show appreciation for the job even if there are aspects of the way in

which it was done that do not meet with your approval. Say "Thanks for washing the counter" rather than "You missed a spot." If you routinely don't like the way your partner does a task, you should have a discussion about it at a time specially set aside for this purpose.

3. Take note of departures from and reunions with your partner. Always greet each other with an acknowledgment and warm hello, and mark a leaving with a tender good-bye. You should not come home, go to bed, or leave the house in silence.

4. Avoid being a "psychopest." Psychopests try to offer insight into their partner's behavior under the guise of being helpful when in fact they are merely being critical. Don't say things like "You're behaving just like your mother" or "Do you know you're being anal retentive about the den?"

5. Always speak for yourself and avoid speaking for your partner. Say "I really want to go to the picnic" rather than "I know you will have a good time at the company picnic."

6. When you have an opinion on something, say what it is rather than fishing around with questions to get your partner to guess what it is. Try "I'd really like to eat at Captain Bob's tonight" instead of "Do you want to eat out tonight?"

7. When all else fails, fall back on the ancient wisdom: "If you don't have anything nice to say, don't say anything" (pp. 77–78).

Box 12-1   Case Study: Confrontation in the Parking Lot

"Boomer" and Helen had been dating for several months when they decided to live together. Boomer earned his nickname on the wrestling squad in high school, where he lettered three years in the heaviest weight class. Boomer became a bartender at an exclusive restaurant where Helen worked as a wine steward. Helen was quite attractive.

Helen knew that being attractive was good not only for her image, but also for the restaurant. So she wore flattering outfits, and she instinctively showed affiliation toward customers by smiling, listening, and sometimes touching them on the arm. This affiliation attracted Boomer to Helen, but it was now driving him crazy.

Boomer found himself trying to see if Helen was flirting with male customers, and there were so many of them that he could not keep track of them all. Many times he thought he had caught her and interrogated her about specific customers. One in particular, a corporate lawyer, was clearly interested in Helen and often dined there on Friday nights. At first, when Boomer asked her about it, Helen assured him nothing was wrong. After a few weeks of interrogation and bickering, however, both Boomer and Helen grew tired of his spying and constant questioning.

So Boomer and Helen started working different days and nights, in hopes that Boomer would not be so jealous of male customers. He worked Monday through

(continued)

Thursday nights, and she worked mainly on weekends, when the restaurant was busiest. Still, Boomer had a tough time keeping away, and he would call or drop by around closing. Helen saw through his "spontaneous" visits. She resented these intrusions and decided to flirt whenever she could.

One Friday night, Boomer somehow sensed the lawyer would be there. He was right, and he saw Helen flirting with the man. Boomer returned home and waited outside for her. As soon as she entered the apartment parking lot, he confronted her:

"I knew you were unfaithful!" Boomer screamed.

"What are you talking about?" Helen asked, although she knew, from previous scenes like this one.

"You know what I'm talking about. I saw you flirting with your lawyer friend," he replied.

She tried to reason with him: "Look, nothing happened."

Boomer felt his heart in his throat, "Yeah, but how do I know that?"

"Well, don't you drive me to it!" she replied.

"Me? I've only been thoughtful of you, you #$%@. And this is how you treat me?! I should kick your @#(*&%!" Boomer yelled.

Helen was quite afraid. "If you lay a hand on me, I'll call the police!"

Boomer couldn't believe this was happening. "I would never hurt you!"

Helen knew Boomer was totally irrational at this point. "Just leave me alone," she demanded.

Boomer panicked, "Listen, honey, I would never hurt you. Please don't leave me." He reached out for her.

"Stop it!" screamed Helen. "Just let me be!"

Boomer worried that he had gone too far. "Helen, listen, I would never hurt you!" This time he grabbed her by the wrist.

"No!" She wrangled to break free. "Help me!" she cried out.

Boomer couldn't believe his ears. "Help you? Help you?!?" he shouted. "Help me, please someone *help me*!!!" He let go of Helen's wrist to plead with the rest of the apartment complex.

Helen now knew for sure that Boomer had lost all ability to reason. She was mad at herself for ever getting involved with him. "Look, I'm leaving you!"

He continued his plea, "Help me, please someone! My baby's leaving me, help me!!"

Helen just shook her head.

Helen ran into the apartment and Boomer followed her, begging for someone to help him. It was quite a sight—this 240-pound athlete imploring someone half his size to help him. Not until she agreed to talk things over did he stop pleading.

This story may sound too melodramatic, but it is largely true. (One of the authors lived next door to "Boomer" and "Helen.") Perhaps even more amazing is the fact that Helen and Boomer replayed a similar scene every two to three weeks. Every time, Helen forgave Boomer and they returned to their usual routine—until Boomer caught Helen flirting with someone else.

Discussion Questions:

1. What advice would you give Helen?

2. What advice would you give Boomer?

RECOGNIZE THE SYSTEMS YOU CREATE

Recognizing that you are part of a system allows you to understand your partner's behavior as a function of your behavior, and vice versa. For example, you see that your partner's withdrawal relates to your confrontation and vice versa, so you do not become angry at the partner for being avoidant or silent. Moreover, you realize that two people are making similar kinds of attributions about the conflict, such that you will rarely find "right" versus "wrong" explanations of conflict causes. This knowledge not only permits you to become more circumspect in analyzing the conflict issue; it also provides flexibility in terms of how you should respond (for example, you do not have to play judge and execute a just response).

Recognizing that you are part of a system allows you to see that your current behavior is also a function of your own previous behaviors. People should acknowledge that they have created their own relational patterns, and that these patterns are self-reinforcing. Research indicates that a person's present conflict behavior has an effect on his or her own future conflict behavior (e.g., Canary et al., 2001; Ting-Toomey, 1983). In other words, people tend to develop consistent patterns of conflict behavior that they repeat over time in different episodes. Breaking the force of habit requires awareness of one's own patterns of behavior. If you see that you tend to respond defensively to conflict, regardless of the issue, you can then assess what alternative ways of responding might be more competent.

If a dysfunctional system cannot be restructured by the adoption of new rules for interaction, then it might need to be dissolved. A relational system is dysfunctional if it impedes someone's growth (for example, adult children who still depend on their elderly parents) or even hurts an individual (for example, physical abuse). Professor Spitzberg's examination of physical aggression (see chapter 10) shows that abusive relationships are not uncommon, and many people appear to be caught in individually destructive relationships. In our view, a person has an ethical obligation (and in some cases, a legal one) to change the system. If the system cannot be changed, and the person continues to suffer, then the system—not the person—should terminate. As Hocker and Wilmot (1995) put it, "you have a responsibility to protect yourself from verbal abuse" (p. 179). Of course, we would argue that this statement extends to physical abuse as well.

Summary

We hope that you understand that your communication during conflict is more important than the mere occurrence or frequency of your disagreements. Communication competence in conflict requires that you communicate in ways that are appropriate as well as effective. Competent communicators are able to influence others successfully, but they attempt to do so in ethical ways. Appropriateness fosters respect and civility, and it mitigates contempt and chaos. Moreover, appropriateness fosters effectiveness insofar as it helps prioritize goals. Competent communication embraces the notion that getting your way usually depends on getting along with others.

No checklist of communication behaviors can guarantee your success in handling conflict. Competent communicators are aware of the distal and proximal factors that affect conflict interaction, and they take them into account when making choices about how to handle specific instances of disagreement. We have offered in this chapter some guidelines that we feel will be useful as you make these choices. In particular, we suggest that you avoid reciprocating negative messages and affect, respond proactively to anger, do not inadvertently reinforce aggressive behaviors, discern and weigh goals, and save face. Above all, recognize that when you interact with others you are part of a communication system. Collaborating with others in that system and adapting your behavior according to the context are hallmarks of the competent communicator.

DISCUSSION QUESTIONS

1. We have argued that ethical codes are part of appropriateness and should guide conflict management. Are there any exceptions, or is this value absolute? Does this statement assume that the relevant moral codes are fair and just? When, if ever, do you think it is justifiable to be socially inappropriate? Can you give examples? In cases where inappropriateness seems justified, would the behaviors be competent? Ethical?

2. Do you agree that checklists of how-to behavior offer little insight about how to manage conflicts when they arise? Why or why not?

3. We stated that the relationships with the greatest intimacy are probably the ones in which we display the least amount of tact, the greatest amount of impoliteness, and the most distressing forms of disrespect. How would you explain this paradox?

4. Pick a close relationship you are currently in. Describe the rules of politeness that you follow (or would like to follow) when you and the other person in this relationship have conflict.

5. We claim that if a system harms the individual, the system should be redefined. We also claim that if the system's rules for interaction do not change, the system should be terminated. What are the critical points that indicate when a system needs to be terminated? How do these compare to times when people need to sacrifice themselves for the sake of their relationships, their organization, or their nation?

6. The fact that you and another person constitute a system when you interact suggests that you never have complete control of what happens to the system—you are only a part of it. Do you agree or disagree? Explain your answer. Can someone else *make you incompetent* during conflict? Or do you have complete control over your own competence?

REFERENCES

ABC News. (2002, October 10). Most say spankings OK by parents but not by grade-school teachers. International Communications Research. Retrieved August 28, 2008, from http://www.icrsurvey.com/Study.aspx?f=ABC_Spanking_1102.html

Afifi, T. D. (2003). "Feeling caught" in stepfamilies: Managing boundary turbulence through communication privacy rules. *Journal of Social and Personal Relationships, 20*, 729–755.

Afifi, T. D., Caughlin, J., & Afifi, W. A. (2007). Exploring the dark side (and light side) of avoidance and secrets. In B. H. Spitzberg & W. R. Cupach (Eds.), *The dark side of interpersonal relationships* (2nd ed., pp. 61–92). Mahwah, NJ: Lawrence Erlbaum.

Afifi, T. D., Hutchinson, S., & Krouse, S. (2006). Toward a theoretical model of communal coping in post-divorce families and other naturally occurring groups. *Communication Theory, 16*, 378–409.

Afifi, T. D., McManus, T., Steuber, K., & Coho, A. (2009). Verbal avoidance and dissatisfaction in intimate conflict situations. *Human Communication Research, 35*, 357–383.

Afifi, T. D., & Schrodt, P. (2003). "Feeling caught" as a mediator of adolescents' and young adults' avoidance and satisfaction with their parents in divorced and non-divorced households. *Communication Monographs, 70*, 142–173.

Ainsworth, M. D. S., Blehar, M. C., Waters, E., & Wall, S. (1978). *Patterns of attachment: A psychological study of the strange situation.* Hillsdale, NJ: Lawrence Erlbaum.

Alberts, J. K. (1988). An analysis of couples' conversational complaints. *Communication Monographs, 55*, 184–197.

Alberts, J. K., & Driscoll, G. (1992). Containment versus escalation: The trajectory of couples' conversation complaints. *Western Journal of Communication, 56*, 394–412.

Aldarondo, E. (1996). Cessation and persistence of wife assault: A longitudinal analysis. *American Journal of Orthopsychiatry, 66*, 141–151.

Alexander, J. F. (1973). Defensive and supportive communications in normal and deviant families. *Journal of Consulting and Clinical Psychology, 40*, 223–231.

Altman, I., & Taylor, D. A. (1973). *Social penetration: The development of interpersonal relationships.* Austin, TX: Holt, Rinehart, & Winston.

Alzenman, M., & Kelley, G. (1988). The incidence of violence and acquaintance rape in dating relationships among college men and women. *Journal of College Student Development, 29*, 305–311.

Amato, P. R. (1996). Explaining the intergenerational transmission of divorce. *Journal of Marriage and the Family, 58*, 628–640.

Amato, P. R. (2000). The consequences of divorce for adults and children. *Journal of Marriage and the Family, 62,* 1269–1287.

Amato, P. R. (2001). Children of divorce in the 1990s: An update of the Amato and Keith (1991) meta-analysis. *Journal of Family Psychology, 15,* 355–370.

Amato, P. R., & Afifi, T. D. (2006). Feeling caught between parents: Adult children's relations with parents and subjective well-being. *Journal of Marriage and Family, 68,* 222–235.

Amato, P. R., & Booth, A. (2001). The legacy of parents' marital discord: Consequences for children's marital quality. *Journal of Personality and Social Psychology, 81,* 627–638.

Amato, P. R., & DeBoer, D. D. (2001). The transmission of marital instability across generations: Relationship skills or commitment to marriage? *Journal of Marriage and the Family, 63,* 1038–1051.

Amato, P. R., & Keith, B. (1991). Parental divorce and the well-being of children: A meta-analysis. *Psychological Bulletin, 110,* 26–46.

Amato, P. R., & Sobolewski, J. M. (2001). The effects of divorce and marital discord on adult children's psychological well-being. *American Sociological Review, 66,* 900–921.

Anda, R. F., Felitti, V. J., Bremner, J. D., Walker, J. D., Whitfield, C., Perry, B. D., Dube, S. R., & Giles, W. H. (2006). The enduring effects of abuse and related adverse experiences in childhood: A convergence of evidence from neurobiology and epidemiology. *European Archives of Psychiatry and Clinical Neuroscience, 256,* 174–186.

Anderson, K. L., Umberson, D., & Elliott, S. (2004). Violence and abuse in families. In A. L. Vangelisti (Ed.), *Handbook of family communication* (pp. 629–645). Mahwah, NJ: Lawrence Erlbaum.

Andes, R. H. (1992). Message dimensions of negotiation. *Negotiation Journal, 8,* 125–130.

Andrews, B. (1992). Attribution processes in victims of marital violence: Who do women blame and why? In J. H. Harvey, T. L. Orbuch, & A. L. Weber (Eds.), *Attributions, accounts, and close relationships* (pp. 176–193). New York: Springer-Verlag.

Arasaratnam, L. A. (2006). Further testing of a new model of intercultural communication competence. *Communication Research Reports, 23,* 93–99.

Arasaratnam, L. A. (2007). Research in intercultural communication competence: Past perspectives and future directions. *The Journal of International Communication, 13,* 66–73.

Archer, J. (2000). Sex differences in aggression between heterosexual partners: A meta-analytic review. *Psychological Bulletin, 126,* 651–680.

Archer, J. (2002). Sex differences in physically aggressive acts between heterosexual partners: A meta-analytic review. *Aggression and Violent Behavior, 7,* 313–351.

Archer, J. (2004). Sex differences in aggression in real-world settings: A meta-analytic review. *Review of General Psychology, 8,* 291–322.

Argyle, M., & Furnham, A. (1983). Sources of satisfaction and conflict in long-term relationships. *Journal of Marriage and the Family, 45,* 481–493.

Argyle, M., Furnham, A., & Graham, J. A. (1981). *Social situations.* London: Cambridge University Press.

Argyle, M., & Henderson, M. (1984). The rules of friendship. *Journal of Social and Personal Relationships, 1,* 211–237.

Arias, I., & Johnson, P. (1989). Evaluations of physical aggression among intimate dyads. *Journal of Interpersonal Violence, 4,* 298–307.

Asante, M., & Asante, K. (Eds.). (1990). *African culture: The rhythms of unity.* Trenton, NJ: African World Press.

Astor, R. A. (1998). Moral reasoning about school violence: Informational assumptions about harm within school subcontexts. *Educational Psychology, 33*, 207–221.

Aubert, B. A., & Croteau, A. (2005). *Information technology outsourcing from business strategy perspective.* HEC Montreal Document #ISSN 0832-7203.

Auerbach, J. S. (1983). *Justice without laws: Resolving disputes without lawyers.* New York: Oxford University Press.

Auwal, M. A., & Singhal, A. (1992). The diffusion of the Grameen Bank in Bangladesh: Lessons learned about alleviating rural poverty. *Knowledge: Creation, Diffusion, Utilization, 14*(1), 7–28.

Averill, J. R. (1993). Illusions of anger. In R. B. Felson & J. T. Tedeschi (Eds.), *Aggression and violence: Social interactionist perspectives* (pp. 171–193). Washington, DC: American Psychological Association.

Babcock, J. C., Green, C. E., Webb, S. A., & Graham, K. H. (2004). A second failure to replicate the Gottman et al. (1995) typology of men who abuse intimate partners . . . and possible reasons why. *Journal of Family Psychology, 18*, 396–400.

Babcock, J. C., Green, C. E., Webb, S. A., & Yerington, T. P. (2005). Psychophysiological profiles of batterers: Autonomic emotional reactivity as it predicts the antisocial spectrum of behavior among intimate partner abusers. *Journal of Abnormal Psychology, 114*, 444–455.

Babcock, J. C., Jacobson, N. S., Gottman, J. M., & Yerington, T. P. (2000). Attachment, emotional regulation, and the function of marital violence: Differences between secure, preoccupied, and dismissing violent and nonviolent husbands. *Journal of Family Violence, 15*, 391–409.

Babcock, J. C., Waltz, J., Jacobson, N. S., & Gottman, J. M. (1993). Power and violence: The relation between communication patterns, power discrepancies, and domestic violence. *Journal of Consulting and Clinical Psychology, 61*, 40–50.

Bach, G. R., & Wyden, P. (1968). *The intimate enemy: How to fight fair in love and marriage.* New York: Avon Books.

Bachman, G. F., & Guerrero, L. K. (2006). Forgiveness, apology, and communicative responses to hurtful events. *Communication Reports, 19*, 45–56.

Bandura, A. (1973). *Aggression: A social learning analysis.* Englewood Cliffs, NJ: Prentice-Hall.

Bandura, A. (1977). *Social learning theory.* New York: General Learning Press.

Bangeman, E. (2006, October 19). HP knocks Dell off its perch. *Ars Technica.* Retrieved January 9, 2008, from http://arstechnica.com/news.ars/post/20061019-8028.html

Bangeman, E. (2007a, February 1). Dell returns as CEO of his namesake company. *Ars Technica.* Retrieved January 9, 2008, from http://arstechnica.com/news.ars/post/20070201-8749.html

Bangeman, E. (2007b, April 19). Dell continues to take market share beating. *Ars Technica.* Retrieved January 9, 2008, from http://arstechnica.com/news.ars/post/20070419-dell-continues-to-take-market-share-beating.html?rel

Bannink, F. P. (2007). Solution-focused mediation: The future with a difference. *Conflict Resolution Quarterly, 25*, 163–184.

Barge, J. K. (2006). Dialogue, conflict, and community. In J. G. Oetzel & S. Ting-Toomey (Eds.), *The Sage handbook of conflict communication: Integrating theory, research, and practice* (pp. 517–544). Thousand Oaks, CA: Sage.

Baron, R. A. (1984). Reducing organizational conflict: An incompatible response approach. *Journal of Applied Psychology, 69*, 272–279.

Baron, R. A. (1985). Reducing organizational conflict: The role of attributions. *Journal of Applied Psychology, 70*, 434–441.

Barrett, J. T., with Barrett, J. P. (2004). *A history of alternative dispute resolution*. San Francisco: Jossey-Bass.

Bartholomew, K., & Horowitz, L. (1991). Attachment styles among young adults: A test of a four-category model. *Journal of Personality and Social Psychology, 61*, 226–244.

Basile, K. C., Arias, I., Desai, S., & Thompson, M. P. (2004). The differential association of intimate partner physical, sexual, psychological, and stalking violence and posttraumatic stress symptoms in a nationally representative sample of women. *Journal of Traumatic Stress, 17*, 413–421.

Basso, K. (1990). "To give up on words": Silence in Western Apache culture. In D. Carbaugh (Ed.), *Cultural communication and intercultural communication* (pp. 303–320). Hillsdale, NJ: Lawrence Erlbaum.

Baucom, D. H., Sayers, S. L., & Duhe, A. (1989). Attributional style and attributional patterns among married couples. *Journal of Personality and Social Psychology, 56*, 596–607.

Baumeister, R. F., Stillwell, A., & Wotman, S. R. (1990). Victim and perpetrator accounts of interpersonal conflict: Autobiographical narratives about anger. *Journal of Personality and Social Psychology, 59*, 994–1005.

Baumrind, D. (1966). Effects of authoritative parental control on child behavior. *Child Development, 37*, 887–907.

Baumrind, D. (1991). The influence of parenting style on adolescent competence and substance abuse. *Journal of Early Adolescence, 11*, 56–95.

Baxter, L. A. (1986). Gender differences in the heterosexual relationship rules embedded in break-up accounts. *Journal of Social and Personal Relationships, 3*, 289–306.

Baxter, L. A., Braithwaite, D. O., & Bryant, L. (2006). Types of communication triads perceived by young-adult stepchildren in established stepfamilies. *Communication Studies, 57*, 381–400.

Bennett, J. M., & Bennett, M. J. (2004). Developing intercultural sensitivity: An integrative approach to global and domestic diversity. In D. Landis, J. Bennett, & M. Bennett (Eds.), *Handbook of intercultural training* (3rd ed., pp. 147–165). Thousand Oaks, CA: Sage.

Berk, S. F. (1985). *The gender factory: The apportionment of work in American households*. New York: Plenum.

Berkowitz, L. (1993). Towards a general theory of anger and emotional aggression: Implications of the cognitive-neoassociationistic perspective for the analysis of anger and other emotions. In R. S. Wyer, Jr. & T. K. Srull (Eds.), *Perspectives on anger and emotion: Advances in social cognition* (Vol. 6, pp. 1–46). Hillsdale, NJ: Lawrence Erlbaum.

Berryman-Fink, C., & Brunner, C. C. (1987). The effects of sex of source and target on interpersonal conflict management styles. *Southern Speech Communication Journal, 53*, 38–48.

Berscheid, E. (1983). Emotion. In H. H. Kelley, E. Berscheid, A. Christensen, J. H. Harvey, T. L. Huston, G. Levinger, E. McClintock, L. A. Peplau, & D. R. Peterson (Eds.), *Close relationships* (pp. 110–168). San Francisco: Freeman.

Berscheid, E., Lopes, J., Ammazzalorso, H., & Langenfeld, N. (2001). Causal attributions of relationship quality. In V. Manusov & J. H. Harvey (Eds.), *Attribution, communication behavior, and close relationships* (pp. 115–133). Cambridge: Cambridge University Press.

Betancourt, H., & Blair, I. (1992). A cognition (attribution)-emotional model of violence in conflict situations. *Personality and Social Psychology Bulletin, 18,* 343–350.

Bethke, T. M., & DeJoy, D. M. (1993). An experimental study of factors influencing the acceptability of dating violence. *Journal of Interpersonal Violence, 8,* 36–51.

Bettencourt, B. A., Talley, A., Benjamin, A. J., & Valentine, J. (2006). Personality and aggressive behavior under provoking and neutral conditions: A meta-analytic review. *Psychological Bulletin, 132,* 751–777.

Bettis, R., Bradley, S., & Hamel, G. (1992). Outsourcing and industrial decline. *Academy of Management Executive, 6*(1), 7–22.

Bickmore, K. (2002). Peer mediation training and program implementation in elementary schools: Research results. *Conflict Resolution Quarterly, 20,* 137–160.

Billings, A. (1979). Conflict resolution in distressed and nondistressed married couples. *Journal of Consulting and Clinical Psychology, 47,* 368–376.

Bippus, A. M., & Rollin, E. (2003). Attachment style differences in relational maintenance and conflict behaviors: Friends' perceptions. *Communication Reports, 16,* 113–123.

Birchler, G. R., & Webb, L. J. (1977). Discriminating interaction behaviors in happy and unhappy marriages. *Journal of Consulting and Clinical Psychology, 45,* 494–495.

Bird, G. W., Stith, S. M., & Schladale, J. (1991). Psychological resources, coping strategies, and negotiation styles as discriminators of violence in dating relationships. *Family Relations, 40,* 45–50.

Blake, R. R., & Mouton, J. S. (1964). *The managerial grid.* Houston, TX: Gulf.

Blake, R. R., & Mouton, J. S. (1970). The fifth achievement. *Journal of Applied Behavioral Science, 6,* 413–426.

Bograd, M. (1988). How battered women and abusive men account for domestic violence: Excuses, justifications, or explanations? In G. T. Hotaling, D. Finkelhor, J. T. Kirkpatrick, & M. A. Straus (Eds.), *Coping with family violence: Research and policy perspectives* (pp. 60–77). Newbury Park, CA: Sage.

Boon, S. D., & Sulsky, L. M. (1997). Attributions of blame and forgiveness in romantic relationships: A policy-capturing study. *Journal of Social Behavior and Personality, 12,* 19–44.

Booth, A., & Amato, P. R. (2001). Parental predivorce relations and offspring postdivorce well-being. *Journal of Marriage and the Family, 63,* 197–212.

Bowen, M. (1978). *Family treatment in clinical practice.* New York: Jason Aronson.

Bowlby, J. (1969). *Attachment and loss: Volume 1: Attachment.* New York: Basic Books.

Bowlby, J. (1988). *A secure base: Parent-child development and healthy human attachment.* New York: Basic Books.

Boxer, D. (2002). Nagging: The familial conflict arena. *Journal of Pragmatics, 34,* 49–61.

Bradbury, T. N., & Fincham, F. D. (1990). Attributions in marriage: Review and critique. *Psychological Bulletin, 107,* 3–33.

Bradley, P. H. (1980). Sex, competence, and opinion deviation: An expectation states approach. *Communication Monographs, 47,* 101–110.

Braiker, H. B., & Kelley, H. H. (1979). Conflict in the development of close relationships. In R. L. Burgess & T. L. Huston (Eds.), *Social exchange in developing relationships* (pp. 135–168). New York: Academic Press.

Braithwaite, D. O., Olson, L., Golish, T. D., Soukup, C., & Turman, P. (2001). "Becoming a family": Developmental processes represented in blended family discourse. *Journal of Applied Communication Research, 29,* 221–247.

Bray, J. H., & Kelly, J. (1998). *Stepfamilies: Love, marriage, and parenting in the first decade.* New York: Broadway Books.

Brenders, D. A. (1987). Perceived control: Foundations and directions for communication research. In M. L. McLaughlin (Ed.), *Communication yearbook 10* (pp. 86–116). Newbury Park, CA: Sage.

Brigg, M. (2003). Mediation, power, and cultural difference. *Conflict Resolution Quarterly, 20,* 287–306.

Brody, G. H. (1998). Sibling relationship quality: Its causes and consequences. *Annual Review of Psychology, 49,* 1–24.

Brody, G. H., Stoneman, Z., & McCoy, J. K. (1994). Forecasting sibling relationships in early adolescence from child temperaments and family processes in middle childhood. *Child Development, 65,* 771–784.

Brody, G. H., Stoneman, Z., McCoy, J. K., & Forehand, R. (1992). Contemporaneous and longitudinal associations of sibling conflict with family relationship assessments and family discussions about sibling problems. *Child Development, 63,* 391–400.

Brown, D. (1982). Divorce and family mediation: History, review, future directions. *Conciliation Courts Review, 20,* 1–37.

Brown, P., & Levinson, S. (1987). *Politeness: Some universals in language usage.* Cambridge: Cambridge University Press.

Bryant, S. A., & Spencer, G. A. (2003). University students' attitudes about attributing blame in domestic violence. *Journal of Family Violence, 18,* 369–376.

Buchanan, C. M., Maccoby, E. E., & Dornbusch, S. M. (1991). Caught between parents: Adolescents' experience in divorced homes. *Child Development, 62,* 1008–1029.

Bunkley, N. (2008, February 12). GM offers more buyouts after $722 million loss. *International Herald Tribune.* Retrieved February 12, 2008, from http://www.iht.com/articles/2008/02/12/business/gm.php

Burggraf, C. S., & Sillars, A. L. (1987). A critical examination of sex differences in marital communication. *Communication Monographs, 54,* 276–294.

Burgoon, J. K., Buller, D. B., & Woodall, W. G. (1989). *Nonverbal communication: The unspoken dialogue.* New York: Harper & Row.

Burgoon, M., Alvaro, E., Grandpre, J., & Voulodakis, M. (2002). Revisiting the theory of psychological reactance: Communicating threats to attitudinal freedom. In J. P. Dillard & M. Pfau (Eds.), *The persuasion handbook: Developments in theory and practice* (pp. 213–232). Newbury Park, CA: Sage.

Burleson, B., Holstrom, A., & Gilstrap, C. (2005). "Guys can't say that to guys": Four experiments assessing the normative motivation account for deficiencies in the emotional support provided by men. *Communication Monographs, 72,* 468–501.

Burman, B., Margolin, G., & John, R. S. (1993). America's angriest home videos: Behavioral contingencies observed in home reenactments of marital conflict. *Journal of Consulting and Clinical Psychology, 61,* 28–39.

Burrell, G., & Morgan, G. (1979). *Sociological paradigms and organizational analysis.* London: Heinemann.

Burrell, N. A., Buzzanell, P. M., & McMillan, J. J. (1992). Feminine tensions in conflict situations as revealed by metaphoric analyses. *Management Communication Quarterly, 6,* 115–149.

Burrell, N. A., Donohue, W. A., & Allen, M. (1990). The impact of disputants' expectations of mediation: Testing an interventionist model. *Human Communication Research, 17,* 104–139.

Bush, R. A. B. (1992). *The dilemmas of mediation practice: A study of ethical dilemmas and policy implications.* Washington, DC: National Institute for Dispute Resolution.

Bush, R. A. B., & Folger, J. (1994). *The promise of mediation: Responding to conflict through empowerment and recognition.* San Francisco: Jossey-Bass.

Bush, R. A. B., & Folger, J. P. (2005). *The promise of mediation: The transformative approach to conflict.* San Francisco: Jossey-Bass.

Byrnes, J. (2003, June 2). Dell manages profitability, not inventory. Harvard Business School. Retrieved February 2, 2008, from http://hbswk.hbs.edu/archive/3497.html

Caetano, R., Ramisetty-Mikler, S., & Field, C. A. (2005). Unidirectional and bidirectional intimate partner violence among White, Black, and Hispanic couples in the United States. *Violence and Victims, 20,* 393.

Caetano, R., Vaeth, P. A. C., & Ramisetty-Mikler, S. (2008). Intimate partner violence victim and perpetrator characteristics among couples in the United States. *Journal of Family Violence, 23,* 507–518.

Caffery, T., & Erdman, P. (2000). Conceptualizing parent-adolescent conflict: Applications from systems and attachment theories. *The Family Journal: Counseling and Therapy for Couples and Families, 8,* 14–21.

Cai, D. A., & Fink, E. L. (2002). Conflict style differences between individualists and collectivists. *Communication Monographs, 69,* 67–87.

Campbell, A., & Muncer, S. (1987). Models of anger and aggression in the social talk of women and men. *Journal for the Theory of Social Behaviour, 17,* 489–511.

Campbell, L. E. G., & Johnston, J. R. (1986). Impasse-directed mediation with high conflict families in custody disputes. *Behavioral Sciences & the Law, 4,* 217–241.

Canary, D. J., & Cody, M. J. (1994). *Interpersonal communication: A goals-based approach.* New York: St. Martin's.

Canary, D. J., Cunningham, E. M., & Cody, M. J. (1988). Goal types, gender, and locus of control in managing interpersonal conflict. *Communication Research, 15,* 426–446.

Canary, D. J., & Cupach, W. R. (1988). Relational and episodic characteristics associated with conflict tactics. *Journal of Social and Personal Relationships, 5,* 305–325.

Canary, D. J., Cupach, W. R., & Messman, S. J. (1995). *Relationship conflict: Conflict in parent-child, friendship, and romantic relationships.* Thousand Oaks, CA: Sage.

Canary, D. J., Cupach, W. R., & Serpe, R. T. (2001). A competence-based approach to examining interpersonal conflict: Test of a longitudinal model. *Communication Research, 28,* 79–104.

Canary, D. J., Erickson, E. L., Tafoya, M. A., & Bachman, G. (2002, November). *Attachment styles, conflict management behaviors, and relational characteristics.* Paper presented at the annual National Communication Association Convention, New Orleans, LA.

Canary, D. J., & Lakey, S. G. (2006). Managing conflict in a competent manner: A mindful look at events that matter. In J. G. Oetzel & S. Ting-Toomey (Eds.), *The Sage handbook of conflict communication* (pp. 185–210). Thousand Oaks, CA: Sage.

Canary, D. J., & Spitzberg, B. H. (1987). Appropriateness and effectiveness perceptions of conflict strategies. *Human Communication Research, 14,* 93–118.

Canary, D. J., & Spitzberg, B. H. (1989). A model of perceived competence of conflict strategies. *Human Communication Research, 15,* 630–649.

Canary, D. J., & Spitzberg, B. H. (1990). Attribution biases and associations between conflict strategies and competence outcomes. *Communication Monographs, 57,* 139–151.

Canary, D. J., Spitzberg, B. H., & Semic, B. (1998). The experience and expression of anger in interpersonal settings. In P. A. Andersen & L. K. Guerrero (Eds.), *Communication and emotion: Theory, research, and applications* (pp. 189–213). San Diego, CA: Academic Press.

Canary, D. J., Weger, H., Jr., & Stafford, L. (1991). Couples' argument sequences and their associations with relational characteristics. *Western Journal of Speech Communication, 55,* 159–179.

Cantos, A. L., & Neidig, P. H., & O'Leary, K. D. (1993). Men and women's attributions of blame for domestic violence. *Journal of Family Violence, 8,* 289–302.

Capaldi, D. M., & Owen, L. D. (2001). Physical aggression in a community sample of at-risk young couples: Gender comparisons for high frequency, injury, and fear. *Journal of Family Psychology, 15,* 425–440.

Caprara, G. V., Regalia, C., Scabini, E., Barbaranelli, C., & Bandura, A. (2004). Assessment of filial, parental, marital, and collective family efficacy beliefs. *European Journal of Psychological Assessment, 20,* 247–261.

Carl, D., Gupta, V., & Javidan, M. (2004). Power distance. In R. House, P. Hanges, M. Javidan, P. Dorfman, & V. Gupta (Eds.), *Culture, leadership, and organizations: The GLOBE study of 62 societies* (pp. 513–563). Thousand Oaks, CA: Sage.

Carson, C. L., & Cupach, W. R. (2000). Facing corrections in the workplace: The influence of perceived face threat on the consequences of managerial reproaches. *Journal of Applied Communication Research, 28,* 215–234.

Carty, S. S. (2007, December 4). UAW contracts may have national ripple effect. Retrieved February 11, 2008, from http://www.usatoday.com/money/autos/2007-12-04-uaw-contracts_N.htm

Cascardi, M., & Vivian, D. (1995). Context for specific episodes of marital violence: Gender and severity of violence differences. *Journal of Family Violence, 10,* 265–293.

Caspi, A., & Elder, G. H. (1988). Emergent family patterns: The intergenerational construction of problem behavior and relationships. In R. A. Hinde & J. Stevenson-Hinde (Eds.), *Relationships within families* (pp. 218–240). New York: Oxford University Press.

Catalano, S. (2006). *Intimate partner violence in the United States.* Retrieved January 3, 2007, from http://www.ojp.usdoj.gov/bjs/intimate/ipv.htm

Cauffman, E., Feldman, S. S., Jensen, L. A., & Arnett, J. J. (2000). The (un)acceptability of violence against peers and dates. *Journal of Adolescent Research, 15,* 652–673.

Caughlin, J. P. (2002). The demand/withdraw pattern of communication as a predictor of marital satisfaction over time: Unresolved issues and future directions. *Human Communication Research, 28,* 49–85.

Caughlin, J. P. (2003). Family communication standards: What counts as excellent family communication and how are such standards associated with family satisfaction? *Human Communication Research, 29,* 5–40.

Caughlin, J. P., & Afifi, T. D. (2004). When is topic avoidance unsatisfying?: Examining moderators of the association between avoidance and dissatisfaction. *Human Communication Research, 30,* 479–513.

Caughlin, J. P., & Golish, T. D. (2002). An analysis of the association between topic avoidance and dissatisfaction: Comparing perceptual and interpersonal explanations. *Communication Monographs, 69,* 275–296.

Caughlin, J. P., & Huston, T. L. (2006). The affective structure of marriage. In A. L. Vangelisti & D. Perlman (Eds.), *The Cambridge handbook of personal relationships* (pp. 131–156). New York: Cambridge University Press.

Caughlin, J. P., & Scott, A. M. (2010). Toward a communication theory of the demand/withdraw pattern of interaction in interpersonal relationships. In S. W. Smith & S. R. Wilson (Eds.), *New directions in interpersonal communication research* (pp. 180–200). Thousand Oaks, CA: Sage.

Caughlin, J. P., & Vangelisti, A. L. (1999). Desire for change in one's partner as a predictor of the demand/withdraw pattern of martial communication. *Communication Monographs, 66,* 66–89.

Caughlin, J. P., & Vangelisti, A. L. (2000). An individual difference explanation of why married couples engage in demand/withdraw pattern of conflict. *Journal of Social and Personal Relationships, 17,* 523–551.

Cavanagh, K., Dobash, R. E., Dobash, R. P., & Lewis, R. (2001). "Remedial work": Men's strategic responses to their violence against intimate female partners. *Sociology, 35,* 695–714.

Chogyam, T. (1976). *The foundations of mindfulness.* Berkeley, CA: Shambhala.

Christensen, A., & Heavey, C. L. (1990). Gender and social structure in the demand/withdraw pattern of marital conflict. *Journal of Personality and Social Psychology, 59,* 73–81.

Cissna, K. N., Cox, D. E., & Bochner, A. P. (1990). The dialectic of marital and parental relationships within the stepfamily. *Communication Monographs, 37,* 44–61.

Clark, R. A., & Delia, J. (1979). *Topoi* and rhetorical competence. *Quarterly Journal of Speech, 65,* 187–206.

Clarke, C., & Lipp, G. D. (1998). *Danger and opportunity: Resolving conflict in U.S.-based Japanese subsidiaries.* Yarmouth, ME: Intercultural Press.

Clore, G. L., & Ortony, A. (1991). What more is there to emotion concepts than prototypes? *Journal of Personality and Social Psychology, 60,* 48–50.

Clore, G. L., Ortony, A., Dienes, B., & Fujita, F. (1993). Where does anger dwell? In R. W. Wyer & T. K. Srull (Eds.), *Perspectives on anger and emotions* (Vol. 6, pp. 57–88). Hillsdale, NJ: Lawrence Erlbaum.

Cloven, D. H., & Roloff, M. E. (1993). The chilling effect of aggressive potential on the expression of complaints in intimate relationships. *Communication Monographs, 60,* 199–219.

Cody, M. J., Canary, D. J., & Smith, S. W. (1994). Compliance-gaining goals: An inductive analysis of actor's goal types, strategies, and successes. In J. Daly & J. Wiemann (Eds.), *Communicating strategically* (pp. 33–90). Hillsdale, NJ: Lawrence Erlbaum.

Coker, A. L., Davis, K. E., Arias, I., Desai, S., Sanderson, M., Brandt, H. M., & Smith, P. H. (2002). Physical and mental health effects of intimate partner violence for men and women. *American Journal of Preventative Medicine, 23,* 260–268.

Coleman, M., Fine, M. A., Ganong, L. H., Downs, K. J. M., & Pauk, N. (2001). When you're not the Brady Bunch: Identifying perceived conflicts and resolution strategies in stepfamilies. *Personal Relationships, 8,* 55–73.

Coleman, S., & Raider, E. (2006). International/intercultural conflict resolution training. In J. G. Oetzel & S. Ting-Toomey (Eds.), *The Sage handbook of conflict communication* (pp. 663–690). Thousand Oaks, CA: Sage.

Collier, M. J. (1991). Conflict competence within African, Mexican, and Anglo American friendships. In S. Ting-Toomey & F. Korzenny (Eds.), *Cross-cultural interpersonal communication* (pp. 132–154). Newbury Park, CA: Sage.

Collier, M. J. (1996). Communication competence problematics in ethnic friendships. *Communication Monographs, 63,* 314–336.

Collins, N. L., & Read, S. J. (1990). Adult attachment: Implications for explanation, emotion and behavior. *Journal of Personality and Social Psychology, 58,* 644–663.

Conrad, C. (1991). Communication in conflict: Style-strategy relationships. *Communication Monographs, 58,* 135–155.

Coogler, O. J. (1978). *Structured mediation in divorce settlements.* Lexington, MA: Heath.

Cook, S. L. (1995). Acceptance and expectation of sexual aggression in college students. *Psychology of Women Quarterly, 19,* 181–194.

Cooks, L. M., & Hale, C. L. (1994). The construction of ethics in mediation. *Mediation Quarterly, 12,* 55–76.

Coser, L. (1956). *The functions of social conflict.* New York: Free Press.

Creasey, G. (2002). Associations between working models of attachment and conflict management behavior in romantic couples. *Journal of Counseling Psychology, 49,* 365–375.

Crocker, C. A., Hampson, F. O., & Aall, P. (Eds.). (1999). *Herding cats: Multiparty mediation in a complex world.* Washington, DC: U.S. Institute of Peace Press.

Crocker, C. A., Hampson, F. O., & Aall, P. (Eds.). (2005). *Grasping the nettle: Analyzing cases of intractable conflict.* Washington, DC: U.S. Institute of Peace Press.

Cross, S. E., & Markus, H. R. (1993). Gender in thought, belief, and action: A cognitive approach. In A. E. Beall & R. J. Sternberg (Eds.), *The psychology of gender* (pp. 55–98). New York: Guilford.

Cui, M., Donnellan, M. B., & Conger, R. D. (2007). Reciprocal influences between parents' marital problems and adolescent internalizing and externalizing behavior. *Developmental Psychology, 43,* 1544–1552.

Cummings, E. M., & Davies, P. T. (2002). Effects of marital conflict on children: Recent advances and emerging themes in process-oriented research. *Journal of Child Psychology and Psychiatry, 43,* 31–63.

Cupach, W. R. (2007). "You're bugging me!": Complaints and criticism from a partner. In B. H. Spitzberg & W. R. Cupach (Eds.), *The dark side of interpersonal communication* (2nd ed., pp. 143–168). Mahwah, NJ: Lawrence Erlbaum.

Cupach, W. R., & Canary, D. J. (1995). Managing conflict and anger: Investigating the sex stereotype hypothesis. In P. J. Kalbfleisch & M. J. Cody (Eds.), *Gender, power, and communication in human relationships* (pp. 233–252). Hillsdale, NJ: Lawrence Erlbaum.

Cupach, W. R., & Carson, C. L. (2002). Characteristics and consequences of interpersonal complaints associated with perceived face threat. *Journal of Social and Personal Relationships, 19,* 443–462.

Cupach, W. R., & Metts, S. (1994). *Facework.* Thousand Oaks, CA: Sage.

Cupach, W. R., & Spitzberg, B. H. (2004). *The dark side of relationship pursuit: From attraction to obsession and stalking.* Mahwah, NJ: Lawrence Erlbaum.

Dailey, R., Lee, C., & Spitzberg, B. H. (2007). Communicative aggression: Toward a more interactional view of psychological abuse. In B. H. Spitzberg & W. R. Cupach (Eds.), *The dark side of interpersonal communication* (2nd ed., pp. 297–326). Mahwah, NJ: Lawrence Erlbaum.

Darley, J. M., & Batson, C. D. (1973). From Jerusalem to Jericho: A study of situational and dispositional variables in helping behavior. *Journal of Personality and Social Psychology, 27,* 100–108.

Davis, A. M., & Salem, R. A. (1984). Dealing with power imbalances in the mediation of interpersonal disputes. In J. A. Lemmon (Ed.), *Mediation Quarterly, 6,* 17–26. San Francisco: Jossey-Bass.

Davitz, J. R. (1969). *The language of emotion.* New York: Academic Press.

Deardorff, D. (2006). Identification and assessment of intercultural competence as a student outcome of internationalization. *Journal of Studies in International Education, 10,* 241–266.

Deaux, K., & Lewis, L. L. (1984). The structure of gender stereotypes: Interrelationships among components and gender label. *Journal of Personality and Social Psychology, 46,* 991–1004.

Deutsch, M. (1973). *The resolution of conflict: Constructive and destructive processes.* New Haven, CT: Yale University Press.

DiCamillo, M., & Field, M. (1997, March 10). Majority of voters continue to approve of abortion during 1st trimester. Opposed to late term abortions, unless woman's health is in danger. *The Field Poll, 1835.* San Francisco: Field Institute.

DiCamillo, M., & Field, M. (2002, May 8). Davis and Simon supporters differ markedly on the issues of abortion and gun control. *The Field Poll, 2043.* San Francisco: Field Institute.

Dillard, J. P. (1990). Primary and secondary goals in interpersonal influence. In M. J. Cody & M. L. McLaughlin (Eds.), *The psychology of tactical communication* (pp. 70–90). Clevedon, England: Multilingual Matters.

Dillard, J. P., Segrin, C., & Harden, J. M. (1989). Primary and secondary goals in the production of interpersonal influence messages. *Communication Monographs, 56,* 19–38.

Dindia, K., & Canary, D. J. (Eds.). (2006). *Sex differences and similarities in communication* (2nd ed.). Mahwah, NJ: Lawrence Erlbaum.

Dobash, R. E., & Dobash, R. P. (1979). *Violence against wives: A case against the patriarchy.* New York: Free Press.

Domenici, K., & Littlejohn, S. W. (2006). *Facework: Bridging theory and practice.* Thousand Oaks, CA: Sage.

Dreyfuss, J. (1990). Get ready for the new workforce. *Fortune,* April 23, 165–181.

Dunn, J., & Munn, P. (1987). Development of justification in disputes with another sibling. *Developmental Psychology, 23,* 791–798.

Dunn, J., & Slomkowski, C. (1992). Conflict and the development of social understanding. In C. U. Shantz & W. W. Hartup (Eds.), *Conflict in child and adolescent development* (pp. 70–92). New York: Cambridge University Press.

Durbin, D. A. (2008, January 24). Ford narrows loss, offers buyouts. Retrieved February 11, 2008, from http://money.aol.com/news/articles/_a/ford-narrows-loss-offers-buyouts/20080124073009990001

Dutton, D. G., & Nicholls, T. L. (2005). The gender paradigm in domestic violence research and theory: Part 1—The conflict of theory and data. *Aggression and Violent Behavior, 10,* 680–714.

Dutton, M. A., Kaltman, S., Goodman, L. A., Weinfurt, K., & Vankos, N. (2005). Patterns of intimate partner violence: Correlates and outcomes. *Violence and Victims, 20,* 483–497.

Eagly, A. (1987). *Sex differences in social behavior: A social role interpretation.* Hillsdale, NJ: Lawrence Erlbaum.

Eagly, A. H., & Chaiken, S. (1993). *The psychology of attitudes.* New York: Harcourt Brace Jovanovich.

Eaker, E. D., Sullivan, L. M., Kelly-Hayes, M., D'Agostino, R. B., & Benjamin, E. J. (2007). Marital status, marital strain, and risk of coronary heart disease or total mortality: The Framingham offspring study. *Psychosomatic Medicine, 69,* 509–513.

Earley, P. C., & Ang, S. (2003). *Cultural intelligence: Individual interactions across cultures.* Palo Alto, CA: Stanford University Press.

Earley, P. C., & Peterson, R. S. (2004). The elusive cultural chameleon: Cultural intelligence as a new approach to intercultural training for the global manager. *Academy of Management Learning & Education, 3,* 100–115.

Eckstein, N. (2007). Adolescent-to-parent abuse: Exploring the communicative patterns leading to verbal, physical, and emotional abuse. In B. H. Spitzberg & W. R. Cupach (Eds.), *The dark side of interpersonal communication* (2nd ed., pp. 363–388). Mahwah, NJ: Lawrence Erlbaum.

Ehrensaft, M. K., & Vivian, D. (1999). Is partner aggression related to appraisals of coercive control by a partner? *Journal of Family Violence, 14,* 251–266.

Eisenberg, A. R. (1992). Conflicts between mothers and their young children. *Merrill-Palmer Quarterly, 38,* 21–43.

Eisenberger, N. I., & Lieberman, M. D. (2004). Why rejection hurts: A common neural alarm system for physical and social pain. *Trends in Cognitive Science, 8,* 294–300.

Eldridge, K. A., Sevier, M., Jones, J., Atkins, D. C., & Christensen, A. (2007). Demand-withdraw communication in severely distressed, moderately distressed, and nondistressed couples: Rigidity and polarity during relationship and personal problem discussions. *Journal of Family Psychology, 21,* 218–226.

Emery, R. E. (1994). *Renegotiating family relationships: Divorce, child custody, and mediation.* New York: Guilford.

Emmers-Sommer, T. M. (2003). When partners falter: Repair after a transgression. In D. J. Canary (Ed.), *Maintaining relationships through communication: Relational, contextual, and cultural variations* (pp. 185–205). Mahwah, NJ: Lawrence Erlbaum.

Epps, J., & Kendall, P. C. (1995). Hostile attributional bias in adults. *Cognitive Therapy & Research, 19,* 159–178.

Epstein, N., Pretzer, J. L., & Fleming, B. (1987). The role of cognitive appraisal in self-reports of marital communication. *Behavior Therapy, 18,* 51–69.

Evarts, W. R., Greenstone, J. L., Kirkpatrick, G. J., & Leviton, S. C. (1983). *Winning through accommodation: The mediator's handbook.* Dubuque, IA: Kendall/Hunt.

Everson-Rose, S. A., & Lewis, T. T. (2005). Psychosocial factors and cardiovascular diseases. *Annual Review of Public Health, 26,* 469–500.

Falbo, T., & Peplau, L. A. (1980). Power strategies in intimate relationships. *Journal of Personality and Social Psychology, 38,* 618–628.

Farhoomand, A. F., Lovelock, P., & Ng, P. (2002). *Dell: Selling directly, globally.* Cambridge, MA: Harvard Business School Press.

Feeney, J. A., & Noller, P. (1990). Attachment style as a predictor of adult romantic relationships. *Journal of Personality and Social Psychology, 58,* 281–291.

Fehm-Wolfsdorf, G., Groth, T., Kaiser, A., & Hahlweg, K. (1999). Cortisol responses to marital conflict depend on marital interaction quality. *International Journal of Behavioral Medicine, 6,* 207–227.

Feinberg, M. E., McHale, S. M., Crouter, A. C., & Cumsille, P. (2003). Sibling differentiation: Sibling and parent relationship trajectories in adolescence. *Child Development, 74,* 1261–1274.

Feldman, C. M., & Ridley, C. A. (2000). The role of conflict-based communication responses and outcomes in male domestic violence toward female partners. *Journal of Social and Personal Relationships, 17,* 552–573.

Felmlee, D. H. (1995). Fatal attractions: Affection and disaffection in intimate relationships. *Journal of Social and Personal Relationships, 12,* 295–311.

Felson, R. B., & Cares, A. C. (2005). Gender and the seriousness of assaults on intimate partners on other victims. *Journal of Marriage and Family, 67,* 1182–1195.

Felson, R. B., & Outlaw, M. C. (2007). The control motive and marital violence. *Violence and Victims, 22,* 387–407.

Feshbach, S. (1986). Reconceptualizations of anger: Some research perspectives. *Journal of Social and Clinical Psychology, 4,* 123–132.

Fiebert, M. S., & Gonzalez, D. M. (1997). College women who initiate assaults on their male partners and the reasons offered for such behavior. *Psychological Reports, 80,* 583–590.

Filley, A. C. (1975). *Interpersonal conflict resolution.* Glenview, IL: Scott, Foresman.

Fincham, F. D., Beach, S. R. H., & Nelson, G. (1987). Attribution processes in distressed and nondistressed couples: 3. Causal and responsibility attributions for spouse behavior. *Cognitive Therapy and Research, 11,* 71–86.

Fincham, F. D., & Bradbury, T. N. (1987). The impact of attributions in marriage: A longitudinal analysis. *Journal of Personality and Social Psychology, 53,* 510–517.

Fincham, F. D., & Bradbury, T. N. (1992). Assessing attributions in marriage: The relationship attribution measure. *Journal of Personality and Social Psychology, 62,* 457–468.

Fincham, F. D., Bradbury, T. N., & Scott, C. K. (1990). Cognition in marriage. In F. D. Fincham & T. N. Bradbury (Eds.), *The psychology of marriage: Basic issues and applications* (pp. 118–149). New York: Guilford.

Fine, M. G. (1991). New voices in the workplace: Research directions in multicultural communication. *Journal of Business Communication, 23,* 259–275.

Fisher, B. A. (1978). *Perspectives on human communication.* New York: Macmillan.

Fisher, D. (1993). *Communication in organizations* (2nd ed.). St. Paul, MN: West.

Fisher, R., & Shapiro, D. (2005). *Beyond reason: Using emotions as you negotiate.* New York: Viking Penguin.

Fisher, R., & Ury, W. (1981). *Getting to yes: Negotiating agreement without giving in.* Boston: Houghton Mifflin.

Fisher-Yoshida, B. (2005). Reframing conflict: Intercultural conflict as potential transformation. *Journal of Intercultural Communication, 8,* 1–16.

Fitness, J., & Fletcher, G. J. O. (1993). Love, hate, anger, and jealousy in close relationships: A prototype and cognitive appraisal analysis. *Journal of Personality and Social Psychology, 65,* 942–958.

Fitzpatrick, M. A. (1988a). *Between husbands and wives: Communication in marriage.* Newbury Park, CA: Sage.

Fitzpatrick, M. A. (1988b). Negotiation, problem-solving, and conflict in various types of marriages. In P. Noller & M. A. Fitzpatrick (Eds.), *Perspectives on marital interaction* (pp. 245–270). Philadelphia: Multilingual Matters.

Fitzpatrick, M. A., Fallis, S., & Vance, L. (1982). Multifunctional coding of conflict resolution strategies in marital dyads. *Family Relations, 31,* 61–70.

Fitzpatrick, M. A., & Ritchie, L. D. (1994). Communication schemata within the family: Multiple perspectives on family interaction. *Human Communication Research, 20,* 275–301.

Fitzpatrick, M. A., & Winke, T. (1979). You always hurt the one you love: Strategies and tactics in interpersonal conflict. *Communication Quarterly, 27,* 3–11.

Folberg, J., & Taylor, A. (1984). *Mediation: A comprehensive guide to resolving conflicts without litigation.* San Francisco: Jossey-Bass.

Folger, J. P., Poole, M. S., & Stutman, R. K. (1993). *Working through conflict: Strategies for relationships, groups, and organizations* (2nd ed.). New York: Harper Collins.

Follingstad, D. R., Laughlin, J. E., Polek, D. S., Rutledge, L. L., & Hause, E. S. (1991). Identification of patterns of wife abuse. *Journal of Interpersonal Violence, 6,* 187–204.

Follingstad, D. R., Rutledge, L. L., McNeill-Harkins, K., & Polek, D. S. (1992). Factors related to physical violence in dating relationships. In E. C. Viano (Ed.), *Intimate violence: Interdisciplinary perspectives* (pp. 121–135). Washington, DC: Hemisphere.

Follingstad, D. R., Rutledge, L. L., Polek, D. S., & McNeill-Hawkins, K. (1988). Factors associated with patterns of dating violence toward college women. *Journal of Family Violence, 3,* 169–182.

Fredrickson, B. L., & Branigan, C. (2005). Positive emotions broaden the scope of attention and thought-action repertoires. *Cognition and Emotion, 19,* 313–319.

Frei, F. X., Edmondson, A. C., & Hajim, C. (2003). *Dell computer: Field services for corporate clients.* Cambridge, MA: Harvard Business School Press.

Freud, S. (1949). *An outline of psychoanalysis* (J. Stracyey, Trans.). New York: Norton.

Freud, S. (1953). *The interpretation of dreams* (J. Stracyey, Trans.). London: Hogarth. (Original work published 1900)

Frijda, N. H., Kuipers, P., & ter Schure, E. (1989). The relationships between emotion, appraisal, and emotional action readiness. *Journal of Personality and Social Psychology, 57,* 212–228.

Fritsche, I. (2002). Account strategies for the violation of social norms: Integration and extension of sociological and social psychological typologies. *Journal for the Theory of Social Behaviour, 32,* 371–394.

Frost, W. D., & Averill, J. R. (1982). Differences between men and women in the everyday experience of anger. In J. R. Averill (Ed.), *Anger and aggression: An essay on emotion* (pp. 281–316). New York: Springer-Verlag.

Fuglesang, A., & Chandler, D. (1988). *Participation as process—What can we learn from the Grameen Bank?* Dhaka, Bangladesh: Grameen Bank.

Funk, J. B., Elliott, R., Urman, M. L., Flores, G. T., & Mock, R. M. (1999). The attitudes towards violence scale: A measure for adolescents. *Journal of Interpersonal Violence, 14,* 1123–1136.

Galambos, N. L., Barker, E. T., & Krahn, H. J. (2006). Depression, self-esteem, and anger in emerging adulthood: Seven-year trajectories. *Developmental Psychology, 42,* 350–365.

Gandossy, R., & Tower, J. (2005, May 22). Strategic sourcing for business results. *Chief Executive Officer.* Retrieved from http://www.the-chiefexecutive.com/features/feature274/

Ganong, L., & Coleman, M. (1994). *Remarried family relationships.* Thousand Oaks, CA: Sage.

Gao, G., & Ting-Toomey, S. (1998). *Communicating effectively with the Chinese.* Thousand Oaks, CA: Sage.

Garcia, A. C., Vise, K., & Whitaker, S. P. (2002). Disputing neutrality: A case study of a bias complaint during mediation. *Conflict Resolution Quarterly, 20,* 205–230.

Garcia, M., Shaw, D. S., Winslow, E. B., & Yaggi, K. (2000). Destructive sibling conflict and the development of conduct problems in young boys. *Developmental Psychology, 36,* 44–53.

Garcia, W. R. (1996). *Respeto*: A Mexican base for interpersonal relationships. In W. Gudykunst, S. Ting-Toomey, & T. Nishida (Eds.), *Communication in personal relationships across cultures* (pp. 137–155). Thousand Oaks, CA: Sage.

Gayle, B. M., Preiss, R. W., & Allen, M. (1994). *Gender differences in conflict management strategy selection: A meta-analytic review.* Unpublished manuscript. University of Portland, Portland, Oregon.

Gayle, B. M., Preiss, R. W., & Allen, M. (2002). A meta-analytic interpretation of intimate and nonintimate interpersonal conflict. In M. Allen, R. W. Preiss, B. M. Gayle, & N. A. Burrell (Eds.), *Interpersonal communication research: Advances through meta-analysis* (pp. 345–368). Mahwah, NJ: Lawrence Erlbaum.

Geis, F. L. (1993). Self-fulfilling prophecies: A social psychological view of gender. In A. E. Beall & R. J. Sternberg (Eds.), *The psychology of gender* (pp. 9–54). New York: Guilford.

Gibb, J. R. (1961). Defensive communication. *Journal of Communication, 3,* 141–148.

Gibson, D., & Barsade, S. (1999). The experience of anger at work: Lessons from the chronically angry. Synopsized in *Yale Bulletin & Calendar, 28*(1). Retrieved March 7, 2009, from http://www.yale.edu/opa/arc-ybc/v28.n1/story1.html

Giles-Sims, J. (1998). The aftermath of partner violence. In J. L. Jasinski & L. M. Williams (Eds.), *Partner violence: A comprehensive review of 20 years of research* (pp. 44–72). Thousand Oaks, CA: Sage.

Gindin, S. (2008). Viewpoint: One-sided class war: The UAW–GM 2007 negotiations. *Labor Notes.* Retrieved February 11, 2008, from http://www.labornotes.org/node/1423

Goffman, E. (1967). *Interaction ritual: Essays on face-to-face behavior.* New York: Pantheon.

Golish, T. D. (2003). Stepfamily communication strengths: Understanding the ties that bind. *Human Communication Research, 29,* 41–80.

Gomulak-Cavicchio, B., Davies, P., & Cummings, M. (2006). The role of maternal communication patterns about interparental disputes in associations between interparental conflict and child psychological maladjustment. *Journal of Abnormal Child Psychology, 34,* 757–771.

Gondolf, E. W., & Beeman, A. K. (2003). Women's accounts of domestic violence versus tactics-based outcome categories. *Violence Against Women, 9,* 278–301.

Goodchilds, J. D., & Zellman, G. L. (1984). Sexual signaling and sexual aggression in adolescent relationships. In N. M. Malamuth & E. Donnerstein (Eds.), *Pornography and sexual aggression* (pp. 233–243). New York: Academic Press.

Goodstadt, B. E., & Hjelle, L. A. (1973). Power to the powerless: Locus of control and the use of power. *Journal of Personality and Social Psychology, 27,* 190–196.

Gortner, E., Berns, S. B., Jacobson, N. S., & Gottman, J. M. (1997). When women leave violent relationships: Dispelling clinical myths. *Psychotherapy, 34,* 343–352.

Gottman, J. M. (1979). *Marital interaction: Experimental investigations.* New York: Academic Press.

Gottman, J. M. (1982). Emotional responsiveness in marital conversations. *Journal of Communication, 32,* 108–120.

Gottman, J. M. (1994). *What predicts divorce? The relationship between marital processes and marital outcomes.* Hillsdale, NJ: Lawrence Erlbaum.

Gottman, J. M., & Carrere, S. (1994). Why can't men and women get along? Developmental roots and marital inequities. In D. J. Canary & L. Stafford (Eds.), *Communication and relational maintenance* (pp. 203–229). San Diego, CA: Academic.

Gottman, J. M., Jacobson, N. S., Rushe, R. H., Shortt, J. W., Babcock, J., La Tailade, J. J., & Waltz, J. (1995). The relationship between heart rate reactivity, emotionally aggressive behavior, and general violence in batterers. *Journal of Family Psychology, 9,* 227–248.

Gottman, J. M., & Krokoff, L. J. (1989). Marital interaction and marital satisfaction: A longitudinal view. *Journal of Consulting and Clinical Psychology, 57,* 47–52.

Gottman, J. M., & Levenson, R. W. (1988). The social psychophysiology of marriage. In P. Noller & M. A. Fitzpatrick (Eds.), *Perspectives on marital interaction* (pp. 182–200). Philadelphia, PA: Multilingual Matters.

Gottman, J. M., & Levenson, R. W. (1992). Marital processes predictive of later dissolution: Behavior, physiology, and health. *Journal of Personality and Social Psychology, 63,* 221–233.

Gottman, J. M., & Levenson, R. W. (2000). The timing of divorce: Predicting when a couple will divorce over a 14-year period. *Journal of Marriage and the Family, 62,* 737–745.

Gottman, J. M., & Levenson, R. W. (2002). A two-factor model for predicting when a couple will divorce: Exploratory analyses using 14-year longitudinal data. *Family Process, 41,* 83–96.

Graham, E. E., & Papa, M. J. (1993). Gender and function-oriented discourse in small groups: An examination of problem-solving processes and outcomes. In C. Berryman-Fink, D. Ballard-Reisch, & L. H. Newman (Eds.), *Communication and sex-role socialization* (pp. 311–336). New York: Garland.

Graham, E. E., Papa, M. J., & McPherson, M. B. (1997). An applied test of the functional communication perspective of small group decision making. *Southern Communication Journal, 63,* 114–132.

Graham, K., Tremblay, P. F., Wells, S., Pernanen, K., Purcell, J., & Jelley, J. (2006). Harm, intent, and the nature of aggressive behavior: Measuring naturally occurring aggression in barroom settings. *Assessment, 13,* 280–296.

Graham, K., & Wells, S. (2002). The two worlds of aggression for men and women. *Sex Roles, 45,* 595–622.

Greene, J., & Haidt, J. (2002). How (and where) does moral judgment work? *Trends in Cognitive Sciences, 6*(12), 517–523.

Grice, H. P. (1975). Logic and conversation. In P. Cole & J. L. Morgan (Eds.), *Syntax and semantics* (Vol. 3, pp. 41–58). New York: Academic.

Grillo, T. (1991). The mediation alternative: Process dangers for women. *Yale Law Journal, 100,* 1545–1610.

Gross, M. A., Guerrero, L. K., & Alberts, J. K. (2004). Perceptions of conflict strategies and communication competence in task-oriented dyads. *Journal of Applied Communication Research, 32,* 249–270.

Grote, N. K., & Clark, M. S. (2001). Perceiving unfairness in the family: Cause or consequence of marital distress? *Journal of Personality and Social Psychology, 80,* 281–293.

Grych, J. H., & Fincham, F. D. (1993). Children's appraisals of marital conflict: Initial investigations of the cognitive-contextual framework. *Child Development, 64,* 215–230.

Gryl, F. E., Stith, S. M., & Bird, G. W. (1991). Close dating relationships among college students: Differences by use of violence and by gender. *Journal of Social and Personal Relationships, 8,* 243–264.

Gudykunst, W., Matsumoto, Y., Ting-Toomey, S., Nishida, T., Kim, K., & Heyman, S. (1996). The influence of cultural individualism-collectivism, self construals, and individual values on communication styles across cultures. *Human Communication Research, 22,* 510–543.

Guerrero, L. K. (1994). "I'm so mad I could scream": The effects of anger expression on relational satisfaction and communication competence. *Southern Communication Journal, 59,* 125–141.

Guerrero, L. K., Andersen, P. A., Jorgensen, P. F., Spitzberg, B. H., & Eloy, S. V. (1995). Coping with the green-eyed monster: Conceptualizing and measuring communicative responses to romantic jealousy. *Western Journal of Communication, 59*, 270–304.

Guerrero, L. K., & Burgoon, J. K. (1996). Attachment styles and reactions to nonverbal involvement change in romantic dyads: Patterns of reciprocity and compensation. *Human Communication Research, 22*, 335–370.

Guerrero, L. K., & La Valley, A. G. (2006). Conflict, emotion, and communication. In J. G. Oetzel & S. Ting-Toomey (Eds.), *The Sage handbook of conflict communication: Integrating theory, research, and practice* (pp. 69–96). Thousand Oaks, CA: Sage.

Gulliver, P. H. (1979). *Disputes and negotiations: A cross-cultural perspective.* New York: Academic Press.

Haefner, P. T., Notarius, C. I., & Pellegrini, D. S. (1991). Determinants of satisfaction with marital discussions: An exploration of husband-wife differences. *Behavioral Assessment, 13*, 67–82.

Hall, E. T. (1983). *The dance of life.* New York: Doubleday.

Hall, J. H., & Fincham, F. D. (2006). Relationship dissolution following infidelity: The roles of attributions and forgiveness. *Journal of Social and Clinical Psychology, 25*, 508–522.

Hamilton, M. A., & Mineo, P. J. (2002). Argumentativeness and its effect on verbal aggressiveness: A meta-analytic review. In M. Allen, R. W. Preiss, B. M. Gayle, & N. A. Burrell (Eds.), *Interpersonal communication research: Advances through meta-analysis* (pp. 281–314). Mahwah, NJ: Lawrence Erlbaum.

Hammock, G. S., Richardson, D. R., Pilkington, C. J., & Utley, M. (1990). Measurement of conflict in social relationships. *Personality and Individual Differences, 11*, 577–583.

Hample, D., & Dallinger, J. M. (1995). A Lewinian perspective on taking conflict personally: Revision, refinement, and validation of the instrument. *Communication Quarterly, 43*, 297–319.

Hannawa, A. F., Spitzberg, B. H., Wiering, L., & Teranishi, C. (2006). "If I can't have you, no one can": Development of a relational entitlement and proprietariness scale (REPS). *Violence and Victims, 21*, 539–560.

Harris, L. M., Gergen, K. J., & Lannamann, J. W. (1986). Aggression rituals. *Communication Monographs, 53*, 252–265.

Harris, M. B. (1993). How provoking! What makes men and women angry? *Aggressive Behavior, 19*, 199–211.

Harris, M. B., & Miller, K. C. (2000). Gender and perceptions of danger. *Sex Roles, 43*, 843–863.

Hayashi, G. M., & Strickland, B. R. (1998). Long-term effects of parental divorce on love relationships: Divorce as attachment disruption. *Journal of Social and Personal Relationships, 15*, 23–38.

Haynes, J. M. (1982). A conceptual model of the process of family mediation: Implications for training. *American Journal of Family Therapy, 10*(4), 5–16.

Hazan, C., & Shaver, P. R. (1987). Romantic love conceptualized as an attachment process. *Journal of Personality and Social Psychology, 52*, 511–524.

Hazleton, V., & Cupach, W. R. (1986). An exploration of ontological knowledge: Communication competence as a function of the ability to describe, predict, and explain. *Western Journal of Speech Communication, 50*, 119–132.

Heavey, C. L., Christensen, A., & Malamuth, N. M. (1995). The longitudinal impact of demand and withdrawal during marital conflict. *Journal of Consulting and Clinical Psychology, 63,* 797–801.

Heavey, C. L., Layne, C., & Christensen, A. (1993). Gender and conflict structure in marital interaction: A replication and extension. *Journal of Consulting and Clinical Psychology, 61,* 16–27.

Heisterkamp, B. L. (2006). Taking the footing of a neutral mediator. *Conflict Resolution Quarterly, 23,* 301–315.

Hellmuth, J. C., & McNulty, J. K. (2008). Neuroticism, marital violence, and the moderating role of stress and behavioral skills. *Journal of Personality and Social Psychology, 95,* 166–180.

Henderson, D. C. (1965). *Conciliation and Japanese law: Tokugawa and modern.* Seattle: University of Washington Press.

Henning, K., & Klesges, L. M. (2003). Prevalence and characteristics of psychological abuse reported by court-involved battered women. *Journal of Interpersonal Violence, 18,* 857–871.

Hetherington, E. M. (1999). Family functioning and the adjustment of adolescent siblings in diverse types of families. *Monographs for the Society for Research in Child Development, 64,* 1–25.

Heyman, R. E. (2001). Observation of couple conflicts: Clinical applications, stubborn truths, and shaky foundations. *Psychological Assessment, 13,* 5–35.

Higgins, T. (2008, February 8). Chrysler to cut model lineup by half. *Detroit Free Press.* Retrieved February 11, 2008, from http://freep.com/apps/pbcs.dll/article?AID=/20080207/BUSINESS01/80207094/1001/NEWS

Hines, D. A., Brown, J., & Dunning, E. (2007). Characteristics of callers to the domestic abuse helpline for men. *Journal of Family Violence, 22,* 63–72.

Hirokawa, R. Y. (1985). Discussion procedures and decision-making performance: A test of a functional perspective. *Human Communication Research, 12,* 203–224.

Hirokawa, R. Y. (1988). Group communication and decision-making performance: A continued test of the functional perspective. *Human Communication Research, 14,* 487–515.

Hobart, C. (1991). Relationships between the formerly married. *Journal of Divorce & Remarriage, 14,* 1–23.

Hochschild, A. (1989). *The second shift: Working parents and the revolution at home.* New York: Viking.

Hocker, J. L., & Wilmot, W. W. (1991). *Interpersonal conflict* (3rd ed.). Dubuque, IA: Wm. C. Brown.

Hocker, J. L., & Wilmot, W. W. (1995). *Interpersonal conflict* (4th ed.). Dubuque, IA: Wm C. Brown.

Hodge, B. J., Anthony, W. P., & Gales, L. M. (2003). *Organizational theory: A strategic approach* (6th ed.). Upper Saddle River, NJ: Prentice Hall.

Hofstede, G. (2001). *Culture's consequences: Comparing values, behaviors, institutions, and organizations across cultures* (2nd ed.). Thousand Oaks, CA: Sage.

Holtzworth-Munroe, A., & Anglin, K. (1991). The competency of responses given by maritally violent versus nonviolent men to problematic marital situations. *Violence and Victims, 6,* 257–269.

Holzner, S. (2006). *How Dell does it.* Boston: McGraw-Hill Professional.

Honeycutt, J. M., Woods, B. L., & Fontenot, K. (1993). The endorsement of communication conflict rules as a function of engagement, marriage and marital ideology. *Journal of Social and Personal Relationships, 10,* 285–304.

Honeyman, C. (1990). On evaluating mediators. *Negotiation Journal, 6,* 23–36.

House, R., Hanges, P., Javidan, M., Dorfman, P., & Gupta, V. (Eds.) (2004). *Culture, leadership, and organizations: The GLOBE study of 62 societies.* Thousand Oaks, CA: Sage.

Howat, G., & London, M. (1980). Attributions of conflict management strategies in supervisor-subordinate dyads. *Journal of Applied Psychology, 65,* 172–175.

Huff-Arneson, R. (1988). *A language of leaders.* Paper presented at the annual convention of the American Library Association, New Orleans, LA.

Hulthén, K., & Gadde, L-E. (2007). Understanding the "new" distribution reality through "old" concepts: A renaissance for transvection and sorting. *Marketing Theory, 7,* 184–207.

Hupka, R. B., Otto, J., Tarabrina, N. V., & Reidl, L. (1993). Cross-cultural comparisons of nouns associated with jealousy and the related emotions of envy, anger, and fear. *Cross-Cultural Research, 27,* 181–211.

Huston, T. L., Caughlin, J. P., Houts, R. M., Smith, S. E., & George, L. J. (2001). The connubial crucible: Newlywed years as predictors of marital delight, distress, and divorce. *Journal of Personality and Social Psychology, 80,* 237–252.

Huston, T. L., Surra, C. A., Fitzgerald, N. M., & Cate, R. M. (1981). From courtship to marriage: Mate selection as an interpersonal process. In S. Duck & R. Gilmour (Eds.), *Personal relationships 2: Developing personal relationships* (pp. 53–88). London: Academic Press.

Huston, T., & Vangelisti, A. (1995). Parent-adolescent relationships. In M. A. Fitzpatrick & A. L. Vangelisti (Eds.), *Explaining family interactions* (pp. 147–177). Thousand Oaks, CA: Sage.

Hydén, M. (1995). Verbal aggression as prehistory of women battering. *Journal of Family Violence, 10,* 55–71.

IBM. (2007). IBM recognizes partners for driving innovation and business impact. Retrieved February 11, 2008, from http://www-03.ibm.com/press/us/en/pressrelease/21586.wss

Ickes, W., & Simpson, J. A. (1997). Managing empathic accuracy in close relationships. In W. Ickes (Ed.), *Empathic accuracy* (pp. 218–250). New York: Guilford.

Igra, V., & Irwin, Jr., C. E. (1996). Theories of adolescent risk-taking behavior. In R. J. DiClemente, W. B. Hansen, & L. E. Ponton (Eds.), *Handbook of adolescent health risk behavior* (pp. 35–51). New York: Plenum.

Infante, D. A., Chandler, T. A., & Rudd, J. E. (1989). Test of an argumentative skill deficiency model of interpersonal violence. *Communication Monographs, 56,* 163–177.

Infante, D. A., & Rancer, A. S. (1982). A conceptualization and measurement of argumentativeness. *Journal of Personality Assessment, 46,* 72–80.

Infante, D. A., & Rancer, A. S. (1996). Argumentativeness and verbal aggressiveness: A review of recent theory and research. In B. R. Burleson (Ed.), *Communication yearbook 19* (pp. 319–351). Thousand Oaks, CA: Sage.

Infante, D. A., Riddle, B. L., Horvath, C. L., & Tumlin, S. A. (1992). Verbal aggressiveness: Messages and reasons. *Communication Quarterly, 40,* 116–126.

Infante, D. A., Sabourin, T. C., Rudd, J. E., & Shannon, E. A. (1990). Verbal aggression in violent and nonviolent marital disputes. *Communication Quarterly, 38,* 361–371.

Infante, D. A., Trebing, J. D., Shepard, P. E., & Seeds, D. E. (1984). The relation of argumentativeness to verbal aggression. *Southern Speech Communication Journal, 50,* 67–77.

Infante, D. A., & Wigley, C. J., Jr. (1986). Verbal aggressiveness: An interpersonal model and measure. *Communication Monographs, 53,* 61–69.

Jacobs, S., & Aakhus, M. (2002). What mediators do with words: Implementing three models of rational discussion in dispute mediation. *Conflict Resolution Quarterly, 20,* 177–204.

Jacobson, N. S., Gottman, J. M., Gortner, E., Berns, S., & Shortt, J. W. (1996). Psychological factors in the longitudinal course of battering: When do the couples split up? When does the abuse decrease? *Violence and Victims, 11,* 371–392.

James, L. R., McIntyre, M. D., Glisson, C. A., Bowler, J. L., & Mitchell, T. R. (2004). The conditional reasoning measurement system for aggression: An overview. *Human Performance, 17,* 271–295.

Jameson, J. K. (1999). Toward a comprehensive model for the assessment and management of intraorganizational conflict: Developing the framework. *The International Journal of Conflict Management, 10,* 268–294.

Jekielek, S. (1998). Parental conflict, marital disruption and children's emotional wellbeing. *Social Forces, 76,* 905–936.

Jenkins, J. M. (2000). Marital conflict and children's emotions: The development of an anger organization. *Journal of Marriage and the Family, 62,* 723–736.

Jensen-Campbell, L. A., & Graziano, W. G. (2000). Beyond the schoolyard: Relationships as moderators of daily interpersonal conflict. *Personality and Social Psychology Bulletin, 26,* 925–935.

Johnson, I., & Sigler, R. T. (1996). Public perceptions of interpersonal violence. *Journal of Criminal Justice, 24,* 419–430.

Johnson, M. P. (2001). Conflict and control: Symmetry and asymmetry in domestic violence. In A. Booth, A. C. Crouter, & M. Clements (Eds.), *Couples in conflict* (pp. 95–104). Mahwah, NJ: Lawrence Erlbaum.

Jones, E., & Gallois, C. (1989). Spouses' impressions of rules for communication in public and private marital conflicts. *Journal of Marriage and the Family, 51,* 957–967.

Jones, R. E., & White, C. S. (1985). Relationships among personality, conflict resolution styles, and task effectiveness. *Group & Organization Studies, 10,* 152–167.

Jones, T. S. (1994). A dialectical reframing of the mediation process. In J. P. Folger & T. S. Jones (Eds.), *New directions in mediation* (pp. 26–47). Thousand Oaks, CA: Sage.

Jones, T. S. (2006). Conflict resolution education: Issues, answers, and directions. In J. G. Oetzel & S. Ting-Toomey (Eds.), *The Sage handbook of conflict communication* (pp. 239–266). Thousand Oaks, CA: Sage.

Jones, T. S., & Brinkert, R. (2008). *Conflict coaching: Conflict management strategies and skills for the individual.* Los Angeles: Sage.

Joshi, A. (2008). Conflict resolution between friends during middle childhood. *Journal of Genetic Psychology, 169,* 133–148.

Kabat-Zinn, J. (1994). *Wherever you go there you are: Mindfulness meditation in everyday life.* New York: Hyperion.

Kahneman, D., & Tversky, A. (1979). Prospect theory: An analysis of decision under risk. *Econometrica, 47,* 263–291.

Kale, P., & Singh, H. (2007). Building firm capabilities through learning the role of the alliance learning process in alliance capability and firm-level alliance success. *Strategic Management Journal, 28,* 981–1000.

Kanin, E. J. (1984). Date rape: Unofficial criminals and victims. *Victimology, 9,* 95–108.

Katz, D., & Kahn, R. L. (1978). *The social psychology of organizations* (2nd ed.). New York: Wiley.

Katz, J., Carino, A., & Hilton, A. (2002). Perceived verbal conflict behaviors associated with physical aggression and sexual coercion in dating relationships: A gender-sensitive analysis. *Violence and Victims, 17,* 93–109.

Katz, J., Kuffel, S. W., & Coblentz, A. (2002). Are there gender differences in sustaining dating violence? An examination of the frequency, severity, and relationship satisfaction. *Journal of Family Violence, 17,* 247–271.

Kaushal, R., & Kwantes, C. (2006). The role of culture and personality in choice of conflict management strategy. *International Journal of Intercultural Relations, 30,* 579–603.

Kelley, H. H. (1979). *Personal relationships: Their structure and processes.* Hillsdale, NJ: Lawrence Erlbaum.

Kelley, H. H., Cunningham, J. D., Grisham, J. A., Lefebvre, L. M., Sink, C. R., & Yablon, G. (1978). Sex differences in comments made during conflict within close heterosexual pairs. *Sex Roles, 4,* 473–492.

Kelley, P. (1992). Healthy stepfamily functioning. *Families in Society: Journal of Contemporary Human Services, 73,* 579–587.

Kernsmith, P. (2005). Exerting power or striking back: A gendered comparison of motivations for domestic violence perpetration. *Violence and Victims, 20,* 173–185.

Kessler, R. C., Molnar, B. E., Feurer, I. D., & Appelbaum, M. (2001). Patterns and mental health predictors of domestic violence in the United States: Results from the national comorbidity study. *International Journal of Law and Psychiatry, 24,* 487–508.

Kiecolt-Glaser, J. K., Malarkey, W. B., Chee, M. A., Newton, T., Cacioppo, J. T., Mao, H. Y., & Glaser, R. (1993). Negative behavior during marital conflict is associated with immunological down-regulation. *Psychosomatic Medicine, 55,* 395–409.

Kiecolt-Glaser, J. K., McGuire, L., Robles, T. F., & Glaser, R. (2003). Psychoneuroimmunology: Psychological influences on immune function and health. *Journal of Consulting and Clinical Psychology, 70,* 537–547.

Kiccolt-Glaser, J. K., & Newton, T. L. (2001). Marriage and health: His and hers. *Psychological Bulletin, 127,* 472–503.

Kiely, L. S., & Crary, D. R. (1986). Effective mediation: A communication approach to consubstantiality. In J. A. Lemmon (Ed.), *Mediation Quarterly, 12,* 37–50. San Francisco: Jossey-Bass.

Kilmann, R. H., & Thomas, K. W. (1977). Developing a forced-choice measure of conflict-handling behavior: The "MODE" instrument. *Educational and Psychological Measurement, 37,* 309–325.

Kim, J., McHale, S. M., Osgood, W., & Crouter, A. (2006). Longitudinal course and family correlates of sibling relationships from childhood through adolescence. *Child Development, 77,* 1746–1761.

Kim, M-S., & Leung, T. (2000). A multicultural view of conflict management styles: Review and critical synthesis. In M. E. Roloff (Ed.), *Communication yearbook 23* (pp. 227–269). Thousand Oaks, CA: Sage.

Kim, Y. Y. (2001). *Becoming intercultural: An integrative theory of communication and cross-cultural adaptation.* Thousand Oaks, CA: Sage.

Kim, Y. Y. (2005). Adapting to a new culture: An integrative communication theory. In W. B. Gudykunst (Ed.), *Theorizing about intercultural communication* (pp. 375–400). Thousand Oaks, CA: Sage.

Kipnis, D., & Schmidt, S. M. (1982). *Respondent's guide to the Kipnis-Schmidt profiles of organizational influence strategies.* Beverly Hills, CA: University Associates.

Kline, S. L., & Stafford, L. (2004). A comparison of interaction rules and interaction frequency in relationship to marital quality. *Communication Reports, 17,* 11–26.

Kochman, T. (1981). *Black and white styles in conflict.* Chicago: University of Chicago Press.

Koren, P., Carlton, K., & Shaw, D. (1980). Marital conflict: Relations among behaviors, outcomes and distress. *Journal of Consulting and Clinical Psychology, 48,* 460–468.

Koski, P. R., & Mangold, W. D. (1988). Gender effects in attitudes about family violence. *Journal of Family Violence, 3,* 225–237.

Koss, M. P. (1989). Hidden rape: Sexual aggression and victimization in a national sample of students in higher education. In M. A. Pirog-Good & J. E. Stets (Eds.), *Violence in dating relationships: Emerging social issues* (pp. 145–168). New York: Praeger.

Kotabe, M. (1992). *Global sourcing strategy: R&D, manufacturing, and marketing interfaces.* New York: Quorum.

Kubany, E. S., Bauer, G. B., Muraoka, M. Y., Richard, D. C., & Read, P. (1995). Impact of labeled anger and blame in intimate relationships. *Journal of Social and Clinical Psychology, 14,* 53–60.

Kuhn, T., & Poole, M. S. (2000). Do conflict management styles affect group decision making? *Human Communication Research, 26,* 558–590.

Kumar, R., & Das, T. K. (2007). Interpartner legitimacy in the alliance development process. *Journal of Management Studies, 44,* 1425–1453.

Kurdek, L. A. (1994). Areas of conflict for gay, lesbian, and heterosexual couples: What couples argue about influences relationship satisfaction. *Journal of Marriage and the Family, 56,* 923–934.

Kurdek, L. A., & Fine, M. A. (1991). Cognitive correlates of satisfaction for mothers and stepfamilies in stepfather families. *Journal of Marriage and the Family, 53,* 565–572.

Lakey, S. G., & Canary, D. J. (2002). Actor goal achievement and sensitivity to partner as critical factors in understanding interpersonal communication competence and conflict strategies. *Communication Monographs, 69,* 217–235.

Langer, E. (1989). *Mindfulness.* Reading, MA: Addison-Wesley.

Langer, E. (1997). *The power of mindful learning.* Reading, MA: Addison-Wesley.

Larzelere, R. E., & Huston, T. L. (1980). The dyadic trust scale: Toward understanding interpersonal trust in close relationships. *Journal of Marriage and the Family, 42,* 595–604.

Laursen, B. (1993). The perceived impact of conflict on adolescent relationships. *Merrill-Palmer Quarterly, 39,* 535–550.

Lavie, D. (2007). Alliance portfolios and firm performance: A study of value creation and appropriation in the U.S. software industry. *Strategic Management Journal, 28,* 1187–1212.

LeBaron, M. (2003). *Bridging cultural conflicts: A new approach for a changing world.* San Francisco: Jossey Bass/John Wiley.

Lefcourt, H. M. (1982). *Locus of control: Current trends in theory and research* (2nd ed.). Hillsdale, NJ: Lawrence Erlbaum.

Lei, D., & Slocum, J. W. (1992). Global strategy, competence-building and strategic alliances. *California Management Review, 26*(4), 81–97.

Leonard, K. E., Quigley, B. M., & Collins, R. L. (2003). Drinking, personality, and bar environmental characteristics as predictors of involvement in barroom aggression. *Addictive Behaviors, 28,* 1681–1700.

LeResche, D. (Ed.). (1993). Special issue: Native American perspectives on peacemaking. *Mediation Quarterly, 10*(4), 321–422.

Lerman, L. G. (1984). Mediation of wife abuse cases: The adverse impact of informal dispute resolution on women. *Harvard Women's Law Journal, 7,* 57–113.

Leung, A. K-Y., Maddux, W., Galinsky, A., Chiu, C. T. (2008). Multicultural experience enhances creativity: The when and how. *American Psychologist, 63,* 169–181.

Leung, K., & Bond, M. (2004). Social axioms: A model of social beliefs in multi-cultural perspective. In M. P. Zanna (Ed.), *Advances in experimental social psychology* (Vol. 36, pp. 119–197). San Diego, CA: Elsevier Academic Press.

Levenson, R. W., Carstensen, L. L., & Gottman, J. M. (1994). The influence of age and gender on affect, physiology, and their interrelations: A study of long-term marriages. *Journal of Personality and Social Psychology, 67,* 56–68.

Lewicki, R. J., & Litterer, J. (1985). *Negotiation.* Homewood, IL: Irwin.

Lieff, Cabraser, Heimann & Bernstein, LLP. (2006). $40 million paid to class members in December 2005 in Abercrombie & Fitch discrimination lawsuit settlement. Retrieved February 11, 2008, from http://www.afjustice.com/

Lippa, R. A. (2002). *Gender, nature, and nurture.* Mahwah, NJ: Lawrence Erlbaum.

Lloyd, S. A. (1987). Conflict in premarital relationships: Differential perceptions of males and females. *Family Relations, 36,* 290–294.

Lloyd, S. A. (1990). Conflict types and strategies in violent marriages. *Journal of Family Violence, 5,* 269–284.

London, M., & Howat, G. (1978). The relationships between employee commitment and conflict resolution behavior. *Journal of Vocational Behavior, 13,* 1–14.

Loudin, J. L., Loukas, A., & Robinson, S. (2003). Relational aggression in college students: Examining the roles of social anxiety and empathy. *Aggressive Behavior, 29,* 430–439.

Lubit, R., & Russett, B. (1984). The effects of drugs on decision-making. *Journal of Conflict Resolution, 28,* 85–102.

Lund, M. (1985). The development of investment and commitment scales for predicting continuity of personal relationships. *Journal of Social and Personal Relationships, 2,* 3–23.

Luthra, R., & Gidycz, C. A. (2006). Dating violence among college men and women: Evaluation of a theoretical model. *Journal of Interpersonal Violence, 21,* 717–731.

Mack, R. N. (1989). Spouse abuse—A dyadic approach. In G. R. Weeks (Ed.), *Treating couples: The intersystem model of the Marriage Council of Philadelphia* (pp. 191–214). New York: Brunner/Mazel.

Maddux, W., & Galinsky, A. (2009). Cultural borders and mental barriers: The relationship between living abroad and creativity. *Journal of Personality and Social Psychology, 96,* 1047–1061.

Makepeace, J. M. (1983). Life events, stress, and courtship violence. *Family Relations, 30,* 97–102.

Malarkey, W. B., Kiecolt-Glaser, J. K., Perl, D., & Glaser, R. (1994). Hostile behavior during marital conflict alters pituitary and adrenal hormones. *Psychosomatic Medicine, 56,* 41–51.

Malis, R., & Roloff, M. (2006). Demand/withdraw patterns in serial arguments: Implications for well-being. *Human Communication Research, 32,* 198–216.

Malle, B. F., Knobe, J. M., & Nelson, S. E. (2007). Actor-observer asymmetries in explanations of behavior: New answers to an old question. *Journal of Personality and Social Psychology, 93,* 491–514.

Manusov, V., & Koenig, J. (2001). The content of attributions in couples' communication. In V. Manusov & J. H. Harvey (Eds.), *Attribution, communication behavior, and close relationships* (pp. 134–152). Cambridge: Cambridge University Press.

Marcus, R. F., & Swett, B. (2003). Violence in close relationships: The role of emotion. *Aggression and Violent Behavior, 8,* 313–327.

Margolin, G., John, R. S., & Gleberman, L. (1988). Affective responses to conflictual discussions in violent and nonviolent couples. *Journal of Consulting and Clinical Psychology, 56,* 24–33.

Margolin, G., & Wampold, B. E. (1981). Sequential analysis of conflict and accord in distressed and nondistressed marital partners. *Journal of Consulting and Clinical Psychology, 49*, 554–567.

Markus, H., & Kitayama, S. (1991). Culture and the self: Implications for cognition, emotion, and motivation. *Psychological Review, 2*, 224–253.

Markus, H. R., & Kitayama, S. (1998). The cultural psychology of personality. *Journal of Cross-Cultural Psychology, 29*, 63–87.

Marshall, L. L. (1994). Physical and psychological abuse. In W. R. Cupach & B. H. Spitzberg (Eds.), *The dark side of interpersonal communication* (pp. 281–311). Hillsdale, NJ: Lawrence Erlbaum.

Marshall, L. L., Weston, R., & Honeycutt, T. C. (2000). Does men's positivity moderate or mediate the effects of their abuse on women's relationship quality? *Journal of Social and Personal Relationships, 17*, 660–675.

Martin, J., Hecht, M., & Larkey, L. (1994). Conversational improvement strategies for interethnic communication: African American and European American perspectives. *Communication Monographs, 61*, 236–255.

Mayer, B. S. (2004). *Beyond neutrality: Confronting the crisis in conflict resolution.* San Francisco: Jossey-Bass.

McCann, C. D., & Higgins, E. T. (1984). Individual differences in communication: Social cognitive determinants and consequences. In H. E. Sypher & J. L. Applegate (Eds.), *Communication by children and adults* (pp. 172–210). Beverly Hills, CA: Sage.

McEllistrem, J. E. (2004). Affective and predatory violence: A bimodal classification system of human aggression and violence. *Aggression and Violent Behavior, 10*, 1–30.

McGonagle, K. A., Kessler, R. C., & Gotlib, I. H. (1993). The effects of marital disagreement style, frequency, and outcome on marital disruption. *Journal of Social and Personal Relationships, 10*, 385–404.

McIsaac, H. (1983). Court-connected mediation. *Conciliation Courts Review, 21*, 49–59.

Mead, D. E., Vatcher, G. M., Wyne, B. A., & Roberts, S. L. (1990). The comprehensive areas of change questionnaire: Assessing marital couples' presenting complaints. *American Journal of Family Therapy, 18*, 65–79.

Medeiros, R. A., & Straus, M. A. (2006). Risk factors for physical violence between dating partners: Implications for gender-inclusive prevention and treatment of family violence. In J. Hamel & T. Nicholls (Eds.), *Family approaches in domestic violence: A practitioner's guide to gender-inclusive research and treatment* (pp. 59–85). New York: Springer.

Meehan, J. C., & Holtzworth-Munroe, A. (2001). Heart rate reactivity in male batterers: Reply to Gottman (2001) and a second look at the evidence. *Journal of Family Psychology, 15*, 415–424.

Meehan, J. C., Holtzworth-Munroe, A., & Herron, K. (2001). Maritally violent men's heart rate reactivity to marital interactions: A failure to replicate the Gottman et al. (1995) typology. *Journal of Family Psychology, 15*, 394–408.

Mehrabian, A. (1997). Relations among personality scales of aggression, violence, and empathy: Validational evidence bearing on the risk of eruptive violence scale. *Aggressive Behavior, 23*, 433–445.

Meloy, J. R. (2002). Pathologies of attachment, violence, and criminality. In A. M. Goldstein & I. B. Weiner (Eds.), *Handbook of psychology: Vol. 11. Forensic psychology* (pp. 509–526). Hoboken, NJ: John Wiley & Sons.

Merkin, R. (2006). Power distance and facework strategies. *Journal of Intercultural Communication Research, 35*, 139–160.

Messman, S. J., & Canary, D. J. (1998). Patterns of conflict in close relationships. In B. H. Spitzberg & W. R. Cupach (Eds.), *The dark side of close relationships* (pp. 121–153). Mahwah, NJ: Lawrence Erlbaum.

Metts, S. (1994). Relational transgressions. In W. R. Cupach & B. H. Spitzberg (Eds.), *The dark side of interpersonal communication* (pp. 217–239). Hillsdale, NJ: Lawrence Erlbaum.

Metts, S., & Cupach, W. R. (2007). Responses to relational transgressions: Hurt, anger, and sometimes forgiveness. In B. H. Spitzberg & W. R. Cupach (Eds.), *The dark side of interpersonal communication* (2nd ed., 243–274). Mahwah, NJ: Lawrence Erlbaum.

Mezirow, J. (2000). *Learning as transformation: Critical perspectives on a theory in progress.* San Francisco: Jossey Bass.

Mikula, G., Scherer, K. R., & Athenstaedt, U. (1998). The role of injustice in the elicitation of differential emotional reactions. *Personality and Social Psychology Bulletin, 24,* 769–783.

Millar, F. E., & Rogers, L. E. (1987). Relational dimensions of interpersonal dynamics. In M. E. Roloff & G. R. Miller (Eds.), *Interpersonal processes: New directions in communication research* (pp. 117–139). Newbury Press, CA: Sage.

Miller, G. E., Dopp, J. M., Myers, H. F., Stevens, S. Y., & Fahey, J. L. (1999). Psychosocial predictors of natural killer cell mobilization during marital conflict. *Health Psychology, 18,* 262–271.

Miller, J. L., & Miller, J. G. (1992). Greater than the sum of its parts. I. Subsystems which process both matter-energy and information. *Behavioral Science, 37,* 1–9.

Miller, P. C., Lefcourt, H. M., Holmes, J. G., Ware, E. E., & Saleh, W. E. (1986). Marital locus of control and marital problem solving. *Journal of Personality and Social Psychology, 51,* 161–169.

Miller, R. S. (1996). *Embarrassment: Poise and peril in everyday life.* New York: Guilford.

Milne, A. (1978). Custody of children in a divorce process: A family self-determination model. *Conciliation Courts Review, 16,* 1–16.

Minuchin, S. (1974). *Family and family therapy.* Cambridge, MA: Harvard University Press.

Moffitt, T. E., Caspi, A., Rutter, M., & Silva, P. (2001). *Sex differences in antisocial behavior: Conduct disorder, delinquency, and violence in the Dunedin longitudinal study.* New York: Cambridge University Press.

Molinsky, A. (2007). Cross-cultural code-switching: The psychological challenges of adapting behavior in foreign cultural interactions. *Academy of Management Review, 32,* 622–640.

Montemayor, R. (1986). Family variation in parent-adolescent storm and stress. *Journal of Adolescent Research, 1,* 15–31.

Moore, C. W. (2003). *The mediation process: Practical strategies for resolving conflict.* San Francisco: Jossey-Bass.

Moore, T. M., Eisler, R. M., & Franchina, J. J. (2000). Causal attributions and affective responses to provocative female partner behavior by abusive and nonabusive males. *Journal of Family Violence, 15,* 69–80.

Moracco, K. E., Runyan, C. W., Bowling, J. M., & Earp, J. A. L. (2007). Women's experiences with violence: A national study. *Women's Health Issues, 17,* 3–12.

Morgan, M., Stephens, C., Tuffin, K., Praat, A., & Lyons, A. (1997). Lawful possession: A constructionist approach to jealousy stories. *New Issues in Psychology, 15,* 71–81.

Morley, I., & Shockley-Zalabak, P. (1986). Conflict avoiders and compromisers: Toward an understanding of their organizational communication style. *Group and Organizational Behavior, 11*(4), 387–402.

Morrill, C., & Thomas, C. K. (1992). Organizational conflict management as disputing process: The problem of social escalation. *Human Communication Research, 18,* 400–425.

Morton, T. C., Alexander, J. F., & Altman, I. (1976). Communication and relationship definition. In G. R. Miller (Ed.), *Explorations in interpersonal communication* (pp. 105–126). Beverly Hills, CA: Sage.

Mouradian, V. E. (2001). Applying schema theory to intimate aggression: Individual and gender differences in representation of contexts and goals. *Journal of Applied Social Psychology, 31,* 376–408.

Muehlenhard, C. L., & Falcon, P. L. (1990). Men's heterosocial skill and attitudes toward women as predictors of verbal sexual coercion and forceful rape. *Sex Roles, 23,* 241–259.

Muehlenhard, C. L., & Linton, M. A. (1987). Date rape and sexual aggression in dating situations: Incidence and risk factors. *Journal of Personality and Social Psychology, 34,* 186–196.

Mullen, P. E. (1996). Jealousy and the emergence of violent and intimidating behaviours. *Criminal Behaviour and Mental Health, 6,* 199–205.

Mummendey, A., Linneweber, V., & Loschper, G. (1984). Aggression: From act to interaction. In A. Mummendey (Ed.), *Social psychology of aggression: From individual behavior to social interaction* (pp. 69–106). New York: Springer-Verlag.

Mumpower, J. L. (1991). The judgment policies of negotiators and the structure of negotiation problems. *Management Science, 37,* 1304–1324.

Murphy, J. E. (1988). Date abuse and forced intercourse among college students. In G. T. Hotaling, D. Finkelhor, J. T. Kirkpatrick, & M. A. Straus (Eds.), *Family abuse and its consequences: New directions in research* (pp. 285–296). Newbury Park, CA: Sage.

Myrtek, M. (2007). Type A behavior and hostility as independent risk factors for coronary heart disease. In J. Jordan, B. Bardé, & A. M. Zeiher (Eds.), *Contributions toward evidence-based psychocardiology: A systematic review of the literature* (pp. 159–183). Washington, DC: American Psychological Association.

National Association of Social Workers. (1991). *Standards of practice for social work mediators.* Washington, DC: Author.

Newell, S. E., & Stutman, R. K. (1988). The social confrontation episode. *Communication Monographs, 55,* 266–285.

Newton, D. A., & Burgoon, J. K. (1990). Nonverbal conflict behaviors: Functions, strategies, and tactics. In D. D. Cahn (Ed.), *Intimates in conflict: A communication perspective* (pp. 77–104). Hillsdale, NJ: Lawrence Erlbaum.

Newton, T. L., & Sanford, J. M. (2003). Conflict structure moderates associations between cardiovascular reactivity and negative marital interaction. *Health Psychology, 22,* 270–278.

Nicotera, A. M., & Dorsey, L. K. (2006). Individual and interactive processes in organizational conflict. In J. G. Oetzel & S. Ting-Toomey (Eds.), *The Sage handbook of conflict communication: Integrating theory, research, and practice* (pp. 293–325). Thousand Oaks, CA: Sage.

Noller, P. (2005). Communication with parents and other family members: The implications of family process for young people's well-being. In A. Williams & C.

Thurlow (Eds.), *Talking adolescence: Perspectives on communication in the teenage years* (pp. 207–227). New York: Peter Lang.

Noller, P., Atkin, S., Feeney, J. A., & Peterson, C. (2006). Family conflict and adolescents. In L. H. Turner & R. West (Eds.), *The family communication sourcebook* (pp. 165–182). Thousand Oaks, CA: Sage.

Noller, P., Feeney, J. A., Bonnell, D., & Callan, V. J. (1994). A longitudinal study of conflict in early marriage. *Journal of Social and Personal Relationships, 11,* 233–252.

Noller, P., Feeney, J. A., Sheehan, G., & Peterson, C. (2000). Marital conflict patterns: Links with family conflict and family members' perceptions of one another. *Personal Relationship, 7,* 79–94.

Notarius, C., & Markman, H. (1993). *We can work it out: Making sense of marital conflict.* New York: Putnam.

Nunamaker, J. E., Dennis, A. R., Valacich, J. S., & Vogel, D. R. (1991). Information technology for negotiating groups: Generating options for mutual gain. *Management Science, 37,* 1325–1345.

Nussbaum, J. F. (Ed.). (1989). *Life-span communication: Normative processes.* Hillsdale, NJ: Lawrence Erlbaum.

O'Connor, T., Hetherington, E., & Clingempeel, W. (1997). Systems and bidirectional influences in families. *Journal of Social and Personal Relationships, 14,* 491–504.

Oetzel, J. G. (1998). The effects of self-construal and ethnicity on self-reported conflict styles. *Communication Reports, 11,* 133–144.

Oetzel, J. G. (2001). Self-construals, communication processes, and group outcomes in homogenous and heterogeneous groups. *Small Group Research, 32,* 19–54.

Oetzel, J. G., Garcia, A., & Ting-Toomey, S. (2008). An analysis of the relationships among face concerns and facework behaviors in perceived conflict situations: A four-culture investigation. *International Journal of Conflict Management, 19,* 382–403.

Oetzel, J. G., & Ting-Toomey, S. (2003). Face concerns in interpersonal conflict: A cross-cultural empirical test of the face-negotiation theory. *Communication Research, 30,* 599–624.

Oetzel, J. G., Ting-Toomey, S., Masumoto, T., Yokochi, Y., Pan, X., Takai, J., & Wilcox, R. (2001). Face behaviors in interpersonal conflicts: A cross-cultural comparison of Germany, Japan, China, and the United States. *Communication Monographs 68,* 235–258.

Ognibene, T. C., & Collins, N. L. (1998). Adult attachment styles: Perceived social support and coping strategies. *Journal of Social and Personal Relationships, 15,* 323–345.

Ohbuchi, K.-I., Kameda, M., & Agarie, N. (1989). Apology as aggression control: Its role in mediating appraisal of and response to harm. *Journal of Personality and Social Psychology, 56,* 219–227.

O'Keefe, D. J., & Sypher, H. E. (1981). Cognitive complexity measures and the relationship of cognitive complexity to communication. *Human Communication Research, 8,* 72–92.

O'Leary, K. D., Smith Slep, A. M., & O'Leary, S. G. (2007). Multivariate models of men's and women's partner aggression. *Journal of Consulting and Clinical Psychology, 75,* 752–764.

O'Leary, R., & Bingham, L. B. (Eds.) (2003). *The promise and performance of environmental conflict resolution.* Washington, DC: Resources for the Future.

Olson, L. N. (2002a). "As ugly and painful as it was, it was effective": Individuals' unique assessment of communication competence during aggressive conflict episodes. *Communication Studies, 53,* 171–188.

Olson, L. N. (2002b). Exploring "common couple violence" in heterosexual romantic relationships. *Western Journal of Communication, 66,* 104–128.

Olson, L. N., & Golish, T. D. (2002). Topics of conflict and patterns of aggression in romantic relationships. *Southern Communication Journal, 67,* 180–200.

Olson, L. N., & Lloyd, S. A. (2005). "It depends on what you mean by starting": An exploration of how women define initiation of aggression and their motives for behaving aggressively. *Sex Roles, 53,* 603–617.

Orbe, M., & Everett, M. (2006). Interracial and interethnic conflict and communication in the United States. In J. Oetzel & S. Ting-Toomey (Eds.), *The Sage handbook of conflict communication* (pp. 575–594). Thousand Oaks, CA: Sage.

Orbe, M., & Spellers, R. (2005). From the margin to the center: Utilizing co-culture theory in diverse contexts. In W. B. Gudykunst (Ed.), *Theorizing about intercultural communication* (pp. 173–191). Thousand Oaks, CA: Sage.

Oreskovich, A. (2007, March 1). Dell's so-called earnings. Retrieved January 16, 2008, from http://www.thestreet.com/story/10341599/1/dells-so-called-earnings.html

Orvis, B. R., Kelley, H. H., & Butler, D. (1976). Attributional conflict in young couples. In J. H. Harvey, W. J. Ickes, & R. F. Kidd (Eds.), *New directions in attribution research* (Vol. 1). Hillsdale, NJ: Lawrence Erlbaum.

Ostermeyer, M. (1991). Conducting the mediation. In K. G. Duffy, J. W. Grosch, & P. V. Olczak (Eds.), *Community mediation* (pp. 91–104). New York: Guilford.

Ostroff, J. (2007, July 16). Can the UAW save Detroit? *The Kiplinger Letter.* Retrieved February 11, 2008, from http://www.kiplinger.com/businessresource/forecast/archive/big_three_negotiations_070716.html

Ostrov, J. M., & Collins, W. A. (2007). Social dominance in romantic relationships: A prospective longitudinal study of non-verbal processes. *Social Development, 16,* 580–595.

Overall, N. C., Fletcher, G. J. O., Simpson, J. A., & Sibley, C. G. (2009). Regulating partners in intimate relationships: The costs and benefits of different communication strategies. *Journal of Personality and Social Psychology, 96,* 620–639.

Papa, M. J., Auwal, M. A., & Singhal, A. (1995). Dialectic of control and emancipation in organizing for social change: A multitheoretic study of the Grameen Bank in Bangladesh. *Communication Theory, 5,* 189–223.

Papa, M. J., Auwal, M. A., & Singhal, A. (1997). Organizing for social change within concertive control systems: Member identification, discursive empowerment, and the masking of discipline. *Communication Monographs, 64,* 219–251.

Papa, M. J., & Canary, D. J. (1995). Conflict in organizations: A competence-based perspective. In A. M. Nicotera (Ed.), *Conflict in organizations: Communicative processes* (pp. 153–179). Albany: State University of New York Press.

Papa, M. J., Daniels, T. D., & Spiker, B. K. (2008). *Organizational communication: Perspectives and trends.* Los Angeles: Sage.

Papa, M. J., & Pood, E. A. (1988a). Coorientational accuracy and differentiation in the management of conflict. *Communication Research, 15,* 400–425.

Papa, M. J., & Pood, E. A. (1988b). Coorientational accuracy and organizational conflict: An examination of tactic selection and outcome satisfaction. *Communication Research, 15,* 3–28.

Papa, M. J., Singhal, A., & Papa, W. H. (2006). *Organizing for social change: A dialectic journey of theory and praxis.* New Delhi: Sage.

Parkhe, A. (1991). Interfirm diversity, organizational learning, and longevity in global strategic alliances. *Journal of International Business Studies, 22,* 579–601.

Parkhe, A. (1993). Strategic alliance structuring: A game theoretic and transaction cost examination of interfirm cooperation. *Academy of Management Journal, 36,* 794–829.

Parks, M. R. (1994). Communicative competence and interpersonal control. In M. L. Knapp & G. R. Miller (Eds.), *Handbook of interpersonal communication* (2nd ed., pp. 589–618). Thousand Oaks, CA: Sage.

Pasch, L. A., & Bradbury, T. N. (1998). Social support, conflict, and the development of marital dysfunction. *Journal of Consulting and Clinical Psychology, 66,* 219–230.

Pavitt, C., & Haight, L. (1985). The "competent communicator" as a cognitive prototype. *Human Communication Research, 12,* 225–242.

Pearce, W. B. (1976). The coordinated management of meaning: A rules-based theory of interpersonal communication. In G. R. Miller (Ed.), *Explorations in interpersonal communication* (pp. 17–35). Beverly Hills, CA: Sage.

Pearce, W. B., & Conklin, F. (1979). A model of hierarchical meanings in coherent conversations and a study of "indirect responses." *Communication Monographs, 46,* 75–87.

Pearce, W. B., & Cronen, V. (1980). *Communication, action, and meaning.* New York: Praeger.

Perlman, D., & Fehr, B. (1987). The development of intimate relationships. In D. Perlman & S. Duck (Eds.), *Intimate relationships* (pp. 13–42). Newbury Park, CA: Sage.

Perlman, M., Garfinkel, D., & Turrell, S. (2007). Parent and sibling influences on the quality of children's conflict behaviors across the preschool period. *Social Development, 16,* 619–640.

Perrow, L. R. (1979). *Complex organizations.* Glenview, IL: Scott, Foresman.

Peterson, D. R. (1983). Conflict. In H. H. Kelley, E. Berscheid, A. Christensen, J. H. Harvey, T. L. Huston, G. Levinger, E. McClintock, L. A. Peplau, & D. R. Peterson (Eds.), *Close relationships* (pp. 360–396). New York: W. H. Freeman.

Phelan, M. B., Hamberger, L. K., Guse, C. E., Edwards, S., Walczak, S., & Zosel, A. (2005). Domestic violence among male and female patients seeking emergency medical services. *Violence and Victims, 20,* 187–206.

Phillips, E., & Cheston, R. (1979). Conflict resolution: What works? *California Management Review, 21*(4), 76–83.

Pike, G. R., & Sillars, A. L. (1985). Reciprocity of marital communication. *Journal of Social and Personal Relationships, 2,* 303–324.

Pinto, M. B., Pinto, J. K., & Prescott, J. E. (1993). Antecedents and consequences of project team cross-functional cooperation. *Management Science, 38,* 1281–1297.

Pistole, M. C. (1989). Attachment in adult romantic relationships: Style of conflict resolution and relationship satisfaction. *Journal of Social and Personal Relationships, 6,* 505–510.

Pondy, L. R. (1967). Organizational conflict: Concepts and models. *Administrative Science Quarterly, 12,* 296–320.

Powers, S. I., Pietromonaco, P. R., Gunlicks, M., & Sayer, A. (2006). Dating couples' attachment styles and patterns of cortisol reactivity and recovery in response to a relationship conflict. *Journal of Personality and Social Psychology, 90,* 613–628.

Putnam, L. L. (2006). Definitions and approaches to conflict and communication. In J. G. Oetzel & S. Ting-Toomey (Eds.), *The Sage handbook of conflict communication: Integrating theory, research, and practice* (pp. 1–32). Thousand Oaks, CA: Sage.

Putnam, L. L., & Bullis, C. (1984). *Intergroup relations and issue redefinition in teacher bargaining.* Paper presented at the annual meeting of the International Communication Association, San Francisco, CA.

Putnam, L. L., & Jones, T. S. (1982). Reciprocity in negotiations: An analysis of bargaining interaction. *Communication Monographs, 49,* 171–191.

Putnam, L. L., & Poole, M. S. (1987). Conflict and negotiation. In F. Jablin, L. Putnam, K. Roberts, & L. Porter (Eds.), *The handbook of organizational communication* (pp. 549–599). Beverly Hills, CA: Sage.

Putnam, L. L., & Wilson, C. E. (1982). Communicative strategies in organizational conflicts: Reliability and validity of a measurement scale. In M. Burgoon (Ed.), *Communication yearbook 6* (pp. 629–652). Beverly Hills, CA: Sage.

Query, L. R. (2001). The quality of family relationships in the prediction of child behavior problems. *Dissertation Abstracts International: Section B: The Sciences and Engineering, 61*(12-B), 6718.

Rahim, M. A. (1983). A measure of styles of handling interpersonal conflict. *Academy of Management Journal, 26,* 368–376.

Rahim, M. A. (1992). *Managing conflict in organizations* (2nd ed.). Westport, CT: Praeger.

Raush, H. L., Barry, W. A., Hertel, R. J., & Swain, M. A. (1974). *Communication, conflict, and marriage.* San Francisco: Jossey-Bass.

Reimer, J. (2006, September 14). Dell goes AMD on the desktop. *Ars Technica.* Retrieved January 30, 2008, from http://arstechnica.com/news.ars/post/20060914-7739.html?rel

Rempel, J. K., Ross, M., & Holmes, J. G. (2001). Trust and communicated attributions in close relationships. *Journal of Personality and Social Psychology, 81,* 57–64.

Renwick, P. A. (1975). Perception and management of superior-subordinate conflict. *Organizational Behavior and Human Performance, 13,* 444–456.

Retzinger, S. M. (1991). *Violent emotions: Shame and rage in marital quarrels.* Newbury Park, CA: Sage.

Retzinger, S. M. (1995). Shame and anger in personal relationships. In S. Duck & J. T. Wood (Eds.), *Confronting relationship challenges* (pp. 22–42). Thousand Oaks, CA: Sage.

Richardson, D. S., & Hammock, G. S. (2007). Social context of human aggression: Are we paying too much attention to gender? *Aggression and Violent Behavior, 12,* 417–426.

Richmond, M. K., & Stocker, C. M. (2006). Associations between family cohesion and adolescent siblings' externalizing behavior. *Journal of Family Psychology, 4,* 663–669.

Ridley, C. A., & Feldman, C. M. (2003). Female domestic violence toward male partners: Exploring conflict responses and outcomes. *Journal of Family Violence, 18,* 157–171.

Riesch, S. K., Bush, L. Nelson, C. J., Ohm, B. J., Portz, P. A., Abell, B., Wightman, M. R., & Jenkins, P. (2000). Topics of conflict between parents and young adolescents. *Journal of the Society of Pediatric Nurses, 5,* 27–40.

Rifkin, J., Millen, J., & Cobb, S. (1991). Toward a new discourse for mediation: A critique of neutrality. *Mediation Quarterly, 9,* 151–164.

Riger, S., Staggs, S. L., & Schewe, P. (2004). Intimate partner violence as an obstacle to employment among mothers affected by welfare reform. *Journal of Social Issues, 60,* 801–818.

Rinaldi, C. M., & Howe, N. (2003). Perceptions of constructive and destructive conflict within and across family subsystems. *Infant and Child Development, 12,* 441–459.

Roberts, J. C. (2007). Barroom aggression in Hoboken, New Jersey: Don't blame the bouncers! *Journal of Drug Education, 37,* 429–445.

Roberts, N., & Noller, P. (1998). The associations between adult attachment and couple violence: The role of communication patterns and relationship satisfaction. In J. A. Simpson & W. S. Rholes (Eds.), *Attachment theory and close relationships* (pp. 317–350). New York: Guilford.

Robin, A. L., & Foster, S. L. (1989). *Negotiating parent-adolescent conflict: A behavioral systems approach*. New York: Guilford.

Robles, T. F., & Kiecolt-Glaser, J. K. (2003). The physiology of marriage: Pathways to health. *Physiology & Behavior, 79,* 409–416.

Rogan, R. G., & La France, B. H. (2003). An examination of the relationship between verbal aggressiveness, conflict management strategies, and conflict interaction goals. *Communication Quarterly, 51,* 458–469.

Rogers, E. M. (2003). *Diffusion of innovations* (5th ed.). New York: Free Press.

Roloff, M. E., & Janiszewski, C. A. (1989). Overcoming obstacles to interpersonal compliance: A principle of message construction. *Human Communication Research, 16,* 33–61.

Roloff, M. E., & Johnson, K. L. (2002). Serial arguing over the relational life course: Antecedents and consequences. In A. L. Vangelisti, H. T. Reis, & M. A. Fitzpatrick (Eds.), *Stability and change in relationships* (pp. 107–128). New York: Cambridge University Press.

Roloff, M. E., & Miller, C. W. (2006). Mulling about family conflict and communication: What we know and what we need to know. In L. H. Turner & R. West (Eds.), *The family communication sourcebook* (pp. 143–164). Thousand Oaks, CA: Sage.

Ronfeldt, H. M., Kimerling, R., & Arias, I. (1998). Satisfaction with relationship power and the perpetration of dating violence. *Journal of Marriage and the Family, 60,* 70–78.

Rook, K. S. (1998). Investigating the positive and negative sides of personal relationships: Through a lens darkly? In B. H. Spitzberg & W. R. Cupach (Eds.), *The dark side of close relationships* (pp. 369–393). Mahwah, NJ: Lawrence Erlbaum.

Rosen, L. N., Parmley, A. M., Knudson, K. H., & Fancher, P. (2002). Gender differences in the experience of intimate partner violence among active duty U.S. army soldiers. *Military Medicine, 167,* 959–963.

Rosenbaum, A., & O'Leary, K. D. (1981). Marital violence: Characteristics of abusive couples. *Journal of Consulting and Clinical Psychology, 49,* 63–71.

Ross, R. G., & DeWine, S. (1988). Assessing the Ross-DeWine conflict management message style (CMMS). *Management Communication Quarterly, 1,* 414–429.

Rudd, J. E., & Burant, P. A. (1995). A study of women's compliance-gaining behaviors in violent and non-violent relationships. *Communication Research Reports, 12,* 134–144.

Rule, C. (2002). *Online dispute resolution for business*. San Francisco: Jossey-Bass.

Rusbult, C. E. (1987). Responses to dissatisfaction in close relationships: The exit-voice-loyalty-neglect model. In D. Perlman & S. Duck (Eds.), *Intimate relationships: Development, dynamics, and deterioration* (pp. 209–337). Newbury Park, CA: Sage.

Rusbult, C. E., Drigotas, S. M., & Verette, J. (1994). The investment model: An interdependence analysis of commitment processes and relationship maintenance phenomena. In D. J. Canary & L. Stafford (Eds.), *Communication and relational maintenance* (pp. 115–139). New York: Academic Press.

Rusbult, C. E., Johnson, D. J., & Morrow, G. D. (1986). Predicting satisfaction and commitment in adult romantic relationships: An assessment of the generalizability of the investment model. *Social Psychological Quarterly, 49,* 81–89.

Rusbult, C. E., Verette, J., Whitney, G. A., Slovik, L. F., & Lipkus, I. (1991). Accommodation processes in close relationships: Theory and preliminary empirical evidence. *Journal of Personality and Social Psychology, 60,* 53–78.

Russell, J. A., & Fehr, B. (1994). Fuzzy concepts in a fuzzy hierarchy: Varieties of anger. *Journal of Personality and Social Psychology, 67,* 186–205.

Sabourin, T. C. (1995). The role of negative reciprocity in spouse abuse: A relational control analysis. *Journal of Applied Communication Research, 23,* 271–283.

Sagrestano, L. M., Heavey, C. L., & Christensen, A. (1999). Perceived power and physical violence in marital conflict. *Journal of Social Issues, 55,* 65–79.

Saltzman, K., Holden, G., & Holahan, C. (2005). The psychobiology of children exposed to marital violence. *Journal of Clinical Child and Adolescent Psychology, 34,* 129–139.

Samter, W., & Cupach, W. R. (1998). Friendly fire: Topical variations in conflict among same- and cross-sex friends. *Communication Studies, 49,* 121–138.

Sander, F. E. A., & Goldberg, S. B. (1994). Fitting the forum to the fuss: A user-friendly guide to selecting an ADR procedure. *Negotiation Journal, 10,* 49–68.

Sanford, K. (2003). Problem-solving conversations in marriage: Does it matter what topics couples discuss. *Personal Relationships, 10,* 97–112.

Sanford, K. (2006). Communication during marital conflict: When couples alter their appraisal, they change their behavior. *Journal of Family Psychology, 20,* 256–265.

Sarantakos, S. (2004). Deconstructing self-defense in wife-to-husband violence. *Journal of Men's Studies, 12,* 277–296.

Satir, V. (1964). *Conjoint family therapy.* Palo Alto, CA: Science & Behavior Books.

Schaap, C., Buunk, B., & Kerkstra, A. (1988). Marital conflict resolution. In P. Noller & M. A. Fitzpatrick (Eds.), *Perspectives on marital interaction* (pp. 203–244). Philadelphia: Multilingual Matters.

Schacter, S., & Singer, J. E. (1962). Cognitive, social, and physiological determinants of emotional state. *Psychological Review, 69,* 379–399.

Scher, S. J., & Darley, J. M. (1997). How effective are the things people say to apologize? Effects of the realization of the apology speech act. *Journal of Psycholinguistic Research, 26,* 127–140.

Schlenker, B. R. (1980). *Impression management: The self-concept, social identity, and interpersonal relations.* Monterey, CA: Brooks/Cole.

Schönbach, P. (1990). *Account episodes: The management or escalation of conflict.* Cambridge: Cambridge University Press.

Schreier, L. S. (2002). Emotional intelligence and mediation training. *Conflict Resolution Quarterly, 20,* 99–120.

Schrodt, P., & Afifi, T. (2007). Communication processes that predict young adults' feelings of being caught and their associations with mental health and family satisfaction. *Communication Monographs, 74,* 200–228.

Schutte, N. S., Malouff, J. M., & Doyle, J. S. (1988). The relationship between characteristics of the victim, persuasive techniques of the batterer, and returning to a battering relationship. *Journal of Social Psychology, 128,* 605–610.

Schütz, A. (1999). It was your fault! Self-serving biases in autobiographical accounts of conflicts in married couples. *Journal of Social and Personal Relationships, 16,* 193–208.

Scott, W. (2008). Communication strategies in early adolescent conflict: An attributional approach. *Conflict Resolution Quarterly, 25,* 375–400.

Segrin, C., Hanzal, A., & Domschke, T. J. (2009). Accuracy and bias in newlywed couples' perceptions of conflict styles and the association with marital satisfaction. *Communication Monographs, 76,* 207–233.

Selman, R. L. (1980). *The growth of interpersonal understanding: Developmental and clinical analyses.* New York: Academic Press.

Senge, P., Scharmer, C., Jaworski, J., & Flowers, B. (2004). *Presence: Human purpose and the field of the future.* Cambridge, MA: The Society for Organizational Learning, Inc.

Sereno, K. K., Welch, M., & Braaten, D. (1987). Interpersonal conflict: Effects of variations in manner of expressing anger and justifications for anger upon perceptions of appropriateness, competence, and satisfaction. *Journal of Applied Communication Research, 15,* 128–143.

Serran, G., & Firestone, P. (2004). Intimate partner homicide: A review of the male proprietariness and the self-defense theories. *Aggression and Violent Behavior, 9,* 1–15.

Shackelford, T. K., Goetz, A. T., Buss, D. M., Euler, H. A., & Hoier, S. (2005). When we hurt the ones we love: Predicting violence against women from men's mate retention. *Personal Relationships, 12,* 447–463.

Shafer, P., Schwartz, D., Kirkson, D., & O'Connor, C. (1987). Emotion knowledge: Further exploration of a prototype approach. *Journal of Personality and Social Psychology, 52,* 1061–1086.

Shan, W. (1990). An empirical analysis of organizational strategies by entrepreneurial high-technology firms. *Strategic Management Journal, 11,* 129–139.

Shantz, C. U. (1987). Conflicts between children. *Child Development, 58,* 283–305.

Shantz, C. U., & Hobart, C. J. (1989). Social conflict and development: Peers and siblings. In T. J. Berndt & G. W. Ladd (Eds.), *Peer relationships in child development* (pp. 71–94). New York: Wiley.

Shehabuddin, R. (1992). *Empowering rural women: The impact of Grameen Bank in Bangladesh.* Dhaka, Bangladesh: Grameen Bank.

Shimanoff, S. (1980). *Communication rules: Theory and research.* Beverly Hills, CA: Sage.

Shuter, R., & Turner, L. (1997). African American and European American women in the workplace: Perceptions of conflict communication. *Management Communication Quarterly, 11,* 74–96.

Sidman, M. (1989). *Coercion and its fallout.* Boston: Author's Cooperative.

Sillars, A. L. (1980a). The sequential and distributional structure of conflict interactions as a function of attributions concerning the locus of responsibility and stability of conflicts. In D. Nimmo (Ed.), *Communication yearbook 4* (pp. 217–235). New Brunswick, NJ: Transaction.

Sillars, A. L. (1980b). The stranger and the spouse as target persons for compliance-gaining strategies: A subjective expected utility model. *Human Communication Research, 6,* 265–279.

Sillars, A. L. (1981). Attributions and interpersonal conflict resolution. In J. H. Harvey, W. Ickes, & R. F. Kidd (Eds.), *New directions in attribution research* (Vol. 3, pp. 281–306). Hillsdale, NJ: Lawrence Erlbaum.

Sillars, A. L. (1986). *Procedures for coding interpersonal conflict (revised)* (Manual). Missoula: University of Montana, Department of Interpersonal Communication.

Sillars, A. L. (1998). (Mis)Understanding. In B. H. Spitzberg & W. R. Cupach (Eds.), *The dark side of close relationships* (pp. 73–102). Mahwah, NJ: Lawrence Erlbaum.

Sillars, A., Canary, D. J., & Tafoya, M. (2004). Communication, conflict, and the quality of family relationships. In A. L. Vangelisti (Ed.), *Handbook of family communication* (pp. 413–446). Mahwah, NJ: Lawrence Erlbaum.

Sillars, A. L., Coletti, S. F., Parry, D., & Rogers, M. A. (1982). Coding verbal conflict tactics: Nonverbal and perceptual correlates of the "avoidance-distributive integrative" distinction. *Human Communication Research, 9,* 83–95.

Sillars, A., Koerner, A., & Fitzpatrick, M. A. (2005). Communication and understanding in parent-adolescent relationships. *Human Communication Research, 31,* 102–128.

Sillars, A., Leonard, K. E., Roberts, L. J., & Dun, T. (2002). Cognition and communication during marital conflict: How alcohol affects subjective coding of interaction in aggressive and nonaggressive couples. In P. Noller & J. A. Feeney (Eds.), *Understanding marriage: Developments in the study of couple interaction* (pp. 85–112). Cambridge: Cambridge University Press.

Sillars, A. L., Pike, G. R., Jones, T. S., & Murphy, M. A. (1984). Communication and understanding in marriage. *Human Communication Research, 10,* 317–350.

Sillars, A., Roberts, L. J., Dun, T., & Leonard, K. (2001). Stepping into the stream of thought: Cognition during marital conflict. In V. Manusov & J. H. Harvey (Eds.), *Attribution, communication behavior, and close relationships* (pp. 193–210). Cambridge: Cambridge University Press.

Sillars, A., Roberts, L. J., Leonard, K. E., & Dun, T. (2000). Cognition during marital conflict: The relationship of thought and talk. *Journal of Social and Personal Relationships, 17,* 479–502.

Sillars, A. L., & Weisberg, J. (1987). Conflict as a social skill. In M. E. Roloff & G. R. Miller (Eds.), *Interpersonal processes: New directions in communication research* (pp. 140–171). Newbury Park, CA: Sage.

Sillars, A. L., Weisberg, J., Burggraf, C. S., & Zietlow, P. H. (1990). Communication and understanding revisited: Married couples' understanding and recall of conversations. *Communication Research, 17,* 500–532.

Sillars, A. L., & Wilmot, W. W. (1989). Marital communication across the life-span. In J. F. Nussbaum (Ed.), *Life-span communication: Normative processes* (pp. 225–253). Hillsdale, NJ: Lawrence Erlbaum.

Sillars, A. L., & Wilmot, W. W. (1994). Communication strategies in conflict and mediation. In J. A. Daly & J. M. Wiemann (Eds.), *Strategic interpersonal communication* (pp. 163–190). Hillsdale, NJ: Lawrence Erlbaum.

Simon, T. R., Anderson, M., Thompson, M. P., Crosby, A. E., Shelley, G., & Sacks, J. J. (2001). Attitudinal acceptance of intimate partner violence among U.S. adults. *Violence and Victims, 16,* 115–126.

Simon, V. A., Kobielski, S. J., & Martin, S. (2008). Conflict beliefs, goals, and behavior in romantic relationships during late adolescence. *Journal of Youth and Adolescence, 37,* 324–335.

Simpson, J. A., Collings, W. A., Tran, S. S., & Haydon, K. C. (2007). Attachment and the experience and expression of emotion in romantic relationships: A developmental perspective. *Journal of Personality and Social Psychology, 92,* 355–367.

Simpson, J. A., Rholes, W. S., & Phillips, D. (1996). Conflict in close relationships: An attachment perspective. *Journal of Personality and Social Psychology, 71,* 899–914.

Smetana, J. G. (1988). Adolescents' and parents' conceptions of parental authority. *Child Development, 59,* 321–335.

Smetana, J. G. (1989). Adolescents' and parents' reasoning about actual family conflict. *Child Development, 60,* 1052–1067.

Smith, J. L. (2005). Effects of parent mediation in sibling disputes on children's socio-cognitive skills and conflict interactions. *Dissertation Abstracts International: Section B. Sciences and Engineering, 66*(6-B), 3470.

Smith, K. A., & Forehand, R. (1986). Parent-adolescent conflict: Comparisons and predictions of the perceptions of mother, fathers, and daughters. *Journal of Early Adolescence, 6,* 353–367.

Smith, P., Dugan, S., Peterson, M., & Leung, K. (1998). Individualism, collectivism and the handling of disagreement: A 23 country study. *International Journal of Intercultural Relations, 22,* 351–367.

Smith, P. H., Thornton, G. E., DeVellis, R., Earp, J., & Coker, A. L. (2002). A population-based study of the prevalence and distinctiveness of battering, physical assault, and sexual assault in intimate relationships. *Violence Against Women, 8,* 1208–1232.

Solidarity. (2007). "Big Three" auto contracts: Was the loss inevitable? Retrieved February 11, 2008, from http://www.solidarity-us.org/node/1236/print

Solomon, D. H., & Samp, J. A. (1998). Power and problem appraisal: Perceptual foundations of the chilling effect in dating relationships. *Journal of Social and Personal Relationships, 15,* 191–209.

Song, M., Dyer, B., & Thieme, R. J. (2006). Conflict management and innovation performance: An integrated contingency perspective. *Journal of the Academy of Marketing Science, 34,* 341–356.

Song, X. M., Xie, J., & Dyer, B. (2000). Antecedents and consequences of marketing managers' conflict-handling behaviors. *Journal of Marketing, 64,* 50–66.

Spitzberg, B. H. (1998). Sexual coercion. In B. H. Spitzberg & W. R. Cupach (Eds.), *The dark side of close relationships* (pp. 179–232). Mahwah, NJ: Lawrence Erlbaum.

Spitzberg, B. H. (1999). An analysis of empirical estimates of rape and sexual coercion. *Violence and Victims, 14,* 241–260.

Spitzberg, B. H. (2000). What is good communication? *Journal of the Association for Communication Administration, 29,* 103–119.

Spitzberg, B. H. (2001). The status of attribution theory *qua* theory in personal relationships. In V. Manusov & J. H. Harvey (Eds.), *Attribution, communication behavior, and close relationships* (pp. 353–371). Cambridge: Cambridge University Press.

Spitzberg, B. H., Canary, D. J., & Cupach, W. R. (1994). A competence-based approach to the study of interpersonal conflict. In D. D. Cahn (Ed.), *Conflict in personal relationships* (pp. 183–202). Hillsdale, NJ: Lawrence Erlbaum.

Spitzberg, B. H., & Chagnon, G. (2009). Conceptualizing intercultural communication competence. In D. K. Deardoff (Ed.), *The Sage handbook of intercultural competence* (pp. 2–52). Thousand Oaks, CA: Sage.

Spitzberg, B. H., & Cupach, W. R. (1984). *Interpersonal communication competence.* Beverly Hills, CA: Sage.

Spitzberg, B. H., & Cupach, W. R. (1989). *Handbook of interpersonal competence research.* New York: Springer-Verlag.

Spitzberg, B. H., & Cupach, W. R. (2002). Interpersonal skills. In M. L. Knapp & J. R. Daly (Eds.), *Handbook of interpersonal communication* (3rd ed., pp. 564–611). Newbury Park, CA: Sage.

Spitzberg, B. H., & Hecht, M. L. (1984). A component model of relational competence. *Human Communication Research, 10,* 575–599.

Sprey, J. (1971). On the management of conflict in families. *Journal of Marriage and the Family, 33,* 722–731.

Stafford, L., & Bayer, C. L. (1993). *Interaction between parents and children.* Newbury Park, CA: Sage.

Stafford, L., & Daly, J. A. (1984). Conversational memory: The effects of recall mode and memory expectancies on remembrances of natural conversations. *Human Communication Research, 10,* 379–402.

Stamp, G. H. (1994). The appropriation of the parental role through communication during the transition to parenthood. *Communication Monographs, 61*, 89–112.

Stamp, G. H., & Sabourin, T. C. (1995). Accounting for violence: An analysis of male spousal abuse narratives. *Journal of Applied Communication Research, 23*, 284–307.

Steinberg, L. (2001). We know some things: Parent-adolescent relationships in retrospect and prospect. *Journal of Research on Adolescence, 11*, 1–19.

Steinberg, L., & Morris, A. S. (2001). Adolescent development. *Annual Review of Psychology, 52*, 83–110.

Steinmetz, S. K. (1977). *The cycle of violence: Assertive, aggressive, and abusive family interaction.* New York: Praeger.

Sternberg, R. J., & Dobson, D. M. (1987). Resolving interpersonal conflicts: An analysis of stylistic consistency. *Journal of Personality and Social Psychology, 52*, 794–812.

Sternberg, R. L., & Soriano, L. J. (1984). Styles of conflict resolution. *Journal of Personality and Social Psychology, 47*, 115–126.

Stets, J. E. (1988). *Domestic violence and control.* New York: Springer-Verlag.

Stets, J. E. (1990). Verbal and physical aggression in marriage. *Journal of Marriage and the Family, 52*, 501–514.

Stets, J. E. (1992). Interactive processes in dating aggression: A national study. *Journal of Marriage and the Family, 54*, 165–177.

Stets, J. E. (1995). Modelling control in relationships. *Journal of Marriage and the Family, 57*, 489–501.

Stets, J. E., & Burke, P. J. (2005). Identity verification, control, and aggression in marriage. *Social Psychological Quarterly, 68*, 160–178.

Stets, J. E., & Pirog-Good, M. A. (1989). Patterns of physical and sexual abuse for men and women in dating relationships: A descriptive analysis. *Journal of Family Violence, 4*, 63–76.

Stith, S. M., Smith, D. B., Penn, C. E., Ward, D. B., & Tritt, D. (2004). Intimate partner physical abuse perpetration and victimization risk factors: A meta-analytic review. *Aggression and Violent Behavior, 10*, 65–98.

Storms, M. D. (1973). Videotape and the attribution process: Reversing actors' and observers' points of view. *Journal of Personality and Social Psychology, 27*, 165–175.

Storti, C. (2001). *Old world/new world.* Yarmouth, ME: Intercultural Press.

Story, L. B., & Repetti, R. (2006). Daily occupational stressors and marital behavior. *Journal of Family Psychology, 20*, 690–700.

Straight, E. S., Harper, F. W. K., & Arias, I. (2003). The impact of partner psychological abuse on health behaviors and health status in college women. *Journal of Interpersonal Violence, 18*, 1035–1054.

Straus, M. A. (1979). Measuring intrafamily conflict and violence: The conflict tactics (CT) scales. *Journal of Marriage and the Family, 41*, 75–88.

Straus, M. A. (1994). *Beating the devil out of them: Corporal punishment in American families.* New York: Lexington Books.

Straus, M. A. (2001). Physical aggression in the family: Prevalence rates, links to nonfamily violence, and implications for primary prevention of societal violence. In M. Martinez (Ed.), *Prevention and control of aggression and the impact on its victims* (pp. 181–200). New York: Kluwer Academic/Plenum.

Straus, M. A. (2006). Future research on gender symmetry in physical assaults on partners. *Violence Against Women, 12*, 1086–1097.

Straus, M. A. (2008). Dominance and symmetry in partner violence by male and female university students in 32 nations. *Children and Youth Services Review, 30*, 252–275.

Straus, M. A., & Douglas, E. M. (2004). A short form of the Revised Conflict Tactics Scales, and typologies for severity and mutuality. *Violence and Victims, 19,* 507–520.

Sue, D. W., & Sue, D. (2003). *Counseling the culturally diverse: Theory and practice* (4th ed.). New York: Wiley.

Sugarman, D. B., & Frankel, S. L. (1996). Patriarchal ideology and wife-assault: A meta-analytic review. *Journal of Family Violence, 11,* 13–40.

Sugarman, D. B., & Hotaling, G. T. (1989). Dating violence: Prevalence, context, and risk markers. In M. A. Pirog-Good & J. E. Stets (Eds.), *Violence in dating relationships: Emerging social issues* (pp. 3–32). New York: Praeger.

Suitor, J. J., & Pillemer, K. (1987). The presence of adult children: A source of stress for elderly couples' marriages? *Journal of Marriage and the Family, 49,* 717–725.

Swan, S., Gambone, L., & Fields, A. (2005, February). *Technical report for "An empirical examination of women's use of violence in intimate relationships"* (NCJ 208611). Washington, DC: U.S. Department of Justice.

Sweeting, H. (2001). Our family, whose perspective? An investigation of children's family life and health. *Journal of Adolescence, 24,* 229–250.

Sycara, K. P. (1991). Problem restructuring in negotiation. *Management Science, 37,* 1248–1268.

Tafrate, R. C., Kassinove, H., & Dundin, L. (2002). Anger episodes in high- and lo-trait-anger community adults. *Journal of Clinical Psychology, 58,* 1573–1590.

Taft, C. T., Vogt, D. S., Mechanic, M. B., & Resick, P. A. (2007). Posttraumatic stress disorder and physical symptoms among women seeking help for relationship aggression. *Journal of Family Psychology, 21,* 354–362.

Tangney, J. P., Hill-Barlow, D., Wagner, P. E., Marschall, D. E., Borenstein, J. K., Sanftner, J., Mohr, T., & Gramzow, R. (1996). Assessing individual differences in constructive versus destructive responses to anger across the lifespan. *Journal of Personality and Social Psychology, 70,* 780–796.

Tangney, J. P., & Salovey, P. (1999). Problematic social emotions: Shame, guilt, jealousy, and envy. In R. M. Kowalski & M. R. Leary (Eds.), *The social psychology of emotional and behavioral problems* (pp. 167–195). Washington, DC: American Psychological Association.

Tavris, C. (1984). On the wisdom of counting to ten: Personal and social dangers of anger expression. *Review of Personality and Social Psychology, 5,* 170–191.

Taylor, C. A., & Sorenson, S. B. (2005). Community-based norms about intimate partner violence: Putting attributions of fault and responsibility into context. *Sex Roles, 53,* 573–589.

Tedeschi, J. T., & Felson, R. B. (1994). *Violence, aggression, & coercive actions.* Washington, DC: American Psychological Association.

Teece, D. (1987). Capturing value from technological innovation: Integration, strategic partnering, and licensing decisions. In B. Guile & H. Brooks (Eds.), *Technology and global industry* (pp. 65–95). Washington, DC: National Academy Press.

Thalhofer, N. N. (1993). Intergroup differentiation and reduction of intergroup conflict. *Small Group Research, 24*(1), 28–43.

Theiss, J. A., & Solomon, D. H. (2006). A relational turbulence model of communication about irritations in romantic relationships. *Communication Research, 33,* 391–418.

Thibaut, J., & Kelley, H. (1959). *The social psychology of groups.* New York: Wiley.

Thich, N. H. (1998). *Mindful living.* Berkeley, CA: Parallax Press.

Thomsen, D. G., & Gilbert, D. G. (1998). Factors characterizing marital conflict states and traits: Physiological, affective, behavioral and neurotic variable contributions to marital conflict and satisfaction. *Personality and Individual Differences,* *25,* 833–855.

Ting-Toomey, S. (1983). An analysis of verbal communication patterns in high and low marital adjustment groups. *Human Communication Research, 9,* 306–319.

Ting-Toomey, S. (1986). Conflict communication styles in Black and White subjective cultures. In Y. Y. Kim (Ed.), *Interethinic communication: Current research* (pp. 75–88). Newbury Park, CA: Sage.

Ting-Toomey, S. (1988). Intercultural conflicts: A face-negotiation theory. In Y. Y. Kim & W. B. Gudykunst (Eds.), *Theories in intercultural communication* (pp. 213–235). Newbury Park, CA: Sage.

Ting-Toomey, S. (1999). *Communicating across cultures.* New York: Guilford.

Ting-Toomey, S. (2004). Translating conflict face-negotiation theory into practice. In D. Landis, J. Bennett, & M. Bennett (Eds.), *Handbook of intercultural training* (3rd ed., pp. 217–248). Thousand Oaks, CA: Sage.

Ting-Toomey, S. (2005a). Identity negotiation theory: Crossing cultural boundaries. In W. B. Gudykunst (Ed.), *Theorizing about intercultural communication* (pp. 211–234). Thousand Oaks, CA: Sage.

Ting-Toomey, S. (2005b). The matrix of face: An updated face-negotiation theory. In W. B. Gudykunst (Ed.), *Theorizing about intercultural communication* (pp. 71–92). Thousand Oaks, CA: Sage.

Ting-Toomey, S., & Chung, L. C. (2005). *Understanding intercultural communication.* Los Angeles: Roxbury.

Ting-Toomey, S., & Kurogi, A. (1998). Facework competence in intercultural conflict: An updated face-negotiation theory. *International Journal of Intercultural Relations* *22,* 187–225.

Ting-Toomey, S., & Oetzel, J. G. (2001). *Managing intercultural conflict effectively.* Thousand Oaks, CA: Sage.

Ting-Toomey, S., Oetzel, J. G., & Yee-Jung, K. (2001). Self-construal types and conflict management styles. *Communication Reports, 14,* 87–104.

Ting-Toomey, S., & Takai, J. (2006). Explaining intercultural conflict: Promising approaches and directions. In J. Oetzel & S. Ting-Toomey (Eds.), *The Sage handbook of conflict communication* (pp. 691–723). Thousand Oaks, CA: Sage.

Ting-Toomey, S., Yee-Jung, K., Shapiro, R., Garcia, W., Wright, T., & Oetzel, J. G. (2000). Ethnic/cultural identity salience and conflict styles in four U.S. ethnic groups. *International Journal of Intercultural Relations, 24,* 47–81.

Tjaden, P., & Thoennes, N. (1998, November). *Prevalence, incidence, and consequences of* *violence against women: Findings from the national violence against women survey.* National Institute of Justice (NCJ 172837). Washington, DC: U.S. Department of Justice.

Tjaden, P., & Thoennes, N. (2000). *Extent, nature, and consequences of intimate partner* *violence: Findings from the National Violence Against Women Survey* (NCJ 181867). Washington, DC: U.S. Department of Justice, Office of Justice Programs.

Tjaden, P., Thoennes, N., & Allison, C. J. (2000). Comparing stalking victimization from legal and victim perspectives. *Violence and Victims, 15,* 7–22.

Tjosvold, D. (1982). Effects of approach to controversy on supervisors' incorporation of subordinates' information in decision making. *Journal of Applied Psychology, 67,* 189–191.

Tjosvold, D. (1983). Effect of supervisor's influence orientation on their decision making controversy. *Journal of Psychology, 113,* 175–182.

Tjosvold, D., & Chia, L. C. (1989). Conflict between managers and workers: The role of cooperation and competition. *Journal of Social Psychology, 129,* 235–247.

Tonizzo, S., Howells, K., Day, A., Reidpath, D., & Froyland, I. (2000). Attributions of negative partner behavior by men who physically abuse their partners. *Journal of Family Violence, 15,* 155–167.

Tracy, K. (1990). The many faces of facework. In H. Giles & W. P. Robinson (Eds.), *Handbook of language and social psychology* (pp. 209–226). New York: Wiley.

Turner, R. J., Russell, D., Glover, R., & Hutto, P. (2007). The social antecedents of anger proneness in young adulthood. *Journal of Health and Social Behavior, 48,* 68–83.

UAW: Contract may yield better products. (2008, January 17). Retrieved February 11, 2008, from http://news.moneycentral.msn.com/ticker/article.aspx?Feed= AP&Date=20080117&ID =8059883&Symbol=GM

Umbreit, M. S. (2001). *The handbook of victim offender mediation.* San Francisco: Jossey-Bass.

U.S. Department of Commerce. (2007). *The road ahead for the U.S. auto market.* Washington, DC: U.S. Government Printing Office.

Utley, M. E., Richardson, D. R., & Pilkington, C. J. (1989). Personality and interpersonal conflict management. *Personality and Individual Differences, 10,* 287–293.

van de Vliert, E., & Euwema, M. C. (1994). Agreeableness and activeness as components of conflict behaviors. *Journal of Personality and Social Psychology, 66,* 674–687.

Vangelisti, A. L. (1992). Communication problems in committed relationships: An attributional analysis. In J. L. Harvey, T. L. Orbuch, & A. L. Weber (Eds.), *Attributions, accounts, and close relationships* (pp. 144–164). New York: Springer-Verlag.

Vangelisti, A. L. (1994). Messages that hurt. In W. R. Cupach & B. H. Spitzberg (Eds.), *The dark side of interpersonal communication* (pp. 53–82). Hillsdale, NJ: Lawrence Erlbaum.

Vangelisti, A. L. (2007). Communicating hurt. In B. H. Spitzberg & W. R. Cupach (Eds.), *The dark side of interpersonal communication* (2nd ed., pp. 121–142). Mahwah, NJ: Erlbaum.

Vincent, J. P., Weiss, R. L., & Birchler, G. R. (1975). A behavioral analysis of problem-solving in married and stranger dyads. *Behavior Therapy, 6,* 475–487.

Vuchinich, S. (1990). The sequential organization of closing in verbal family conflict. In A. D. Grimshaw (Ed.), *Conflict talk: Sociolinguistic investigations of arguments in conversations* (pp. 118–138). New York: Cambridge University Press.

Wahyuni, S., Ghauri, P., & Karsten, L. (2007). Managing international strategic alliance relationships. *Thunderbird International Business Review, 49,* 671–687.

Walton, R. E. (1969). *Interpersonal peacemaking: Confrontations and third party consultation.* Reading, MA: Addison-Wesley.

Walton, R. E., & McKersie, R. B. (1965). *A behavioral theory of labor negotiations: An analysis of a social interaction system.* New York: McGraw-Hill.

Ward, C. (2004). Psychological theories of culture contact and their implications for intercultural training and interventions. In D. Landis, J. M. Bennett, & M. J. Bennett (Eds.), *Handbook of intercultural training* (3rd ed., pp. 185–216). Thousand Oaks, CA: Sage.

Watzlawick, P., Beavin, J., & Jackson, D. D. (1967). *Pragmatics of human communication.* New York: Norton.

Weary, G., & Reich, D. A. (2000). Attribution theories. In A. E. Kazdin (Ed.), *Encyclopedia of psychology* (Vol. 1, pp. 320–325). Washington, DC: American Psychological Association.

Weider-Hatfield, D., & Hatfield, J. D. (1995). Relationships among conflict management styles, levels of conflict, and reactions to work. *The Journal of Social Psychology, 135*, 687–698.

Weiner, B. (1995). *Judgments of responsibility: A foundation for a theory of social conduct.* New York: Guilford.

Weinstein, E. A. (1969). The development of interpersonal competence. In D. A. Goslin (Ed.), *Handbook of socialization theory and research* (pp. 753–775). Chicago: Rand McNally.

Weiss, R. L., & Summers, K. J. (1983). Marital interaction coding system-III. In E. E. Filsinger (Ed.), *Marriage and family assessment: A sourcebook for family therapy* (pp. 85–115). Beverly Hills, CA: Sage.

Whitson, S., & El-Sheikh, M. (2003). Marital conflict and health: Processes and protective factors. *Aggression and Violent Behavior, 8*, 283–312.

Wiehe, V. R. (1990). *Sibling abuse: Hidden physical, emotional, and sexual trauma.* New York: Lexington Books.

Wiemann, J. M. (1977). Explication and test of a model of communicative competence. *Human Communication Research, 3*, 195–213.

Williams, S. L., & Frieze, I. H. (2005). Patterns of violent relationships, psychological distress, and marital satisfaction in a national sample of men and women. *Sex Roles, 52*, 771–784.

Wilmot, W. W., & Hocker, J. L. (2007). *Interpersonal conflict* (7th ed.). New York: McGraw Hill.

Wilson, M., & Daly, M. (1993). Spousal homicide risk and estrangement. *Violence and Victims, 8*, 3–16.

Wilson, S. R., & Morgan, W. M. (2004). Persuasion and families. In A. Vangelisti (Ed.), *Handbook of family communication* (pp. 447–471). Mahwah, NJ: Lawrence Erlbaum.

Winslade, J., & Monk, G. (2000). *Narrative mediation: A new approach to conflict resolution.* San Francisco: Jossey-Bass.

Winstock, Z. (2006). The why and what of intimate conflict: Effect of the partners' divergent perceptions on verbal aggression. *Journal of Family Violence, 21*, 461–468.

Winstock, Z. (2007a). Perceptions, emotions, and behavioral decisions in conflicts that escalate to violence. *Motivation and Emotion, 31*, 125–136.

Winstock, Z. (2007b). Toward an interactional perspective on intimate partner violence. *Aggression and Violent Behavior, 12*, 348–363.

Wiseman, R. (2003). Intercultural communication competence. In W. B. Gudykunst (Ed.), *Cross-cultural and intercultural communication* (pp. 191–208). Thousand Oaks, CA: Sage.

Witte, T. H., Schroeder, D. A., & Lohr, J. M. (2006). Blame for intimate partner violence: An attributional analysis. *Journal of Social and Clinical Psychology, 25*, 647–667.

Witteman, H. (1992). Analyzing interpersonal conflict: Nature of awareness, type of initiating event, situational perceptions and management styles. *Western Journal of Communication, 56*, 248–280.

Witteman, H., & Fitzpatrick, M. A. (1986). Compliance-gaining in marital interaction: Power bases, processes, and outcomes. *Communication Monographs, 53*, 130–143.

Wolf-Smith, J. H., & LaRossa, R. (1992). After he hits her. *Family Relations, 41*, 324–329.

Wood, J. T. (2004). Monsters and victims: Male felons' accounts of intimate partner violence. *Journal of Social and Personal Relationships, 21*, 555–576.

Yaffe, J. (1972). *So sue me! The story of a community court.* New York: Saturday Review Press.

Yoshioka, M. R., & DiNoia, J., & Ullah, K. (2001). Attitudes toward marital violence: An examination of four Asian communities. *Violence Against Women, 7,* 900–926.

Young, S. L. (2004). What the _ _ _ _ is your problem?: Attribution theory and perceived reasons for profanity usage during conflict. *Communication Research Reports, 21,* 338–347.

Zaffar, E. (2008, June). Context is king: A practical guide to reframing in mediation. Center for Dispute Resolution and Conflict Management. Retrieved September 22, 2008, from http://www.mediate.com

Zelenski, J. M., & Larsen, R. J. (2000). The distribution of basic emotions in everyday life: A state and trait perspective from experience sampling data. *Journal of Research in Personality, 34,* 178–197.

Zillmann, D. (1988). Cognition-excitation interdependence in aggressive behavior. *Aggressive Behavior, 14,* 51–64.

Zillmann, D. (1990). The interplay of cognition and excitation in aggravated conflict among intimates. In D. D. Cahn (Ed.), *Intimates in conflict: A communication perspective* (pp. 187–208). Hillsdale, NJ: Lawrence Erlbaum.

INDEX

Accommodation, 61, 80, 148, 153
Action readiness plans, 100
Activeness and disagreeableness, 48
Activity bias, 105
Actor-observer bias, 104–105
Adaptability, 32, 158–159
Adolescence and family conflict, 199
African American conflict styles,
    154–155
Aggravation, 244
Aggression, 92
    avoiding inadvertent reinforcement
        of, 292
    children's, 202–205
    communicative, 69, 218, 220,
        233–235
    diminishing through conflict man-
        agement, 5–6
    environmental factors contributing
        to, 95
    goal attainment through, 29
    impact of pain on, 95
    intimate, interactional model of,
        237–250
    myths and maxims of, 214–237
    reasons explaining the use of, 70
    skill deficiency model of, 70
Alliances, strategic, 184–189
Alternative dispute resolution (ADR),
    256. *See also* Mediation
Analytic remarks, 47–48
Anger
    causes of, 91–93
    communicating, 52–53
    emotions associated with, 95–97

scripts, 100, 102
    types of, 93–95
Appropriateness, 3–4, 27–29, 123–126,
    141–142, 185, 288–289
Arguing, serial, 9
Argumentativeness, 69–71
Arousal, 6–7, 35, 98–99, 129, 133, 240
Asian American conflict orientations,
    155–156
Attachment styles, 67–69
Attachment, two-dimensional model of,
    69
Attribution(s)
    bias, 104–107, 121, 236–237
    as cognitive outcomes, 121–122
    dimensions, 103–104
    linguistic forms of, 105
    model of responsibility attribution,
        appraisal, and response, 107
    parallel thoughts and meanings in
        couple interaction, 106
    as proximal consequences, 120–122
    research on marital relationships
        and, 126, 130
Attributional locus, 105

Bargaining
    collective, 180–181
    distributive vs. integrative, 178–179
Behavior(s)
    communicative, competence as eval-
        uative judgment of, 29
    conflict level and, 10
    contexts of, 22
    defining conflict through, 7–9

as form of disagreement necessary in interpersonal conflict, 9
interconnectedness between cognitions and emotions, 122
nonverbal, link with conflict strategies, 53
relationship outcomes and, 20–21
transparency in, 187
Belief asymmetry, 105
Belief markers, 105
Benevolent approach, 148
Bias, in prospect theory, 108–109
Blameworthiness, 93–94, 103

Case studies
Confrontation in the Parking Lot, 295–296
Grameen Bank versus Moneylenders, 164–165
Phone Calls at 1:00 AM, 37
Planning a Romantic Evening, 96–97
Working for the Minimum Wage, 15–16
Cautious disengagement, 250
Children
conflict/aggression in, 202–205
modeling effective conflict competencies with, 194
triangulation of, in family conflict, 196–197
Code-switching, in intercultural conflict, 158–159
Cognitive deficits, 102–103
Collaboration/integrating style, 50–51, 53, 56, 68, 123, 130, 143, 149, 153, 173, 237, 244, 250, 273
Collective bargaining, 180–181
Collectivism, 145, 148–149, 153–157
Commitment, 84
Communal approach, 146, 148–149, 195
Communication
adaptability of, 158–159
appropriate, rules governing, 27–28
competence. *See* Competence
constructive, in intercultural conflict, 143
contexts of, 22
dimensions of, in conflict, 48–50

effectiveness and appropriateness of, 3–4
in organizational conflict, 166
skills, 32–33
Communication interaction, low- vs. high-context, 144–145
Communication satisfaction, 36, 126–127
Communicative aggression, 69, 218, 220, 233–235, 246
Competence
appropriateness of communication and, 27–29
in communicating, 3–4
criteria for and components of, 141–143
defining, 29
disputant, skills and knowledge contributing to, 281–282
effectiveness and, 28–29
facilitating factors for, 29–33
goal achievement and, 23–27
importance of, 20–21
in intercultural conflict, 139–161
in interpreting/performing conflict behaviors, 22
judgments of, 20–22, 29, 123–126
knowledge and, 31–32
motivation and, 30–31
in negotiating intimate violence, 241–246, 251
perceptions of, guiding criteria for, 22–29
skills, 32–33, 143
value in managing interpersonal conflict, 287–289
Complementarity, 60
Composure, 33
Compromising conflict style, 56, 68, 153–154
Conciliatory remarks, 47–48
Conflict
actual vs. perceived, 11–13
anger/anger-like responses to, 92–93
attributions about causes of, 103–107
background influences on, 65–86
behavioral and episodic features of, 7–9
competence-based approach to, 19–38
contexts of, 22, 33–36, 90–116

cumulative nature of, 122–123
defining, 7–10
explanatory model of, 33–38,
    167–170
family, 192–209. *See also* Family con-
    flict
frequency/pervasiveness of, 4–5, 8
guidelines for managing, 290–297
importance of, 1–17
inevitability of, 286–287
interaction, 35
intercultural competence in, 139–161
intergroup, 179–182
interpersonal, explanatory model of,
    33–38, 167–170
intimate violence. *See* Intimate vio-
    lence
levels of, 10–11, 13–14
mediation, 256–282
messages, 41–63. *See also* Conflict
    communication
organizational. *See* Organizational
    conflict
outcomes of, 119–136
personal development and, 2–3
proximal influences on, 90–117
reasons to study, 3–7
recognizing the systems inherent in,
    297
spontaneous reactions to, 90–117
types of, 13–14
Conflict communication
cross-cultural national/ethnic styles
    and patterns of, 152–157
dimensions of, 47
impact on proximal and distal rela-
    tional outcomes, 130
messages, 41–63
nonverbal, 52–55
rules governing, 28
strategies of, 50–52
styles of, 55–57
tactics of, 46–47
Conflict face-negotiation theory, 151–153
Conflict interaction(s)
communication dimensions of,
    48–50
communication tactics of, 46–47
distal consequences of, 130–135

distal individual factors affecting,
    66–76
distal relational factors affecting, 76–85
dyadic systems, 112–116
in organizational conflict, 169
patterns of, 57, 60–62
proximal consequences of, 120–130
satisfaction, 127
topical content of, 42, 45
Conflict locus of control (CLOC) scale,
    72–73
Conflict management
diminishing aggression through, 5–6
facework in, 128–129
health improvement through, 7
personal development and, 5
sex differences in, 73–76
Conflict situation, initial reactions to
physiological, 97–100
scripts, 100–102
temporary response mode, 100
Conflict strategies, 50–52
avoidance, 50–52
distributive, 50–51
integrative, 50–51
Conflict styles, 56–57
cross-cultural, 152–154
cross-ethnic, 154–157
dispositional, situational, and sys-
    tems approaches to, 152
Conflict tactics
categories of, 49–50
classification of, 46–48
disagreeableness and activeness of, 48
typology of/dimensions underlying,
    48–49
Confrontational remarks, 47–48
Confucianism, 149, 155
Consequences
distal, 130–135
proximal, 120–130
Contempt and disgust, communicating,
    52, 132
Context(s)
cultural, 22, 160
distal, 33–35, 167–168, 289
impact on future conflicts, 36
proximal, 35, 90–116, 122, 168–169
Control mutuality, 84

Control, locus of, 71–72, 289
Conversational recall, 11
Cooperative tactics, 173
Corporate conflict approaches, 146–150
Couple interaction, parallel thoughts and meanings in, 106
Couple systems, 115. *See also* Marital relationships
Criticism, 131–132
Cross-cultural code-switching model, 158–159
Cross-cultural ethnic/national communication styles, 152–157
Cultural context, 22, 160
Cultural values grid, 146–149
Culture
    communication style and, 144–150
    definition of, 142
    violence influenced by, 221
Culture-based value dimensional patterns, 144–145
Culture-sensitive knowledge, 142–143

Defensiveness, 132
Demand-withdraw patterns, 60, 133–134, 197, 245–246, 250
Denial and equivocation, 46
Differentiation
    conflict phase of, 170–172, 183
    group, 179, 182
    in organizational conflict, 179, 185–186
    in sibling treatment, negative impact of, 206
    strategic alliances and, 185–186
Directness, 48
Disagreeableness and activeness, 48
Disagreement, explicit/expressed, 8–9, 11
Disgust and contempt, communicating, 52
Displaced conflict, 12–14
Dispositional approach to studying conflict style, 152
Distal context
    in interpersonal conflict, 33–35
    in organizational conflict, 167–168, 189
Distal individual factors affecting conflict interaction, 66–76
    argumentativeness, 69–70

attachment styles, 67–69
locus of control, 71
sex differences in conflict management, 73–76
taking conflict personally, 70–71
Distal outcomes/consequences, 36
divorce as, 135
effects of the demand-withdraw pattern, 133–134
in organizational conflict, 169–170
relational satisfaction and stability as, 134–135
relationship (dis)satisfaction and (in)stability, 130–132
Distal relational factors affecting conflict interaction, 76–85
Distributive conflict strategies, 51, 53, 121, 130, 151, 173
Distributive vs. integrative bargaining, 178–179
Divorce, prediction through types of communication, 135
Dominating conflict strategies, 5–57, 153–154
Dyadic relationships/systems
    dysfunctions in, 114–116
    interaction in, 112
    in interpersonal organizational conflict, 175
    parent-child relationships, 206–207
    properties of, 112–114

Effectiveness, 24–28
    assessing communication competence through, 123–126
    in communicating, 3–4
    communication assessment criterion of, 23–29
    intercultural conflict and, 141–142
    in organizational communication, 166, 185
    personal, vs. appropriateness, 289
Egocentric motives, incompetence due to, 93
Emotions
    conflict severity escalated by, 240–241
    contagious nature of, 101, 112
    negative, avoiding reciprocation of, 291

negative, evoking through transgressions, 240
as proximal consequences, 122–123
tone of conflict episode set by, 35
Entropy, 113
Environmental context, 22
Episode(s), 7, 9, 35–36
Equifinality, 27, 113
Equilibrium/homeostasis, 113
Equivocation and denial, 46
Ethnic conflict communication styles, cross-cultural, 154–157
Ethnorelativism/ethnocentric perspective, 140
Exit-voice-loyalty-neglect responses, 84–85
Expectancy value, goals, and assessments, 108, 111–112
Expectations, 108–110, 143
Explanatory model of interpersonal conflict, 33–38, 167–170
    conflict interaction in, 35, 169
    distal context in, 33–34, 167–168
    proximal and distal outcomes in, 36
    proximal context of, 35, 168–169
Expressiveness, 33

Face
    importance in Asian American conflict orientations, 155–156
    saving, 294–295
    self-face and mutual-face concern, 151
    self-presentation goals and, 26–27
    threat and restoration, as proximal consequences, 127–129
Fairness, lack of, 93
False conflict, 12–14
Family conflict
    adolescent, 199
    blended family problems, 197–198
    children's aggression, impact on other family members, 202–205
    competent management of, 207–209
    constructive vs. destructive, 193–195, 198, 290
    examining in families as a whole, 205, 207
    interparental, impact on children, 195–198

misunderstanding as a source of, 199–201
parent to child, 198–199
parenting style's role in, 201–202
systems approach to, 192–193
systems perspective of, 205–207
Fatal attractions, 77–78
Fear, 96
Feelings. *See* Emotions
"Fight or flight" orientation, 98–99
Flaming, 22
Flooding, 98–99, 103
Four Horsemen of the Apocalypse, 131
Friendship, sources of conflict in, 44
Frustration, 92, 94
Functional context, 22

Gender
    differences in conflict management, 73–76
    physiological responses to conflict and, 98–99
    relationship blueprints, 73–76
    violence and, 221–228
Globality, 103
Goals
    appropriate means of achieving, 27–29
    discerning others', 292–294
    expectations for achieving, 108–112
    hierarchy of, 24
    instrumental, relational, and self-presentational, 110–111
    nature of, 23–26
    transactive, 123–124
    types of, 26–27
Group differentiation, 179, 182

Health
    conflict interactions and impact on, 129–130
    family conflicts and impact on, 194–197
    improving through conflict management, 6–7
    negative consequences of physiological reactions to conflict, 99
    physical, as proximate consequence, 129–130

Higher-ordered thoughts, 102–112
Homeostasis/equilibrium, 113
Hostile episodes, interpersonal conflict
 as, 8–9
Hostility, 8–9, 47, 196
Hyperarousal, 133

Identity management, 92
Identity negotiation adaptation process,
 158–159
Ignorance, 76, 93
Impartial approach, 146, 148
Incompetence, 93
Independent/interdependent construal
 of self, 150–151
Individual personality tendency pat-
 terns, 150–151
Individualism, 145, 148, 153–155
Information sharing/seeking, 170–171
Instrumental goals, 26–27, 110–111
Integration, 170–174
Integrative vs. distributive bargaining,
 178–179
Intent, importance of, 103
Interaction goals, 23–26
Interaction management, 33
Intercultural (IC) conflict
 antecedent factors, 143–151
 code-switching/communication
  adaptability in, 158–159
 communication, process factors of,
  151–157
 competence, 158, 139–161
 corporate approaches, 146
 cross-cultural national communication styles in, 152–154
 cross-ethnic communication styles
  in, 154–157
 face concern in, 151–152
 mindful transformation in, 159–161
 nature of, 140–141
 process, factors, and outcome of,
  158–161
Intergroup conflict, 179–182
Interorganizational conflict, 182–189
Interparental conflict, impact on children, 195–198
Interpersonal conflict
 definitions of, 10

explanatory model of, 33–38,
 167–170
 See also Conflict
Interpersonal relationships, importance
 of conflict in, 1–17
Intimacy
 social penetration theory of, 79
 trajectories for, 78–79
Intimate partner violence (IPV), 218,
 222–223, 226, 228–229, 232–233,
 246
Intimate violence, 212
 assessing existence and justification
  of, 215–217
 model of intimate partner aggression
  and violence, 248
 myths and maxims of, 213, 217–218,
  220–221. See also Aggression;
  Myths and maxims of intimate
  violence and aggression
 physiological reactivity during,
  99–100
 sexual coercion as, 218–219
Involvement, communication of, 53–54
Irreverent remarks, 46

Judgments of competence, 20–22, 29,
 123–126

Knowledge
 culture-sensitive, 142–143
 facilitating competence through,
  31–32

Latent conflict, 12–14
Latino(a) American conflict practices,
 156–157
Life span changes, conflict interaction
 affected by, 79–80
Listening, mindful, 160
Locus of control, 71–72, 289
Locus, attribution dimension of,
 103–105

Macromotive commitment, 85
Marital relationships
 common conflict rules in, 126
 demand-withdraw pattern's effects
  on, 133–134

predicting divorce through conflict
communication patterns, 135
relationship (dis)satisfaction and
(in)stability in, 130–132
stress, anger, and violence in, 95
violent, impact on children, 195–198
Marital types, 80–81
Marriage systems, traditional vs. egalitarian, 115
Mediation
definition and purpose of, 256–259
dilemmas for mediators, 280
disputant competence in, 281–282
goals of, 260–262
perceived competence as tool of,
20–21
principles of, 259–260
process of, 262–278
skills and knowledge for competence
in, 278–280
Message variety and accommodation,
61
Metaconflict, 43
Mexican American conflict practices,
156
Mindful transformation, 159–161
Mindfulness, 143
Misattributed conflict, 12–14
Model of responsibility attribution,
appraisal, and response, 107
Monitoring mechanisms, 174
Moods/response modes, 100
Motivation, 30–31
Multifinality, 113
Mutual problem definition/description,
170–172, 179, 186
Mutual-face concern, 151
Myths and maxims of intimate violence
and aggression, 213–214
female violence is motivated by self-
defense, 226–228
intimate violence by males is about
power, 229–232
intimate violence is an incompetent
approach to conflict management, 235–237
intimate violence is chronic, 229
intimate violence is harmful and
traumatizing, 232–233

intimate violence is more harmful
and traumatizing than communicative aggression, 233–235
intimate violence is unilateral, 228
violence is gendered, 221–226
violence is obvious, 214–221

Nagging, 62
Native American conflict practices, 157
Negative arousal, 98–99
Negative attributions
distributive behavior and, 121
divorce predictable by study of, 131
self-perpetuating nature of, 121
Negative conflict patterns, reacting to,
61–62
Negative interactions and messages,
105
Negativity, physiological impact of, 6–7,
99
Negotiation and bargaining, 178–179
Noncommittal remarks, 46
Nonsummativity, 114
Nonverbal conflict communication,
54–55
behavior link with conflict strategies,
53
communicating involvement, 53–54
positive vs. negative affect, 52–53, 55
ways of showing protest and anger,
102
Norms and roles, 10

Obliging conflict style, 56–57, 153, 156
Organizational conflict
applying the phase model to,
175–189
competence-based approach to, 166
and the explanatory model of interpersonal conflict, 167–170
four arenas of, 165–166
interpersonal, 175–178
phases of, 170–174. *See also* Phase
theory/models
Other orientation, 33
Other-face concern, 151
Outcomes, proximal and distal. *See* Distal outcomes/consequences; Proximal outcomes/consequences

Pain, impact on aggression, 95
Parallel conflict, 12–14
Parent-child conflict, 198–199
Parentification of the child, 116
Parenting style, 201
Parents. *See* Family conflict
Passive inhibition, 250
Patriarchal terrorism, 223, 226
Perception
    of competence, 21–29
    impact on interpersonal conflict,
        11–12
    role in interpersonal conflict, 9
Personal characteristics and attitudes,
    11
Personality, individual tendency pat-
    terns of, 150–151
Phase theory/models
    applying to organizational conflict,
        175–189
    bargaining and negotiation in,
        178–179
    differentiation and integration in,
        170–171
    extended research example of,
        176–178
    integration phase, 172–174
    intergroup conflict application,
        179–184
    mutual problem description phase,
        171–172
Physical health, as proximate conse-
    quence, 129–130
Physical violence, 220, 233–235
Physiological/psychological responses
    to conflict, 6–7, 98–100
Power
    control mutuality and, 84
    cultural differences in, 145
    distance value patterns, 148
    ethnic value patterns, 148, 154–157
    value orientation, 148–149
    violence and, 229–232
Praiseworthiness, 103
Predispositions, 93
Prospect theory, 108–110
Proximal context, 35, 90–116, 122,
    168–169
Proximal influences, 90–117

Proximal outcomes/consequences, 36
    attributions as, 120–122
    communication satisfaction as,
        126–127
    cumulative nature of, 130
    emotions as, 122–123
    face threat and restoration as,
        127–129
    judgments of competence as,
        123–126
    in organizational conflict, 169
    physical health as, 129–130

Reason bias, 105
Reciprocity, 22, 57–59
Reflexivity, mindful, 161
Relational development, effects on con-
    flict interaction, 76–80
Relational goals, 26, 110–111
Relational interdependence, recogni-
    tion of, 172
Relational rules, 11
Relational satisfaction, 7, 12, 36, 45, 74,
    80, 82–83, 105, 130–132, 134–135,
    232
Relationship blueprints, 73–76, 80–85
Relationship context, 22
Relationships, characteristics of, 82–85
Reproach, 94
Resentment, 94
Response modes/moods/tendencies,
    100–101
Responses, anger-like, 91–97
Responsibility, 103–104
Responsibility attributions, 106–107
Restructuring the problem, 172
Rigidity, 61
Role strain, 115
Romantic relationships, trajectories for
    intimacy in, 78–79
Rules
    determining appropriateness
        through, 124–126
    relational, transgressions of, 11

Scripts, 100, 102
Self, independent/interdependent con-
    strual of, 150–151
Self-construal, 150–151

Self-face concern/self-voice assertive focus, 151
Self-presentation goals, 26–27, 110–111
Self-silencing, negative physiological impact of, 99
Selfishness, 103–104
Serial arguing, 9
Sex differences
    in conflict management, 73–76
    and physiological responses to conflict, 98–99
Sexual coercion, 218–219
Situational approach to studying conflict style, 152
Skills
    communication competence, 32–33, 143
    intercultural (IC) conflict, 143
    mediation, 281–282
Social categorization, 181–182
Social confrontation episodes, 125
Social interaction, rules governing, 27–28
Social penetration theory, 79
Solutions, alternative, 173–174
Stability, 4, 103, 130, 134–135, 229

Status-achievement approach, 146, 148–149
Stereotypes, sex role, 73–74
Stonewalling, 132
Strategic alliances, 184–189
Stress, 95–96, 115

Taking conflict personally (TCP), 70–71
Threats, 93
Topical continuity, 60–61
Transactional redundancy, 114
Transactive goals, 25, 123–124
Transformation, mindful, 160–161
Transgressions, as cause of intimate conflict, 238–240
Triangulation, 196–197
Trust, 83–84, 106
Two-dimensional model of attachment, 69

Valence, 48–49
Value dimensional patterns, culture-based, 144–145
Veridical conflict, 12
Violence, definition and types of, 218
    intimate. See Intimate violence